IRELAND AND SCOTLAND

IRELAND AND SCOTLAND

Order and Disorder, 1600–2000

R.J.Morris, Economic and Social History,
University of Edinburgh

Liam Kennedy, School of History,
Queen's University Belfast

First published in Great Britain in 2005 by
John Donald, an imprint of Birlinn Ltd

West Newington House
10 Newington Road
Edinburgh
EH9 1QS

www.birlinn.co.uk

ISBN 10: 1 904607 55 1
ISBN 13: 978 1 904607 55 7

British Library Cataloguing-in-Publication Data
A catalogue record for this book is available on request from the British Library

Typeset by Carnegie Publishing Ltd, Lancaster
Printed and bound by Bell & Bain Ltd, Glasgow

Table of Contents

Acknowledgements

Early versions and precursors of many of the papers in this volume were first presented in the fifth of a longstanding series of occasional meetings of historians of Scotland and Ireland held in Belfast from 23 to 25 June 2000. The British Academy was a major supporter of both the meeting and this subsequent publication. The conference was also supported by the Economic History Society and by Queen's University, Belfast. The publication of the 'photo-essay' was made possible by the Carnegie Trust for the Universities of Scotland. We are grateful to Barbara Morris for expert assistance in the preparation of the manuscript. We thank them all. Last, and in many ways most importantly, our thanks to all who came to the conference and took part in the discussions which had such a formative effect on the papers in this volume.

RJM
LK

Contributors and Editors

Professor R.J. Morris, Economic and Social History, Edinburgh University

Professor Liam Kennedy, School of History, Queen's University Belfast

Dr David J. Menarry, Wigan, formerly Department of History, Aberdeen University

Dr W.H. Crawford, Newtownards, formerly Ulster Folk and Transport Museum

Dr Rosemary Richey, Dunfermline, formerly School of History, Queen's University Belfast

Dr Jonathan Bell, Ulster Folk and Transport Museum

Professor Andrew Blaikie, Department of Sociology, Aberdeen University

Dr Paul Gray, Belfast, formerly School of History, Queen's University Belfast

Dr Eilidh Garrett, Sheffield, formerly Senior Research Fellow, Department of Geography, University of Portsmouth

Ms Ros Davies, Cambridge Group for the History of Population and Social Structure

Dr Roisín Higgins, Humanities Institute of Ireland, University College, Dublin

Dr Cathal McCall, School of Politics and International Studies, Queen's University Belfast

Dr Kevin James, Department of History, University of Guelph, Canada

Dr Alan O'Day, Fellow in Modern History, Greyfriars, University of Oxford

Dr Máirtín Ó Catháin, Institute of Ulster Scots Studies, University of Ulster

Professor Donald M. MacRaild, History Programme, Victoria University of Wellington, New Zealand

Dr John A. Burnett, School of Psychology and Sociology, Napier University, Edinburgh

Dr Iain Robertson, School of Environment, University of Gloucestershire, Cheltenham

Dr Alastair Durie, History Department, University of Stirling

Dr Christopher Finlay, Dublin European Institute, University College, Dublin

Introduction

The papers in this volume were derived from the fifth of a series of meetings of historians of Ireland and Scotland. These meetings were initiated in 1976 by Louis Cullen and Chris Smout[1] in the belief that the experiences of two countries modest in size and deeply influenced by their very different links and proximities with a major metropolitan power could be compared and illuminate the understanding of each. At that time the major questions centred on economic growth and economic development – different but related concepts; the one concerned with questions of the measurement of wealth creation and accumulation, the other with more value-laden questions of the structures, conditions and social and cultural changes associated with sustained growth.

Since then the agenda has widened – notably in matters of cultural and social experience. The agenda of the group has always been driven by historians associated with the exploitation of the social sciences to increase historical understanding. In the 1970s, that meant economics and a limited number of associated social questions. By 2000, assumptions of the primacy of economics in historical explanation have long been abandoned. Indeed there is a danger that curiosity regarding the material and economic logic of the past has now faded too far in the historian's imagination. Cultural questions, especially those of cultural representations and their place in the creation and sustaining of identities, have come to the fore. Political institutions and direction have taken a more central role.

A number of clear themes emerge from these articles. The first is land. Land was not simply a factor of production but an aspect of political, military and social power, and as such, formed one aspect of the diverging fortunes of the two countries. The seventeenth-century foundations of the two societies were very different, and these were reflected in different attitudes to law, to authority and to market processes.

Land was the basis of the elaborate social structure that characterised Irish rural society from plantation in the seventeenth century to partition in the early twentieth. Bill Crawford directs attention to the differing legal structures in the two societies. Under Scottish law landlords had extensive powers to control and discipline their tenants. A vital part of this was the landlord's ability to eject a tenant at the end of a lease without much fuss. So far was this from being the case in Ireland that the Earl of Abercorn, who owned estates in the two countries, could complain of the 'oppression I lie under from the tenants'.[2] Even when a long lease had come to an end, the expectation in Ireland, often backed up by the threat of protest, was that the sitting tenant had a right of renewal. This difference was of protean significance. In Scotland, as Tom Devine has argued, landlords could pursue a 'gigantic strategy of social and economic engineering' in the closing decades of the eighteenth century and the early years of the nineteenth.[3] In Ireland, by contrast, no such recasting of the social landscape was possible. Tenant-dominated juries were quick to frustrate landlord ambition, where a clash of economic interests might threaten. The stereotypical image of the landlord might therefore be turned on its head. It is not that Irish landlords were overbearing but rather that they were too weak to intervene effectively in relation to the long-term economic and demographic development of the rural economy. Stretching the point further, over-population, poverty and social stress were the eventual, and possibly inevitable, outcomes. If so, then differing institutional structures may have been decisive in shaping the long-run evolution of the two societies. Cullen and Smout have argued that Ireland and Scotland diverged economically and demographically in the later eighteenth century.[4] It might be hypothesised that a substantial part of the explanation lay with differences in property rights, the incentives embodied in those structures, and the differing costs of enforcing property rights.

Rosemary Richey's account of the land agents in County Down illustrates one aspect of the manner in which power in Ireland had to be carefully negotiated. David Menarry's account of the manipulative use of debt against landowners in seventeenth-century Scotland shows that under conditions of contested, and in this case temporary, military conquest, power and authority also required negotiation as well as imposition by the courts.

While the land agent had a role in diffusing knowledge of new tech-niques in agriculture, it was the stronger tenant farmers who were the key innovators. The sources of agricultural innovation, in Ireland more so than in the case of Scotland, were from outside Irish society. In the eighteenth century, English farming was the primary source of ideas and techniques. But as the nineteenth century dawned, Scottish practices were increasingly emulated. This shift is explicable in terms of the dynamism of Scottish farming and also a similarity in topography and social conditions between Ireland and Scotland. Jonathan Bell extends the range of conventional enquiry in agricultural history by bringing a material culture perspective to the issue of technology transfer. Migratory labourers, it is interesting to note, were sometimes the conveyors of improvements in hand technology and, at least in the case of West Donegal, of co-operative organization as well.[5] The traffic in ideas and techniques seems to have been largely one way, which raises deeper questions about the *capacity*, or rather lack of capacity, for autonomous innovation within the Irish agrarian sector.

The continual challenge and conditional nature of authority over land in Ireland gave rise to a number of quasi-secret societies for which violence was part of the standard repertoire of negotiation. Two of the contributions here show the manner in which these traditions were transferred to urban environments. The importance of the Orange Order in Belfast and Liverpool has long been recognised, but MacRaild maps the extensive nature of their influence in the industrial towns of north-east England. Ó Catháin demonstrates that the Ribbonmen, also of rural origin, transferred themselves both to urban Ulster and Scotland. Although they presented themselves as defenders of Catholic populations, they were as ready to take aggressive action as their Orange counterparts. A traditional view of Ribbonism is that it was engaged primarily in regulating relations between the landed elite and Catholic small farmers, covertly representing the interests of the latter. Ó Catháin views the Ribbon organization as a kind of Catholic defence association, initially in rural areas but later in the densely packed slums of Belfast, Londonderry and Glasgow. Ribbonmen, in his view, were as much aggressive as reactive participants in the sectarian street fights of the decades after 1850. The defining feature of the loosely linked Ribbon groups was not 'victimhood' but anti-Orangeism; attacking Orange parades and thumping Orangemen was a good day's sport in Ulster and Scotland, despite occasional fatal consequences. In the 1880s Ribbonmen reinvented themselves as stewards marshalling home rule demonstrations, impressively armed with heavy blackthorn sticks. While the Ribbonmen disturbed public order, the Fenian organisation offered a more fundamental challenge to the whole political and constitutional order. Ribbon organisation re-emerged after the debacle of the Fenian rising. There was no neat progression to a more 'advanced' form of political subversion.

Land remains an issue in the politics of both countries. In Scotland, land reform was one of the first topics to be tackled in distinctive ways by the devolved parliament.[6] In the north of Ireland, land struggles have been transmuted into the often violent struggles over urban turf and the ethnic marking of space, while in Scotland such struggles tend to be about distribution, access and something called 'community'. Is there still a land issue in the Republic of Ireland? In Dublin, 'land' struggles have been subsumed under debates over the control of property development. Those who face the traffic congestion and house-price inflation of Dublin are exploited by developers, heedless of negative externalities, with greater precision than anything in the experience of nineteenth-century landlords and their agents.[7]

Political and social violence and its contestation was only one aspect of the manner in which the two societies constructed disciplines and subordinations. Blaikie and Gray examine the impact of the Kirk Sessions upon the sexual activities before marriage of their congregations. Ulster Presbyterian ministers and Kirk elders took a close and obsessive interest in sexual discipline and seem to have 'caught' the bulk of offenders. This did not prevent Presbyterian populations displaying a much higher rate of illegitimacy than their Catholic neighbours. In eighteenth-century Ulster, when Presbyterian church organisation and discipline seems to have been at its height – constituting a 'state within a state' as Anglican critics sourly claimed – the majority of those brought to account were actually men, suggesting a concern with welfare and fairness along gender lines, far removed from the image of patriarchal church elders indulging their prurience at the expense of vulnerable women. Such discipline broke down under the impact of the forces of commercialisation and urbanisation, which gave rise to increased mobility. The result was that by the mid-Victorian period the putative father had frequently absconded, leaving the woman to face Kirk and community. This was very different from the early modern period, when apparently the authority of the Kirk was capable of producing a more egalitarian outcome. The course of modernisation had produced greater inequality.

One of the most formidably internalised disciplines was evidenced by the demographic regime of late marriage, high levels of celibacy and high marital fertility often identified with Ireland after the 1840s. Garrett and Davies trace the course of marriage, celibacy and fertility on the island of Skye in the late Victorian period, using Ireland as the comparator. The manuscript base of this study is remarkably rich, linking not only the household returns for the population censuses of 1881 and 1891 but also the parish registers for the intervening years. The picture that emerges is one of high fertility, late and infrequent marriage, and a (relatively) low incidence of illegitimacy. This certainly resembles Ireland. It is also consonant with a 'peasant' demographic regime which Guinnane has identified for peasant farming areas more generally in western Europe in this period, thus suggesting that Ireland was less of a demographic outlier than is sometimes claimed. Moreover, the fact that the population of Skye was Protestant might suggest that the Irish demographic experience had little to do with Roman Catholicism and much more to do with a smallholding economy in which there were few alternatives to working on the land or at sea. But there is a major anomaly. In terms of economic characteristics and circumstances – peripheral location, dependence on smallholding agriculture, reliance on fishing – Skye had much more in common with the west of Ireland than it had with Ulster and the eastern counties of Ireland. Yet the demography of Skye turns out to be much closer to that found in the east of Ireland rather than along its Atlantic seaboard. This is a puzzle which is not easily resolved, but it may be that cultural factors, including the heritage of traditional behaviours embedded in Gaelic language and culture, are more important than the economistic models deployed by Guinnane would seem to allow.

One new element which was present at the conference and in the papers was the sense of history in the present and the agency of history and understandings of history. This was especially appropriate in a meeting held in Belfast where understandings of history play an important role in the legitimising of current political positions and, by implication, the violence with which many of those positions were and are associated. For this reason we have included a photographic essay on the contrasting historical narratives contained in the wall murals of Republican and Loyalist Belfast. Each in different ways was crafted to legitimise the political claims of those who dominated these patches of urban turf. Scotland, appropriately given the themes coming out of these papers, demonstrated a more douce attitude to its history, but no-one who has followed the campaign for and creation of the devolved parliament in Edinburgh can doubt the agency of historical interpretations of history.[8]

This sense of historical understandings as active and powerful agents in present actions, attitudes and relationships lies behind two innovatory papers in this collection. Roisín Higgins explores the relationship between the current sense of epochal and contested change and the normative and analytical concepts of civil society. This leaves issues of contested legitimacy implied in many of the papers to be explored. Cathal McCall uses interview material to explore the crisis of identity amongst Ulster Unionists. This insecure and troubled group has lost the old certainties of the monopolistic claims of the 'Orange' state[9] and finds that the claim to be 'British' resonates hollowly in the England and Scotland and Wales of devolution, the European Union and globalisation. Nor do claims to be 'Protestant' have much meaning in polities which are largely secularised and have largely forgotten their own intensely Protestant pasts. Ironically, it is only the Black and Asian populations of England who share this desire to be British, a reminder that such claims for citizenship are aspects of a post-imperial situation with all the ethnic tensions implied.[10] Readers of theories of nationalism can watch an 'imagined community' being imagined from the slender material of a fading linguistic variant of Scots English and the creation of a mythical past of the Scots Irish in a narrative of blood and soil. Readers unfamiliar with theories of nationalism should note that the concept of 'imagining' does not imply that such nationalism is more or less real, nor more or less legitimate than any other social and cultural manifestation. It does imply that the creation of national consciousness was and is a social and cultural process requiring careful analytical study.[11]

O'Day provides a careful and scholarly demolition of any potential myth-making around a Celtic alliance or a homogenous centre-periphery model for constitutional change. Despite occasional mutual interest, devolution means very different things in Cardiff, Edinburgh and Stormont, just as home rule clearly did in Ireland, Scotland and Wales in an earlier debate.

How should we begin to assess these themes of contest and discipline and the varied patterns of change identified in this and earlier volumes? Twentieth-century historiography might tempt us to look to the history of class conflict and resolution. More broadly, the move from pre-capitalist to capitalist forms may provide elements against which the experience of both Scotland and Ireland might be judged. Confidence in these and in any single-path story has rapidly waned in the 1990s. In part, this has been due to philosophical moves in western Europe; in part, to the collapse and discrediting of the authority derived from teleological histories in fascist, soviet and other regimes; and in part from the legitimising of violence and exclusion by particularist versions of history in a wide range of societies. Such single-path notions of history were challenged by both feminist and post-colonial demands for 'alternatives' and, indeed, a parity of esteem for such alternatives.[12] Such contests may well have started with usurpatory demands – my history replaces your history, my Ireland replaces your Ireland – but in many cases this has led to a search for multiple histories and identities with attendant problems of philosophy and governance. These have appeared in many forms, from the surveys of nationalism in Scotland which offer 'do you feel both Scottish and British?' as an option, to the powerful presentation of the two traditions of Ireland.[13]

In light of this, historians who wish to try and summarise and give direction to their understanding of change over the last four hundred years have been left with a number of much weaker and less structured notions. Modernisation as a historical narrative is much tainted by its life as a right-wing alternative to the materialist vision of history based upon capitalism and class. Modernisation theory does invite a search for key features such as the accumulation of knowledge, the dominance of rationality, the growth of market- and cash-based economies, an increasing sense of individuality, the testing of legitimacy through universality, and the preference for civic nationalism over particularist and ethnic nationalisms.[14] Closely linked is the notion of modernity, which might be defined in shorthand as the experience of such changes, which, with deliberate paradoxicality, offers an experience of fragmentation, the dominance of the surface experience of consumption and the attribution of meanings to signs, together with a tendency to reject analysis based on materiality and production for those of representation and consumption.[15]

A case of an Ulster Presbyterian community's encounter with modernity and modernisation is sketched in Kevin James' account of Ballymena at the time of the well-known revivals. The Presbyterians of Ballymena had to deal with the growing intensity of market forces, urban growth and the institutionalisation of education with a fairly weak and unstable structure of civil society. The revivals were only one aspect of this.

The Gaelic and Gallic languages present themselves as repositories of memory, tradition and the irrational. Modernisation, by contrast, involves rational calculus, forethought, and the accumulation of knowledge. Burnett charts the confrontation between Highland Gaelic-speaking society and modernity. This opposition was not a normative one. Clearly there is still a sense of pride in the worth of 'traditional' society and language, but in this confrontation it is the modern language, English, which was seen as the future, as the key to wider economic opportunities. There was no such thing as a 'pure' folk culture. Highlanders had been negotiating the boundaries of different cultures and economies since at least the eighteenth century by virtue of their involvement in migratory labour and, of course, the same is true of Irish rural communities, especially those of the north-west, which had a long tradition of seasonal working in Scotland. The long mutual interaction of the 'isolated' rural community and the modern urban was common to both Ireland and Scotland.[16]

Iain Robertson's account of the land raids in the post-1918 islands of Scotland also involves outside influences such as the experience of fighting in France during the First World War and the migratory workers' experience of urban labour. Peasant and community consciousness was structured by the class divisions of crofter and cottar with their own views of the legitimacy of claims to land.

The nature and awareness of modernity has privileged consumption and experience over structure and production in the historian's imagination. We have two contributions here. Finlay produces a reading of David Hume which relates his ideas closely to the experience of a socially competitive, commercial and consumer society. Durie examines a key leisure and service industry in which Scotland clearly triumphed over Ireland in the production of exactly the sort of experience required by consumers.

Both countries retain stories of conquest in their histories. In both Scotland and Ireland, the military might of England, when properly organised, was always able to dominate the major sites of power. In Ireland, that domination was turned into forms of governance and land ownership which created a ruling class alienated by identity from the bulk of the population. In Scotland, the English armies of conquest, like that of 1641, withdrew.

The Scots were drawn into Union with England not by military power but by negotiation and, some would say, bribery and the economic misfortunes of the 1690s. Many Scots sing the unofficial anthem with some relish, especially the line 'sent him homewards to think again'. But few reflect on Burns' rewrite of a popular eighteenth-century refrain:

> We're bought and sold for English gold
> Such a parcel of rogues in a nation!

This negotiation created a ruling class which became firmly identified with 'Scotland'. This process was neither inevitable nor linear. The rebellions of 1715, 1745 and the Covenanter wars were dangerous and disruptive. Earlier volumes and other recent work suggest that the stable conditions for economic growth and development for the Scotland of enlightenment and improvement did not appear until the 1760s. The eighteenth century saw the establishment of a dominant and managed politics which collapsed with a legalised suddenness in the reform of 1832. The result was the wholesale ejection of the Scottish Tory interest from much of the country's political life, followed by the creation of a Unionist Nationalism.[17] This was quite different from Ireland, where the relative stability of the early eighteenth century was followed by a period in which violence became first a standard mode of negotiation and then the basis of nation building. This was a part of the process of creating order in both countries The concept of the creation of order leaves the question – whose order? In many instances the legitimising of violence was the creation of an alternative form of order. These essays, together with key articles in earlier volumes, suggest that it may well be that it is in the ability to impose, negotiate, legitimise and internalise discipline and order that the experience of the two countries in part diverged.

PART ONE

THE LAND

I

Rural Change in Ulster and Scotland, 1660–1815[1]

W.H. Crawford

An earlier conference concluded that 'at the heart of the problem was the inability of the [Irish] landlords to exercise real control over patterns of land occupation and land use on their estates' but admitted that 'assertions that Irish landlords failed to manage their estates in such a way as to maintain a profitable balance between population and resources seemed to run ahead of explanations as to why this should have been so.'[2] In *The Transformation of Rural Scotland* Devine and his team tested many historical general-isations about the nature of social control in Scotland.[3] In their light we need to re-examine certain aspects of Ulster's experience that were discussed by Roebuck and by Kirkham.[4] Whereas Devine focused on four counties across the Lowland belt of Scotland, this study concentrates on Ulster, the most northerly of the four provinces in Ireland, both because its settlement history displays several unique characteristics and because of the accessibil-ity of the estate records in the Public Record Office of Northern Ireland. Heavy immigration from England and then Scotland to Ulster throughout the seventeenth century affected the development of Ulster society and exacerbated the tensions produced by the clash of English and Scottish cultures with the indigenous Irish culture.

This discussion about the nature of social control in Lowland Scotland and Ulster needs to be placed in the context of a recent publication analysing the character and the history of the great variety of peasantries throughout Europe from the fourteenth to the eighteenth centuries. Scott stresses that 'to explain the survival of peasantries in the Celtic regions of the British Isles alongside their apparent disappearance in much of England is a task of comparative historical research which needs urgently to be addressed.'[5] The analysis of legal developments is central to this task.

The major factor in the creation of a distinctive legal culture in Ulster was the Ulster Plantation scheme in the early seventeenth century, which imposed the contemporary English system of estate management on a Gaelic society that was in the process of shedding its tribal characteristics and copying practices introduced to Leinster and Munster by the Anglo-Normans.[6] As the English government was determined to civilise Ulster, no account was taken of the native customs and concepts of land tenure, and the Ulster Irish were compelled to adopt English legal practices. Although this approach was modified during the seventeenth century by acts passed in the Irish parliament, the legislation appears to have been designed not so much to cope with specific Irish circumstances as to bring Ireland into line with the reforms in England. This legislation produced different effects in Ireland.

> From the ashes of the system of feudal or freehold tenure there arose in Ireland (much more so than in England) a system of leasehold tenure. A direct factor was the confiscation and resettlement of Irish land during the seventeenth century. It is true that the original crown grants created feudal tenure, because invariably the freehold was granted subject to a rent, called in Ireland a 'crown' or quit rent. These grants, given in letters patent, in turn entitled the grantees to subinfeudate non obstante Quia Emptores ['notwithstanding the Quia Emptores act' of 1290 which forbade sub-infeudation in England]. Subinfeudation was the process by which a person to whom lands had been granted, made a grant of those lands or part of them to another person in return for feudal services or a money rent. It was not a transfer of the lands but a further or sub-grant of them. This gave rise to the creation of one type of fee farm grant which is unique to Ireland. The grantees, or their agents, also embarked upon a process of leasing and sub-leasing the land into sub-divided parts, in an effort to extract as much income from it as possible. The result was a rapid growth in Ireland of leasehold tenure to an extent never experienced in England, a generalization that remains true to this day in respect of urban land. Finally, it has also been suggested that the terms and conditions of the letters patent given to the seventeenth century settlers, especially in Ulster, may have been responsible for the introduction of special kinds of leases in Ireland, such as the lease for lives renewable for ever.[7]

Another government initiative had very important historical consequences. The Crown was determined to ensure that Ulster would attract enough immigrants to introduce and sustain English culture, so it ordained that the new landlords should retain only a small proportion of their estates as demesne lands while leasing the remainder to British colonists by any forms of tenure then current in England. This unwise move discouraged major investors from Britain and left the responsibility for realising the project in the hands of men with little capital or social standing, often army officers and government officials. In their efforts to enforce this policy, the government over the first fifteen years of the Plantation dispatched four successive parties of commissioners who toured the counties to examine, supervise and report on its progress.[8] These reports provide much information about the initial development of estates on the six escheated counties (those forfeited by the Irish chiefs who fled from Ulster in 1607) and can be supplemented by documentation about the more heavily colonised counties of Antrim and Down comprising the eastern seaboard. The general impression from these reports is that too many landlords had to compete to secure British tenants and were forced to offer leases on attractive terms even to doubtful individuals.[9] The new Ulster colony was constructed on unsatisfactory foundations.

The unit of leasing that the English government adopted was the Irish traditional concept of the townland, for it considered that, in the majority of cases, the townland could be equated to sixty acres of profitable land based on an Irish Plantation perch of seven yards.[10] Indeed, it used this assumption to calculate the size of land grants for each estate. In the circumstances of the Plantation the townland proved to be a flexible and convenient unit that all parties could comprehend, even if they continued to apply their own interpretations. Around the new settlements, or 'estate towns', townlands were allocated and enclosed into fields, known as 'town parks', for the use of the townspeople. Beyond these town parks lay the remaining townlands whose boundaries were defined either by streams, bogs, stone walls, or newly planted whitethorn hedges.[11] Descendants of English tenants would subdivide them into compact enclosed farms, notably in County Armagh, whereas both native and Scottish tenants often perpetuated their traditional farming practices in hill country such as County Antrim. Even in the early years of the Plantation, commentators drew attention to the problem of protecting settlers who lived on isolated farms among the Irish at some distance from the estate towns.

Although several of the estates granted in the counties of Antrim and Down were very large (notably those of the Earl of Antrim, Sir Edward Conway and Sir Arthur Chichester),[12] those in the six counties comprising the Ulster Plantation project were much smaller and contained between one and two thousand Irish Plantation (= 1.6 to 3.2 thousand statute) acres of profitable land. They were allocated to one hundred English and Scottish 'undertakers' and about fifty 'servitors' (government officials and army officers) among whom were few men of substance, although the lands required considerable investment in capital and manpower. The City of London was coerced by King James I to 'take on the entire county of Londonderry in an effort to bring capital and economic prosperity to a commercial backwater'.[13] Even from the early years of the Plantation, a considerable market in property had developed, although money to buy it or mortgage it was often in short supply.[14]

The fortunes of the new landlords suffered in both the 1641 Rising and its long aftermath and in the Williamite Wars. Landlords soon learned that if their lands were not to lie waste, they would have to attract potential tenants by granting them beneficial leases in return for promises to build houses and enclose farms. By the end of the seventeenth century, the traditional English copyhold lease for lives had been adapted as the common improvement lease in Ulster, whereas the longest term for Scottish leases in the eighteenth century was nineteen years. This traditional copyhold lease for lives, however, required interpretation when applied to Irish estates because it differed from the copyhold of inheritance common in the Midlands, and in the east and south-east of England, in that there was no automatic right of renewal.[15] Both these forms of the leases for lives were adopted in Ulster but they were not held according to 'the custom of the manor' but as written contracts signed and sealed by both parties and witnessed by third parties. The lease for three lives was not renewable automatically but it was assumed from an early date that the sitting tenant had the first right to renegotiate the terms of the new lease. To encourage potential tenants to build houses in the Ulster towns, leases for three lives were made renewable by the tenant on the death of each one of the lives, on payment of a year's rent. By law the landlord could not break the lease even if the tenant failed to insert a new name on the death of an old one, paying the renewal fine: his only redress was to sue the tenant for debt. The real nature of this lease was recognised in 1849 by the enactment of the Renewable Leasehold Conversion Act, which converted it into a fee farm grant.[16]

Under the Plantation scheme, Crown grants to undertakers and officials had created a system of landholding that contained some of the elements of feudal tenure. The Crown also, by setting aside the statute of *Quia Emptores* of 1290, introduced a manorial system with tenants bound 'to do suit at' (i.e. required to attend and use) the manor courts and mills. The tenants they brought with them or attracted to their estates were bound to their new lords by something like the feudal tenure that many of the immigrants had known before they left England. After the Restoration, however, by the Tenures Abolition Act (Ireland) of 1662,[17] such feudal tenures were converted into freeholds and leaseholds, although some of the old paraphernalia such as 'suit to court and mills' and heriots were not abolished. Although this act cut any traces binding tenants to their lords, many tenants continued to appreciate the traditional ties and to value support and patronage in the colonial world. Those instincts were expressed in their claim to remain under their landlord and to hold their property from him, which is the essence of the concept of tenant right, known to us as the Ulster Custom.[18] This concept had its origins in medieval England but it was modified by circumstances in colonial Ulster.[19] Until parliament and the lawyers undertook to define tenant right in the nineteenth century, its practice differed widely from estate to estate throughout Ulster. It was sold by tenants with (or sometimes without) the knowledge of their landlords.

No evidence can be found in Ulster of the Scottish 'steelbow' tradition by which the landlord provided his tenant with capital equipment, including livestock and seed corn, at the entry of a lease, to be returned at its expiry.[20] Ulster landlords, especially in the early years of the colony, did not have the resources to assist in this manner, and circumstances provided no subsequent opportunities to invest in farm improvements.

In Scotland, there had long been a culture of landlord paternalism which placed the Scottish landlord in a very powerful position against the people on his estate. He presided over his own baron courts, the lowest levels of the judicial hierarchy.[21] In practice, he had the legal right of eviction at the end of a lease, including not only the tenant but also the subtenants and cottars, a procedure prescribed by an act of 1555. Although baron courts were abolished in 1747, along with 'heritable jurisdictions', the eviction procedure was clarified by the Act of Sederunt in 1756, and the baron court replaced by a much more effective legal instrument, the sheriff court.[22] When a lease terminated, the landlord was required only to give the tenant a summons of removal forty days notice before Whitsunday.[23]

In eighteenth-century Ulster, possession of a lease did not end when the term of the lease expired. The sitting tenant might claim a right to negotiate new terms for its renewal. In 1705, for example, the leading Belfast merchant who was anxious to become a tenant of Lord Conway and prepared to lay out £1,200 to £1,500 in the purchase of leases, insisted in a letter that he 'would not meddle with any lease that the tenant thinks he has a right to renew and is willing to do it'.[24] An agent explained about tenants on a County Antrim estate in 1722 as follows: 'If they do not come to a new agreement you need not fear tenants, but [deal with] none until they have left the land for our foolish people in this country think it a great sin to take land while the other tenant is in possession.'[25] Possession of the lease had an economic value, and its current 'interest' was calculated on the number of lives or years that it might have to run, together with a sum reflecting the state of demand in the property market. The sitting tenant was recognised as such by his fellows, and they were ready to support him if they considered that he was not receiving fair and understanding treatment at the hands of the landlord. Tenants often tried to take advantage of this understanding and presented serious problems to the agent pondering how to *distrain* [sell up the assets of] tenants who had fallen heavily into arrears.

If I could once get a farm sold cleverly, I am very confident that some would struggle to pay, who as your Lordship observes are waiting the event, but the loss I am at is getting purchasers while the tenant is in possession. If he himself is not earnest in selling, not a man will offer to buy, and to bring the tenant to consent I must either take off all he has, or bring a writ for him and send him to gaol. I will indeed do everything in my power. I will go on and seize the crops and cattle, and if I can, get sufficient security for their being delivered to me on the grounds in eight days. I will set up notices to sell them and the farm at that time. If I cannot get security I must I believe impound the cattle and sell them in six days after they are impounded, and then if there will not be sufficient, sell the farm if I can. [26]

Because Irish landlords were advised by their lawyers to avoid law cases, they acted cautiously in handling such troublesome tenants. The agent on the Barrett-Lennard estate in Clones, County Monaghan, explained to his master in 1760:

I shall so far take care as you desire not to proceed nor to take any step rashly or inconsiderately and expose ourselves to the hazard of being defeated, for if we proceed at law for breach of covenant, it must be tried by a jury, who perhaps may be for the most part tenants themselves, and if so, will most probably favour the tenant or incline to do in all such actions, and all which ought to be considered and thought of beforehand.[27]

A further major difference between the legal circumstances of Scotland and Ireland emerges with Devine's discovery that the Scottish landlord was allowed by law to build into the contract of the lease 'mandatory improving clauses which were enforceable at law'.[28] As he admits, 'these were major advantages for a social class intent on radical change. But, in addition, they had considerable seigneurial authority.' In contrast, Irish landlords found it very difficult to enforce covenants, even when they were traditional clauses in leases. The Scottish Earl of Abercorn, who owned estates at Duddingston in Midlothian and Paisley in Renfrewshire as well as in the Counties of Tyrone and Donegal in Ireland, was exasperated when he wrote to his Irish agent in 1773: 'I think it an act of lunacy to enter into covenants, for a long term, which I am bound and intend to perform, with people who profess not to think of themselves bound on their part.'[29] Eight months later he was still fulminating in a letter to Jemmy's brother, John Hamilton, his agent in Strabane: 'The great consolation I have in the oppression I lie under from the tenants is the resolution I have taken not to let farms any more for such long terms. Long leases are the ruin of Ireland and of every man in it and the great obstruction to improvement.'[30] His verdict on Irish tenants was pithy: he had become 'more and more convinced of the total ignorance of the tenants of the principles of justice and common sense upon which the contract of a lease is founded'.[31] Although Abercorn's solution would have been to reduce the term of leases to seven years, his agent convinced him that no tenant would take the farm on those terms and he would have them lying on his hands.

Two methods of dealing with this problem were suggested by contemporaries: inserting into leases penal clauses prescribing fines for the non-performance of covenants, or charging high rents with rebates for the performance of each covenant. That the first solution was not effective was the opinion of the Abercorn agent in 1772.

> I did not think that covenants in the leases for additional rents were nugatory and it is no doubt proper to convince the tenant they are not. Yet in the cases your Lordship was pleased to send me, the penalty (if I might so call it) seems rather more than exemplary, and on the other hand if nothing could be recovered but the damages, it would give frequent room for litigation.[32]

Both methods were considered too complicated and ponderous to cope with the problem. When a tenant was in arrears with his rent, the lease contract gave the landlord or his agent the right to seize, or *distrain* (the official term) property belonging to the tenant in lieu of the debt; this action was known as *distress*. On many estates a practice arose of sending out the estate bailiff to seize cattle: the arrival of the bailiff prompted many tenants to pay their rent. After a certain period allowed to the remaining debtors for paying off their debt (known as recovery, or *replevin*), their cattle or other chattels could be sold in public to pay the debt. If the property seized was not sufficient to pay the arrears, the landlord had the right to *re-enter* and resume his property, but only after every opportunity to repay the debt had been afforded to the tenant. Anyone dispossessed on such an ejectment, however, had the legal right to repossess his property if he paid the debt and costs within six months. In such circumstances, a culture developed of delaying the payment of rent as long as possible. The Abercorn agent reported in 1767:

> It must be allowed even by the tenants themselves, that their bargains under your Lordship are good, which is very evident by the high prices given by anyone purchasing into your Lordship's estate, and I am persuaded that few amongst them, but could pay much better, and that it is now high time to oblige them, their leases having run so far. The richest among them plead for time to enable them to carry on trade, others that if they are obliged to pay they will be forced to sell their stock, or that they have their yarn ready to weave and that if they got some time they would make considerably by it.[33]

Abercorn instructed Jemmy to inform all tenants who were in arrears that their claim to tenant-right would not be recognised when their leases expired.

Devine showed that in late eighteenth- and early nineteenth-century Scotland the landlords used the mechanism of the improving lease for the dissemination of improved practices[34] and enforced the covenants through 'a zealous group of estate factors, agents and surveyors in partnership with enterprising tenants'.[35] 'The commitment of the landlords to improvement was based on the expectation of hugely increased profits from their lands which would cover the cost of their investment in a relatively short time.'[36] Crucial was the availability of a pool of tenants sufficient to replace those who failed.[37] Devine's major points can be used to highlight the differences between circumstances in Scotland and Ulster.

As the early eighteenth-century Ulster linen industry developed, farmers began to sublet portions of their farms to skilled weavers who wanted small-holdings to maintain their families during downturns in trade. Such farmers tried to safeguard their own claim to tenant right by setting 'five or six years short of the tenure they have. Besides, they bind them under a penalty, and sometimes by oath, to give up peacably when their turn is expired and that they are not to petition or otherwise apply for any tenant right.'[38] In time landlords began to realise how much potential rent they were losing and so, as the head leases to the farmers expired, they began to let the smallholdings direct to the weavers, cutting out the middlemen and expanding the number of rentpayers. There were no significant changes in the covenants in the leases. Indeed, the terms in leases had become standardised, and many land-lords used printed versions purchased from stationers. Conditions were advertised as in the *Belfast News-Letter* in the summer of 1769:

> To be let from the first of November 1769 for the term of three lives, twenty-two farms of land in the townland of Corromannon and county of Armagh, part of the estate of Sir Archibald Acheson, Bart. Each farm is enclosed by a new ditch, quicked and planted, and contain variously from thirteen to fifteen [statute] acres a piece, with sufficient meadow, good water, and excellent turf bog. Such persons as become tenants, shall have liberty to build their houses this ensuing summer, and be furnished with principal timber, and allowed to cut turf. Samuel Wilson of Lurgiross will show these farms, and proposals will be received by Mr George Sinclair, and Mr Mark Brown at Market Hill. Such persons as intend to treat (if strangers) must fetch certificates, signed by responsible people, for their honesty and good behaviour.

As early as 1739 William Henry, a dean of the established church, had commented on 'the happy success which this method of dividing the land into small partitions and encouraging the cottager and the manufacturer has had in enriching both landlord and tenant'.[39] By 1759 Edward Willes, the chief baron of the exchequer, noted that along the sixty miles of road from Monaghan to Carrickfergus:

One is scarce ever 200 yards from a neat cabin, or a manufacturer's house or a gentleman's seat. And what adds greatly to the beauty, every little cabin has an orchard or garden belonging to it, and spinning or weaving or some branch of the linen trade going on in every one of them. The multitude of bleach yards adds greatly to the prospect. They look like so many patches of unmelted snow upon a thaw.[40]

The success of this policy made other landlords aware of its potential to increase their rent rolls at little cost to themselves. Especially significant was the reclamation of the upland country in South Armagh. The catalyst was the application of water power by Ulster bleachers to drive machinery for the bleaching and finishing of linen: in 1743 the first of these bleachgreens had been constructed on the River Callan; by 1771, there were another thirty-five of them.

And the [linen] manufacture gaining strength about fifty years ago [1745] they began to push their improvements into the mountains which separates the low country from Louth, and by the assistance of turf, fuel being convenient and good constant rivers for feeding bleachyards and working machinery, they were enabled greatly to extend their improvements in the mountains, and many wealthy farmers and manufacturers were induced by the low price of them – about a shilling to half a crown an acre – to take farms, lime and burn them, although the limestone quarries were distant from the centre of the mountains measuring from the quarries at Armagh or those on the Louth side towards Dundalk at least eight or nine miles either way but their spirited industry has surmounted all difficulties, and within these forty years Newtown Hamilton a considerable town has been established in the centre, and a weekly linen market well supplied established. A strong yeomanry and many excellent houses and roads leading through the country in all directions have been made here, formerly a perfectly 'black' mountain. This is an example worthy of the attention of the landed interest and landholders of Ireland as these mountains were lofty without any internal manures and generally very wet and bad stuff to work on, and yet it is no exaggeration to say those inhabitants have reduced more mountain to profitable and excellent tillage ground than any other county in Ireland can boast of. The small pot kill [kiln] is what they mostly all use to burn their lime.[41]

The establishment of Newtownhamilton in 1748 might be said to mark the beginning of two decades of major urban development in Ulster. Landlords tried to attract tenants to build in their estate towns by providing facilities such as inns and market-houses for the sale of linen yarn and cloth and by promoting markets and fairs as collecting points for cattle after the ban on exporting live cattle to Britain was lifted in 1759.[42] There were attempts to encourage weavers to move into some of the small market towns, but in general they failed before the end of the century.[43]

The development of Ulster towns was related to the expansion of the road network. Although the attempt to introduce the turnpike system into Ireland in the 1730s had been underwritten by the Dublin government, it was very limited in its success and the burden for the upkeep of the roads continued to fall on the public by the traditional six days' scheme managed by the parishes. In 1765, however, a road act made the county grand juries responsible for the construction and maintenance of the roads in their several baronies and allowed them to impose an extra charge on the county cess. This effectively placed the supervision for the expansion of the road network under the control of the landlords. It proved to be a great success and employed the poor in the construction of new roads and bridges throughout the province. Nowhere is this better illustrated than by a comparison of the 1780 and 1808 versions of the grand jury map for County Antrim, where the revision of 1808 depicts the new roads constructed in the intervening years. The rapidly rising expenditure by the grand juries of the counties indicates the increasing prosperity of the local economy.[44]

Table 1.1. Grand jury expenditure in £000s in Ulster, 1770–1840

County	1770	1780	1790	1800	1810	1820	1830	1840
Antrim	4	6	8	13	29	33	43	66
Armagh	–	5	8	8	19	21	24	32
Cavan	3	–	–	–	17	17	24	37
Donegal	5	6	10	16	21	19	–	41
Down	–	4	7	12	27	30	36	52
Fermanagh	2	2	4	5	11	13	15	28
Londonderry	4	5	8	13	24	19	28	30
Monaghan	2	3	5	7	12	15	19	25
Tyrone	–	–	–	–	–	–	45	48

Source: Appendix to Minutes of Evidence taken before Her Majesty's Commissioners of Inquiry into the state of the law and practice in respect to the occupation of land in Ireland, pt. IV [672], B.P.P., 1845, XX, No. 70.

In 1772 'an act for the making of narrow roads through the mountainous unimproved parts of this kingdom' (11&12 GIII c.20) stated in its preliminary that 'it would greatly contribute to the improvement thereof, if roads were made through the same'. The next act in the statute book, 'an act to encourage the reclaiming of unprofitable bogs' (c.21), noted that 'it hath been proved by experience, that such bogs are capable of improvement, and to be converted into arable or pasture land, if encouragement was given to the lower class of people to apply their industry to the reclaiming of the same'. Owners of this marginal land advertised their intention to create new market towns and required the county grand juries to link them with roads to neighbouring market towns. The landowners were then in a position to encourage settlement by leasing new farms at low rents alongside new access roads on which lime and timber could be imported to build a cottage and outbuildings. Techniques for draining and improving marginal lands were propagated in the mid-eighteenth century, and the potato crop was found to be especially effective for their initial cultivation. Cultivating these marginal lands provided one of the very few opportunities afforded to the less well-off to lift themselves out of the massed ranks of the poor. As long as landlords were prepared to lease marginal lands there would always be potential tenants.[45] Problems arose when lands were leased to groups rather than individuals: on the Abercorn estate this style of holding land was referred to as 'rundale' because the boundaries between the 'dales' were not marked by hedges or stone walls. The practice of leasing to partners had been used by landlords to secure their rents because they held the partners jointly responsible for payment. As individual farmers struggled to gain independence from their partners, however, they needed someone to champion them. On a well-organised estate such as the Abercorn, the agent James Hamilton was able to request his master to regulate the division of such holdings between partners.[46] Abercorn responded quickly. 'Any tenants desirous of a division, may put their leases into your hands, under assurance of having them restored when the division shall be made under my order, without any advance or expense to them of any sort, and as conveniently as may be. And I will support no division made after by themselves.'[47] The number of small farms continued to increase rapidly also because, in contrast to the Scottish situation, there were few opportunities outside farming for the rising generations. Provision for them had to be made. As Jemmy Hamilton explained to the Earl of Abercorn: 'These debts that become burdens on the farms are very ruinous. If the daughter at her marriage does not get a bit of the farm, her portion is borrowed and becomes in the end a demand on the farm. They seldom make any other provision for son and daughter than the land.'[48]

The contrast between Scotland and Ireland was considerable. Although Scottish landlords recognised that colonies of small tenants practising intensive agriculture were ideal for the reclamation of marginal land,[49] they concentrated on withdrawing tenants. While communities continued to work in rural linen and cotton mills, mines and quarries, more of the hill country was given over to sheep farming, and so tenants were cleared off the hill country or concentrated around a smaller tenant elite.[50] Devine's verdict is 'the removal of the cottiers was concentrated in the last few decades of the eighteenth and the early years of the nineteenth century. In its scale, speed and effect it was more reminiscent of the patterns of clearance in the Highlands than any other aspect of lowland social change in this period ... The Highland Clearances have stimulated a veritable scholarly industry but the Lowland Clearances still await their historian.'[51] He adds, however, 'It was fundamental to the emergence of a predominantly landless labour force, the migration process within the countryside and the dissolution of the older settlement pattern. An entire tier of the traditional social order was removed in many areas over the space of a few decades.'[52]

In 1821, when the population of Scotland was 2,091,000, the population of Ulster reached 1,998,494, making it the most densely populated province in Ireland. In 1841 the average number of people per square mile of 'arable' (or improved) land in the whole of Ireland was 335, equivalent to about 60 families. In Leinster the rural density was 247, in Munster 332, in Connaught 386 and in Ulster 406 per square mile. It reached 511 per square mile in the handloom linen weaving county of Armagh.[53] Most of the Ulster farms supported a single household: 265,000 families in 234,000 farms.[54] The proportion of landless labourers in the population was small. Only 4 per cent of the farms exceeded 30 acres, while 43 per cent comprised 1–5 acres.[55] Ulster had evolved into the province of the independent small farmer. After the 1793 Catholic Relief Act, Catholic tenants moved on to the same legal footing as their Protestant neighbours. Leases gave them a considerable degree of legal security in their holdings due to the social pressure they were able to exert on landowners, whose incomes depended on the regular payment of rents. Economic security was based on oatmeal and the potato, which had allowed more land to be brought under cultivation, while the expanding market in Britain for Irish cattle and pigs promised prosperity.[56] The successful domestic linen industry was providing employment for all.

After 1800 the Ulster population began to overflow into Scotland, attracted by job opportunities for seasonal labour. These migrants would have found that the cultures of Scotland and Ulster were diverging. Scotland was industrialising and urbanising; by contrast, families in the poorer regions of Ulster were beginning to suffer from the decline of the domestic industry of handspinning linen yarn, which forced them to compensate for their losses by farming more intensively or emigrating to Britain. Like their landlords, most of the stronger tenant–farmers were Protestants, while the majority of the small farmers and the cottiers who held land from them were Catholic. The resurgence of the Catholic church, reflected in the Catholic Emancipation Act of 1829 and the subsequent campaign against the Act of Union, began to politicise the Catholic tenants. 'The North of Ireland was becoming during the nineteenth century an ethnic frontier between the British and Irish nations.'[57]

2

Debt and the Scottish Landed Elite in the 1650s

David J. Menarry

This essay is drawn from a broad study of the political accommodation reached between the English governments of the Commonwealth and Protectorate and the Irish and Scottish landed elites during the Interregnum.[1] It focuses on the role played by private debts in shaping the settlement between the Cromwellians and Scotland's political leaders after the English conquest of the Scots in the early 1650s. Traditionally, in the absence of a large standing army and a centralised administration, the government of Scotland relied upon the support of regional power brokers, whose power came both from their leading role within kin groups as well as their legal rights as tenants-in-chief, to maintain law and order in the localities. Following its army's attainment of military superiority over the Scots in the autumn of 1651, the English parliament set about trying to break the economic and political power of the Scottish landed elite. The Cromwellians thought they possessed the muscle and policies to reduce and replace proprietors opposing their agenda. Such a belief proved misplaced.

The Commonwealthsmen blamed Scottish proprietors for provoking the conquest, branding them a 'wicked and perfideous generation'.[2] They argued Scotland's landowners retained an unjustifiable and overbearing influence within society, which they had exploited to push the country into the arms of Charles II and ruin any possibility of partnership. Against this background the English parliamentary commissioners, who arrived in Scotland in January 1652 to take over civil government, found that, because of the nature of the Scottish debt laws, they could exploit indebtedness among the landed elite to undermine them. As a consequence, debt emerged alongside sequestration as one of the main weapons used by the English to reduce the power of the landed elite. The policy of reduction and replacement, however, by helping to fuel a Royalist rebellion, which proved costly and threatened the continuation of the regime in Scotland, caused a rethink. The republican government found itself forced to recognise the limits of its authority and accept existing power structures. In offering a specific example of a situation where debt represented an important political issue, this article complements recent publications on the Scottish and Irish elites.[3] It also stands as an addition to works on the New British and Irish Histories in the seventeenth century.[4]

In response to the regicide of late January 1649, the radical regime, which had been in power in Edinburgh since the previous autumn, declared Charles II King of Great Britain, France and Ireland on 5 February 1649. This, a natural response given the imperatives of covenanting, placed it on a collision course with the Independent faction in England, on whose military support it relied when it had assumed control of Scotland, wresting power from supporters of the Royalist Engagement.[5] While the king remained in exile and the radical regime denied him executive power, the republican government in London pretty much accepted the Edinburgh administration's argument that it did not seek to alter England's constitutional settlement by force. But when, in the spring of 1650, it became clear that the radical regime, unpopular and keen to return to more traditional modes of government to bolster its position, intended inviting Charles II to Scotland to rule as a covenanted monarch, the English Commonwealth took fright and took the decision to launch a pre-emptive strike against the Scots.[6]

Charles II signed the Covenant at Speymouth on 23 June 1650. Cromwell crossed the Tweed with an army a month later.[7] The Rumpers knew the king aimed at the recovery of his English and Irish thrones from a Scottish base and believed the radical regime, notwithstanding the conditions it tried to impose on him, might not simply be dupes. As far as the English parliament was concerned, the very fact that the Edinburgh government made contact with Charles II cast doubt upon its claim to accept the existence, if not the legitimacy, of the Commonwealth.[8] Faced with an English invasion, covenanting purists within the radical regime doubled their efforts to remove Engager influence completely from the Scottish army.[9] Defeat of the purged army at Dunbar on 3 September, though, undermined the purists' position and persuaded pragmatists within the administration in Edinburgh to move towards a patriotic accommodation with former Engagers as the only way to defend Scotland against English republicanism. In the closing months of 1650, the covenanting mainstream, the radical regime being its public face, split. The purists found themselves sidelined. Notwithstanding the transformation of the army and its command promoted by Charles II and Scottish Royalists during the first half of 1651, the patriotic cause collapsed in the autumn.[10]

At Worcester on 3 September Cromwell smashed the Royalist force that Charles II had led out of Scotland in August. In the following couple of months, the commanders of the English army, who had remained in Scotland to pacify the country, extended the area under their control to the fringes of the Highlands (which remained passively opposed to the

Commonwealth).[11] The extension of English authority did not simply result from military might. Accompanying the strongarm tactics, English officers in essence kicked off the formal process of accommodation with the Scottish landed elite, negotiating terms of surrender guaranteeing security of estate with, most prominently, John Murray, second Earl of Atholl, Lewis Gordon, third Marquis of Huntly, and Alexander Lindsay, first Earl of Balcarres, all leading Royalists and important regional power brokers.[12] Such agreements, which effectively offered protection from sequestration at this early stage, the English parliament hoped later to subvert with its policy on debt.

The 'Declaration on the Government of Scotland', published by the parliamentary commissioners in February 1652 along with an ensuing 'explanation', revealed whom the English intended holding to account for the preceding wars.[13] After imposing religious toleration and 'inviting' the Scots to join England in a political union, the Declaration claimed for the English parliament the estates, 'real and personall', of 'the chief Actors' in the hostile invasions of England by James, first Duke of Hamilton in 1648 and Charles II in 1651. Initially the English government offered pardon and protection only to Scots who had deserted the patriotic cause after Dunbar, but the 'explanation' changed the emphasis, assuring all those in the counties who accepted the change in government, 'not having lands and goods above the clear value of two hundred pounds sterling', that they would be 'freed and discharged from all Forfeitures and confiscations of their estates'.[14] The average annual income of a Scottish laird in 1640 has been estimated to have been 83*l.* The primary targets of the English were the greater landlords.[15] The final say on which individuals would face forfeiture lay with the English parliament but, while the enabling legislation was under discussion, the parliamentary commissioners in Scotland received the power to sequestrate the revenues of the Scots they felt would be acted against.[16]

Sequestration, as a forerunner to confiscation, might have represented the most overt expression of English policy toward the landed elite, but it would be used sparingly. Against the background of war with the Dutch, so fearful were the parliamentary commissioners in Scotland of provoking resistance that they confined sequestration to the estates of Scottish prisoners of war, the people whom they felt would most likely be among the Scots the Rump would decide to forfeit.

The extent to which the English government backed away from sequestration during 1652 can be most clearly viewed from its dealings with the Highlands. In the summer of that year, the parliamentary commissioners oversaw a campaign to bring the Highlanders to heel. Instead of extending sequestration, the army commanders promoted a policy of self-regulation. The terms that Archibald Campbell, Marquis of Argyll, secured on 19 August, after some skirmishing in his bounds with the English army, exemplified this. Under the deal the Marquis essentially guaranteed his dominant position within the western Highlands. The fourth article of the agreement asserted 'the said Lord Marquesse of Argyle shall enjoy his liberty, estate, lands, and debts, and whatever duty belongs unto him, free from sequestration or molestation from the Parliament of the Commonwealth of England, or any by aucthority [sic] for them.'[17] While sequestration only came to cause a problem for a small section of the elite, the difficulties that the English created through the debt laws were almost universal. This, in turn, led the English to draw back from sequestration still further. Why should the English government move against estates when they could leave other Scots to do it for them? They might even gain some political support from creditors recovering money they were owed.[18] Landowners often borrowed money from other landowners, but, increasingly through the turmoil of the 1640s and early 1650s, debt chains had their origins in the burghs, which the English were particularly eager to court.[19] Also, the English government became disillusioned with sequestration because it subordinated its right to revenues from the sequestrated estates to the creditors of those estates, and it often found that sequestration only led to it incurring greater costs with no reward.

From the time of the arrival of the parliamentary commissioners in January 1652, the problems that the elite suffered as a consequence of indebtedness increased. One of the first things the commissioners did was abolish all jurisdictions not sanctioned by the Commonwealth.[20] Scotland's greatest landowners had until then been able to use their position within the judicial system to delay the payment of money they owed and temper the rigour of any process of diligence against them. The best example of this was the advantages brought by the existence of heritable jurisdictions, such as a regality or barony courts. Those in possession of such jurisdictions were able to repledge cases brought against them in other, higher courts back to their own courts on the undertaking that they would hear the particular case within a year and a day. Of course, once within their jurisdiction suspensions against creditors could be granted and the whole process slowed down. Heritable jurisdictions were not completely reduced, but (leaving the unique case of the Marquis of Argyll aside, as he did attain a limited degree of immunity from his creditors under the terms of his articles) as far as the powers that the remaining holders of such jurisdictions had to help them avoid paying their debts, they might as well have been. The judicial advantage enjoyed by the elite prior to the English takeover was not just confined to those presiding over courts, either, as those without heritable jurisdictions used their political networks to gain favourable decisions from the courts. As Smith has demonstrated, the judges, primarily English, appointed under the Commonwealth were detached from the interest of the

Scottish elite and therefore the system was not as susceptible to manipulation, at least not in the same way as before.[21]

When in May 1652 the parliamentary commissioners appointed the 'Commissioners for the Administration of Justice to the people of Scotland' as the new top tier of the judicial system, they made certain they would not help preserve the financial position of Scotland's indebted landowners.[22] This policy, which amounted to conquest by stealth, proved so potent because landowners found it difficult to service their debts. The devastation of the Scottish rural economy by over a decade of warfare and the cost of sustaining English occupation left them unable to raise the necessary money either from their revenues or new sources of credit. The level of the monthly assessment that the English government imposed on Scotland reveals the scale of the problem the Scots faced as, by February 1652, the parliamentary commissioners had still only stabilised it at a rate of 10,000*l*.[23] Such a sum, even taking into account the fifth, allowed in abatements, was 500*l* more per month than the radical regime had set out to collect in 1649. It represented an annual burden equivalent to just under a quarter of the rental of Scotland in 1649, and that, of course, before the dislocation caused by the conquest.[24] It proved impossible to gather.

As soon as the justice commissioners had been appointed in May, the government in Edinburgh became well aware it was onto a winner with its policy on debt; it proudly reported from Leith that the Scottish people were beginning 'to meddle with many of their Grandees agt whom heertofore they durst nott complaine'. Mentioned were suits against the Earls of Loudon, Huntly, Murray, Morton, Balcarres and Crawford Lindsay, and the parliamentary commissioners did not doubt 'but justice will be administered to all without respect of persons'.[25] The problems faced by Huntly, for instance, were well known. At the beginning of February 1652, *Mercurius Politicus* reported that 'Huntley is a man more in Debt then his whole Estate, a man infinite proud and ambitious; vastly expensive'. The correspondent went on to comment on the reason for Huntly's peaceful deportment, writing 'he is in possession of his whole Estate; neither *Sequestration* nor *Law* troubles him, and he hath by him Companions for any adventure.'[26] The English expected resistance to arise in Scotland as a result of their policy; what they did not anticipate was the scale of the problem it would create and the change in approach it would force upon them.

The parliamentary commissioners in 1652 did not alter the fundamental legal relationship between debtor and creditor, nor did they remove the obstacles lying in the way of creditors gaining legal redress against those that failed to honour bonds by making sure that the courts acted against the elite. Rather, procedures were altered which tweaked the Scottish debt laws more to the advantage of creditors. For example, heirs and executors of deceased creditors were saved the customary long court case to prove their right to claim the debts before moving to recover any money owed.[27] The English also appear actively to have persuaded creditors to go to law. For instance, the head of the Jesuit house in Paris – a Scot, Father Robert Gall, who was in constant contact with his homeland – wrote in September 1652 of how the English intended 'to give full power agayne Martinmasse next to all Merchands & Creditores, to whom any of the Gentry or Nobility ar endebted, to compryle [i.e. comprise] their lands & tak seizing [i.e. seisine] yrof, if they be not satisfied before that tyme'.[28]

The ruin of John Stewart, Earl of Traquair, by his creditors in the 1650s would have been regarded by the English as a perfect example of what they hoped to see happen in Scotland as a consequence of their changes to the judiciary. Traquair represented a soft target. Not only a prisoner of war, he also occupied an exposed position within Scottish Lowland society, having been a target of the Covenanters for many years. From the charters registered under the Great Seal during the 1650s, the alienation of the Earl of Traquair's property to satisfy his creditors can clearly be seen.[29] While most members of the landed elite, including prisoners of war, avoided the loss of their estates, Traquair's isolation meant that he found it impossible to delay his creditors. Traquair was allowed to return to Scotland on parole for six months in March 1653, but he was unable to prevent his fall into penury.[30] By the time the English changed their stance on debt, he had lost too much to reverse the process. Huntly and John Erskine, ninth Earl of Mar, also suffered from early onslaughts from their creditors, but neither fared as badly as Traquair. While in the long term Traquair's fate might have proved rare, the fear of suffering such an indignity exercised the minds of the majority of the landed elite in the early 1650s, causing them to contemplate armed resistance.

The measures employed against the Scottish elite remained, more or less unchanged, throughout 1653. It was by the late summer of that year that the policy really began to bite, causing many among Scotland's landed elite to join the Royalist force that had emerged in the Highlands during the previous few months. It was the threat of arrest and imprisonment under letters of caption (the primary method of enforcing payment of debts adopted in the early 1650s by creditors, as the political turmoil in Scotland and the country's poor financial state made other forms of diligence less attractive), no doubt coupled with the prospect of their estates being apprised by creditors when land values were low, that pushed landowners into the arms of the rebels.[31] At first, the English ignored the proprietors joining the Royalists led by William Cunningham, eighth Earl of Glencairn, in the hills. To the authorities, their flight merely confirmed the belief they had been right to allow proceedings against them. Although the numbers involved increased, along with the problems posed by the rebellion, things changed. The role that debt played in helping Royalist recruitment was not lost on an anonymous Scottish chronicler, who described the leaders of the Royalist army in the late summer of 1653 as being made up of 'highlanders, and some noblemen, whereof some were fled for debt'.[32]

On 3 October 1653 Colonel Robert Lilburne, commander-in-chief of the English forces in Scotland from the end of 1652, granted protections to Huntly and Mar against their creditors.[33] Lilburne feared that, without such an olive branch from the government, Huntly and Mar would join Glencairn's rebellion, which, because of their influence in the north-east, could have caused great problems for the English.[34] In Mar's case there does not seem to have been much more behind the protection than the need to prevent him joining the rebels. He had simply reached the end of his tether, having already witnessed the loss of large parts of his estate to his creditors.[35] More, though, lay behind Huntly's experience. Huntly found himself tied to Argyll, who remained acquiescent to English rule, as he believed the rebellion would 'ruine more Scottes then Inglish'.[36] Argyll was Huntly's major creditor, having bought up the debts of his brother-in-law George, seventh Earl of Huntly.[37] Argyll, therefore, to some extent dictated the way Lilburne treated Huntly, offering a way of controlling his nephew through his debts. The protections that Huntly and Mar secured were of the same style as the concessions that Argyll had gained the previous year on his debts – they did not represent a change of policy by the English on debt. However, just six weeks later Lilburne advocated just that.

In the second half of October and November 1653, the rebels plundered and caused widespread destruction outside the Highlands while managing to elude the English soldiers stationed specifically to prevent incursions into the Lowlands.[38] Shocked, Lilburne responded with a wholesale review of policy. Accompanying calls for a bolstering of the English military establishment, Lilburne questioned the whole basis of the Commonwealth's approach to the Scottish elite.[39] Lilburne's change of heart manifested itself in his call for an act of oblivion to include all but those who refused to lay down their arms and just five or six 'grand offendors', as well as his arguments to ease the plight of debtors.[40]

In his letter to the Council of State of 12 November, Lilburne described how 'Lords and gentlemen (that have had good fortunes)' had been reduced to 'great extremity' by their creditors. He explained that these men were often inclined to give what satisfaction they could, but 'theyre creditors sometimes refusing putts some upon desperate courses, and in these broken times constrains them to lay hold upon any advantage to save themselves, and therby … join with those parties [the rebels] out of meere necessity, to the disturbance of the peace'. Lilburne informed the Council that he was in no position to stop such situations arising as he did not have the power to grant protections or suspensions. The only thing he could do, he said, was present their cases to the justice commissioners, but as they were 'tied uppe much to the letter of the law', the debtors were often left 'in an unsatisfied condition'.[41] He made clear the scale of the problem when he reported in December 1653 that there were '35,000 captions out against men'.[42]

At first it looked to Lilburne as if his requests had fallen on deaf ears. The silence most probably resulted from the turmoil in London surrounding the creation of the Protectorate. By January, he had heard from London that his proposals were receiving consideration as part of a whole raft of measures designed by Cromwell and his supporters to bring about 'healing and settling' across the three kingdoms.[43] While Lilburne instigated the changes which occurred in policy in Scotland during the spring of 1654, General George Monck, who had commanded the English forces in Scotland in the autumn and winter of 1651, returned on the back of successes against the Dutch to oversee their implementation.[44] Monck's appointment reflected the fact that, while the London government was ready to make concessions in Scotland to promote peace and stability, it did not completely concur with Lilburne's suggestions. In the Ordinance of Pardon and Grace to the people of Scotland of 12 April, some ninety-nine Scots were excepted by name from pardon – twenty-six of them faced definite forfeiture, while seventy-three had the opportunity to avoid that fate by paying a fine – in addition to the Scots remaining in arms against the Commonwealth.[45] Monck found himself rather overawed by the situation he encountered in Scotland, and consequently he quickly adopted much of Lilburne's more pragmatic programme, which included him offering strong backing to the Ordinance on Debt being discussed in London and which appeared at the end of May.[46] By the summer, only the rebel leaders remained in Monck's sights. After an otherwise successful summer campaign failed to bring their defeat, and the financial drain that Scotland represented to the Commonwealth increased further (in July it was estimated that the monthly charge of the military establishment in Scotland exceeded 41,000*l.*), the status of the rebel leaders changed in Monck's eyes. In the autumn he treated with Glencairn, Atholl and Kenmore, agreeing articles guaranteeing that their estates would not be forfeited.[47]

The Ordinance on Debt gave the justice commissioners the power 'to moderate Decrees to be by them given out against such Debitors as shall manifestly appear to them not to bee able to procure money for paying such Debt, by allowing som fit and convenient time or dayes for payment ... with interest for the same, until such time or dayes of payment'.[48] If the time elapsed without payment, the judges were authorised 'to appoint and set out lands of such Debtors, for the satisfaction of the Debt'. For this purpose the land was to be valued at its 1648 level, at a price of twenty years' purchase. This was an extremely 'debtor-friendly' move, not only because land values had dropped during the intervening period but also because, by giving such an inflated value to the lands of debtors, it made creditors who could afford to wait a little longer for their money think twice before moving against the Scots who owed them money while the measure was in force.[49] The Ordinance was to remain operative until 12 May 1655, by which time the government must have been hoping that the rebellion would have ended so there would not be such a pressing political need to give concessions to debtors. In addition, there were thoughts that land values would have recovered enough to return the debtor–creditor relationship to a more balanced state, and/or that the government by then might have brought Scotland's legal practice on debt into line with England's, which was always on the agenda but never carried out.

The legislation, championed by Lilburne and Monck because of the role indebtedness played in feeding the rebellion, was designed to reassure the landed elite. However, the justice commissioners were not as quick to use their new powers as they might have been. The diarist John Nicoll tells us the judges granted many suspensions, and not only to 'persones of meane rank'. He mentions Argyll and James Murray, second Earl of Tullibardine, among the elite.[50] The records of the central courts 'indicate that the judges made little change in practice, and continued to issue letters of horning without an extended date for the payment of the debt'.[51] For example, the Earl of Crawford's cautioner failed to gain a suspension, despite arguing that the creditors of the forfeited persons should gain satisfaction out of the forfeited estates and that he could not pay the money, as he had recently paid off his own creditors.[52]

Monck's efforts to persuade the justice commissioners to make more use of the powers they had been given by the Ordinance centred initially, during the autumn of 1654, around the cases of rebels that submitted under articles. On 18 September he wrote to the judges on behalf of David Creighton, Laird of Lugton, Glencairn's representative in the negotiations leading to Glencairn's capitulation.[53] Robert Gordon, fourth Viscount Kenmore, Richard Murray, heir to the Laird of Broughton, James Gordon of Cardines and James Baillie, second Lord Forrester, also received Monck's backing for suspensions to be granted against their creditors and for protection from arrest under letters of caption.[54] It must have been on the back of Monck's successful interventions on behalf of former rebels that the likes of James Home, third Earl of Home, Sir William Baillie of Lawington and Charles Seton, Earl of Dunfermline approached him for similar aid. Having remained detached from the uprising, they felt that they deserved equal if not better treatment than former rebels, and Monck agreed.[55] The justices remained reticent, and in the end Home had to approach the government in London for help. In his letter of recommendation for him on 20 March, Monck stated 'truly if the Judges would bee more forward in disposing Gentlemens lands for satisfying their creditors according to the said ordinance it would keepe this cuntry much more in Peace then it is'.[56] The Council of State only dealt with the case after the 1654 legislation had expired.[57] Home, joined by James Johnston, second Earl of Hartfell and Sir Robert Douglas of Blackerstoune, 'acting for themselves and other nobles and gentlemen of Scotland', persuaded the Council of State in the summer of the need to bring in new measures. They no doubt did so with the help of Roger Boyle, Earl of Broghill, who had been appointed president of the new Scottish council and who, through his wife, was related to Home and Hartfell.[58] Broghill arrived in Scotland in September 1655 with the primary intention of securing the Protectorate by making it more appealing to the Scots. Alongside Monck, he promoted the involvement of the Scottish elite in the administration, tying their interest to that of the Protectorate. Most clearly this manifested itself in the reduction of fines and retreat from the policy of forfeiture imposed by the Ordinance of Grace. On 25 September, the Council of State ordered the Scottish council to move toward the adoption of English practice in debt cases, but in the meantime they authorised the justice commissioners to proceed as if the former ordinance had not expired, with problematic cases to be referred to government in London.[59] On 5 October, it effectively reversed its decision by asking the Scottish council to look into the problem of debt and suggest a solution.[60]

In the ensuing debate in Scotland, the Scottish council accepted many of the arguments put forward by Home, Hartfell and Douglas, although it also listened to creditors, who had opposed the 1654 legislation.[61] The Scottish council sent its recommendations to the Council of State on 21 February 1656.[62] The Edinburgh government's proposals were quickly accepted. The Council of State passed an 'order for the relief of debtors' in Scotland on 15 April. It received its final approval on 12 May and was proclaimed in Edinburgh ten days later.[63] The Order was loosely based on the Ordinance of 1654, but it was significantly more generous to debtors; in particular, it did not, as its predecessor had done, afford the justice commissioners discretionary powers over the granting of suspensions. The Order of 15 April 1656 stated that 'every debtor of Scotland – giving in a list of his just debts' to the judges, 'swearing his inability to pay in money or personal estate', and who also declared that he had 'lands or other real estate' which he was 'willing to have set out in compensation to his creditors', was to be granted a suspension 'for a convenient time, not more than a year', in which time he was to 'convey the lands to the creditors according to priority'. In an attempt to show that creditors had not been forgotten, the Order provided that the lands they were to receive would be valued by 'indifferent persons' appointed by the courts, rather than using their 1648 value, and they were to be the lands nearest to where they lived and in the Lowlands, unless creditors specified to the contrary.[64]

The registration of debts began on 18 June 1656. There are some 571 entries in the books of debts, which contain the inventories of sums owed presented by debtors.[65] Among them are the lists of debts registered by twenty-six of the ninety-nine Scots excepted by name by the Ordinance of Grace in 1654. This group, along with the forty-four members of the peerage who registered their debts, can be used as pre-selected samples to illustrate the scale of the difficulties faced by the Scottish landed elite. The mean of the debts registered by the twenty-six, who included nineteen of the peers, was 14,100l. The range lay between the Earl of Roxburgh's massive 35,800l. debt and John Renton of Lamberton's more modest 1,500l.[66] The mean of the debts of the forty-four peers was 15,800l. and ranged from the Marquis of Argyll's 44,600l. to James, Lord Lindores' 300l.[67]

In spite of all the arguments put forward declaring that the Order of 15 April was just, creditors remained unreconciled to it.[68] Distressed creditors approached the courts for redress in the autumn and managed to delay the execution of the procedures set up by the Order, presenting their case through the burgh representatives to the Second Protectorate Parliament. While parliament was receptive to their arguments and a bill addressing their predicament emerged, the situation did not improve markedly for them. The legislation quickly faltered as Home successfully petitioned the Council of State once again and won the full implementation of the Order of April 1656.[69] In spite of all the creditors' efforts, debtors remained the priority for the English government. Policy had been turned completely on its head by Glencairn's rebellion, which had been fuelled by the problems associated with debt. The Cromwellians' need to promote peace and stability and address the Commonwealth's chronic financial situation in Scotland forced them to continue to develop a policy of accommodation with the members of the Scottish elite whom, initially, they had set out to destroy.[70] Monck's employment of Glencairn and other former Royalist rebels as intermediaries to liaise with the rest of the Scottish elite as he marched into England in 1660 offers a clear view of the extent of the compromise reached by the end of the decade.

3

The Eighteenth-Century Estate Agent and His Correspondence. County Down: A Case Study

Rosemary Richey

This essay examines the role and persona of the 'agent' whose one-sided correspondence with his master dominates so many estate papers and provides a basis for understanding landlord–tenant relationships and eighteenth-century estate management, particularly as other evidence, including landlord instructions to representatives, letters from the tenantry, rent rolls and lists of arrears, has largely disappeared. Examples are taken from County Down, principally the estates of the Annesley, Blundell, Downshire and Ward families. As a consequence of the circumstances of colonisation in the seventeenth century, subsequent land purchases and the break-up of estates, Down was unusual in having a large gentry class of some ninety families, nearly all Protestant, from which the larger landholders could recruit agents.[1] Other Irish counties had fewer upper-class candidates to act as stewards for absentee magnates. The linen industry in north-east Ulster also gave rise to regionally specific agricultural and economic conditions, producing as it did smaller holdings and a more affluent tenantry.

The duties of an Irish agent were diverse. As a result, their letters contain information on nearly every aspect of estate life: the receiving of rent or suing for rents and debts; the appointment of bailiffs; the signing of legal documents; the issuing of receipts, keeping of accounts and payment of any surplus to the landlord; adjudication in relation to mearings and the cutting of turf; and the schooling of farmers in how to improve land. Land agents tried to prevent tenants running into arrears, reported to the landlord who was a good tenant and who was unworthy, protected tenants from encroachments from outside the estate boundaries and transposed cash rents into bills of exchange for transmission to England. Absentee landlords visited their estates only sporadically, and their agents were expected to fulfil a wider role in society: organising manorial courts, cultivating electoral interest, nominating church wardens, cracking down on crime, sitting on grand juries, representing the interests of the estate (often sitting as a justice of the peace to prevent unnecessary taxation being levied on an estate), or being clerks of works on building projects (obligations often performed by the gentry themselves).[2]

Nevertheless, absentee landlords scrutinised the business of their distant holdings with an insatiable curiosity. Agents were rebuked for not sending detailed descriptions of local events at regular intervals. This attention to detail and the regular and copious provision of information make stewards useful witnesses for modern historians. In the period between 19 September 1747 and 16 December of the same year, Robert Isaac, the local agent on Lord Blundell's estate at Dundrum, wrote to Henry Hatch, the Dublin agent, at least five times: on 19 September, 3 October, 21 November, 28 November and 16 December.[3] One shortfall is the absence of letters written by agents to a disinterested third party describing their life in the frank tones reserved for correspondence with a friend.

This regular exchange between steward and proprietor was part of the necessary checks on the conduct of stewards and other paid servants. The agent on the Castleward estate was evicted from his holding in 1734 after continually failing to make tenants pay their rents in full.[4] For a period in the 1740s the Blundell estate at Dundrum was not closely monitored and, in 1746, there were repeated arrears, late payments and complaints from the tenantry. It was alleged that most of the Dundrum estate had been let either to James Gwyn, the local agent, or to his relatives, so that no one would bid against them and Gwyn was free to charge whatever rent he pleased. Gwyn was required to send his accounts to the Dublin agent. He enclosed arrears from 1744, the 1745 rent roll, his receipts for both, a list of the present arrears owing and an abstract of accounts between himself and Lord Blundell. He gave a detailed description of the tenants' financial position, the state of the linen industry and how the weather was affecting crops, in order to explain why some payments might be late.[5] The Dublin agent remained unconvinced and resolved to travel to Dundrum himself, both to collect the remaining arrears and to audit the estate, which, in his opinion, was not well managed.[6] Shortly afterwards Gwyn was dismissed and a replacement installed.

Gwyn is a particular example of a disreputable steward, but even those of a higher calibre were carefully circumscribed to forestall similar lapses in estate discipline. Power to do anything, whether collecting rents, renewing lives on leases or holding courts, had to be justified by an attorney's letter. Tenants were suspicious of an unsupervised representative and did not want to risk having to pay rent twice over because the first instalment had gone to an impostor. When Robert Isaac assumed his position as receiver at Dundrum, the Dublin agent travelled to the north to introduce him to the tenantry so that no-one would have cause for concern. Following his ultimate dismissal, Isaac remained to foment trouble for his replacement,

James Savage, by hinting to the local farmers that Savage was not qualified to accept remittances.[7] In many cases this accusation fell on willing ears, for Savage, as well as being a Roman Catholic amongst an almost exclusively Protestant tenantry, had a vigorous approach to estate management. Soon after his appointment he marched from farm to farm, flanked by bailiffs and threatening to distrain immediately if the rent were not paid. This provoked complaints from the tenantry and caused estate discipline to erode yet further.[8]

Tenants knew the limits of the agent's authority, and relations could be fraught as some sought to test his power to the limit. The agent would have kept the landlord informed of proceedings in order to maintain his authority over the tenantry. In the above case the Dundrum tenants refused to pay rent to Savage, and one applied to the Dublin lawyer to know if the local agent really had the power to force them to cut down the trees growing on their farms. (Legal convention in the eighteenth century stated that any trees growing on an estate belonged to the landlord.[9]) Fifteen years earlier these same tenants had petitioned Lord Blundell to prevent Isaac becoming a receiver.[10] If relations between agent and tenants deteriorated beyond repair, tenants could and would threaten to transfer their loyalty to another estate once their leases fell in unless a more amenable agent was found. As the eighteenth century was a time of high emigration from north-east Ireland, landowners often found prospective tenants in short supply. They could not afford to antagonise reputable leaseholders.[11] In England tenants commonly played agents and landlords off against each other, either complaining about a tyrannical steward or bypassing him to negotiate leases with the landlord themselves.[12] Similarly, in Ireland relationships were less heavily weighted in favour of the landed interest than has previously been assumed.[13]

In 1747, Robert Isaac's letter to Henry Hatch, the Dublin lawyer employed to supervise the Dundrum estate, hinted at this delicately maintained balance. 'Favour of you in all your letters where you state the rents being due, to give me the most strict charge you think proper to me immediately to collect them, which I can read to the tenants that are indebted, which will show to them the urgent occasion for the money being paid as desired and no excuse can avail them.' Later, when Hatch obligingly sent his firm instructions, Isaac summoned all the local farmers to a court leet, where he stressed, 'if you fly in my face the consequence will be that you also fly in the face [of] my Lord Blundell your landlord by whose authority I act.'[14]

Although the agent was not considered to be a man of the highest social standing, he was still well placed in the lower ranks of the gentry. The steward was a middleman between two conflicting interests, the landlord who wanted rents to rise or at least remain the same, and the tenant who wanted them to fall. It was feared that agents selected from the tenantry would be too sympathetic to other farmers and, as local men, be subject to peer pressure from neighbours.[15] It was also necessary that the agent keep the respect of the tenantry. When James Savage, a Roman Catholic, was appointed receiver at Dundrum he experienced considerable resistance from the Protestant tenants who said they would rather be in 'Egyptian bondage' than under his power.[16] The large number of minor landholders in County Down helped make the selection of upper-class stewards easier. Agents' letters were therefore written by men of education with knowledge of estate management as well as gentlemen who were at ease with members of the upper classes. In Ireland the agent's background was often of greater consequence than in England, with younger family members frequently being employed. Robert Ward served on his brother Michael's estate and, of other Castleward agents, Henry Waring was in all likelihood a relative of the Warings of Waringstown. Charles Echlin occupied a sizeable estate at Echlinville, and John Jolly's daughter, Susannah, married into the Montgomery family of Rosemount, Greyabbey.[17] In general, as the social eminence of the employer increased, so did that of his agent.[18] William Sinclair, agent to David Ker of Comber, saw all three of his daughters marry into the Irish establishment: Elizabeth to the Rev. Edward May, rector of Belfast, brother of Sir Stephen May and brother-in-law to the second Marquess of Donegall; Charlotte to Conway Richard Dobbs of Castle Dobbs; and a third daughter to the Rev. James Strange Butson, Archdeacon of Clonfert.[19] John and Edward Trotter, who managed the Southwell estate at Downpatrick, owned lands at Oakley and claimed descent from the Earls of Gowrie, and John Moore, agent to the Earl of Annesley and his various relations, was a country gentleman with a small fortune who could claim descent from the Muire family of Rowallane in Ayrshire. He had received a military education but in later life retired to farm. His wife, Debra, was the daughter of Robert Isaac of Holywood House and sometime agent to Lord Blundell.[20]

Others combined commerce with agencies. William Sinclair, son of Thomas Sinclair – a substantial Belfast linen merchant – and Hester Eccles Pottinger of Mountpottinger, and husband to Charlotte Pollock, whose father John served as Crown Solicitor, became a founder member of the Belfast Chamber of Commerce in 1783. By 1804 he was its president. In 1784 he pioneered the use of American potash in the bleaching of linen, and by the early 1790s his extensive bleach works at Ligoniel on the outskirts of Belfast were reputed to be the largest, most mechanised and most technically advanced in the region. A year after his marriage in 1784 at the age of twenty-four, he built an impressive house for himself and his family in Donegall Place, the most fashionable and expensive thoroughfare in Belfast, and as a leading figure in the town he was involved in setting up the Belfast Society for Promoting Knowledge, which later became the Linen Hall Library. He was a member of the Belfast Reading Society and was active in the first and third Presbyterian congregations in Rosemary Lane. In 1792 he was appointed to the committee of the newly formed Belfast dispensary. In the nineteenth century the Sinclair family continued to be among the leading families in Belfast.[21]

Other agents were clergymen. Edward Bayly, minister at Killinchy, administered his brother's estate in Louth in the years following Sir Nicholas Bayly's inheritance. James Clewlow, Minister at Bangor, managed the Ward estate in that town, and George Vaughan, Vicar of Donaghmore, was agent to William Mussenden of Larchfield.[22] Clerics were often related to the landed elite and already earned about £50 p.a. in their capacity as clergymen. They would already control parish relief and vestry decisions on parish administration through their clerical role, and as such would be well known to the tenantry. [23]

Alternatively, agents might be middlemen. John Jolly of Rathmullen, County Down, leased land from Lord Limerick and Michael Ward for the use of himself and his under-tenants but also worked as a land agent for Ward, as did Thomas Squire, another middleman on that estate.[24] This simplified estate discipline. When one of Squire's under-tenants stole some timber, his family was immediately evicted, an action for which no permission was sought from Ward nor legal advice taken, for under-tenants seldom had the advantage of a lease.[25]

Material advantage and conspicuous consumption would also have made the agent visibly the 'better' of the tenantry he supervised. George Vaughan occupied Larchfield House while William Mussenden was absent, and this was by no means unusual. John Moore's lodgings, the agent's dwelling owned by the Annesleys on the Clough estate, though less ambitious and in desperate need of repair, was still substantial and was described in correspondence as a mansion house.[26] In Downpatrick, John and Edward Trotter, father and son, both agents to the Southwell family, resided in a long, two-storey slated house at the head of Irish Street with a large expanse of ground at the back. The Southwells stayed there themselves in 1749 when they came to inspect the town. In his own right John Trotter acquired further property in the borough and, in his time as owner, Edward built an extension to the family home in order to accommodate a library.[27]

Agents received considerable salaries, usually 5 per cent of the annual rental of the estate. Moore claimed that he had turned down an offer of £300 p.a. to work on Lord Clanbrassil's estate at Dundalk. The man who eventually accepted the position was created collector of the port, increasing his yearly stipend to £500. Another collected £900 p.a. as the combined agent of Lords Granard and Moira.[28] James Crawford received only £60 p.a. from the Maxwells, but this was still a substantial sum.[29] Multiple agencies were common. At Dundrum, Robert Isaac, agent for Lord Blundell, also oversaw land for the Annesley family at Clough. A later agent for the Annesleys, Isaac's son-in-law Moore, was administrator for Lords Glerawly and Clanbrassil.[30] Sharing agents produced a greater uniformity of estate management throughout the county and allowed the agent to maintain his status of gentleman without his employers having to pay him an exorbitant amount.[31]

The convention of only appointing agents of high social standing was reinforced by the custom requiring would-be agents to give security in money and personal assurances before they commenced their responsibilities. At Dundrum, James Savage obtained affirmation from a Mr Crombie and Sir Robert Blackwood of Bangor, whose descendants became the Marquesses of Dufferin and Ava.[32] On the same estate Robert Isaac provided a personal recommendation from Hans Bailie, the proprietor of an estate at Inishargy, County Down, as well as paying £600 collateral, twice the sum of the annual rent roll. For a major agent such as Henry Hatch, the Dublin lawyer employed by the Blundells, this sum rose to £5,000.[33]

As many agents were landlords in their own right, if on a much smaller scale than their employers, class identity as much as money bound them to their employers. John Moore, who served Arthur Annesley for over two decades before the estate was sold in 1785, saw the master–servant relationship as one of longstanding trust enduring from generation to generation. He had ambitions of procuring his clergyman son a provision in a nearby diocese so that he would be on hand to succeed Moore in the event of his father's death.[34] In return for these services, the agent's family often prospered. The post of estate manager provided security of employment and status as well as an annual income. Mrs Annesley took an active interest in the education of Moore's sons, earning Moore's untold gratitude as 'we cannot all be great scholars but we are certainly inexcusable if we want good manners and such are only to be learned in good company'.[35]

Mrs Annesley dispatched sheet music from England, to be performed by Moore's daughters when she was next in Ireland.[36] Encouraged by their cordial relationship, Moore was persistent in requesting patronage and entreated Arthur Annesley to send a letter of recommendation on his son's behalf to Lord Hillsborough. Moore had ensured this would be met with favourably, as in the proceeding year he had provided political service to the Hill family.[37]

This investment proved worthwhile as, in later life, Moore's children followed responsible professions. His eldest boy, William, entered the church, while his second joined the army and travelled to Gibraltar. His daughters were accorded a high enough position in society to enable them to attend the local balls and assemblies, where, no doubt, their connection with the Annesleys made them sought after as possible brides.[38] Similarly, Edward Trotter's son, Edward Southwell Trotter (later Ruthven), sat for the Southwell family's borough of Downpatrick in 1806, while the second son, John Bernard Trotter, became private secretary to Charles Fox, and also penned a *Letter to Lord Southwell on the Catholic Question* in 1808.[39]

Status and a congenial manner were essential for an agent as he was the absent landlord's representative amongst the local resident gentry, especially if the landlord was away for prolonged periods.[40] During the progress of a boundary dispute, John Moore transacted with the Earl of Moira personally and a compromise was reached over dinner at the Earl's home.[41] John Trotter found himself involved in intricate manoeuvrings between Cromwell Price, Edward Southwell and Lord Annesley in 1761. Price had previously sat for the Southwell's borough of Downpatrick but had been asked to stand down in favour of Lord Annesley's son. In return, Price asked Trotter to negotiate compensation of £300. When Trotter approached Annesley the latter agreed, but later Price raised the ante to £400. At this point Trotter retreated from the proceedings.[42]

Being on friendly terms with local families was particularly important in election years, when an agent might act on a magnate's behalf and exhort the lesser gentry or freeholders to place their interest behind a favoured candidate.[43] From 1718 to 1739 Charles Echlin acted as provost of Michael Ward's borough of Bangor and thereby permitted Ward to control the election of a candidate to serve the borough in parliament, while another Castleward agent, Ward's brother Robert, was responsible for organising the registration of voters in 1745.[44] Edward Corry, an agent for the Needham family of Newry, was active in the management of that relatively open borough. He was the town's MP from 1775 to 1776, until his son Isaac replaced him.[45] Agents were often responsible for entertaining voters during the poll. In 1771 Edward Trotter wrote to his master that 'we have not yet fixed the mode of entertainment for our vile potwallopers but from the various methods proposed I fear it cannot be done for under £150'. In 1783 Lord Downshire's agent requested £3,000 for similar purposes.[46] Agents could be elected High Sheriff, a post that required the holder to organise the county elections. Henry Waring, a land agent to Lord Bangor, was High Sheriff in 1750, and William Montgomery, agent to Lord Hillsborough, held the post in 1755, as did John Moore in 1768, a general election year.[47]

In the intervening periods between elections stewards were still active. John Slade, Lord Hillsborough's agent, had political duties and was responsible for recommending people to fill the vacant posts for burgesses in the borough of Hillsborough. In the 1790s Thomas Lane served on Lord

Downshire's behalf on the County Down grand jury. As one of only twenty-three men he helped decide how the £2,400 allocated to county funds should be spent on constructing roads and bridges, supporting the militia and, more particularly, ensuring that as much money as possible was allocated to the Downshire estate. He assisted the touring judge in trying cases, some as serious as murder or treason, and allotted funds for the transportation of prisoners and for the local infirmary. In 1780 John Slade was quick to report to Lord Hillsborough that Robert Stewart was attempting to turn a section of the jury against the Hillsborough interest, and the following year John Moore was appointed treasurer of the county by the same institution.[48] William Montgomery, agent to the Downshires, sat for the borough of Hillsborough and helped forward the Downshire family's political aims in parliament.[49] In the late 1770s and early 1780s popular politics grew in influence, and at this point William Moore, Edward Trotter and George Vaughan all organised Volunteer companies. These corps were designed to channel the tenantry's newfound political interest into conventional modes.[50]

Gentlemen of 'good' background had many necessary skills, a fine writing hand, a knowledge of accountancy and a thorough acquaintance with surveying and drawing, often accompanied by experience on their own estates.[51] William Sinclair was reported by Theobald Wolfe Tone to resent the resistance to innovation shown by his contemporaries, and William Ogilvie, while agent to his stepson, the younger brother of the Duke of Leinster, was responsible for building the pier at Ardglass. Another land agent, John Sloan of Comber, Co. Down and later Glenavy, Co. Antrim, is also recorded as being a surveyor in 1753.[52] In 1764, Bernard Ward's land agent at Rathfriland, Henry Waring, proposed the construction of a market house and the rebuilding of the town's houses and workshops, in order to bring linen drapers to the village. On the outlying estate he recommended resetting farms so that no-one had more land or bog than strictly necessary, thereby prohibiting subletting, and also recommended the establishment of farmhouses containing workshops for linen weavers.[53] Five months later Waring sent a progress report to Ward. The market was increasing but the traders were concerned that no market house had been built. Waring suggested that a few stones be quarried to give the appearance of activity although work could not start for some months as a suitable site had yet to be decided. He advised that the town's customs duties be decreased so that any discouragement to trade in Rathfriland would be removed.[54]

Other instances of agents advising their employers are recorded. After he came of age, Arthur Annesley was instructed in the practices of Irish estate management by John Moore and, before the Dundrum lands were set, Robert Isaac promised to advise the Dublin agent, Henry Hatch, on any rent proposals tenants might put forward and to make a report of what he felt they could pay.[55] In his turn, Hatch counselled Lord Blundell that he should set leases for three lives rather than thirty-one years so that tenants would be more likely to improve the land. Guidance was also proffered when tenants proved obstreperous. James Savage urged Hatch to take strong measures against late payers on the Dundrum estate.[56]

Though social status and experience favoured identity with the landlord, many agents sought good relations with the tenantry. John Moore remarked of the farmers of Clough: 'They are a decent set of people, in general pay their rents well, have in many instances limed and improved their lands since the late Mr Annesley's demise, on my assuring them no unfair advantage would be taken of their improvements to enhance the value of their lands when the present Mr Annesley came of age.' Moore congratulated himself on rescuing under-tenants from an overbearing middleman by giving out individual leases, likening it to delivering them 'from bondage', and criticised the practice of advertising townlands in local papers in order to get the highest bid as an act carried through 'without regard or indeed humanity to the old tenants'.[57]

Part of an agent's duties was to harass tenants for arrears and carry through distraint and eviction. After 1765 the growth in population created pressure on land, and subdivision became increasingly common. The agent had a rising number of tenants to deal with, multiplying opportunities for conflict, and, in times of crisis, the tenantry openly demonstrated their belief that the agent was clearly positioned in the landlord's camp, widening the gap between the two social categories even further. In the early 1770s the Hearts of Steel outrages erupted, in a lower-class response to levies of cess designed to finance road construction in the county, and Edward Southwell's agent, John Trotter, was threatened. He discovered that by refusing to react when the first two letters were sent to him a third did not appear.[58] George Vaughan, as agent to William Mussenden, a Presbyterian proprietor at Larchfield, three miles east of Hillsborough, and probably the most domineering landlord in the county, was less fortunate. In early February 1772 he heard that the Hearts of Steel planned to attack Larchfield the following week. Vaughan returned to the house, hoping that his presence would prove a deterrent, but to no avail. In the dead of night 300 armed men, almost certainly local, surrounded the house, swearing they would see it in flames before they left. Attempts at pacification proved useless, only provoking warnings that the door would be burned down to make Vaughan swear oaths on peril of death. After shots had been fired at the defenceless house, Vaughan agreed to come out and write to Mussenden, stating the determination of the Hearts of Steel to lay waste the estate and their threat to Mussenden's life, to Vaughan's if he remained, and to any bailiff or agent who attempted to collect the county cess. The situation was so intimidating that it was impossible to employ a guard: no-one could be appointed from so uncertain a tenantry.[59] It took a proclamation from thirty-five County Down landlords and an act of parliament before the Steelboys were subdued.[60]

Twenty-five years later, James Porter, the local Presbyterian minister at Greyabbey, was hanged for treason following the publication of his letters between 'Billy Bluff and the Squire' in 1797. Bluff is reputed to have been the local bailiff on the Montgomery estate at Rosemount; Squire Firebrand, the Rev. John Cleland, agent to Lord Londonderry. The letters were a Presbyterian satire on the gentry and aristocracy of County Down, which clearly included Cleland – who later sat on the jury that condemned Porter to death – in their number. Cleland was portrayed as a malevolent character who made it his business to spy on the tenantry and to use any irregularity as evidence of sedition. In one section the Squire berated the education of the common people, who now thought for themselves rather than obeying compliantly. He longed for the 'old days' when one could put people in jail or the stocks for the flimsiest of reasons, horsewhip tradesmen when they presented their bills, take a tenant's daughter or shoot dogs for barking.[61]

These agents embodied landed power on many estates as well as providing detailed historical evidence in their reports. Although many were substantial gentry and yeomen with considerable income and high-status consumption patterns, they never constituted a separate class with any real say in the governance of rural Ireland. The gentry sought high-status agents because this would gain respect from the tenantry and lesser gentry on neighbouring estates and, hopefully, provide a loyal and honest servant who would consistently reflect the landlord's position and wishes in his dealings with the tenantry. In practice the agent had little real power of his own. His ability to act independently was limited by law. He could threaten distraint or eviction, but only the landowner could carry this out. Any influence the agent might have on estate management came from his role as on-the-spot adviser to an absent proprietor. The tenant would still have regarded his landlord as the true master of his fate, and this must influence the historian's use of agents' letters and reports.

4

Scottish Influences on Irish Farming Techniques

Jonathan Bell

This essay examines some historical relationships between Irish and Scottish farming at the level of implements and techniques, an area of study usually described as 'material' culture. The general statements of the great cultural theorists regarding the relationship between social organisation and its material base have proved difficult to apply to concrete situations. A level of mediating connections has to be identified which links empirical data and theoretical abstractions, but attempts to do this often achieve little more than facile generalisations, or the postulation of relationships which, in the end, imply technological determinism.[1] The difficulties become clear when we try to link Irish farming techniques to the social organisation of a particular period. The most striking feature of the application of technology to Irish farming during the last three centuries has been the flexibility and inventiveness with which farmers overcame resource limitations in order to gain access to machinery and techniques, once convinced of their value.[2]

Discussion of the relationship between social and economic change and technical development in farming is least problematic when the former is viewed as the context in which technological systems can be understood. In Scotland, a broad and useful overview has been suggested by Fenton:

> In every community there are layers of agricultural implements (as well as house types, domestic paraphernalia etc.) stratified according to the status of the users. At the top are the elite, the innovators, those who can afford to experiment; next comes a broad group, the ordinary farmers, who ... are able to take advantage of these innovations ... Finally there are the small-holders or crofters ... who might be able to take advantage of new machinery by clubbing together and sharing, but very often ... have to be content with hand tools or small scale horse-drawn equipment of their own.[3]

A similar pattern can be identified in many parts of Ireland, where 'small farms on marginal land were worked using highly localised techniques, relying on ingenuity and intensive manual labour, while prosperous mixed farms show the early application of standardised, improved machinery and methods. The richest farms more often provide evidence for expensive and risky experimentation.'[4]

In attempting to understand the choices of technology made by farmers, a model of rational decision making can be useful. This can take into account farm size, capital and labour resources, and situation in relation to markets. Contemporary discussion from the eighteenth century on shows that Scottish and Irish farmers operating at the three main socioeconomic levels identified by Fenton were aware of these factors to some extent. Using the model, differences between Scotland and Ireland in the rate of adoption of new implements and techniques before the mid-nineteenth century can usefully be related to the relatively small size of Irish farms compared with Lowland Scotland, and the availability of cheap labour in Ireland, both factors reducing the impetus towards mechanisation.

Social and economic issues defined the context within which farmers operated, but it is the more easily identified technical issues which are the focus of this essay. At this level there is clear evidence that a number of developments in Scotland were particularly attractive and successful for Irish farmers. The widespread use of Scottish methods reflected the general importance of Scottish contributions to international developments in farming but, in some instances, Scottish-designed implements, and their associated techniques, were better suited to conditions throughout much of Ireland than their English equivalents.

The foundation of the Dublin Society in 1731 marks the beginning of organised, large-scale attempts to improve Irish agricultural practices. The society aimed to improve the system of farming in Ireland as followed by the gentry, but also by 'the poorer sort'.[5] Early projects of the society tended to focus on English developments. One of its first initiatives was the publication in 1731 of Jethro Tull's *Horse Hoeing Husbandry*. In 1749, it was announced that an Englishman, Mr John Cam, had been engaged 'as an itinerant husbandman, to advise [farmers] … in the right way of ploughing their land for the growth of corn'.[6] In 1763, another Englishman, John Wynn Baker, established a farm at Laughlinstown, near Cellbridge, County Kildare. The society began to pay him a salary in 1769, and in 1771 he received a grant to open an implement factory. Arthur Young commented that 'nothing was ever better imagined, than the plan of fixing an English farmer in the Kingdom.'[7] In 1780 the society employed another Englishman, Mr Thomas Dawson, as an itinerant instructor, but he did not seem to develop any projects as ambitious as those of Baker.

The tendency for Irish agriculturists to aspire to best English practice remained pronounced during much of the eighteenth century, but by 1800 there was a marked swing towards the discussion of Scottish developments and their application in Ireland. The first two examples outlined below describe Scottish technical innovations which were part of international exchanges in which Scots took a lead and which had major impacts in Ireland. These relate to the threshing of grain and drainage of fields.

Threshing Machines

Harvested grain is beaten, or threshed, to separate the seed from the straw. Before eighteenth-century developments in mechanisation, the most common method used throughout Europe was to beat the seed out of the heads of grain, using two sticks tied together to form a flail. Most of the successful early development of machines for threshing occurred in Scotland, and these dominated early developments in both Britain and Ireland. Early inventions included an attempt to attach a series of flails to a revolving drum, but breakages were so common that the idea was abandoned. In 1786, Andrew Meikle of Midlothian produced a design which became basic to many later machines (Fig. 4.1). Here grain was separated from the straw by a revolving cylinder, along which four bars of wood had been placed at regular intervals. Water power was used to turn the cylinder – or threshing drum as it became known – inside a metal casing set around the drum, about one inch away from its surface. Sheaves were fed into the drum, and the grain was beaten out of the sheaves by the bars on the cylinder. In later designs (such as that illustrated in Fig. 4.1), another drum containing revolving rakes was added, to rake off the straw once the seed had been removed. Meikle was given a patent for his threshing machine in 1788, and from this time on threshers of his design began to be used on some large farms in Scotland and the north of England.[8]

By 1800, threshing machines had been installed on some large Irish farms. A Mr Christie of Kirkassock, near Magheralin, County Down, claimed to be the first proprietor in Ireland to have installed a thresher. In 1796 he inspected machines in Scotland, and had drawings and a model made of one of these. A local workman used the plans to construct a similar machine on Mr Christie's farm.[9] Christie's machine, and at least some other early installations, were driven by horses. Mr Ward, of Bangor, County Down, for example, had a 'horse engine', or gearing system around which the horses were driven in order to turn the thresher, set below the machine.[10]

Surveyors working for the Dublin Society reported that, by the first decade of the nineteenth century, threshing machines had been installed on farms in several counties, including Cavan, Louth, and Dublin. In the last county, it was claimed that the machines were coming into use 'very fast'.[11] By 1811, it was estimated that the cost of machines bought in Scotland and erected in Ulster by Scottish workmen had dropped to 50 per cent of the 1800 price.[12] Despite this early activity, threshing machines seem to have

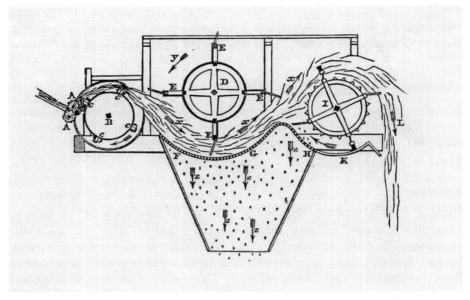

Fig. 4.1. A developed version of Meikle's threshing machine, as illustrated in David Low's *Elements of Practical Agriculture* (Edinburgh 1834), p.118

been confined to large farms during the first half of the nineteenth century. The Ordnance Survey Memoirs recorded few threshing machines in the north of Ireland even by the 1830s.[13] The slow rate of adoption of mechanical threshing in Ireland can be related to the limited scale of grain cultivation on small farms, as well as the availability of cheap labour. In 1849, the Irish *Farmer's Gazette* advised farmers to use manual labour in threshing. 'In order to give employment, we would prefer thrashing [with flails] at 3*d* a barrel than using a machine.'[14] More widespread use of threshing machines only came when smaller horse-driven and hand-operated machines became available and labour became more scarce.

The slow spread of the new threshing technology can also be related to technical problems. In 1854, the Irish agriculturist John Sproule claimed that many threshing machines were so inefficient that four horse-power machines required three horses to turn them, even when they were empty.[15] Agriculturists were also concerned about the use of horses to drive early threshing machines, as they were thought to put an uneven strain on the animals and to cause giddiness.[16] Martin Doyle believed that a contrivance invented by a Scot, Walter Samuel of Niddry, which allowed the horses to pull with a continuous and equal draught, lessened the problem,[17] but as late as 1863 a classic Irish farming text described the use of horses to power threshing machines as 'most objectionable'.[18]

These technical problems were lessened with the development of smaller barn threshers, which were being manufactured by local foundries in Ireland from the 1830s.[19] The latter also provided the infrastructure necessary for the maintenance of the machines. Between 1860 and 1940, the firm of Kennedy's of Coleraine manufactured and sold about 2,000 machines throughout the north of Ireland. By 1912, there were more than 30,000 threshing machines of various kinds operating in Ireland.[20] Barn threshers, and portable threshing machines of Scottish design, had become an everyday part of harvest technology throughout most of Ireland.

Drainage

The development of field drainage provided a clear example of developments which involved an ongoing international exchange of ideas, largely between English and Scottish agriculturists, which again profoundly influenced Irish farming methods. Around 1800, many Irish agriculturists were enthused by the drainage system advocated by Joseph Elkington of Warwickshire. This method centred on the release of underground springs using an auger, the water then being carried away by drains. However, by the 1840s the drainage system advocated by a Scot, James Smith of Deanston, was enthusiastically embraced by agriculturists. The Devon Commission found that on most large-scale schemes on Irish farms, Smith's plan of closed drains placed twenty-one feet apart, at a depth of two feet six inches, was commonly followed. By the 1860s, however, Smith's layout was perceived as overly rigid, and a more flexible layout was followed, of a kind advocated by the Englishman Josiah Parkes. 'People began to see that, owing to the diversified character of the soils, subsoils and substrata of the land in this country [Ireland], it was impossible to fix any one uniform depth or distance apart for the drainage of soils.'[21]

One of the most interesting aspects of improved drainage in Ireland was the modifications made by Irish farmers to the prescribed methods. In achieving drainage, the application of Smith of Deanston's methods did not usually include the subsoil plough, which he had developed as part of his system. In 1845, Lambert pointed out that 'though admirably adapted to good flat ploughlands, such as the carses of Scotland, [the subsoil plough] is suitable here only in similar cases, and to proprietors and extensive farmers who keep strong horses and powerful teams. It is altogether out of the reach of the peasantry; and there are few large farmers who are so systematically extensive in tillage as to have the horse power necessary for the work.'[22]

The solution adopted by most Irish farmers was to achieve subsoiling using spades, in some cases combining thorough drainage with the ancient technique of ridgemaking (Fig. 4.2). The application of new ideas about

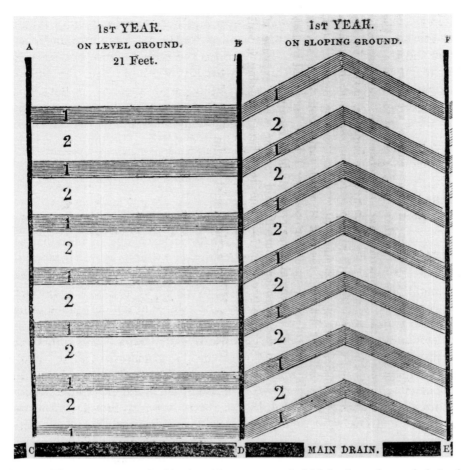

Fig. 4.2. The arrangement of cultivation ridges on ground which has been thorough drained as described in the Devon Commission *Digest of evidence* vol.1 (Dublin 1847), p.101.

drainage is typical of the history of technological change in Irish farming throughout the last three centuries. Improvements were often achieved by modifying established techniques to suit local conditions and resources. As in the development of threshing technology, however, many of the new ideas adopted originated in Scotland.

Ploughs

The impact of Scottish developments on Irish farming was greatest in plough design. This was the clearest instance where Scottish developments were particularly suited to conditions on farms in most of Ireland. Systematic experiments aimed at improving plough design were attracting interest in Ireland by the 1750s. Once again, Irish improvers initially looked towards English ideas. Thomas Hale's *A Compleat Body of Husbandry* was reprinted in Dublin in 1757 'at the request ... of several Members of the Farmers' Societies in Ireland'.[23] This work described and illustrated several experimental wheel ploughs (Fig. 4.3). By 1767, John Wynn Baker was manufacturing eleven types of plough in his factory at Cellbridge, including two wheel ploughs. Baker expressed doubts:

> Wheel ploughs ... cannot be so effectual in general use, as ploughs without wheels, for this plain reason; that as the wheels are the gauge for the depth of the plough, whenever they meet with anything which raises them, the plough consequently rises so as to plough shallow ... at other times, when the wheels sink into any declivity, the plough sinks in proportion, so the ploughing is render'd irregular by those kinds of accidents ... Another consideration is, that they are in general complicated, and not a little expensive.[24]

Despite Baker's doubts, Arthur Young found that some landlords were importing English wheel ploughs from Norfolk, Suffolk and Kent.[25] He also found wheel ploughs being used by the Palatines in Arbella, County Kerry.[26]

Revolutionary developments in Scottish plough design began with James Small, who designed implements using 'scientific' principles. One of Small's most important contributions was the development of mathematical formulae for designing the best curvature for plough mouldboards.[27] A mouldboard pushes newly cut furrow slices over as the plough moves through the ground. The degree of curvature in the mouldboard determines

Fig. 4.3. Wheel plough illustrated in Thomas Hale *A compleat body of husbandry* vol.2 (Dublin 1757), p.80.

how effectively the sod is turned. Small's early ploughs had wooden mouldboards, but after 1763 he began to manufacture them from iron. His designs were later modified by Wilkie of Uddingston, and the ploughs developed changed very little before the late nineteenth century. By the early nineteenth century, the consensus among agriculturists was that improved Scottish swing (wheelless) ploughs were best suited to Irish conditions. In the barony of Imokilly, County Cork in 1810 a 'good many Scottish ploughs had been introduced, but only a few English wheel ploughs'.[28]

The early history of the adoption of Scottish ploughs was not one of uncritical enthusiasm. Agriculturists like Hely Dutton thought that the reluctance to adopt them was to a large extent due to ignorance and prejudice.[29] Before the Scottish ploughs could be successfully used, new skills had to be learned by ploughmakers, blacksmiths, and ploughmen.[30] The curved mouldboards had to be cast in a foundry, and blacksmiths had to learn how to make very sensitive adjustments to the angle of the wing on the share, and its relationship to the angle of the coulter. Apart from the infrastructure required for manufacturing and setting the ploughs, there were also practical problems arising from the way in which the ploughs turned the ground. Richard Thompson commented 'I am, and have been, since I first saw the Scotch plough, a very great advocate for its being generally adopted, yet I confess that in this country there are many soils in which it will not answer for the summer's gorrowing [cross ploughing summer fallows].'[31] In 1819, Mason reported that in County Kilkenny

> [although] some of the respectable farmers have introduced Scotch ploughs ... they are not suited to wet grounds, which are so stiff and adhesive, that the sod requires to be raised as much as possible, in order that the air may get through it to pulverise it. The Scotch plough is thought to lay the sod too flat, while the Irish plough raises it, and breaks it more; while the superiority of the Scotch plough in dry grounds is fully acknowledged, a dislike to it in the former instance may have some foundation in reason.[32]

Despite these reservations, the adoption of Scottish ploughs was widespread by the early nineteenth century. The enthusiasm of farming societies, and their success in persuading Irish farmers to adopt the new ploughs, is well illustrated by accounts of ploughing matches in the *Munster Farmer's Journal*.

In 1812, the Cork Institution decided that its ploughing matches in the following year would have two classes: one for 'gentlemen and farmers', the other for 'working farmers'. Irish ploughs could only be used in the second category. Ploughs of Scottish design, some made locally, were given as prizes. In the same year, the Farming Society of Ireland employed a champion ploughman, William Kippie, to instruct farmers in the use of both

Irish and Scottish ploughs. Kippie would 'attend any farmer who wishes to employ him at 2s.6p. per day with his diet and lodging'.[33] In a ploughing match at Fermoy, County Cork in 1813, separate prizes were given for Irish and Scottish ploughs, but by 1816 Scottish ploughs were becoming dominant.[34] At a ploughing match at Kinalea, County Cork, on 13 March, twenty-one ploughs were entered, twenty of them of Scottish design. A report concluded: 'The rapid improvement in ploughing ... and the very general adoption of Scotch ploughs which have been introduced into this district within the last few years, afforded a most satisfactory evidence of the utility of ploughing matches.'[35]

By the mid-nineteenth century, all-metal Scottish swing ploughs had become the most common plough type in Ireland. The Irish Industrial Exhibition catalogue of 1853 described the Scottish swing plough as 'almost universally employed'.[36] The cast metal mouldboards and shares of the improved Scottish ploughs were suited to large-scale industrial production, and foundries began to produce standardised ploughs and plough parts. The best known foundry manufacturing ploughs in the north of Ireland was set up by Robert Gray in Belfast in 1840, initially as a subsidiary of its parent company in Glasgow. Other large foundries producing swing ploughs at this time were Paul and Vincent of Dublin, and W. & J. Ritchie of Ardee, County Louth. Foundries also sold plough parts to blacksmiths, who constructed implements from them. In the later nineteenth century, for example, blacksmiths in north Antrim bought sole plates, mouldboards, and roughly blocked-out shares and plough bodies from the firm of Kennedy and Sons of Coleraine.[37]

The technical advances represented by even the earliest improved Scottish ploughs were clear. Because of their mathematically designed

Fig 4.4. Scottish swing plough, illustrated on a medal of the Farming Society of Ireland, 1815 (Ulster Folk and Transport Museum photo L2318/32).

mouldboards, they turned sods over much more effectively than the common Irish ploughs which they replaced. There were two main types of furrow slice turned using Scottish swing ploughs: rectangular, and high-crested work. Both furrow patterns provided an excellent bed for seed, sown broadcast. The linear pattern produced by the furrow slices meant that seed sown broadcast over them tended to fall into long straight lines, which were then covered by knocking off the tops of the slices using harrows. This produced a pattern roughly similar to that produced by a seed drill. The Scottish ploughs also had the advantage of being operable by only two horses or oxen and one ploughman. Common Irish ploughs required four horses and up to three operators. Another major factor in the adoption of Scottish rather than English plough types in Ireland was the absence of wheels on the best-known Scottish improved ploughs.

Swing ploughs remained popular in many parts of Ireland until well into the twentieth century. This was especially true on small farms in hilly areas. Oral testimony confirms the advantages of swing ploughs which had been identified by John Wynn Baker. Using a wheelless swing plough, the ploughman could adjust the draught (or strain on the horses) on the plough at will. When he lifted the handles up, the share turned downwards, cutting a deeper furrow slice and also increasing the draught. The width of the furrow slices could also be adjusted by deflecting the handles to left or right. Going uphill, the plough could be made to cut shallower, narrower slices, thus easing the draught on the horses. On ploughs with wheels – that is, most English improved ploughs of the period – the width and depth of the furrow slice were set by adjusting the wheels at the front of the plough before ploughing started. This made the ploughs easy to use on level ground, where long straight furrows could be turned. On hummocky or sloping land, where it was necessary to change the draught, the ploughman had to stop and readjust the wheels. This also made wheel ploughs less attractive on rough, stony land. Swing ploughs could be eased over large stones by lowering and raising their handles as they were driven along, whereas wheel ploughs, being fixed, would bounce off large stones and sometimes miss pieces of ground.[38] In the north of Ireland, English wheel ploughs only became common in the 1920s and 1930s, when consolidation and levelling of fields meant that fixing the dimensions of furrow slices could ease the ploughman's task.

It is beyond the scope of this essay to detail all of the influences that improved Scottish techniques had on Irish farming practice. Scottish implements and techniques were adopted when they suited Irish conditions and farmers' resources, and where there was a technical and marketing infrastructure to support their use. There are instances where Scottish developments were not adopted, one being early reaping machines. Reaping machines, as in Britain, became the subject of widespread debate in Ireland during the 1850s, after the American Hussey and McCormick machines were displayed in Belfast and Dublin in 1852 and 1853 respectively. The machines developed by Patrick Bell in Scotland in the late 1820s were also known in Ireland. In tests associated with their display at the Belfast and Dublin shows, the Scottish machine was judged to have performed better.[39] Despite the opinions of early observers, it was the American machines that were successfully developed by manufacturers. This can probably be related to the efficient commercial operation of the Americans.

Migration and Technology Transfer

The movement of implements and techniques between Ireland and Scotland occurred at all levels of farming society. At the level of seasonal workers, there is some evidence of a two-way movement. Irish workers probably learnt a number of improved manual farming techniques while working in Scotland. The use of the scythe was mastered by many seasonal migrants during their time in Scotland, and in the north of England during the late nineteenth century. It is also possible that the relative absence of potato ridges in County Donegal in recent decades, compared with neighbouring counties of Fermanagh, Cavan and Leitrim, may reflect the large numbers of migrants who went from Donegal to Scotland and the techniques of drill cultivation that they learnt there. On the other hand, at the level of what agriculturists described rather dismissively as 'common' practice, there is evidence from Scotland that Irish migrant workers influenced the techniques of cutting grain adopted by their Scottish counterparts. This evidence suggests that, although toothed sickles were the tool favoured by Irish reapers, smooth-bladed hooks may also have been fairly common. It has been claimed that from the eighteenth century onwards Irish migrant workers in Scotland favoured smooth-bladed hooks,[40] and in 1831 Loudon claimed that hooks had actually been introduced into the south-west of Scotland by Irish harvesters.[41] However, so far, this evidence all seems to come from Scotland. Written and oral testimonies from Irish sources all affirm that the sickle remained the tool most used by Irish harvesters.[42]

Tractors

The biggest impact which Irish technical and industrial developments had on Scottish farming was the introduction of Ferguson's revolutionary three-point hydraulic linkage to tractor design (Fig. 4.5). The first Scottish trials of tractors were held near Perth in 1904, but even the impulse provided by compulsory tillage during the First World War did not lead to their

Fig. 4.5. Ferguson Brown tractor, during tests in the 1930s (photo: courtesy of Museum of English Rural Life).

widespread adoption.[43] Before Ferguson, tractors had simply pulled implements along, and the ability of the tractor driver to control their movement was limited. There was serious contemporary debate about the potential usefulness of the heavy, cumbersome machines compared with horses. Ferguson began experiments to improve tractor design in 1919, and during the next decade he perfected his revolutionary system, which became an integral part of tractor construction. The linkage at the back of the tractor allowed a large number of complex movements to be controlled by the driver. The versatility of the Ferguson system allowed tractor power to be applied to a variety of tillage, harvest and processing operations. In 1934, the system was installed in tractors manufactured by David Brown in Birmingham. Tractor sales in Scotland boomed after the Second World War, and these were dominated by the purchase of Ferguson models.[44]

Conclusion

It was emphasised at the beginning of this essay that technological change cannot be understood without reference to wider social and economic contexts. The need to make these links is clearly shown by considering the direction in which different kinds of agricultural exchange between Ireland and Scotland occurred. Technological exchanges during the eighteenth and nineteenth centuries were overwhelmingly from Scotland to Ireland. However, exports of grain, cattle, horses and other farm produce largely went the other way.[45] This was also the direction in which most labour flowed between the two countries. During the early nineteenth century, the number of seasonal migrant workers who travelled from Ireland to Scotland each year for harvest work increased, reaching 35,000 in 1835 alone.[46] Technological exchanges have to be seen within this overall context.

The impact of improved Scottish farming methods and implements on Irish techniques was primarily a reflection of the central importance of Scottish developments to the international discourse on agricultural improvement in the eighteenth and nineteenth centuries. From an Irish perspective, the acceptance or rejection of these techniques reflects the state of development of industrial infrastructure within Ireland, the availability of unskilled or skilled labour, and the resources of land and other capital within holdings. Within these parameters, technical developments within Scotland often provided the best option available to Irish farmers.

PART TWO

DISCIPLINES AND DEMOGRAPHIES

are rare and Irish [illegible] comparisons [illegible]
abiding in agony is one of [illegible] Kafka [illegible]

Archives of Abuse and Discontent? Presbyterianism and Sexual Behaviour during the Eighteenth and Nineteenth Centuries

Andrew Blaikie and Paul Gray

Introduction

Our essay title derives from a quotation in which Hufton alludes to the annals of church history in Europe as indices of social indiscipline and irregularity.[1] We aim to identify the shifting impact of ecclesiastical control over the sexual behaviour of parishioners by addressing who were the victims and who the dissatisfied. While the issues we raise have considerable implications for reading the bald facts of population history, our primary aim is to compare the regulatory efforts of the Presbyterian Kirk in two settings, namely eighteenth-century Ulster and nineteenth-century north-east Scotland.

Although historical research into British church court material provides a contextual backdrop, systematic and quantitative studies at the parish level are rare and Irish–Scottish comparisons of this period unknown.[2] The abiding imagery is one of ruthless Knoxian discipline, of sackcloth and ashes, penance at the cutty stool and draconian measures such as the lacteal test, whereby in the event of a foundling being placed at the kirk door, all unmarried women 'come to perfection' had to assemble to have their breasts examined by parish 'gentlewomen' for signs of milk.[3] However, close scrutiny of the parish minutes themselves, in conjunction with the contextual details of sexual behaviour, suggests a rather different reality.

Eighteenth-Century Ireland: 'Overarching Gospel and Social Control'

The sexual misdemeanours of a people are in many instances, and by their very nature, hidden from history. Although the relatively uncharted waters of illicit sexuality in Ireland in the eighteenth century do not lend themselves to anything other than general comment, it appears that illegitimacy was low, and if it increased at all it is unlikely to have reached anything resembling mainland European levels. The major exception that emerges to an almost universal portrayal in the literature of the chaste and pure Irish is the north-east of the island. O'Riordan's somewhat mischievous quotation that 'it seems ... Orangeism and illegitimacy go together, and that bastards in Ireland are in proportion to the Orange Lodges'[4] finds an echo in other observations of the character of Ulster. Forbes noted the 'inferior standard of morals among the young women';[5] Lynd commented on the 'social conditions in which the sexes meet on easy and intimate terms' but also noted that 'Ulster pays for its greater sexual freedom by a frequency of illegitimate births unknown in the other provinces'.[6] The Ordnance Survey Memoirs also contain intimations of a freer morality in Ulster, with the suggestion that this may also have prevailed in preceding generations.[7]

Scholarly literature points to a cultural differential, with areas of mainly Protestant Lowland Scots settlement operating a different morality from the rest of the island. Connolly observes that inhabitants of certain parts of Ulster were an exception to contemporary generalisations concerning Irish chastity,[8] and Akenson, in his study of Islandmagee, found widespread premarital sexual intercourse, suggesting Lowland Scottish rather than general Irish patterns of behaviour.[9] Protestant clergy – or more specifically Presbyterian clergy – had methods of enforcing sexual morality that would have made their Catholic counterparts envious, notably the public humiliation in front of their peers at Sunday service of those accused of sexual sins.[10] Herein lies a paradox. If areas of Scottish settlement were mainly Presbyterian, and if Presbyterians exercised stringent sexual discipline amongst their membership, why was there apparently greater moral laxity in areas where Presbyterians predominated?

This part of the essay will shed light on aspects of illicit sexuality in Presbyterian communities in Ulster in the eighteenth century by analysing sexual discipline cases in the Presbyterian church courts.

The Context of Presbyterian Church Discipline

The eighteenth century for Presbyterianism was summed up by Holmes as one of discomfort, division and disillusionment. Under the Penal Laws Presbyterians faced discrimination, and the Anglican church declared those married according to Presbyterian custom fornicators and their children illegitimate. This was not how Presbyterians viewed their own marriage partners and their children, but in an era of insecurity and mistrust Anglicans continued to condemn Presbyterians, branding them as a state within a state, disloyal and seditious, with their Synods, Presbyteries and Kirk Sessions exercising an unlawful jurisdiction in defiance of the authority of church and state.[11]

In terms of administration the Presbyterian church in the eighteenth century had three levels of church court. At congregational level, a local church (or Congregation) would have a number of individuals (or Elders) who would constitute the governing body of the Congregation and were known as the Session (or Kirk Session). The representatives from Session, together with those from Sessions of other Congregations, combined together to form a Presbytery. Finally, representatives from Presbyteries came together to form the General Synod. The complicating factor in this analysis is the existence of two major strands of Irish Presbyterianism in the eighteenth century – those Presbyterians under the General Synod, and Seceders who had their own Congregations, Presbyteries and Synod.

Much of the tenor of church discipline in Presbyterian church courts has been subject to caricature and misrepresentation, and although there appears to have been a preoccupation with cases of a sexual nature, this was not the Sessions' sole area of operation. Sessions dealt with drunkenness, theft and libel. Circulating scandal was forbidden, as was misbehaviour at wakes and playing cards and dice. A man was also forbidden to beat his wife on the Sabbath (although whether he was permitted to do so on other days is unclear). Session also governed the Congregation's spiritual affairs and ensured that the poor and needy were cared for.[12] Sexual discipline was not a practice confined to Irish Presbyterians; other denominations exercised their own sexual control in Ireland.[13]

Disciplining by Presbyteries

The Presbyteries featured here (Table 5.1),[14] which dealt with more difficult or more serious sexual misdemeanours referred by Sessions, examined a small number of cases overall. Tyrone Presbytery dealt with only six cases (0.2 per annum) from 1781 to 1809; due to the small number of cases involved, Tyrone is excluded from the remainder of the analysis. Over the century the trend in the number of cases dealt with was downwards. Route and Down Presbyteries dealt with an average of 5.2 and 3.9 cases per annum respectively for the early part of the century, while the Moira and Lisburn and Down (Associate) Presbyteries each dealt with only 1.9 cases per annum towards the end of the century. Route Presbytery in the early nineteenth century dealt with only 1.3 cases per annum, compared to the 5.2 cases which it recorded in the early eighteenth century. There is a suggestion of change over time in the data and, although the mechanisms are unclear, it does not appear that the decreasing caseload was due to a rebellious laity. The visitation by Presbytery (which was in reality an audit of Congregational affairs) of various Congregations in the Route Presbytery in the late 1820s and early 1830s, when ascertaining whether the members of

Table 5.1. *Sexual discipline cases brought before the presbyteries of Route, Down, Tyrone, Down (Associate) and Moira and Lisburn (Seceder)*

	Route Presbytery 1701–6	Route Presbytery 1811–34	Down Presbytery 1707–15	Down (Associate) Presbytery 1785–95	Moira and Lisburn (Seceder) Presbytery 1774–1786	Tyrone 1781–1809
Number of cases						
Total number of cases	31	30	35	21	25	6
Average cases per annum	5.2	1.2	3.9	1.9	1.9	0.2
Types of case (%)						
Fornication	19.4	16.7	22.9	9.4	24.0	33.3
Fornication with birth of bastard child	6.5	13.4	–	14.3	12.0	16.7
Antenuptial fornication	–	–	–	33.3	–	–
Fornication and adultery	9.7	–	–	4.8	–	–
Adultery	48.4	60.0	62.8	14.3	36.0	16.7
Adultery and bastard child	–	–	–	14.3	–	–
Other	16.0	9.9	–	9.6	28.0	33.3
Cases involving adultery*	70.9	60.0	62.8	33.3	40.0	16.7
Cases involving fornication*	35.6	30.0	22.9	61.9	36.0	50.0
Gender of defendants						
Male	48.4	73.3	51.4	71.4	72.0	100.0
Female	29.0	26.7	40.0	23.8	20.0	–
Joint	22.6	–	8.6	4.8	8.0	–

Adultery cases+						
Married man cited	81.0	N/A	N/A	42.9	50.0	N/A
Married woman cited	23.8	N/A	N/A	–	30.0	N/A
Action to be taken						
Acknowledge sin and be rebuked (c)	67.5	–	–	–	16.0	–
Acknowledge sin and be rebuked (p)	–	–	94.2	–	20.0	33.3
Take oath of purgation	5.0	16.7	–	–	–	–
To be dealt with by Session	15.0	6.7	–	28.6	32.0	–
Innocent	2.5	3.3	–	–	8.0	33.3
Further action/defer/other	10.0	13.3	5.8	33.3	24.0	33.3

Notes: (p) is Presbytery; (c) is Congregation. In the case of Route 1701–6 appearances are used and not cases.

Of the twenty-seven who were to acknowledge their sin in the congregation and be rebuked, seventeen (63.0%) were reported to have done so.

* May include cases in the 'other' category

the Congregation submitted to discipline, usually received an affirmative reply. This might suggest, if the response was not merely formulaic, there was at minimum an acquiescence in the disciplinary procedure of the Congregation, at least in the Route area.

The data presented do not point to a uniform procedure in operation in all Presbyteries regarding sexual discipline. However, common features included referring the case back to the Session to be dealt with, the rebuke of the individual or individuals concerned before either the Congregation or the 'bar of Presbytery', and their repentance before being admitted to 'sealing ordinances'. The minutes of the Presbytery of Down in 1710 stated that 'Agnes Wilson being referred hither from the Session of Ballee for the sin of adultery with James Wylie, and Mary Ure for a relapse into fornication, being called, they appeared, were rebuked for yir sins and remitted to the Session of Ballee'.[15] From the Presbytery of Moira and Lisburn the case of Janet Harriet provided a variant: 'Janet Harriet, otherwise Young, as was appointed in former minutes, appear'd and was dealt wt. by ye Pby.

concerning her sense of her sin in being guilty of Adultery, and her sorrow for it, which she expressed to satisfaction. The Session of Gilnahirk was appointed to take her satisfaction before the Congregation three several Sabbaths in the course of the next half year.'[16] In over 67 per cent of cases in Route (1701–6), the individual was to be rebuked by the Congregation. In Down, over 94 per cent were rebuked by the Presbytery, and in the case of Route (1811–34) the figure was 60 per cent. In some instances a case was deferred, further enquiry was requested or the individual was deemed to be innocent. In many cases guilt appears to have been proven and therefore repentance, rebuke and referral were the salient features. The only major exception occurred when individuals were willing to take a 'purgation oath' to purge them from the sin and assert their innocence, although this was usually only permitted when Presbytery could be sure that perjury would not be an unwelcome addition to the original crime.

The overarching control of the church authorities was exemplified by a Down Presbytery minute for 1706, noting a letter from Galloway in Scotland that 'there are many grossly scandalous persones fled from thence to Ireland to escape Church censures … there are others already excommunicated with the highest excommunication' and recommending all ministers to be 'very strict in observing all strangers that come within their bounds … that if the aforesaid scandalous persones or any of them be within the bounds of this Presbytery, they may be discovered.'[17]

The startling variation in the types of sexual misdemeanour illustrated the wide range of behaviour encountered and the apparent ingenuity of the prosecuting authorities. In addition to the perennial fornication and adultery may be added criminal conversation, uncleanness, incest, fornication including the conception of an illegitimate child, fornication before marriage, indecent behaviour and whoredom.[18] Around 71 per cent of cases in Route (1701–6), 63 per cent in Down and 60 per cent in Route (1811–34) dealt with adultery, and although the percentages in the Seceder Presbyteries of Moira and Lisburn and Down (Associate) were lower, around 40 and 33 per cent respectively, they still represent a sizeable proportion of all cases. Fornication in all the Presbyteries ranged from around 23 to 36 per cent of all cases, the only exception being the Presbytery of Down (Associate), where they accounted for around 62 per cent of cases. The evidence points to adultery as a major area of concern to Congregations, who therefore appear to have referred it to Presbytery.

In cases where an illegitimate child was born, proceedings could be complex, with both parties being cited to appear by Presbytery. Sessions and Presbyteries appear to have embraced the moral quagmire of paternity cases with a sense of bounden duty which appears to reflect a collective concern about the perceived subversive nature of sexual intercourse outside marriage.

The Code of Discipline of the General Synod of Ulster (1825), representing the accumulated wisdom on Church procedures, noted that 'as fornication is a crime peculiarly injurious to the best interests of society, it is the duty of the session to mark it with the strongest disapprobation'. It continued, in the case of fornication, 'if a woman refuse to name the father of an illegitimate child, she is to be held contumacious [stubbornly disobedient], and not only cut off from privileges, but held incapable of restoration until she declare the father'. Both parties in such cases might be confronted, and if they persevered in their assertions, Presbytery's advice was sought.[19] The final stage in such a process involved the summoning of witnesses who were examined on oath as to the truth or falsehood of the matters before them.

Despite the relentless pursuit of single pregnant females, most of the defendants were men. In three of the five Presbyteries almost three quarters were men, while in the other two the number of male defendants outweighed female defendants. The evidence is unsettling, given the stereotype of male-dominated church courts pillorying vulnerable unmarried mothers; moreover, in cases of adultery it appeared that the married man was the defendant rather than the married woman. In a male-dominated society it might be suggested that it is surprising to find males being held accountable for their sexual misdemeanours. There is no evidence to suggest why this should be so. Despite its obvious failings, the Presbytery displayed a less partisan approach than might be expected. This observation is further strengthened when it appears that the cases of clergymen's sexual misdemeanours were dealt with on the same basis as the laity.[20]

Discipline by Kirk Sessions

In both Session and Presbytery minutes, fornication and illegitimate offspring were major items, but in the Session minutes the emphasis was more on fornication or fornication before marriage rather than adultery. The occupation of women cited in proceedings was rarely given, but where it appears it was invariably given as servant. In Cahans Congregation in 1753, William Stevenson was charged with adultery with his servant girl.[21] The same year John Craford was rebuked before the Congregation for fornication with a servant maid.[22] In Connor, James Grahams was accused of fornication with Mary McComond, 'his own servant'.[23] The wide variety of sexual misdemeanours was more apparent in Session than in Presbytery minutes – cases of rape, promiscuous dancing, lewdness, repeated acts of fornication, the bad disorder (presumably venereal disease), being a whore, fornication, adultery, illegitimate children and fornication before marriage were all brought before Session.

Baptism in the context of illicit sexuality was an important issue in so far as it was connected with church discipline. It is because of rigid church discipline that 'it is perhaps not surprising that many women chose to baptize their illigitimate children in neighbouring churches'.[24] The issue of baptism arose at various times in Connor Kirk Session, the minutes noting in April 1708 that 'Samuell Parker and his wife have agreed upon it that their child shall not be baptised until he be admitted to hold up his own child seeing he is willing to submitt to what church censer either presbytery or sess[ion] shall enjoyn upon him'.[25] Baptism was at times refused, the Connor minutes noting that as one individual was 'unwiling to apear in public to make confession of his sin they could not admit him baptism to his child and he left the sesion abruptly'.[26] In the case of Elizabeth Campble, who appeared before Session 'Desiring Baptism to her child and signifying her willingness to give satisfaction to ye congregation for her sin of fornication', the Session judged that because she had often fallen into this 'snare of the Devill' and her previous confessions had clearly been unsatisfactory, she could not hold her child up for baptism. They did however offer her the opportunity to obtain a sponsor.[27]

Childbirth in the case of the unmarried became an occasion for discovery as well as suffering. For instance, 'Cathren Nemans ... when she was in Laboure to bring forth her child the medwife and other weman prefent refufed their afsiffance untill she declared who was the father of her child'.[28] An unfortunate woman, clearly vulnerable, could therefore be quizzed about the child's paternity and used to provide evidence which in various instances would be used by Session in its examination of her case. Although vulnerable, women used sexual bargaining, as in the case of Joan Brown, who defended herself when being accused of fornication by stating that 'it was only to gett marriage of him that confed hir to keep company with him'.[29] How common such a strategy was is not known, though in the parish of Carnmoney it was noted that premarital intercourse had been used for the ulterior motive of securing and increasing dowries and that such occurrences were not unusual.[30]

The minutes of the Session of Carnmoney have been quantified to provide a more detailed analysis of sexual discipline within an individual Congregation (Table 5.2). Between 1767 and 1805, 171 cases came before the Session, although the annual average decreases over time, reinforcing the impression created by the Presbytery minutes of change over the years. The analysis confirmed that in Carnmoney fornication, and in particular fornication before marriage, formed the majority of cases.

In Carnmoney, the transcripts of baptisms and marriages make it possible to trace prenuptial pregnancies. Even allowing for the possibility of premature birth, it was clear that many baptisms related to births prenuptially

Table 5.2. Sexual discipline cases, Carnmoney Presbyterian congregation, 1767–1805

Years	Number of new cases	Number of new cases per annum	Fornication (%)	Illegitimate child and fornication (%)	Illegitimate child (%)	Fornication before marriage (%)	Other (%)	Adultery (%)
1767–75	47	5.2	38	9	6	34	–	13
1776–85	37	3.7	32	3	3	51	11	–
1786–95	57	5.7	35	9	5	47	4	–
1796–1805	30	3.0	28	23	–	43	3	3

Source: Data compiled from Carnmoney Session Minutes, 1767–1805.

conceived, the baptism being recorded within six months of marriage. Baptisms which might have attracted suspicion were then checked back to the antenuptial sexual discipline cases to see if the offenders had been brought before the session. The results gave a prenuptial pregnancy rate of 13 per cent (1767–75), 12 per cent (1776–85), 19 per cent (1786–95) and 11 per cent (1796–1805). The data contrasted markedly with an exceptionally low illegitimacy ratio of 0.8 per cent (1767–75) and 1.3 per cent (1786–95), although both illegitimacy and prenuptial pregnancy move together upwards between the two periods. The evidence revealed that Carnmoney Session brought before them to answer the charge 96 per cent of those who were married in Carnmoney and might be suspected of sexual intercourse before marriage.

Akenson has indicated that it might be a reasonable guess that in mid-nineteenth-century Ireland, only one half of all pregnancies resulted in live births.[31] If this is accepted for eighteenth-century Ireland, and there is little to presume that it would be any less than in the nineteenth, it would appear that around one quarter of women in Carnmoney Congregation had been pregnant at some time before their marriage. Although unspectacular by eighteenth-century English standards, it provides a perspective on a Presbyterian community that would be masked by an apparently low level of illegitimacy.

The evidence suggests that Presbyterian church discipline in north-east Ulster was strict and that the laity generally acquiesced to church authorities in their exercise of sexual discipline. The Anglican view that Presbyterians provided a rival jurisdiction to that of the established church, a state within a state, is strengthened by the impressions gained from the minutes of Presbytery and Session.[32] With regard to the exercise of sexual discipline, Stone has contended that by 1740, shame punishments for fornication or prenuptial conceptions had virtually ceased in England.[33] In Scotland, Boyd notes that by the early years of the nineteenth century 'in many parishes public penance was now a rare if not an unknown event'.[34] Though cases declined, sexual discipline was still administered by Irish Presbyterians until the early twentieth century and, exceptionally, into the 1960s.[35] Why were sexual discipline cases so prevalent, especially in the absence of any particular biblical emphasis? Were they 'easier both to detect and condemn',[36] or did the encroachment of the civil authorities in other areas lead the church courts to specialise in the area of sexual sins?

There are a few possibilities regarding the paradox of strict Presbyterian sexual discipline and freer sexual morality in Presbyterian areas. The Presbyterian system of sexual discipline with a public penance and absolution may have purged not only the spiritual aspect of the sin but also its social stigma. The community were involved in the absolution and therefore could not malign the individual later, at least not in public, for fear of being subject to Session for their own slanderous actions. Ironically, the frequent highlighting of sexual misdemeanours might denote the ordinary. Sexual misdemeanours that are not special but commonplace are less likely to incur popular disapprobation. This does not mean they were viewed as morally right or that the disciplinary process was derided. It may simply have been that, in contrast to a disciplinary system – such as the confessional in the Catholic church, where the spiritual sin was forgiven but its social stigma left extant – the Presbyterian system left little room for the rumour and innuendo which secrecy and taboo engender. This argument, though speculative, may help at least to open further lines of enquiry into the nature of this specific aspect of illicit sexuality in Ireland.

A Harsh Discipline?

The nature of church discipline within the Irish Presbyterian community in the eighteenth century has been caricatured as the searching out and punishing of fornicators and adulterers. Accepting this distorted picture misunderstands the Presbyterian mindset, which, however limited in its practical implementation of church discipline, was dedicated to maintaining a standard of behaviour to be upheld by servant and master, clergy and laity alike. Both of our studies indicate the application of social control in an egalitarian manner. This egalitarian discipline helped to lose Presbyterianism some of its remaining members among the gentry who could not easily submit to the rebukes of minister and Session.[37]

Illegitimacy was severely dealt with, but so too was slander, stealing and other non-sexual sins. Sessions strove, as far as possible, to see that illegitimate children were supported.[38] The midwife's role during labour in obtaining the name of the father in cases of illegitimacy, although hardly good obstetric practice, ensured that the male culprit was brought to justice, as well as perhaps ensuring the practical support of the child. Both parents were held accountable. The double standard of sexual conduct did not pertain in the dealings of Session or Presbytery.

Irish Presbyterians were characterised by a lack of ostentation, plain speaking and puritanical dourness.[39] However, what emerges from Presbytery and Session minutes was a breadth of human behaviour within the Presbyterian community and a greater light and shade in the area of sexual relations than hitherto acknowledged. Citations in Session minutes, such as that of Grissel Curry, who confessed 'fornication with William Parker, which was committed in a field near his fathers about daylight going the latter end of harvest',[40] or Agness Mason's assertion that she told the father of her illegitimate child 'in harvest in the time of her Fathers shearing',[41] evoke the rural idyll of any peasant society. Presbyterian peasantry at times portrayed this role of earthy rebellion, sceptical of church and state. Their scepticism and rebelliousness was vividly portrayed by Sam Hanna Bell when he stated that:

> Men or women determined to pursue some selfish course, hardened their hearts with an ancient knowledge that the world did not behave as the clergy wanted it to or, worse still, said it did. In a drought the peasants might flock to church with every mark of fervour to pray for rain, but they knew that when the rain did come, it would come vast, rolling, drenching the world from horizon to horizon and not seeking out, with scrupulous justice, the meadows of the pious.[42]

Other currents of this Presbyterian mindset produced a studied system of justice with the acceptance or acquiescence of the community. 'The object of the Kirk Session' in cases of paternity of an illegitimate child was to 'ascertain the truth in a scriptural and peaceful way'.[43] Discipline was to be maintained within the community but under the sacred canopy of biblical truth. Overarching Gospel and social control went hand in hand. Rebelliousness and redemption, conscience and coercion, were captured in the oath taken by Mary Taggart that her child was not the product of illicit sexual intercourse.

> I Mary Taggart being called in question on the occasion of having brought forth my first child after marriage sooner than ye ordinary time do put an end to ye process now depending before ye session concerning me, I do

hereby solemnly swear in ye sight of a heart searching God the awful avenger of all falsehood yt I had no carnal dealing before marriage with John Wilson my husband or any other man and this I declare to be the truth as I shall answer it to God and as I hope for his mercy in time and eternity.[44]

Victorian Scotland: Declining Social Control or Cultural Resilience?

In Ireland, good Presbyterian records survive for the eighteenth century. However, across Scotland the written record was largely abandoned around 1780.[45] Before then north-east Scotland appears to have resembled many parts of north-east Ireland in that illegitimacy levels were low and the great majority of 'offenders' who could have been disciplined were in fact brought before the Session. We might suppose a cultural homogeneity on both sides of the North Channel that was attributable to common faith and practice. However, when Scottish records resume in the 1820s the pattern shifts appreciably, for although both of our studies indicate a willingness to apply social control in an egalitarian manner (the relatively affluent undergoing the same rigorous scrutiny as the relatively poor), the Scottish example demonstrates a pronounced trend towards decreased levels of surveillance and discipline as the nineteenth century progressed.

In their study of early-modern Scotland (1660–1780), Mitchison and Leneman remark that material drawn from Kirk Session minute books provides comprehensive coverage of sexual licence. 'It is our claim that for a considerable period the system of discipline in Scotland has left records which show investigation into all unmarried pregnancies once they reached a fairly advanced stage, and also into pregnancies preceding marriage.'[46] This is in line with the near total coverage of prenuptial fornicators by the Carnmoney Session, and suggests that Irish and Scottish trends were in close harmony.

Because of the paucity of Old Parish Register coverage of births, Mitchison and Leneman use the numbers of sexual offenders appearing before the Session on charges of 'fornication' and 'antenuptial fornication' as a surrogate measure for the illegitimacy level. However, this indicator takes no account of the efficiency of the Session. During this period, bastardy levels were not high. In north-east Scotland, for example, the illegitimacy ratio was calculated as being just 4.9 per cent (1760s), while the proportion of cases where the mother was pregnant at marriage is given as less than 2 per cent. In these circumstances, surveillance appears to have been high.[47] However, as levels of illegitimacy rose, it is plausible to assume that Sessions would find it increasingly difficult to contain sexual irregularity. There is also the matter of cultural context, for even though reliable measures of bastardy can later be obtained from parish and civil registers, their interpretation will depend upon the extent to which declining marriage was perceived to be a significant indicator of underlying cultural change. We must therefore consider first the pattern of sessional activity, and second the meaning of such surveillance.

Declining Sessional Activity

The Presbyterian Form of Process had since 1707 employed a system of delation and citation whereby each district elder patrolled his patch and reported scandalous findings to the Session, which would then summon the persons suspected to appear before them after the service on a stated Sunday.[48] The lesser excommunication of most sexual offenders required them to forego communion privileges as penitents while undergoing public humiliation before the Congregation (although by 1804 the Presbytery of Strathbogie had decreed the replacement of public appearance by private appearances before the Session), the number of appearances being consistent with the severity of the offence. Thereafter they were absolved.[49] In Rothiemay, Banffshire, no disciplinary details exist for the years between 1751 and 1827. On 9 September 1827, the Kirk Session minutes resume by recording an agreement 'to dismiss none from church censure upon his or her first appearance'.[50] During the 1830s, fines for fornication (£1.3s.4d.) and, less frequently, adultery (£2.10s.) were considerable, although at 5s. the fine for antenuptial fornication was less than half that for irregular proclamations of banns – irregular marriages were extremely rare – and some fornicators were remitted parts of their fines 'in consequence of their being servants' or apprentices and allowed to pay by instalments (wages by the half-year for single farm servants were just £6 for men and around £3 for women).[51] Although in 1835 the Presbytery ordained an end to fines for

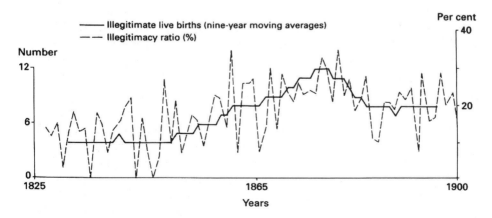

Fig. 5.1. *Rothiemay: illegitimacy trends, 1827–1900.* Sources: OPR 165/2, 4; civil registration certificates, 165.

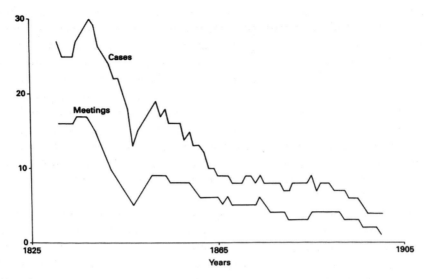

Fig. 5.2. *Rothiemay: frequency of meetings for discipline and no. of cases dealt with per meeting, 1827–1904* (nine-year moving averages).
Sources: CH2/416/5,6; *Vestry*, minutes 3 Aug. 1872 – 2 Nov. 1945.

antenuptial fornication, with other offences soon following suit, the minutes continue to give every appearance of the machinery being well organised.[52] However, as the century progressed the system gradually broke down: the Session met less frequently to enact discipline, cases were increasingly dropped as offenders failed to appear and, when they did show up, appearances were sporadic and inconsistent.

The number of cases for both 'antenuptial fornication' and fornication dealt with by the Rothiemay Session fell from eighty-two in 1831–40 to just thirty-three in the closing decade of the century, a decline in disciplinary surveillance rendered all the more striking when set against a protracted rise in the numbers of *de facto* miscreants as the bastardy ratio rose from 13.4 per cent to 21.2 per cent over the same period. Juxtaposed, Figures 5.1 and 5.2 clearly indicate the divergence between illicit sexual behaviour and the Kirk's ability to contain it.

The fall-off in disciplinary activity after the mid-1840s was partly due to the Disruption of the Church of Scotland (1843), when upwards of half of the congregation seceded to form the Free Church. Free Church minutes for Rothiemay have not survived, but comparable samples from the adjacent parish of Marnoch indicated clear declines in discipline amongst both denominations.[53] The mid-1840s saw the final demise of the parish state in Scotland as the Kirk's welfare functions became secularised with the advent of the New Poor Law (1845), and in 1855 the registration of births, marriages and deaths became a civil procedure. Both of these measures freed the church to deal more with pastoral matters, yet with its central role in local affairs diminished, its power over the dealings of parishioners crumbled. The uncoupling of the welfare and disciplinary functions only formalised an already attenuated reciprocity. Local charity was no longer supported by fines for fornication. Meanwhile, settlement arrangements under the New Poor Law facilitated greater mobility amongst applicants (those born in the parish being able to claim despite living far away), thus breaking the link between parochial welfare provision and local residence. Unmarried mothers prevailed amongst the non-resident applicants since, although many came home to bear their children, they later returned to service elsewhere.[54]

Between 1827 and 1830 there were twice as many fornication cases as there were registered illegitimate births in Rothiemay (Table 5.3), whereas by the 1890s there were more than three times as many recorded bastard births as disciplinary cases appearing in the minute book of the Established Church. This remarkable *volte-face* demonstrates the protracted failure of the Session to perform its disciplinary role as proportionately more 'offenders' escaped during each decade between the 1820s and 1880. Cross-matching tests indicate consistently accurate levels of registration both before and after 1855.[55] Thus, even if the Free Church dealt with half of all post-Disruption cases, there was still a considerable fall-off in ecclesiastical capture.

Table 5.3. *Fornication cases (Church of Scotland) relative to illegitimate births, Rothiemay, 1827–1900*

Decade	No. of fornication cases	No. of recorded illegitimate births	Fornication cases as percentage of recorded illegitimate births
(1827–1830)	28	14	200.0
1831–1840	58	40	145.0
1841–1850	45	43	104.6
1851–1860	46	60	76.7
1861–1870	40	82	48.8
1871–1880	27	111	24.3
1881–1890	36	78	46.2
1891–1900	24	77	31.2
TOTALS	304	505	60.2

Sources: CH2/416/5, CH2/416/6 (SRO); Vestry, Minutes 3 August 1872 to 2 November 1945; 165/4, civil registration certificates (New Register House); OPR.

When a couple asked for their child to be baptised and the mother was found to have borne the child within nine months of marriage, sessional rebuke was supposedly inevitable. Nevertheless, the minutes indicate a fall in the number of recorded antenuptial cases from 73 between 1827 and 1860 to just 28 between 1861 and 1900. Given the nature of this offence, appearance by both partners was overwhelmingly the norm (70 out of 101 cases). With extramarital rather than premarital liaisons, however, the demise of discipline was decidedly gendered in its impact. In the 1830s, denials of paternity were a frequent occurrence, not least because financial penalties disinclined men to admit their 'guilt'. A proportion of putative fathers did eventually appear, often following a second or third summons, in order to refute the woman's accusation. Some changed their plea and were duly absolved; others pledged to remain silent until the birth, perhaps in the perverse hope that the woman would miscarry or the child be stillborn, thus letting them off the hook of paying aliment.[56] If the male party persisted in his denial, a mother could apply for a certificate of poverty, permitting her to bring a civil action in the Sheriff Court.[57] Yet men increasingly failed to appear at all: in Rothiemay the number of extramarital fornication cases where both partners appeared more than once and were absolved fell from 33 couples between 1831 and 1840 to just 5 between 1891 and 1900. Although in 118 instances in total (1827–1900) both parties satisfied discipline, women alone underwent the full diet in 150 cases, compared to just 44 cases where men did so.

Our Irish data indicated that most defendants were men. Contrastingly, in Scotland the growing absence of men during the nineteenth century was reflected in two trends: increasingly paternity was acknowledged by letter, or men simply absconded. Whereas men living outwith the parish had once been summoned to attend by ministers exchanging written summons, by the 1860s it was conventional for non-resident men to plead in writing. Rising numbers simply disappeared. Phrases like 'failed to appear despite summons' became common. Often women were unable to ascertain a fleeting partner's residence and were thus unable to obtain letters acknowledging paternity, while comments such as 'who has absconded but admits his guilt' and 'has gone abroad, but a letter was produced which showed that he admitted the paternity' offered little succour.[58]

By far the great majority of putative fathers were farm servants who moved between farms every six months, as did the female domestics who formed the bulk of unmarried mothers. This pattern reflected changes in the system of hiring which had occurred between the 1790s and 1840. As subtenants were squeezed out of the system, farmers increasingly relied on full-time unmarried servants, male and female, billeted on the farm, rather than cottagers and married men.[59] Not only did these servants move frequently, but the apparent eradication of the old 'kindly relations' between employer and servant as the cash nexus took hold effected a weakening of the quasi-parental control of the farmer.[60] In such a shifting and morally vacant context, it was scarcely surprising that partners quickly lost contact with one another. Moreover, as emigration increased after the onset of agrarian depression during the 1870s, it became unrealistic to expect to track down parties living in Canada, Australia or South Africa.[61] A father's signature on a birth certificate came to be considered sufficient proof of paternity, yet by the 1870s less than 30 per cent of unmarried fathers signed. The women were left quite literally holding the baby, as necessity forced them to return home to raise their offspring. Between 1861 and 1904, four-fifths of female offenders brought before the Kirk Session lived within the parish. The corresponding score for males was only 20.3 per cent.

Between 1851 and 1900, 32 per cent of bastard-bearing women who married in Rothiemay already had two or more illegitimate children, a statistic that was clearly related to a rise in absconding fathers. When it came to repeat offences, it also tended to be women who had their cases remitted to the Presbytery for further deliberation ('grave dealings') or whose period of penitence was extended: it was far easier to enumerate consecutive offences for women who reappeared in the same parish than it was to catalogue the misdemeanours of men who, though they were equally if not more copious, moved regularly between districts.[62] Meanwhile there were examples of partners appearing together, each admitting to having indulged in second, third, and fourth 'lapses'. Remarks such as 'John Hay, guilty of the sin of fornication with Jane Smith ... now confesses himself guilty of the same sin with Anne Largue' were by no means rare, and comments like 'his being a second case with her and hers being a case of quadrilapse' allude to both the complexity of sexual behaviour and the fluidity of social ties.[63]

Given that the Form of Process decreed that 'only sins which had outward and physical manifestations were to be dealt with', Kirk Sessions lost their power over the inner souls of their parishioners and no longer dealt with sins such as pride or avarice.[64] By contrast, pregnancy provided tangible evidence of guilt. It is thus hardly surprising that fornicators came to dominate the minute books, albeit in lessening numbers, while women were disproportionately represented.[65]

Communities in Crisis?

Yet how far does the decline of church discipline, combined with the protracted rise in illegitimacy, reflect any real rupture in the social consensus of such rural communities? Was it true, as Victorian moral reformers were wont to imply, that the men and women whom the church censured as fornicators were practitioners of a sexual code at odds with the tenets and usages of the parish at large? Or were they mostly just young adults acting out a time-honoured ritual common to this stage in the life cycle? What was the goodness of fit between formulaic church discipline and habitual popular culture?

Local synods were much exercised over the rise in non-churchgoing amongst farm servants, and congregations were enjoined to halt the seepage. Session clerks noted that some adherents had lapsed from membership on account of their lapses in morality.[66] As they could not expect to reclaim the heathen by adopting an overtly punitive stance, the churches were effectively in a buyer's market where sexual offenders could 'shop around' for the most sympathetic treatment.[67] While the local Free Kirk in Marnoch sometimes gave absolution to non-adherents, the Established Church in Rothiemay drove a tougher bargain: when one woman 'stated that she had often made application to the Free Church minister in this parish to deal with her case but had met with refusal, she again expressing her wish to join the Established Church', the Session 'resolved to admit her on proba-tion for a year, informing her that if her conduct were satisfactory during that time she might then be freed from church censure'.[68] However, farm and domestic servants were not unduly disaffected or disaffiliated. The Communion Rolls between the years 1873 and 1881 – a period when ille-gitimacy levels peaked in Rothiemay (34.8 per cent in 1879) – show that servants, who comprised 28 per cent of all persons in the 15–49 age range, represented approximately one-third of Rothiemay's Established Church membership. Church connection was not really the nub of the problem.

The decadal bastardy ratio in Rothiemay between 1851 and 1901 never fell below 18.1 per cent. Many couples indulged in premarital intercourse, and four-fifths of first children born to women who had married in the parish were either illegitimate or conceived before wedlock. Although such patterns suggest deviance from High Victorian sexual behaviour, within the cultural frame of Rothiemay and many surrounding agricultural districts a rather different standard of morality (or at least practice) prevailed. In parts of Banffshire and Aberdeenshire, the very frequency of illicit sexual behaviour denoted its ordinariness.

In such a climate, the biographical details of the Kirk elders are revealing, for although they were sanctioned to uphold the virtues of the local congregation, Table 5.4 illustrates that at least half were connected, either directly or via their families, with sexual impropriety. Elected by male communicants over 21, and composed overwhelmingly of small-to-middling tenant farmers, the eldership was broadly representative of the peasant nature of the parish. By contrast, MacLaren's work on Aberdeen revealed

Table 5.4. Biographical details of elders serving on the Kirk Session of Rothiemay (Church of Scotland), 1827–1904

Name	Ordained	Age	Occupation	Relevant information
John Allan	1882	30	Farmer	Sister bears bastard (1837)
John Begg	1832	36	Farmer	
Alex Mackie	1832	58	Farmer	Fined for irregular proclamation of banns (1805); son fathers bastard (1836); daughter bears bastard (1832)
John Murray	1832	61	Stonemason and crofter	Mother pregnant at marriage; sister bears bastard (1819); daughter bears bastard (1861)
Alex MacWilliam	1832	34	Farmer	
William Petrie	1832	30	Farmer	
Alex Skinner	1832	44	Stonemason	Brother fathers bastard (1807)
Alex MacGregor	1832	61	Merchant	Daughter bears bastard (1823)
John Sharp	1832	?	Farmer	
William Wilson	1832	?	Blacksmith	Daughter bears bastard (1834)
Thomas Duncan	1845	35	Farmer (40 ac.)	
George Howie	1845	61	Farmer (31 ac.)	
William Mackie (son of Alex Mackie, see above)	1845	38	Farmer (75 ac.)	Parents fined for irregular proclamation of banns (1805); sister bears bastard (1832); brother fathers bastard (1836); daughter bears bastards (1862, 1863); son fathers bastard 1879)
John Pirrie	1845	54	Master miller	
John Smith	1845	37	Farmer (7 ac.) (vintner)	Mother pregnant at marriage
James Weir	1875	52	Farmer (94 ac., 1871/ 114 ac., 1881)	
Peter Clark	1875	41	Master shoemaker	Resigns from eldership having been disciplined for antenuptial fornication
James Horne	1875	55	Farmer (20 ac.) (road contractor)	Illegitimate (1819); fathers bastard (1844); sons father bastards (1868, 1872)
Alex Smith	1875	56	Farmer (56 ac.)	Illegitimate (1819)

Name	Ordained	Age	Occupation	Relevant information
William Walker	1875	28	Farmer (landed proprietor 1899)	
William Wilson	1875	45	Farmer (52 ac.)	
James Cruickshank	1894	42	Farmer (300 ac.)	
George Mackie	1894	47	Farmer (50 ac.)	Mother pregnant at marriage; brother fathers bastard (1858)
John Mitchie	1894	51	Farmer	
Elders already ordained in 1827:				
Alex Weir		?	?	
James Taylor		?	?	
Alex Anton		45	Farmer	
James Reid		?	Farmer	

Sources: CH2/416/5, CH2/416/6 (SRO); *Vestry*, minutes 3 August 1872 to 2 November 1945; OPR 165/4; civil registration certificates; census enumerators' books (New Register House).

the membership of urban vestries was drawn largely from the upwardly mobile middle classes.[69] Their lament at the growing distance between their own exemplary piety and the uncultured mores of the masses found little credence in the rural hinterland, where social background regarding breaking the Seventh Commandment did not prevent men becoming elders. James Horne fathered a bastard when in service as a young man, but he went on to hold office for over thirty years. Nevertheless, the fate of Peter Clark indicates that, once elected, elders could not fall from grace, even in a minor way, and expect to continue as moral guardians.

Smout once averred that sexual morality in Victorian Scotland was 'in practice largely a function of the authority relationship between parents and children, and the economic situation of both'.[70] Our analysis for Scotland has demonstrated that most sexual 'defaulters' were life-cycle servants in agriculture. These individuals left home in their teens to labour, moving between farms every six months. The sons and daughters of peasant elders were no different from the rest in this regard, and the impossibility of maintaining strict parental control over their behaviour beyond the family farm was eloquently reflected in the nine sons and daughters of elders who bore illegitimate children.

Arguably, in early-modern Scotland, 'the morality of the Church, and its methods of enforcing it, were accepted, "internalized" by both sexes'. Before the 1780s, approximately 75 per cent of fathers admitted paternity of their bastard offspring. Yet by 1850 only around a third did so, and a high proportion simply evaded summons.[71] Public penance became rare in Scotland and non-existent in many parts of the north-east, while fines were a thing of the past. In 1895, the Rothiemay Session resolved that the minister might henceforth admonish antenuptial fornicators privately, and in 1902 the General Assembly authorised the names of offenders across Scotland to be scrubbed from the record once five years had elapsed.[72] There was no written evidence of discipline in Rothiemay after 1904. The tightly administered machinery of surveillance and public shaming had collapsed into a largely voluntaristic system of private confessional. That process can be construed as liberating, in that individuals were gradually freed from the tyranny of ecclesiastical control, although it was decidedly one-sided in that it was men rather than women who benefited from the slackening of moral oversight. Mitchison and Leneman found that the early-modern Kirk 'by its authority, was able to go a long way towards equality of treatment of the sexes'.[73] However, by mid-Victorian times the absence of authority was indicated by a marked imbalance.

Social historians have generally regarded any decline in the social control of the church as symptomatic of growing individualism, with the mechanisms of sexual surveillance shifting from community controls to couples working out their own courtship and family-building strategies.[74] The risks implied through absence of family supervision, increased mobility and the rest were all too evident in the upswing of illegitimacy, as contemporaries readily pointed out. Demographic patterns were also indicative of responses to changing material conditions as crofts and holdings became scarce and marriage thus became untenable for many. However, the sexual culture of north-east Scotland was not simply reducible to economic rationality.[75] While Shorter's South German communities 'bifurcated' as economic modernisation freed the proletariat from peasant traditionalism and bastardy levels rocketed,[76] our analysis shows no such transformation; but rather an established moral economy accommodating shifting sexual patterns. Although the scale of sexual nonconformity shifted markedly, sexual customs themselves do not appear to have changed. Indeed, long-term persistence of regional differences in sexual behaviour across Scotland suggests that underlying cultural precepts remained remarkably resilient.[77] Discontinuous though the scale of illegitimacy was, the continuity of distinctive regional cultures explains the patterns themselves. That is why, despite regional variation in early-modern 'illegitimacy' levels, these figures 'show no regional or secular correlation with economic growth or the expansion of domestic industry'.[78]

The arguments for cultural continuity are as follows. First, Victorian social investigators have suggested that both bastardy and bridal pregnancy had long been endemic in north-east Scotland. William Alexander remarked:

> Not even in relation to the sore subject of bastardy did the people of last century in the northeast of Scotland hold a greatly more favourable position than their descendants do ... although the absence of sufficient numbers of reliable parish registers precludes such an investigation. But of one thing we may hold ourselves assured – that at no period known to history was the proportion of bastard births other than considerable.[79]

Mitchison and Leneman suggest that before 1790 it was 'unlikely that any sizeable part of the population regarded sexual intercourse as a normal prelude to marriage'.[80] This was perhaps so over much of the country. However, in Rothiemay nearly a third of brides were pregnant at marriage as early as the 1770s. *Pace* the modernisation theorists, it was improbable that all or even most intercourse was motivated by self-interest. A more plausible account would be that an enduring custom of 'fertility-testing', of premarital sex with conception followed by marriage, was supplanted by unmarried motherhood because the other prerequisite for settling down to marry, namely independent housing, became increasingly scarce. Although the rising illegitimacy levels in Scotland's other high-bastardy region, the south-west, may have reflected a long tradition of resistance against the authorities, in many north-eastern rural communities they more readily represented adaptations of a resilient popular culture to economic change.[81] In such circumstances, church influence over sexual behaviour was something of a red herring.

Conclusion

A number of shared characteristics are apparent from our comparative studies. By the later eighteenth century the great mass of cases dealt with by the Kirk were of a sexual nature. In both north-east Ireland and north-east Scotland, levels of illegitimacy at this period appear to have been low, with discipline largely accepted and commonly adhered to. Declines ensued in the numbers of cases dealt with relative to the numbers of people indulging in illicit behaviour – a trend that was particularly dramatic in Scotland during the nineteenth century as men increasingly evaded all censure and women underwent an increasingly privatised diet of absolution.

In both study areas, the common factor of Presbyterian faith lent a cultural dimension to the context in which sexual behaviour was socially perceived and treated. However, common predispositions cannot be straightforwardly read off from the records of ecclesiastical social control. In both countries, if in differing degrees at different times, a paradox emerges between the apparent rigour with which the Form of Process was applied and an equally lively popular toleration of sexual licence. The apparent continuity of such a paradox belied rather different sets of social conditions operating at different periods. By the late eighteenth century, the system was already largely unworkable in the towns and becoming so in much of the countryside. The decline in numbers undergoing discipline was not due to any greater efficiency in techniques of reformation; on the contrary, it was because 'there were too many weak spots in the communication network for all sinners to be traced'. While this does not mean that sexual irregularity was accepted or approved, disapproval had increasingly to be 'expressed in private and personal ways, not with authority'.[82] At the same time, the shift from congregational humiliation and rebuke to private dealings between minister and parishioner has to be seen in the context of an Enlightenment ethos of civic humanism and individualism.[83]

Our Irish evidence suggests that sexual discipline cases decreased as the eighteenth century progressed. There were many instances of irregular marriage.[84] This was in marked contrast to Scotland, where by the 1860s the Registrar General calculated irregular marriages to be just 0.18 per cent of the total.[85] Various references to those who denied crimes, disputed the jurisdiction of Session or Presbytery, or merely refused to be summoned or accept punishments made it clear that a number of individuals lived a more colourful life than that of the obedient or penitent. The frequency of irregular marriage, usually conducted by the Church of Ireland clergyman, highlighted one difference between the two countries. In Ireland the Presbyterians maintained church courts which rivalled ecclesiastical courts of the Established Church, the Episcopalian. In Scotland, the Presbyterian Kirk *was* the Established Church. It is possible such a difference in standing between Presbyterian churches on either side of the Irish Sea helped frame the cultural context of church discipline and the peculiarities of control in both jurisdictions. More generally, we can conclude that there was certainly a downward trend in sexual discipline cases in Ireland, although this was less pronounced than that later experienced in Scotland.

The distinction between shame culture and guilt culture may aid the explanation for Scotland. Benedict argues that while shame cultures are ritually policed through external sanctions on individual behaviour, guilt cultures rely on their members internalising norms of right and wrong within their own consciences.[86] With the instigation of the Form of Process in the early eighteenth century, the Kirk began to lose ground. A guilt culture, reliant upon internalised sanction within each individual's soul, gave way to a system of public penance which visibly purged not just the sin but – to the extent that parishioners accepted discipline and were absolved – its social stigma too. By the mid-nineteenth century, such shaming obtained less purchase, particularly as its crucially public character was eroded. As a mechanism for social control, public shaming requires a cohesive congregational culture in which all people know one another well and continually live and move within daily sight of each other. The intensification of farm servant mobility and the supplanting of quasi-familial conditions of peasant farming by anonymous master–servant relations attenuated such a sense of local belonging. Increasingly men absconded, and women underwent discipline in private, first before the Session and latterly simply by interview with the minister. Ironically, however, this turn to a confessional mode was no longer accompanied by the mechanisms for instilling deep guilt used in the days of the Reformers. Instead, the formal phraseology of the minute books, wherein offenders 'expressed their deep sorrow and were absolved from the scandal of their sin' was so much empty words, the formal husk of a system increasingly without meaning.

The democratic nature of dealings under the Presbyterian system suggests that the relationship between Kirk and community was a consensual one. Neither doctrinal differences, as represented in the events of the Disruption, nor shifts in welfare, nor, directly at least, economic changes, were the basis of profound cultural schism. Instead, the rift lay between the increasingly anachronistic and centrally imposed formality of Presbyterian process and the underlying precepts of a vigorous and locally variable popular culture. Our findings have implications for the secularisation debate among social historians. For instance, Brown contends that, contrary to the received wisdom which holds that Christianity in Britain has been in decline since the Industrial Revolution disrupted older ties of community, its true demise has been short-lived and began only in the 1960s.[87] His argument turns on the claim that religiosity should be measured in terms of cultural predisposition rather than attendance figures. Thus, it may be instructive to apply his logic to the shifts in the balance between cultures of discipline and popular culture, although our inferences may shed doubt on his periodicity.

6

More Irish than the Irish?
Nuptiality and Fertility Patterns
on the Isle of Skye, 1881–1891

Ros Davies and Eilidh Garrett[1]

Irish demography in the post-Famine era has been described as an outlier in the European context.[2] Many theories and explanations have been offered for the island's high levels of out-migration, low levels of nuptiality, high rates of marital fertility and the virtually non-existent rates of birth outside marriage. In *The Vanishing Irish*, Guinnane argued that 'the most important feature of Irish land tenure', with a direct bearing on the island's demographic regime, was neither Catholicism nor 'the existence of landlords or the lack of leases but the fact that most agriculturalists in Ireland were peasants or relatively small farmers'.[3] This was 'very different from England's agrarian structure, where most agriculturalists were landless labourers working for farmer-entrepreneurs'. Comparison of the demographies of England, even rural England, and Ireland is therefore unlikely to uncover the detailed mechanisms of the demographic adjustments underway in the latter country. Such comparisons are made doubly difficult by the fact that the enumerators' books compiled during the taking of the 1861–91 censuses of Ireland failed to survive and the civil registers of Ireland, like those of England and Wales, are closed to detailed academic inspection.[4]

One area of mainland Britain where the economy and culture could, in the second half of the nineteenth century, still be described as that of a 'peasant society' is the crofting counties of Scotland. A study of this area could elucidate whether Guinnane's theory tying demography to the 'peasant' nature of Irish society, and the very close ties to the land associated with this mode of living, held true elsewhere in the British Isles. In demographic terms were the Scottish crofters as Irish as the Irish?

The demography of the Scottish Highlands and islands has been detailed from aggregate sources by both Anderson and Morse, and Flinn *et al.*[5] Anderson, both alone and in collaboration with Morse, has highlighted the unusual demography of the crofting population, and the similarities with Ireland.[6] The present paper draws from the early stages of a study designed to reconstruct the population history, from 1861 to 1901, of the seven

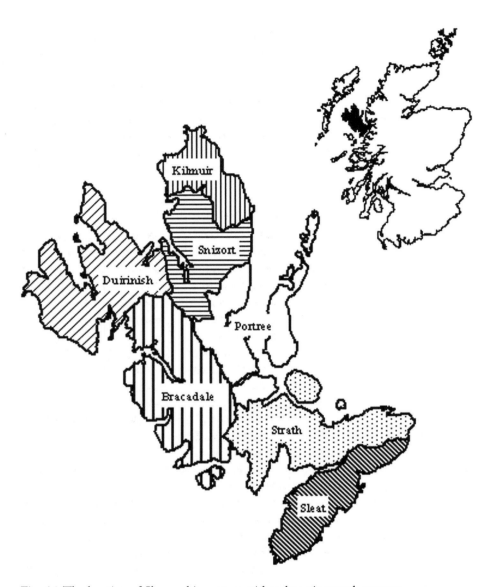

Fig. 6.1 The location of Skye and its seven parishes, late nineteenth century

Note: The map is based on data provided with the support of the ESRC and JISC and uses boundary material which is copyright of the Crown and the Post Office.

Source: Digitised boundaries for Scotland and Skye, 1892: UKBORDERS™ facility, University of Edinburgh, 2001.

parishes of the Isle of Skye, i.e. Bracadale, Duirinish, Kilmuir, Snizort, Portree (including the island of Raasay), Strath and Sleat, shown in Figure 6.1.[7] Our intention is to link the individual census records from the 1861, 1871, 1881, 1891 and 1901 censuses to the civil registers of vital events for the intervening decades.[8] So far the enumerators books' of 1881 (encompassing approximately 17,700 individuals) have been linked to those of 1891 (approximately 16,500 individuals) and to the births, marriages and deaths (approximately 4,300, 600 and 3,000 events respectively) occurring between April 1881 and March 1891.[9] Such linkage is akin to that employed in family reconstitution, but it has two distinct advantages. First there is the level of detail available in both sources. The occupation, age and relationship data given in late nineteenth-century censuses are well known. The Scottish civil registers of birth record the occupation of the child's father, the mother's maiden name, and the date and place of the parents' marriage. The death certificates indicate the names of the deceased's father and mother, as well as that of any spouse. The occupation of the father and mother were also requested (although seldom given in the case of mothers) and statement had to be made as to whether these individuals were still alive. Similar information was requested on the certificates of marriage, in addition to an indication of the religious denomination under whose auspices the marriage ceremony was conducted.[10] Second, the inclusion in the censuses of all individuals resident on census night, not just those experiencing demographic events, makes the linked dataset for Skye very rich in economic and social detail, thus providing a more intimate picture of the demography of the community than that usually wrested from cross-sectional studies of late nineteenth-century censuses. [11]

At present, our study only covers one decade and is subject to considerable problems of 'censoring', i.e. we have little knowledge of people's lives before March 1881 or after April 1891, but it goes some way towards illustrating the potential of the Skye data, and Scottish civil register material in general, for improving our understanding of the interaction between social, economic and demographic processes in the latter half of the nineteenth century. Here we use the linked data for the 1880s to explore whether the crofting communities of Skye had a demographic profile akin to that of the 'peasant' economy of rural Ireland.

In common with both Ireland and many of the other islands off Scotland's west coast, Skye suffered dramatic out-migration across the second half of the nineteenth century.[12] The 16,500 inhabitants in 1891 represent a fall of 28 per cent from the 1841 peak in population numbers of 23,000. The outflow continued unabated into the twentieth century; by the outbreak of the Second World War the population numbered only around 10,000.[13] By the latter decades of the nineteenth century there had been noticeable ageing of the population structure.[14] It is likely, although not conclusively demonstrable from the census returns, that, as well as the absence from home of the island's many fishermen and seafarers, the population was periodically further depleted by marked seasonal migration of young adults. That the outflow was more male than female is suggested by the island's low sex ratio. Amongst individuals aged 25–29 in England Wales in 1891 there were 879 men for every 1,000 women. In Scotland as a whole this fell to 867, but in Skye the sex ratio in this age group was just 672.[15] In the parish of Portree the ratio fell to just 477 men per 1,000 women, although this may have been due as much to the influx of young women to jobs in service, in the houses of the well-to-do who congregated on the outskirts of the small town of Portree, as to a mass exodus of males.

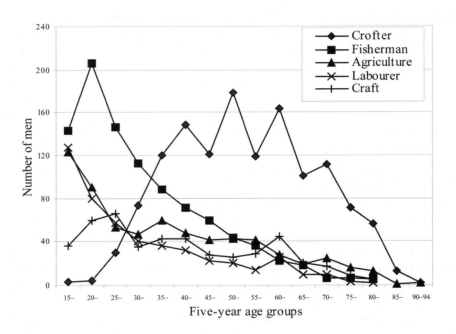

Fig. 6.2. The number of men in selected occupational classes, by five-year age group 15-94, Skye 1881

Note: Agriculture = all forms of agriculture except crofters, cottars and agricultural labourers. The latter are classified as labourers.
Source: Data from census enumerators' books.

The importance of fishing to the island's economy is demonstrated in Figure 6.2, which shows that it was the main occupation for men up to the age of thirty-five. Thereafter crofting became the main occupation.[16] This life-cycle element to occupation on Skye has to be borne in mind throughout any analysis of demographic processes. In the 1881 census 48 per cent of male heads of household were crofters, and only 10 per cent were fishermen, yet in the island's marriage registers for the 1880s, 32 per cent of grooms were fishermen and only 17 per cent were crofters.[17] The marriage registers further reveal that in 81 per cent of the marriages where the groom was a crofter his father was deceased; only 36 per cent of the grooms who were fishermen had lost their fathers.

These figures do not indicate that a better living was to be made from fishing than from crofting, but rather that if one married young on Skye then one was more likely to be a fisherman, and because one was young, the chances of having lost one's father were smaller than among the grooms who were crofters. The number of crofter grooms who did not marry until their father had died, and presumably left them the family croft, highlights the importance of inheritance as a means of becoming a crofter and having the wherewithal to support a family. Table 6.1 indicates that of over 1,100 crofters recorded on Skye by the 1881 census fewer than one tenth had never married, whereas 64 per cent of the 900 or so fishermen were still single. Admittedly the crofters were almost twenty years older on average; fifty rather than thirty years of age. The linkage process identified 65 per cent of the crofters listed on the island in the 1881 census as still resident in 1891. A further 30 per cent could be linked to the pre-1891 death registers, suggesting the remaining 5 per cent had left the island.[18] Amongst fishermen, only 9 per cent were observed in the death registers and 61 per cent were identified in the 1891 census. Applying the same logic, some 30 per cent may have been assumed to have left Skye in the decade following the 1881 census.[19] Of the crofters still resident on the island in 1891, 87 per cent still gave 'crofter' as their occupation. Those who registered another occupation were mostly recorded as 'farmers'. Amongst 1881 fishermen, only 41 per cent of those remaining on Skye in 1891 retained that occupation. Virtually four in ten had become crofters, presumably on the death of their father. Of the remaining 20 per cent a few maintained a connection with the sea as 'sailors' but the others had become 'cottars' or 'agricultural labourers'; lowly occupations, without any land to call their own. Fishing was a young man's occupation, part of the life cycle, and men who could not make the transition from 'fisherman' to 'crofter' had few options other than out-migration.

The average age of marriage for men marrying for the first time on Skye in the 1880s was 31.0 years, and for women it was 26.6, very much within

Table 6.1. Occupation and the life cycle on Skye: crofters and fishermen in the 1881 census linked across the civil registers for the 1880s to the 1891 census

Occupation in 1881	No.	Unmarried in 1881 (%)	Dying 1881-91 (%)	Linked to 1891 census (%)	Leaving (or unlinked) (%)
Crofter	1122	9.6	30.3	65.1	4.6
Fisherman	927	64.0	9.3	60.8	29.9

Of those still resident on Skye in 1891

Occupation in 1881	No.	'Crofter' in 1891 (%)	'Fisherman' in 1891 (%)	'Other' in 1891 (%)
Crofter	730	87.3	2.9	9.9 (mostly 'farmer')
Fisherman	564	38.7	41.1	20.2 (mostly 'cottar', 'agricultural labourer' or 'sailor')

Source: Record linkage of census enumerator's books and civil registers of Skye, 1881 to 1891

the range presented for the 'crofting counties' at this time by Anderson.[20] Both sets of figures are comparable to the 30.3–31.7 range of singulate mean age at marriage (SMAM) for men and the 26.9–27.8 range of SMAMs for women calculated for the 1861 birth cohort in Ireland by Fitzpatrick.[21] Across the parishes of Skye the range of ages at first marriage was 29.0–32.3 for men and 25.6–28.3 for women.

Fishermen married at earlier ages than crofters, walking up the aisle for the first time, on average, at the age of 30.1. Their brides had an average age of 25.3. On average crofter bachelors were aged 33.3 on their wedding day, the spinsters they married being 27.3 years old. Their relative ages suggest that there was an agreement between the crofter and his intended bride to delay their union until the man had achieved crofter status. If the groom had waited until he secured his croft before choosing a bride, it seems likely that he would have opted for a younger woman, given the surplus of single females.

Widow remarriage on Skye was relatively rare. Only 2 per cent of all marriages on the island between March 1881 and April 1891 involved widows, compared with 5–6 per cent in Ireland in the 1880s.[22] In contrast, 11 per cent of the ceremonies involved the remarriage of a widower, identical to the Irish figure of 11–12 per cent. The figure for Skye hid considerable variation amongst crofters registering their marriage: 30 per cent were widowers, yet only 7 per cent of fishermen were being married for a second or subsequent time.[23] The occupational specificity of remarriage suggests that crofting households relied heavily on the work of wives and mothers. If a crofter lost his wife he often wasted little time in acquiring another one. Of the thirty men observed remarrying in the study population where the date of the first wife's death is known, the average gap between the latter event and the new marriage was 22.4 months. For the nineteen crofters in this group the average gap to remarriage was just 16.6 months.

The rate of remarriage amongst crofters meant that when the average age of all crofter grooms and all fisher grooms is compared, the difference is virtually seven years: on average a fisherman marrying on Skye in the 1880s would be aged 30.4 but a crofter would be 37.3. The fact that so few cases of remarriage involved widows meant that the average age of brides scarcely alters whether first or all marriages are considered.[24]

A further feature of marriage, less often commented on by nineteenth-century demographers, is the gap in ages between spouses. On the island as a whole grooms were on average 5.8 years older than their wives; 5.2 years if they were bachelors and 10.9 years if they were widowers. Bachelor crofters were 6.0 years older than their wives, and widower crofters 11.6 years older. Thus the wife of a crofter had, on average, a husband who was 7.7 years older than herself. The wives of fishermen were, on average, 5 years younger than their husbands (4.8 years if he was a bachelor, 9.0 years if he was a widower). In virtually a quarter (24 per cent) of the Skye marriages observed, grooms were 10 years or more older than their brides. Not only does this suggest that relations within the household were probably highly patriarchal and might offer a distinct contrast to the 'companionate' marriage thought to typify much of England at this time, but it also has important implications both for the island's demography, in terms of the number of marriages curtailed by death of the husband, and its social structure, particularly the proportion of women left to rear relatively young families on their own.[25]

The late age at marriage said to characterise Ireland is thus reflected on the Isle of Skye. The 'wait' to inherit the 'family land' and the consequent delay in marriage are conspicuous amongst the crofters who so closely equate to Guinnane's 'peasant' agriculturalists.[26] The next aspect of nuptiality to consider is that of 'celibacy'.

Celibacy is most often measured as the proportion of those aged 45–54 who have never married.[27] At these ages on Skye in 1881, 26 per cent of the female population and 19 per cent of the male population were reported to be 'unmarried'.[28] The male celibacy rate is again on a par with figures for Ireland in 1881.[29] Guinnane quotes an all-Ireland figure of 17 per cent unmarried men aged 45–54, with a range across the four provinces of 11–22 per cent. Only 9 per cent of women in the relevant age group were unmarried in Connaught in 1881, and in Leinster and Ulster 20 per cent of similarly aged women had not made it to the altar. In all, like their men, 17 per cent of Irish women were 'never married'. Female celibacy was therefore a more prominent feature of life on Skye in the 1880s than it was in Ireland, despite the latter's notoriety in this respect.[30] Why the very rural counties of western Ireland, which might be expected to be most like the crofting counties of Scotland, should display the lowest rates of celibacy is a puzzle which might reward further research. In counties such as Kerry, Clare, Galway and Mayo, lying along Ireland's Atlantic coast, fewer than 5 per cent of women aged 45–54 were unmarried in 1881.[31] It is of interest that the counties of the north-east, Tyrone, Londonderry, Antrim and Down, in closest proximity to the west coast of Scotland, had female rates of celibacy of between 10 and 15 per cent. Given the relatively strong presence of Scots in this part of Ireland, it is tempting to suggest that they had some influence over these figures.

When reproductive regimes are being compared in a historical context, the most common measures used are those known as the 'Coale' or 'Princeton' indices. These compare the nuptiality and fertility of a study population with the equivalent behaviour amongst the Hutterites, an Anabaptist sect living in North America, who had the highest recorded rates of marital fertility ever known.[32] The index I_m uses hypothetical fertility levels to calculate a measure of nuptiality. First, the number of children that *married* women aged 15–49 in a study population would have if they followed the Hutterite fertility schedule is calculated followed by the number of children that *all* women in that age group would bear. The first figure divided by the second gives I_m, an indication of the proportion of women contributing to the population's capacity for reproduction, assuming of course that marriage is the main arena for procreation. The reciprocal of I_m can be viewed as indicative of the degree to which the study population's reproductive capacity is depleted through celibacy or late age at marriage. I_f indicates the level of overall fertility by comparing the number of births occurring within a study population to that which would occur if the same population experienced Hutterite marital fertility rates, while I_g, the index of marital fertility, compares the number of legitimate births with the number of children which married women in the population would produce if they followed Hutterite marital fertility patterns. An I_f of 1 indicates that a particular population are bearing children at the same rate as married Hutterites: virtually eleven children per woman marrying aged twenty and surviving to celebrate her fiftieth birthday. The fourth index gauges levels of childbearing outside marriage by expressing the number of illegitimate births occurring in the population under observation as a proportion of the births which would occur if all unmarried women in the population were bearing children at the same rate as the married Hutterites.[33] The indices for England and Wales, Scotland and Ireland in 1891 are provided in Table 6.2. The figures emphasise that Ireland's overall fertility levels were driven by its low nuptiality regime. Within marriage, fertility in Ireland (I_g) was somewhat higher than that of either England and Wales or Scotland, but the Irish I_m is well below those of the other two countries and reduces the overall fertility of Irish women, as measured by I_f, to exceptionally low levels within the context of late nineteenth-century Europe.

Table 6.2. *The reproductive regime of Skye, compared to those of England and Wales, Scotland and Ireland in the late nineteenth century*

	I_m	I_f	I_g	I_b
England and Wales, 1891	.477	.310	.621	.026
Scotland, 1891	.420	.317	.696	.042
Ireland, 1891	.336	.245	.709	.010
Skye, 1880s	.344	.299	.812	.031
Bracadale, 1880s	.238	.226	.853	.031
Duirinish, 1880s	.341	.310	.856	.029
Kilmuir, 1880s	.380	.343	.842	.040
Portree, 1880s	.353	.320	.846	.035
Sleat, 1880s	.381	.288	.712	.028
Snizort, 1880s	.295	.247	.770	.028
Strath, 1880s	.362	.290	.754	.028
Ireland, 1881	–	–	.841	–
Co. Dublin	–	–	.615	–
Co. Mayo	–	–	.910	–
Co. Clare	.961	–	–	–
Co. Antrim	.742	–	–	–

Sources: Figures for England and Wales, Scotland, Ireland 1891 from Coale and Treadway, 'Changing distribution'. Figures for Ireland 1881 from Ó Gráda, 'Ireland before and after the famine', Table A5, quoted in Guinanne, *The Vanishing Irish*, Table 8.2. Figures for Skye parishes calculated from 1881 census, 1891 census and civil registers of Skye, April 1881 to March 1891.

The indices in Table 6.2 also demonstrate that nuptiality on the Isle of Skye lay well below the national figure for Scotland, at a level close to that of Ireland. Marital fertility on Skye was very high indeed, outstripping even the Irish figure as calculated by Teitelbaum in the course of the Princeton project.[34] On the basis of these levels of I_g the inhabitants of Skye could be said to be more Irish than the Irish.

Ó Gráda has taken issue with the figures for I_g calculated by Teitelbaum, stating that the latter did not take into account the under-registration of births occurring in the early years of Ireland's registration system. Ó Gráda proceeded to recalculate measures of I_g, producing a figure of 0.841 for Ireland as a whole. He also revised the figures at county level, and those he calculated for a selection of four counties are shown in Table 6.2. The latter display a considerable range, and therefore fuel Ó Gráda's arguments for marked variation in fertility behaviour within Ireland, particularly along urban–rural lines. The figures for Co. Clare and Co. Mayo come very close to 1.0, indicating levels of fertility close to the maximum known.[35] According to these figures, Skye does not come close to the fertility of Ireland's 'really rural' counties.

There are, however, reasons to question Ó Gráda's assumptions for the calculations of his I_gs, not least amongst them being the levels of child and infant mortality he chose to work with. Infant mortality for Skye in the 1880s lay at just over 100 deaths per 1,000 births, so Ó Gráda's assumption of an infant mortality rate of 165 for the western provinces of Connaught and Munster and of 135 for Leinster and Munster in the east seem rather pessimistic for the most rural counties within them.[36] If this is indeed the case, then Ó Gráda's fertility estimates for such counties may well be inflated and the true figures more akin to those of the crofting parishes of Skye.

Finally, the very low level of illegitimate fertility amongst the Irish in 1891 stands out in the I_h figures given in Table 6.2. Illegitimacy in Skye was considerably higher, although lower than for Scotland as a whole. In total, some 6.4 per cent of births were registered as illegitimate on Skye 1881–91 (ranging from 9.6 per cent in the parish of Bracadale to 5.2 per cent in Sleat). Illegitimate fertility is, however, notoriously difficult to measure accurately. No doubt on Skye some mothers came home to give birth to babies conceived elsewhere, and others left the island to have babies conceived locally. A few Skye grandmothers may have registered an illegitimate grandchild as their own.[37] Calculations suggest that there were 13.0 births out of wedlock per 1,000 single women each year on Skye during the 1880s.[38] This is a slightly higher figure than the 11.7 quoted by Flinn et al. for the Highland counties, but the latter calculation included both single and widowed women in the denominator.[39] The Highland region figure was the lowest of all the regional illegitimacy rates calculated by Flinn and his team:

the north-east was highest at 33.9, while the overall Scottish figure lay at 20.2. Amongst the parishes of Skye, the illegitimacy rate was as low as 10.2 in Strath, while in Kilmuir it was as high as 16.8. One might speculate on the relationship between theses figures and the distance which had to be travelled to the mainland.

To return to the question of marital fertility, our linkage of the various sources gives us the opportunity to monitor fertility levels in a more longitudinal fashion than is normally possible with late nineteenth-century sources. Information given in the census returns and on the marriage certificates allow us to gauge a woman's age at the birth of all children she had over the course of the 1880s, and not just those surviving to be recorded by the enumerators. In addition, the registers allow us to observe if the woman's marriage ends at any point through either her own death on Skye or that of her husband. In-comers and out-migrants are identified by failure to link them between the 1881 and 1891 censuses. Such couples are excluded from analysis as we only know of their presence on the island through births of further children, and their inclusion would bias any fertility measures against those migrants who did not have children and thus cannot be observed. We are therefore able to calculate such measures as age-specific marital fertility rates (ASMFRs) for our population and can compare these with the ASMFRs for other populations for which such measures exist. The ASMFRs can be summarized by the total marital fertility rate (TMFR), i.e. the number of children a woman would achieve if she were to marry at age twenty and continue through her childbearing years, experiencing the ASMFRs of a particular population.

As can be seen from Figure 6.3, members of the Skye population were far more fertile within marriage than their peers in selected agricultural districts of England and Wales in 1891, and indeed much more fertile than the women bearing children in the years 1800–24 when fertility peaked in the twenty-six English parishes studied by Wrigley et al. using family reconstitution.[40]

According to ASMFRs provided by Flinn et al., the TMFR for married women aged 20–49 in Scotland in 1855 was 7.3 children per woman.[41] Even if the 1855 births were under-registered by some 8 per cent as Anderson suggests, the national TMFR still languishes well below the 9.4 children we estimate Skye women were achieving in the 1880s.[42] The latter figure lies very close to that calculated by Vann and Eversley for Irish Quakers in the first half of the nineteenth century. Skye women in their twenties were rather more fertile than the Quaker women, in their thirties the position is reversed, and by their forties the Skye women's fertility had fallen to levels on a par with the English populations shown. This may have been the result of a social taboo on the production of children at later reproductive ages, or the increasing proportion of women being affected by the menopause having

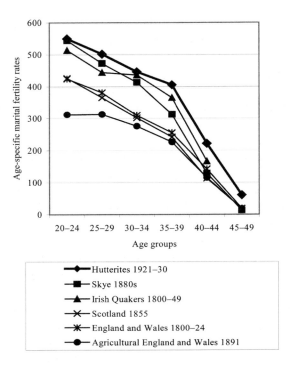

Fig.6.3. Age specific marital fertility rates for selected populations

Notes and sources:

ASMFRs are expressed per 1000 married women:

Figures for the *Hutterites* taken from A.J. Coale and R. Treadway, 'A summary of the changing distribution of overall fertility, marital fertility and the proportion married in the provinces of Europe' in A.J. Coale and S.C. Watkins, *The Decline of Fertility in Europe* (Princeton, 1986), p. 154. J.W. Eaton & A.J. Mayer 'The Social Biology of very high fertility among the Hutterites' *Human Biology* 25,3 (1953), p.227, report an 'annual age specific nuptial birth rates' for the 1926-1930 cohort of 406, 452, 415, 355, 239 and 24.

Figures given for *Skye* are calculated excluding marriages where the union was ended by the death of one or other spouse in the 1880s. When these marriages are included the figures are scarcely altered; the greatest discrepancy is shown by the 40-44 age group where the ASMFR falls to 122, a 5% decrease.

Figures for the *Irish Quakers* are taken from R.T. Vann, & D. Eversley, *Friends in life and death: the British and Irish Quakers in the demographic transition* (Cambridge, 1992), p. 134 Table 4.2. Note the authors did not present an ASMFR for the 45-9 age group. The TMFR for the Irish Quakers is thus an underestimate.

Figures for *Scotland 1855* are taken from Flinn *et al Scottish Population History*, Table 5.3.6 Anderson, *Fertility decline*, p.11, suggests that there was 8% under-registration of births in Scotland in 1855.

Figures for *England and Wales 1800-24* are taken from E.A. Wrigley, R. Davies, J. Oeppen and R.S. Schofield *English population history from family reconstitution* (Cambridge, 1997). Figures for a selection of *Agricultural districts in England and Wales, 1891*; Garrett *et al Changing family size*, pp.240-41.

a more dramatic effect amongst the highly fertile mothers on Skye.[43] Certainly none of the populations shown can compete with the 30– and 40–year-old women amongst the Hutterites: it is little wonder that the latter group achieved virtually eleven children.

The close to Hutterite fertility levels observed amongst both the Irish Quakers and the inhabitants of Skye suggest that these individuals were a) not contracepting or abstaining from marital relations in any way (except perhaps when the women reached their forties and many of their husbands would have been approaching, if not already in, their fifties); b) cannot have been breastfeeding for extended periods; and c) were probably generally fitter and better fed than their urban counterparts and could better withstand the rigours of multiple, rapid pregnancies. The peasant diet of potatoes, oats and milk supplemented, perhaps, with fish on Skye and bacon in Ireland had reputedly fostered some of the tallest men in Britain, if nineteenth-century military records are to be believed.[44] It would not be too large a leap to assume that it was also of benefit to the islands' mothers.

The final slant we can take on the high fertility levels to be found in Skye is a comparison of the percentage of women achieving given numbers of births within a particular marriage cohort, those married between 1881 and 1885. Small numbers mean that we can only consider married women aged 20–24 and those aged 25–29. Even then the results must be treated with

Table 6.3. *The percentages achieving given parities, by the succeeding census, by age at marriage, for those married in 1881–85 in Skye, and 1901–06 in 'rural Ireland' and a selection of English and Welsh communities*

	Marriage Age	Parity						
		0	1	2	3	4	5	6+
Skye	20–24	1	3	7	28	38	17	6
Rural Ireland	20–24	7	6	16	28	24	19	
England & Wales	20–24	8	17	25	24	17	6	3
Skye	25–29	7	7	18	27	22	12	6
Rural Ireland	25–29	10	7	16	26	23	19	
England & Wales	25–29	15	24	27	18	10	3	2

Note: All figures have been rounded to the nearest whole number

Sources: Skye figures calculated from linked civil register and census data. Rural Irish figures from P.A. David and W.C. Sanderson, 'Measuring marital fertility with CPA', *Population Index* 54, 4 (1988), pp. 691–713, Table A. Percentages for parities beyond 5 are not provided. England and Wales represented by figures derived from the 1911 census returns of thirteen communities; see Garrett *et al.*, *Changing Family Size*.

caution.[45] The percentages can be compared with those reported from around Britain during the 1911 Fertility census. The figures for 'rural Ireland', that is, excluding the major towns, have been discussed extensively both by David and Sanderson and Ó Gráda. While the numbers from Skye are small in comparison with the Irish figures, the distribution of achieved parities looks remarkably close, particularly in the case of the women married in their late twenties.

The high fecundity of the younger married Skye women, hinted at in previous figures, shows in the smaller proportions achieving only 0 or 1 birth. This could be ascribed to higher rates of prenuptial pregnancy amongst these women, but as 31 per cent of the younger wives gave birth within nine months of marriage and 25 per cent of the older wives did so this seems unlikely. Virtually the same percentage in each age group (61 versus 62 per cent) had a child within one year of marriage. The women of Skye must either have enjoyed a frequent sex life, enhancing their chances of conceiving, or they were a naturally very fecund population – suggesting once again that they were a healthy group of women.[46]

If the Skye population were not *more* Irish than the Irish they were certainly *as* Irish as the Irish, and in light of the lack of census material for Ireland they may well provide an insight into the demography of a 'peasant' Britain which, Guinnane's work not withstanding, has been somewhat neglected and dubbed 'atypical'. Guinnane's thesis that Irish demography represented a 'peasant' rather than a 'Catholic' demography has been entirely borne out by our work on Skye. All the women we have observed on 'the Island of the Mists' married under the auspices of the Church of Scotland or the one of the Free Churches. There was not one bride who had her marriage blessed by the Church of Rome.

PART THREE

CONFLICTS
AND IDENTITIES

7

Creating New Forms:
Civil Society in Northern Ireland

Roisín Higgins

It has been said that 'Ireland is almost a land without history because the troubles of the past are relived as contemporary events'.[1] Indeed to many observers, Northern Ireland seems lost to modernity, adrift in the Dark Ages. We may not be alone. Umberto Eco has argued that the end of the twentieth century had developed into a world that corresponded in certain moments to his abstract model of the Middle Ages. In asking what is required to make a good Middle Ages, Eco begins with the ending of an existing order.

> Its collapse is precipitated because the 'barbarians' are pressing at its borders. These barbarians are not necessarily uncultivated, but they are bringing new customs, new views of the world. These barbarians may burst in without violence, because they want to seize a wealth that has been denied them, or they may steal into the social and cultural body of the reigning Pax, spreading new faiths and new perspectives on life.[2]

At the collapse of the great Pax, crisis and insecurity ensue. Within the context of contemporary society, Eco considers the result of the breakdown of consensus as 'theatres of permanent tension' where cities 'tend more and more to become ... inured to guerrilla warfare'.[3] Underlying this new condition is an insecurity which is both 'historical' and psychological. 'In the Middle Ages a wanderer in the woods at night saw them peopled with maleficent presences; one did not venture lightly beyond the town; men went armed.'[4] The final touch to this collective insecurity is 'the fact that, now as then, and contrary to the usage established by modern liberal nations, war is no longer declared and you never know if there is a state of belligerence or not'.[5]

Eco's allegory is useful as a reminder of the way in which we assume the presence and logic of modernity in recent history. Northern Ireland appears as an anomaly in the 'West', preoccupied as it is with tribal and nationalistic identities. Ennui with Northern Irish affairs in the British press is explained by the simple belief that 'they don't understand it'.[6] This wilful refusal to comprehend the ongoing conflict facilitates the idea that the inhabitants in

Northern Ireland are somehow irrationally obsessed with old battles and that the problem is ultimately cultural. Not only are the problems in Northern Ireland structural rather than cultural,[7] but they can also be seen as the result of the social and economic consequences of 'modernisation'.[8] This essay is concerned with the organisational nature of Northern Irish society and the way it is configured within the concept of civil society – which is itself concerned with representation and modernity.

In seeing the 'Atomic Age' as a sort of reliving of the Middle Ages, Eco depicts the end of the twentieth century as a period of transition – a new era of revolution in which 'new forms, new social, technological and philosophical forms are invented', coupled with a sense of apocalyptic breakdown.[9]

Eco draws his parallel with the contemporary collapse of Pax America. However, it could more easily be read globally – as the collapse of European imperialism – or locally – as the challenge to English hegemony in Britain or the dismantling of Stormont in Northern Ireland. Indeed, the period following the collapse of the Northern Irish Government in 1972 has been described as an interregnum: understood in the Gramscian sense of the signal that 'the ruling class has lost its consensus i.e. is no longer "leading" but only "dominant", exercising coercive power alone'. Out of this breakdown a new 'arrangement' must be found; Gramsci contended that within this context there exists 'the possibility and necessity of creating a new culture'.[10] In fact, the removal of power from Stormont and the imposition of direct rule from Westminster was a recognition of the failure of the Northern Irish state as a hegemonic force. The integrity of that state had always been contested by a minority of the population of Northern Ireland; their economic and political exclusion and self-exclusion precluded the possibility that the state as it existed would constitute a commonsensical or logical option.[11] The escalation of state and civilian violence since 1969 did represent a crisis of governance and in that sense appeared as an elongated disjuncture or interregnum, which eventually led to the formulation of a 'new arrangement' at Stormont.

In 1998 the Good Friday (Belfast) Agreement was mandated by almost 72 per cent of the population in a vote that was largely one for peace, for a new beginning. The leader of the Social Democratic and Labour Party (SDLP), John Hume, described it as 'neither victory nor defeat', but something which created 'the circumstances in which we will use our energies to enable us to leave the past behind'.[12] Eco's central dialectic between order and chaos implies that the history of the old order shaped the nature of disruption, and this disruption must be understood in the shaping of the new order.

The attempt to resolve conflict and difference in Northern Ireland coincided with the new Labour government's devolutionary strategy for Scotland and Wales. It reflected the language of the 'new politics' of that administration. The rhetoric is confident and does not entertain alternatives. The Prime Minister, Tony Blair, speaking during the visit of President Clinton, reasserted the view that

> The Good Friday Agreement ... is the only way forward. Because the principles at the heart of it ... are the right principles. The principle of consent, the principle of devolution and power-sharing, the principles of justice and equality and recognition of different identities, the principle that whatever our differences, whatever the problems within communities, those differences should only be resolved ... by peaceful and democratic and non-violent means ... the principles are agreed and therefore what we need now is the will – and not only the political will, but the will in the community, each part of the community to integrate the agreement we have made.

Blair outlines the perfect model of a traditional civil society, one in which, as Adam Ferguson outlined it in the eighteenth century, liberty was maintained by 'continued oppositions and differences', a system which necessitated 'manly apprehension of personal independence, which render(s) every individual ... the guardian of freedom of fellow citizens'.[13] The implication of devolved power is that the individual, in exercising more power, will also exercise a greater sense of responsibility: not just for him- or herself, but to the organic whole.

The resumption of a vaguely understood and even more vaguely remembered sense of civil society lies at the heart of the devolution project. However, civil society is itself a highly contested term. It has its roots in the Enlightenment but has enjoyed a reconsideration since the 1980s, particularly in its application to the extrapolation of Eastern Europe from Soviet influence. As a theory, civil society has been criticised for lacking empirical evidence, for adding nothing that more familiar concepts (such as constitutionalism, citizenship and democracy) do not already cover, for being at best part of the 'magic' of the transition of states from violence and, although a 'shining emblem', in reality a chimera.[14] The error is to see the term as a neutral, decontextualised concept.[15] Rather than setting it up as a definitive model, the theory can be used to interrogate the relationships of state, society, economy and individual. It is also instructive on current thinking on notions of democracy and citizenship. Within the context of Northern Ireland, the theory of civil society has had significance in policy making, particularly in the area of conflict resolution.[16]

In a general sense, the term 'civil society' is used to describe networks of association that are independent of the state and that are social or economic rather than party political (sport, education, welfare, media). Despite their autonomy, it is the relationship of these bodies to the state that determines the way in which the civil society model operates. In its traditional sense (based on the work of Ferguson and de Toqueville), it can be used to describe associational bodies that foster a sense of community and citizenship. They can be seen, in Robert Putnam's phrase, to supply a source of 'social capital': 'features of social organisation such as networks, norms, and social trust that facilitate coordination and cooperation for mutual benefit'.[17] Ultimately, this type of civic membership enhances democratic governance in acting as a counterweight to the state. Alternatively (as it is used in the context of Eastern Europe and Latin America), it describes those bodies that act as a challenge to the tyrannical state. Under these circumstances, civil society is not only independent of the state, but resistant to it.[18]

This tension in the definitions of civil society is particularly significant for the case of Northern Ireland. Foley and Edwards have unpicked some of the weaknesses in logic and evidence of both schools of thought. The contradictions in the first model are underlined by the existence of the second: if civil society is a vehicle for the overthrow of a tyrannical state, its ability to overthrow a democratic state is also present. There is therefore a tendency to emphasise those associations that conform to whichever model is being described. Foley and Edwards contend that 'the civil society argument hinges on the virtues of association and of organised society per se; it cannot confront the conflictual potential thereof by definitional sleight of hand, but neither can it ignore the conflict at the heart of the modern "organizational society"'.[19] Theirs is an argument against the prescription of which associations should and should not be included in an understanding of civil society. The model should address conflicts among groups (which may well lead to civil disruption and violence), and these must be understood within the specific political settlements. It is this prevailing political settlement that 'governs who plays, the rules of the game, and acceptable outcomes. Numerous examples from recent history show that such settlements are the work of political parties and of the best financed, and often best armed, elements of civil society.'[20] In advocating a model that recognises the 'political variable', Foley and Edwards argue that civil society should include political groupings as well as being understood within the political settlement.

The ambiguity at the heart of civil society can be seen in the recent history and politics of Northern Ireland. In Robert Putnam's model, only those associations that cut across social cleavages – horizontally organised groups – can be included, 'like sports clubs, cooperatives, mutual aid societies, cultural associations, and voluntary unions'. Furthermore, these associations should not be 'polarised' or 'politicised'. In Northern Ireland, this would exclude sporting bodies such as the Gaelic Athletic Association (GAA), many local soccer teams, the Northern Ireland football team, church groups, the Boy Scouts, the Girl Guides and many more. Rather than the 'problem' being Northern Ireland's peculiarity, the 'problem' lies with Putnam's faith in the apolitical. Putnam presupposes a society in which the political structure is settled (as in the USA) and in which the decline in occasional civic conversation over beer and pizza among members of bowling leagues is lamented as part of the decline in civil society.

This type of 'apolitical' inclusiveness is immediately problematic in a society like Northern Ireland in which there is no dominant consensus. The politics of the place infuses all aspects of cultural life and individual identity. The practice of community relations and cultural traditions offers a useful example. The Community Relations Council (CRC) was formed as an independent charity in 1990 'to promote better community relations between Protestants and Catholics in Northern Ireland'. It professes 'no view on what form of political solution should take place'. The CRC presented anti-sectarian work as pre-political and important 'no matter what political solution people want to see put in place'. On the CRC's promotion of accommodation, David Miller has argued that 'in a conflict where the key dispute is over the very existence of the state, it is hardly apolitical to advocate accommodation within its structures.' Much of the criticism of the CRC has been directed towards its political naiveté. Giving equal merit to two traditions did not confront the power dynamic within the society. Moreover, an approach to community relations which views sectarianism as the result simply of ignorance and hatred deletes economics from the equation and operates a 'deficit model of working class culture ... in which there is a heart-felt plea for more civilised behaviour'.[21]

Civil society is a heavily weighted term. Those associations it delineates not only mediate the power of the state, but mediate its meaning. It is

> The sphere of culture in its broadest sense. It is concerned with the manners and mores of society, with the way people live. It is where values and meanings are established, where they are debated, contested and exchanged. It is the necessary complement to the rule of class through its ownership of the means of production and its capture of the apparatus of the state. By the same token it is the space that has to be colonised – the famous 'war of position' – by any new class seeking to usurp the old.[22]

The Opsahl Commission was an attempt to give articulation to the values and meanings in Northern Ireland's civil society and to give voice to an active citizenry. The fear that political deadlock had reduced the people of Northern Ireland to 'mere spectators at their fate' was the impetus for the setting up of the Opsahl Commission and publication of the subsequent *Report* of 1992–93. The Commission represented an ambitious and important attempt to rescue the concept of civil society in Northern Ireland. It was hoped that an independent commission of inquiry with no limitation on the ideas submitted to it would help answer 'a widespread desire among all kinds of people for a new means of expressing their views and hopes for the future'. The Commission gathered 554 written and taped proposals, and the recommendations of the subsequent *Report* correlate at many points to the measures outlined in the Good Friday Agreement. In its Introduction, the *Report* drew a clear distinction between conflict and violence. 'Conflict is neither good nor bad, but intrinsic in every social relationship from marriage to international diplomacy ... the real issue is not the existence of conflict, but how it is handled ... rather than solved.'[23]

The *Report* presented the view that 'both communities in Northern Ireland should have equal voice in making and vetoing laws and should equally share administrative authority'. It argued that Northern Ireland 'as currently constituted' is not like any other part of the United Kingdom and that 'majority rule ... whether simple or proportionate, is not currently a viable proposition. The nationalist population has no reason to agree to it and the critical mass to prevent its imposition.'

Majority rule is not simply a challenge to the governance of Northern Ireland. In his account of the United States, de Toqueville noted the 'tyranny' of majority rule, and this has been recognised as 'the hardest question in democratic theory'.[24] In order to achieve a sustainable peace in Northern Ireland, it was necessary that its structures should be reconfigured to extend the reach of 'political' and 'civil' society and, thereby, extending the obligations of all those living within the state. For Locke, civil society was dependent upon the circumstance when 'any number of Men have so consented to make one Community or Government, they are therefore presently incorporated, and make one Body Politick, wherein the Majority have a Right to act and conclude the rest'.[25] In having failed to create a single community, 'one body with the power to act as one body', in Northern Ireland, a structure was created that acknowledged the existence of at least two distinct communities and which would abide by the wishes of 'two majorities'.[26]

The Good Friday Agreement proposed a form of power sharing that was based on cross-community support for legislation. To this end, the Agreement stated that 'at their first meeting members of the Assembly will register a designation of their identity – nationalist, unionist or other – for the purposes of measuring cross-community support for Assembly votes'.[27] The constitution of Northern Ireland, therefore, simplifies and solidifies identity in order to deliver the democratic process from the 'tyranny of the majority'. The wording of the Agreement demands a designation of identity rather than political affiliation. Within this framework, only those who designate themselves 'other' (The Women's Coalition and the Alliance Party) do not define themselves in terms of their relationship to the state. In signing up to the Agreement, all parties collectively affirmed their commitment to 'the mutual respect, the civil rights and the religious liberties of everyone *in the community*'. The Good Friday Agreement, in recognising the existence of a Holy Trinity of nationalists, unionists and the non-aligned, hopes to create, if not one body, then one consensus. And like the mystery of the Holy Trinity, it requires great faith.

This attempt to address the division – and the fusion of politics and identity – reveals the dialectic between political structures and civil society. 'Civil' shares its linguistic root with 'civic'; both come from the Latin *civis*, meaning citizen. Northern Ireland raises the basic question of who has the right to citizenship. The current tenuous nature of political structures can be read both as the self-exclusion of bodies associated with 'private' arms of the civil and political community and the determination of Unionists and the British government to assume the right to confirm or deny citizenship of elected representatives and of those who have voted for them.

These questions of legitimacy, authority and civic inclusion are as old as the state itself. Northern Ireland was established by the Government of Ireland Act (1920). It comprised six counties in the north-east and had an in-built Protestant and Unionist majority. Partition was not initially conceived as a permanent solution to the governance of Ireland, with the consequence that the Northern Irish state felt itself to be under constant threat from its own Catholic and Nationalist minority and from critics in Britain and the Free State. Defensiveness over its legitimacy led the state to defend itself aggressively with permanent 'emergency' legislation in the form of the Special Powers Act.

The creation and execution of the state consolidated the understanding of identity in terms of Catholic–Nationalist and Protestant–Unionist polarities. The state was Unionist by definition and Protestant by design. Catholics were excluded and discriminated against socially and economically, and they absented themselves from participation in civic life and, in large part, abstained from political participation. This consolidated the role of the Catholic Church in its community, as it provided many of the outlets for civic expression from the St Vincent de Paul Society to fundraising for Catholic schools and the Mater Hospital. Corpus Christi processions, investitures and the funerals of bishops have been likened to alternative state occasions for Catholics.[28] The power of the Church reinforced the perception by others of Catholics as a centralised, monolithic group with an allegiance that circumvented the state.

Northern Ireland's existence was peppered with paramilitary, state and sectarian violence. By 1962 the IRA ceased operations, and it appeared that certain sections of the Catholic population were beginning to accept the reality of partition by involving themselves more fully in the affairs of the state. The Butler Education Act had been extended to Northern Ireland in

1947 and facilitated an increase in the Catholic middle class. A change in approach came with the disentanglement of the desire to overthrow the state from the civil rights question. The Northern Ireland Civil Rights Association would later claim that 'Unionism had become synonymous with the denial of civil rights and the non-Unionist political organisations fought for the removal of Unionism – by the abolition of the state – and ignored the civil rights question.' This remained the situation until the 1960s, 'the era of the ecumenical movement, when the Beatles came to Belfast, men went into space and Lord Brookborough went into retirement. It was a period of change.'[29]

This interregnum was characterised by a breakdown not simply of the existing order but of social and political order in a more general sense. Frustration over the pace of the government's movement on civil rights (too slow for Nationalists, too quick for some Unionists), the state's handling of civil rights protests and widespread urban disorder (with many families being burned out of their homes) led to an increase in Loyalist and Republican paramilitary violence. The story of the conflict in Northern Ireland cannot be presented in a linear narrative. The positions of all sides shifted and responded to changing events. Attempts to create a new constitutional order included the imposition of Direct Rule from Westminster (1972), the Sunningdale Agreement (1973–74), the Constitutional Convention (1975–76), proposed Rolling Devolution (1982–84), the Anglo-Irish Agreement (1985), the Downing Street Declaration (1993) and the Good Friday Agreement (1998). Attempts to provide a security solution included the deployment of British troops (1969), internment without trial (1971–75) and Ulsterisation (1976). Even the role of the state and the constitutional position of the North were constantly under review.

Within this context, Northern Ireland poses conceptual and empirical questions of the civil society model and underlines Foley and Edwards' contention that civil society can only be understood within the framework of the political settlement in which it is formed. Within the conventional model of civil society, Republicans are excluded (prior to the current IRA ceasefire) because they are usurpatory – they dispute the state's claim to the monopoly of legitimate violence rather than representing an 'interest' in the public sphere of debate. Within the model of civil society as it is applied to Eastern Europe, the need to challenge the state (crucially, in non-violent forms) is seen as its strength. Clearly the state also has responsibilities and must demonstrate (not simply assert) its legitimacy to govern. It is not, therefore, Republicans' struggle against the state that determines their position within the model of civil society, it is their method of struggle. By any definition, civil society requires the resolution of conflict and difference through non-violent means.

The position of the Unionists and Loyalists is equally problematic. Their loyalty to the Northern Irish state from 1921 to 1972 was not automatically transferred to that of the British state[30] after the imposition of direct rule and has been conditional in the subsequent period. Despite their name, Ulster 'Loyalists' are less loyal to Britain than British Unionists (Ulster Unionists who see themselves as British) and have allegiance to the British Crown (a symbol of the British Union) rather than Parliament on condition that it is seen to protect Protestant liberties in the Northern Irish state.[31] The fact that the constitutional position of Northern Ireland often appears negotiable is one of the main reasons for their distrust. Opposition to the Power Sharing Executive and the 'Irish dimension' led to the 1974 Workers' Strike, which has been the most serious single challenge to the rule of the British state throughout the conflict. The strike, run by the Ulster Workers' Council[32] with support increasing among the broader Unionist community as the strike progressed, brought Northern Ireland to a standstill for fifteen days in May 1974 and ultimately brought down the power-sharing initiative. It exposed the lack of reciprocity in the relationship between the British government and Ulster 'Loyalism', with Prime Minister Harold Wilson notoriously attacking the strikers as 'people who spend their lives sponging on Westminster and British democracy and then systematically assault democratic methods. Who do these people think they are?'[33] A willingness to usurp the democratic will of the state with the backing of Loyalist paramilitaries raises questions of the right of certain Unionists to be seen as consistently a part of civil society throughout conflict.

The position of all political groupings in Northern Ireland underlines Michael Walzer's argument that 'the paradox of the civil society argument' is that a democratic civil society seems to require a democratic state, and a strong civil society seems to require a strong and responsive state.[34] One of the problems for those trying to resolve the conflict in Northern Ireland was this mutuality: the democratic deficit and the civil society deficit had to be addressed in parallel. This required a more flexible understanding both of democracy (beyond straightforward majoritarianism) and civil society/ citizenship. Seamus Mallon has called the Good Friday Agreement 'Sunningdale for slow learners', but it can also be argued that the slow learners were in fact the participants in Sunningdale who thought they could set up an institution without bringing in the political representatives of mainstream paramilitary groups. In a conflict resolution situation, a rigid or prescriptive model of civil society is counterproductive. If paramilitary groups are as representative of their community as any other more acceptable institution,[35] then it is necessary that the 'more acceptable institutions' attempt to understand the context and politics of paramilitarism. This is not to say that paramilitarism has any part in a working civil society, but that failure to engage with Republicanism and Loyalism is a failure to understand the history and structure of the conflict and a failure to engage with dynamics that are particularly resonant among working-class communities. A political solution and its attendant civil society that does not include all sections of the community raises the question: in whose image is civil society created?

The current attempt to resolve the conflict in Northern Ireland is, therefore, both an attempt to apply an abstract model of civil society and an example with which to interrogate that model. Without a critical engagement with the concept of civil society, it simply becomes another term for middle-class hegemony. The issues at the heart of the conflict, rather then being arcane, are fundamental to modern democratic structures. It is the acceptance of this that has made the current peace process possible and it is why it will continue to encounter difficulties. This period of the North's recent history is no longer easily described with breathtaking understatement as the 'Troubles' (it might easily have been called 'the Trouble with …'). Northern Ireland was involved in a violent conflict – of interests, ethno-national, economic and cultural. The term 'peace process' is significant in that it signals a recognition that there was a conflict and that its resolution requires a process of negotiation among all parties.

An examination of an industrial society that is not at ease with itself lays bare many of the assumptions at the heart of modern governance. In order to confront the violence in Northern Ireland, it was necessary to confront the politics of violence. In 1991 the journalist Hugo Young wrote: 'The condition of Ulster defeats every liberal device. It nullifies language, repudiates politics. To some extent, however, Ulster wallows in this state. An irresolvable conflict is what gives the place its uniqueness, we hear. But how long can this self-glorying, this claim on our awe, survive events elsewhere: in Yugoslavia, for example?'[36]

Young's piece assumes that 'every liberal device' had been pursued in Northern Ireland prior to 1991. It assumes that conflict over constitutionality, legitimacy, authority, exclusion and representation are a repudiation of politics. It asserts that the residents of Northern Ireland wallowed in and glorified brutality, and finally it assumes that Britain has the luxury of becoming uninterested in a state over which it has sovereign responsibility.

The current 'condition of Ulster' is one of not peace/not war. This does not absolve the state or the residents of the six counties from the responsibility of constituting a structure that is democratic and pluralist. The history of dysfunction makes this difficult, but it also casts light on what 'functional democracy' and 'pluralism' mean in practice. The peace process was an exercise in demonstrating that democratic politics were an alternative to violence. That violence is a means of achieving ends is axiomatic in

Northern Ireland.[37] The structure created has, therefore, to be robust, representative and accountable. It requires a civil society that is both an arena in which community and citizenship are made meaningful, and that is an area which challenges the tyranny within the state.

The media play a vital role as civil society's public sphere: the space in which the activities of the state can be confronted and subjected to criticism. In Northern Ireland, the autonomy and legitimacy of the media have been heavily criticised in the recent past. State censorship and a nervous or deliberate self-censorship have gained the area the reputation as a 'training ground in blandness'. Such was the pessimism of a leading commentator in June 1995 that he contemplated a sustained campaign to disband the BBC and the Independent Television Commission in Northern Ireland with the hope of facilitating an indigenous media which would be rigorous and relevant in its questioning.[38] Within the complexities of the conflict, institutional bias from 1971 onwards reduced the role of broadcasting to that of descriptive capacity rather than one of analysis.[39] In attempting to represent the views of all sides, broadcasting in Northern Ireland has moved to a system of 'balanced sectarianism', which is a recognition of the lack of consensus in Northern Ireland politics and society.[40] It has been suggested that liberal democracy in the context of antagonistic pluralism must have another function beyond the expressive, but it must facilitate a relationship of 'ideal discourse' between elected representatives.[41]

The failures on the part of the political structures, civil society and the public sphere in Northern Ireland have potentially extreme consequences. This does differentiate the place from its neighbours to the south and east. Shared problems include broadcasting in Britain and the Republic of Ireland, which falls short of rigorous reporting and is often little more than the presentation of views within a limited frame of reference. Even in a 'non-antagonistic pluralism', liberal democracy is not simply a 'common-sense' position to be described and expressed, it must be constantly constructed. There is a bluntness to debate in Northern Ireland, which is not without its merits. At least there is an understanding that there is no such thing as neutral language.[42]

There must be room in liberal democracy for voices that challenge the 'rationality' and 'logic' of 'the liberal state', even when these voices are located within a form of unionist or Irish nationalism. There must be room for voices to challenge the agencies (armed and unarmed) that defend that logic. In Northern Ireland, we are dealing with the politics of fear, bitterness, and communal grief. In the midst of this, Northern Ireland is working through fundamental structural issues. It is a society that is now well versed in the language of civil rights and 'parity of esteem' and in which the reality behind the easy rhetoric is bitterly contested.

The difficulty for Northern Ireland will be to find political structures to which everyone can agree. This is slowly being achieved. Then the real challenge will be to construct within this an idea of pluralism beyond the twin pillars of nationalism and unionism; to challenge the now constitutionally enshrined idea that forms of identity – gender, class, disability, non-Irish ethnicity – are 'other'.

If we style our present in the fashion of Eco's self-styled past we might remember the Middle Ages as a time of vision. Under its apparent immobility and dogmatism there was, paradoxically, a moment of 'cultural revolution' in which different civilisations clash and slowly the image of a new man is outlined.[43] It was a period which 'preserved in its way the heritage of the past but not through hibernation, rather through a constant retranslation and reuse; it was an immense work of bricolage, balanced among nostalgia, hope and despair'.[44]

Religious friction should not conceal the way in which the conflict in Northern Ireland and its resolution expose the recesses of power in modern societies – political, social and economic. In the aftermath of the events in the United States on 11 September 2001, world powers have made much of the language of civilisation, with no attempt to address or problematise this concept. The history of Northern Ireland is a complicated one, and rather than being dismissed as anomalous, it should offer an important vehicle with which to complicate notions of 'modernisation', 'progress', and that which we consider 'civilised'.

8

Arise therefore Ulster-Scot: Ulster Unionist Identity and the Reconfiguration of the Isles

Cathal McCall

Introduction

Two hundred years after the Act of Union (1800), the British Isles were again in the throes of major administrative upheaval. The devolved parliament of Scotland and the Welsh Assembly experienced initial difficulties because of the inexperience of members and the centrist instinct of the United Kingdom Prime Minister, Tony Blair, but the devolutionist course was irreversible. Development is likely to be more than 'merely the delegation of power from a superior political body to an inferior' and result in either a fully-fledged federation or separation.[1]

Establishing devolution and transterritorial 'British Isles' institutions for Northern Ireland has been fraught with more difficult problems. They stem from a history of conflict between communities that have complex political loyalties – with religious, ethnic, national and ideological dimensions – anchored in Ulster unionism and Irish nationalism. These problems have impeded the smooth implementation of the 'Good Friday', 'Belfast' or 'Multi-party' Agreement (1998)[2] provisions for a new legislative Northern Ireland Assembly, power-sharing Executive and Civic Forum; institutionalised North/South (island of Ireland) and British–Irish spaces; and reforms in the areas of equality, policing and criminal justice. UK devolution and the Agreement, with their promises of overhaul for governance in the British Isles, are crucial to the renegotiation of communal identities in Northern Ireland, as well as in the rest of the Isles.[3]

The territorial, economic and cultural resources of communal identities in Northern Ireland are being renegotiated in light of changing Northern Ireland, island of Ireland, British–Irish, European Union (EU) and global contexts. While the economic resource is important, it is the territorial and cultural resources of identity, with their integration of history, place, religion, language, myths, symbols, institutions and commemorations that are the essential stock which require accommodation in new Isles spaces. With a political psychology firmly embedded in a potent mix of territorial and cultural insecurity and siege,[4] Ulster unionists baulk at the implications of changing spaces for the resources of their identity but it is unlikely that they can remain impervious to these changes.

For many unionists, Ulster Protestantism is a central, steadfast cultural resource, but under the impact of devolution, other cultural resources are being renegotiated, notably Britishness, Ulster-Scots and Irishness. The cultural rise of Irishness in Northern Ireland and the decline of 'Britishness' in Britain has helped generate the invention of a 'new medieval' Ulster-Scots tradition, opening a new front in the quest to provide the unionist identity with legitimacy, differentiation and continuity. On the other hand, changing politics and structures of governance may enable more unionists to reclaim a sense of Irishness in an evolving British–Irish context. Others may make an even greater investment in Ulster Protestantism, its corollary, Orangeism, and a sense of territorial siege.

Primary evidence from semi-structured interviews with political representatives from across the unionist spectrum, and from political party and interest group literature, is used here to gauge initial shifts between the cultural variables of Protestantism, Britishness, Irishness and Ulster-Scots. The study draws on recent theoretical work in the fields of territorial autonomy and identity politics to provide a conceptual framework for the fluid structural context and concepts involved. The structural and political changes within the Isles take place within broader structural changes. Globalisation, EU multilevel governance and cosmopolitan localism offer differing but complementary theoretical ideas on the causes and consequences of structural and political change and their implications for territorial space and cultural identity.

Globalisation, EU Multilevel Governance and Cosmopolitan Localism

Globalisation, defined by the late twentieth-century information technology, communications and transport revolution with the resulting media culture, information flows and the compression of time and space in commerce and finance, has challenged the integrity of the modern state. The shift in attention from boundaries to flows has challenged the claim of the nation state to contain the processes of governance within its boundaries and threatens territorial conceptions of economy, politics, culture and identity.[5] The expanding regulatory power of the European Community (now the European Union) was a response to this.[6] Neo-functionalist theorists understand this as a fundamental reordering of European economic, political and cultural space, with the nation state being superseded by a supranational entity.[7] Intergovernmentalist theorists, on the other hand, believe that the EU is the saviour of the nation state, providing an additional platform for a national government to control its territorial domain. Nevertheless, the leading intergovernmentalist, Andrew Moravcsik, concedes that the national government has had to step outside its territory and enter into an ever more complex web of interstate bargaining and compromise in the effort to exercise control.[8]

National governments have sought to maintain the veneer of control over affairs within their respective territorial spaces. However, much of the substance of policy making has been transferred, often camouflaged in technical detail, to the EU policy space where it is then subject to a consensual decision-making procedure involving all member state governments.[9] EU governance is characterised by informal links and social partnerships between the Commission, the subnational level and the voluntary and community sector, especially in the area of the Structural Funds.[10] Nevertheless, despite the transterritorial, multilevel, non-state, social partnership polity of the EU, the nation state remains pivotal.[11] For Scotland, multilevel governance involves complex and dynamic links between local government, Edinburgh, London and Brussels, but in the absence of a Scottish place on the EU Council of Ministers the connection with Westminster remains vital to Scottish interests.[12]

Cosmopolitan localism pursues the global–local nexus and the multilevel governance theme from a particularist perspective. Cosmopolitan localism understands globalisation not as the instigator of a 'dehumanising and undemocratic Brave New World' where unaccountable bureaucrats rule from centres like Brussels, but as a dynamic whereby the local can be enjoined with the global in a meaningful and empowering way.[13] Despite positive implications of this paradigm shift in the relationship between governance, identity and the nation state, many minority secessionists still hold to the ideal of an exclusivist modern nation state. Globalisation is a complex and uneven process that affects or disaffects identities depending on their economic, social and geographic circumstances. The insecurity it invokes leads to disorientation, estrangement and traditional nationalist reaction rather than reappraisal and realignment. Nevertheless, globalisation has initiated a period of transition that has induced self-reflexivity for many communities and individuals, raising questions about the relationship between the state and identity.

Some premodern ethnicities and 'civic–institutional' identities have already seeped through the cracks in the modern state and are poised to stake their claim in the emerging system of governance. Stateless nations like Scotland have been inspired by small EU member states such as the Republic of Ireland, which now enjoys a certain 'parity of esteem' with larger EU neighbours. Consequently, Scottish nationalists have embraced the European project and have attempted to redefine their nationalism as 'liberal' through the goal of 'independence in Europe', with the broader interdependence that entails. Their goal would appear to be equal partnership status at the national level for Scotland in an EU multilevel system of governance. 'World Cities' such as Brussels, Berlin, Milan and London appear to be readjusting to the shifting paradigm of governance with distinctive political communities and leaders like the London cosmopolitan localist Ken Livingstone, who became the city's first elected mayor in May 2000. This 'new medievalism' exists in a multilevel governance paradigm marked by interconnectedness – empowered cities forming poles of interconnection.

Ulster unionists have little regard for ideas like globalisation, EU multilevel governance or cosmopolitan localism. These concepts have tended either to be dismissed as abstractions from the reality of the Union between Great Britain and Northern Ireland and the sovereignty of Westminster or characterised as part of a Papist plot and, therefore, a threat to unionist cultural identity. Sir Reg Empey (Minister for Enterprise, Trade and Industry, MLA),[14] a leading pro-Agreement member of the Ulster Unionist Party (UUP), dismissed the idea of a paradigm shift in the EU state system by claiming that 'there is not the remotest prospect of the nation states fundamentally disposing of their sovereignty'.[15] The Reverend Dr Ian Paisley (MP, MEP, MLA), leader of the anti-Agreement Democratic Unionist Party (DUP),[16] has railed against what he believed to be the inherent threat of the 'Treaty of Rome' for Ulster Protestants and has drawn attention to the fact that the EU has an overwhelming Catholic majority.[17]

Unionists and Protestantism

The significance of Protestantism for the unionist identity is emphasised by the interchangeable way in which the terms 'Ulster Protestant' and 'Ulster Unionist' are used and accepted. The Reverend Ian Paisley is the leader of the DUP and the self-professed defender of 'Protestant Ulster'. The nominally socialist Progressive Unionist Party (PUP) is less concerned with working-class issues per se than with Protestant working-class issues. The 'liberal' unionists claim to eschew sectarianism but are disposed to 'play the Orange Card'[18] for the purposes of electoral gain and political mobilisation. The UUP has retained its link with the exclusively Protestant Orange Order despite conference votes to break the connection.

The conditional nature of the British–Northern Ireland link has brought an exaggerated reliance on Protestantism as the symbol and substance of

Ulster unionist identity.[19] This despite the fall in formal religious observance in both Protestant–unionist and Catholic–nationalist communities. With Britishness insecure, unionists rely on shared symbolic memories of Protestantism: the massacre of Protestants by Catholic rebels in 1641, the Siege of Derry in 1689, the Battle of the Boyne in 1690, as well as the contemporary annual summer siege of Drumcree.[20] These landmarks lack the sense of historic continuity and place required for the survival of an ethno-national identity. In contrast, weaving the thread of continuity in the political, territorial and cultural goals of the United Irishmen in the eighteenth century, the Young Irelanders in the nineteenth century, the IRA in the early twentieth century and the Provisional IRA in the late twentieth century has been the preoccupation of traditional Irish nationalist cultural determinists[21].

Ulster Protestantism provides the marker of a distinctive ethnic group. In Northern Ireland, the juxtaposition of Ulster Protestantism and Irish Catholicism has precipitated endogamy, residential segregation and segregated schools. Ethnic differentiation is perpetuated by these practices. Crucially, most unionist identities believe that their ethnic and cultural distinctiveness is also bound up in a heavily qualified British identity which they understand to be the shared 'national' identity of the UK. Therefore, their cultural identity is underscored by an essential Protestant–British ethos which most judge to be best served by a devolved form of government for Northern Ireland operating within the UK context.

A much smaller number of self-styled 'liberal' unionists profess little or no allegiance to Ulster Protestantism and prefer to subscribe mainly to an anti-Irish nationalist British political identity founded in the Act of Union (1800) and reinforced by the Government of Ireland Act (1920). This definition of liberal unionist identity based on citizenship has championed the total integration of Northern Ireland into the UK. Some prominent anti-Agreement UUP members hold to this idea of Britishness that was imparted to them in the 1980s by the right-wing visionary and exile from the mainstream British political system, Enoch Powell. Antipathy towards devolution because of an aversion to sharing power with Irish nationalists has been the primary motivating factor for the subscription of these unionists to this politically top-heavy version of Britishness. In 1989, Jeffery Donaldson (UUP, MP) denounced the concept of devolution if it meant sharing power 'with the likes of John Hume and Seamus Mallon', leaders of the liberal Irish nationalist Social Democratic and Labour Party (SDLP).[22] In the context of contemporary restructuring and the EU regard for minority and regional nationalism, this vision of a sovereign integrated UK based on a singular British political identity appears unattainable.

Unionists and Britishness

The insecurity of the Unionist identity relates directly to its sense of isolation on the island of Ireland and the perceived weakness of its British political and cultural dimensions. Although Northern Ireland is part of the UK, there is no adjective to describe this condition. The UK construct lacks the offer of security provided by the nation's sense of historic community and continuity.[23] Consequently, unionists subscribe to the adjective 'British' in an effort to give symbol and substance to their UK political allegiance and security to their identity. Their complex mix of political allegiance and cultural identity is illustrated by DUP deputy leader Peter Robinson's self-description as 'a Unionist in terms of my politics and a Protestant in terms of my beliefs ... but from the point of view of being an Ulster Protestant Unionist, there is a complexity to that identity because we are British by way of our nationality yet we live on the island of Ireland'.[24]

British identity has become more noticeable in recent years because it is under threat from devolution and EU development. The origins of British state nationalism were in popular Protestantism, a massive overseas empire and recurrent war with France.[25] With all of these now gone, new coordinates are urgently needed if Britishness is to survive as a political and cultural identity.[26]

New coordinates could include ideas of interconnection, plurality, Europe, multiculturalism and the liberal democratic tradition, with Britain recast as 'Multicultural Britain', 'Multinational Britain', 'European Britain' or even reconfigured in the 'British–Irish Isles'. So far, there is little evidence of new coordinates emerging. British nationalism's cadre of right-wing interest groups, politicians and journalists still harbours ideas of a hegemonic Great Britishness of Protestant Crown and Empire, and appears to be intent on replacing France with the EU as its 'other'. Tony Blair's effort at 'rebranding Britain' has yielded little of substance.[27] However, the emphasis on allegiance endows Britishness with the capacity to be a dimension of multiple identity within an overall European framework. In the 1950s and 1960s, Asian and Afro-Caribbean immigrants formed an attachment to their British citizenship and consequently developed a 'Black British' dimension to their identity.[28]

Many traditional and modern Ulster unionists, including former UUP leader David Trimble, prefer a traditional British identity with Protestantism at its core.[29] For others, like Robert McCartney (leader of the fringe United Kingdom Unionist Party (UKUP)), Britishness as a cultural identity survives on a Second World War sensibility derived from family involvement, boyhood heroes and a nostalgia for the period.[30] Most Britons have no experience and a dissolving communal memory of Popular

Protestantism, Empire and World War. Their political and cultural reality is of empowered sub-state nationalities and localities, a national state Westminster government locked into the EU, a global–local nexus and multiple identities. Younger Britons may well relegate a depleted sense of Britishness in favour of other global, national or local identification with Europe; Scotland, England or Wales; the Highlands, Cumbria or Cornwall; London, Manchester or Glasgow. The cultural commentator Joyce McMillan maintains that 'most Scots under 35 now say that they do not feel British at all, not even as a subsidiary or second identity'.[31] The Scottish people may have swallowed the 1990s new Hollywood medievalism of films such as *Rob Roy* and *Braveheart* with tongues planted firmly in cheeks, but there is no denying the 'glory in defeat' pride in national sports teams or the substantive intellectual, material and emotional investment in the Scottish Parliament.

Preoccupation with the Irish nationalist 'other' and the convulsions induced by the prospect of structural change for Northern Ireland provided for in the Agreement (1998) have blinkered many unionists to the possible decline of Britishness and the break-up of Britain. The poet Gerald Dawe, from a unionist background, has remarked on how the Second World War blackout blinds did not come down in his house until the late 1950s, a useful metaphor for this blinkeredness.[32] The rise of cultural nationalism in the UK, the shrivelled imperial Protestant cultural core of Britishness, and the conditionality and tenuous nature of British political allegiance for unionists threatens the long-term survival of the unionist identity as an exclusively British ethno-national identity.

Unionists and Irishness

This ambiguous and negotiable link with Britain provides none of the historical continuity and sense of place available in nationalist discourse.[33] EU success in gradually uncoupling territory and nationalism through the development of multilevel governance, as well as the UUP's acquiescence to the Agreement's North–South institutions, may offer an opportunity for a cultural connection to be made, which at the same time provides a place for unionists on the island of Ireland and enables them to maintain their political allegiance to the union with Britain and a cultural connection to Britishness. However, ideas such as globalisation, EU multilevel governance and words like 'dynamic' and 'change' run counter to the grain of unionism. Zygmunt Bauman's warning of some nationalist disorientation and disaffection in the face of rapid change pertains to many unionists.[34] Unionism is an ideology built on the perceived maintenance of a 'privileged way of life' imparted through union with Britain. Resistance to change and the defence of the status quo are the central tenets of unionist mythology.[35] The multiple processes of change may produce a unionist reaction rather than a reappraisal and realignment.

Unionism was a relatively stable monolith prior to the 1960s because state boundaries were secure, especially the all-important one with the Republic of Ireland, and any threat to that boundary easily neutralised. In the rapidly changing world that was to come, immobility was not an option. Fissures first appeared in the aftermath of Northern Ireland Prime Minister Terence O'Neill's attempts at socioeconomic 'modernisation' during the 1960s and the consequent upheaval of the civil rights campaign at the end of the decade. With the 'Irish peace process' of the 1990s, Irish nationalism began to coalesce, or at least acquiesce, around the principles of consent, equality, interdependence and transterritorialism. Irish republicans, and the Sinn Féin leadership in particular, were essential to the formation of a coherent Irish nationalist discourse because of their process of transition from 'militant' to 'civic' republicanism through an ideological shift in emphasis from territorialism to culture, justice and equality issues. Consequently, it may be claimed that the Irish nationalist discourse proved adaptable to the paradigm shift in contemporary European politics, from territorial boundaries to political and economic flows, through its shift in emphasis from independence to interdependence; from exclusion to inclusion; and from territorialism to transterritorialism. The fissures within unionism multiplied and deepened as a result, with factional division on the Agreement's ability to fulfil unionism's raison d'être – resistance to change, especially change perceived to be driven by Irish nationalism.

Exclusion and inclusion were the lines along which the post-Agreement unionist ideological battle was drawn. In their effort to restructure unionist ideology on the principle of inclusion and to secure the Union, albeit a confederal one, pro-Agreement unionists recognised the need for a 'historic compromise' and coalition government with nationalists. This pro-Agreement unionism represented a shift towards the civic unionism described by Norman Porter[36] that recognised the Britishness and Irishness of Northern Ireland. Exclusivists rejected this realignment, citing religious or national domination by 'the other' – Irish Catholic nationalists – as the only outcome of such a venture. Victory or defeat, rather than compromise and accommodation, are the only viable outcomes for exclusivist unionists.

A form of civic unionism can be incorporated within the increasingly diverse and intricate UK state being created by devolution and the Agreement (1998). However, even for pro-Agreement unionists the journey towards a civic unionist position was littered with potential pitfalls and ambushes. The implementation of the Agreement represented the active route map for this journey. Most unionists believed that the Agreement concealed an agenda for the erosion of the symbols of Britishness in Northern Ireland, hence the campaign launched by UUP leaders in May 2000 to retain the name and badge of the Royal Ulster Constabulary through the police reform process and the flying of the Union Flag from public buildings on designated days. Elsewhere in the UK, such symbols of Britishness were gradually being complemented and even superseded by national and supranational ones. The Scottish Parliament flies the national flag alongside the Union flag on most official occasions, and in an act of potent symbolism it was the Union flag that was lowered on the Scottish Parliament building to make way for the EU flag on Europe Day in 2000.[37]

The traditional interpretation of Britishness posits it as a pluralist, civilising and democratic identity that is the antithesis of, and superior to, nationalism. In the past, this interpretation has enabled unionists to deny equivalence to Irish nationalists and avoid negotiation and accommodation with them. Having made an agreement on the course for the political future of Northern Ireland with Irish nationalists and republicans, the unionist self-definition of Britishness is shifting for pro-Agreement unionists, replacing privilege with multiethnic and multinational inclusivity. A changing sense of Britishness, together with the development of an increasingly secular, diverse, pluralist and inclusive southern Irish society, the ending of the violent conflict in Northern Ireland and the changing nature of governance in the EU have enabled some pro-Agreement unionists to locate their identity on the island of Ireland and be reconciled with an idea of British Irishness. Sir Reg Empey has described his identity as 'Irish–Unionist' with Irish and British dimensions.[38] For other unionist identities the pursuit of premodern ethnic ties with Scotland and the invention of a tradition, embodied in the Ulster-Scots language, heritage and culture, offered the preferred route towards a secure cultural identity.

Arise therefore Ulster-Scot?

Ulster-Scots is worn increasingly by some Ulster unionists as badge of identity. The Ulster-Scots cultural narrative originates in the idea of a 'Dalriadian Sea cultural province' that extended from Ulster to the Argyll and Galloway region of Scotland. Dr Ian Adamson (UUP, MLA) is a leading exponent of this cultural province. Despite the ridicule of historians and anthropologists he has continued to invent a narrative of continuity linking a contemporary Ulster identity with medieval and ancient times. His central claim is that prior to the arrival of the Celts (Gaels) in Ireland, Ulster was under the control of an Ulster-Scots province. The invading Gaels forced back the indigenous Ulster-Scots – the *Cruthin* – to what is now Down and Antrim. In this narrative, the seventeenth-century Protestant Plantation of

Ulster is reworked as the cultural reunification and reconquest by the ancestors of the *Cruthin* rather than as the settlement of an alien population which is central to the nationalist discourse[39].

The contemporary Ulster-Scots cultural narrative takes its cue from a neglected folk, literary and linguistic tradition associated with the eighteenth-century Rhyming Weaver poets of Antrim and Down. After the Act of Union and the onslaught of modernisation in the north-east of Ireland, Ulster-Scots became stigmatised as 'bad English'. For many of the 'educated classes' it was symbolic of a backward, premodern rural existence.[40] The postmodern rise of Ulster-Scots during the 1990s and into the twenty-first century is symptomatic of the contemporary crisis of identity experienced by unionists. Investment has been made in Ulster-Scots by some unionists for the return of a distinctive cultural identity that can counteract an increasingly assertive northern Irish nationalist identity, legitimise Northern Ireland as a nation state, compensate for a general decline in Britishness and provide a secure identity for unionists. However, the stigma shared by dialects and cants is likely to undermine any serious revival.[41] In Europe and beyond, dialects and cants are perceived generally to be an impediment to the social and economic progress of the individual. Parents are unlikely to risk the future social and economic prospect of their children in order to distinguish or invent ethnicity.

Attempts at the contemporary revival of Ulster-Scots have been linked, somewhat benignly, to the growth of the UK government-sponsored culture and heritage industry and the growing awareness of linguistic and cultural diversity.[42] The likely catalyst is the successful politicisation of the Irish language in the 1980s and 1990s.[43] During the past two decades, the Irish language has undergone a form of cultural revival in Northern Ireland. It became a key cultural marker for Northern Irish nationalists and is no longer viewed as a marginal and eccentric activity.[44] Most *bunscoileanna* (Irish-language primary schools) and *meánscoileanna* (Irish-language secondary schools) were in receipt of UK or EU funding by the 1990s.[45] With the Irish language viewed widely as a Catholic–nationalist language, Ulster-Scots has become the beacon for many unionists in search of recognition and funding reciprocity. The Reverend William McCrea (DUP, MP) complained in the House of Commons of the 'constant bombardment' from a 'foreign' Irish culture, and demanded that the government support Ulster-Scots to counteract this 'foreign' influence.[46] For the Rhyming Weavers of the eighteenth century, Ulster-Scots was a means of protecting a regional identity from the 'foreign' influence of England and Englishness.[47] In the postmodern political climate, Ulster-Scots is being mobilised by some unionists as a means of countering the assertion in Northern Ireland of what they perceive to be a 'foreign' Irish language and culture. Ian Paisley Jnr.

(DUP, MLA) conceded that the mobilisation of Ulster-Scots is 'largely reactionary'. According to Paisley, 'the reality is that the unionist community is neither convinced by Ulster-Scots or exposed to it sufficiently to underpin it'.[48] While Robert McCartney (UKUP, MLA) understood that people can be 'in search of roots', he believed that 'Ulster-Scots is being raised as a form of Ulster nationalism which, like Irish nationalism, requires its symbols in order to establish its own identity and is, therefore, a rather ersatz idea'.[49]

The Agreement (1998) conferred a parity of esteem on Irish and Ulster-Scots in stating that 'all participants recognise the importance of respect, understanding and tolerance in relation to linguistic diversity, including in Northern Ireland, the Irish language [and] Ulster-Scots'.[50] During the negotiations leading to the Agreement, the letters page of the *Belfast Telegraph* newspapers generated ridicule and intolerance rather than respect and understanding for Ulster-Scots. When the DUP published sections of its 1997 General Election manifesto in Ulster-Scots, proclaiming that 'we hinnae bin feared tae tak a stan agin the sell-oot', the *Irish Times* pursued Peter Robinson (DUP, Deputy Leader) for a comment but, failing to secure one, jibed that he was 'awa hame for his tae'.[51] Ulster-Scots experimental texts of the 1990s have been largely artificial and have provided entertainment in newspaper columns, so much so that there have been accusations that opponents of Ulster-Scots are inventing words with the intention of discrediting the attempted revival.[52]

While the North–South and British–Irish institutions of the Agreement (1998) and the EU Bureau for Lesser Used Languages provided the potential infrastructure for the nurture of this new medieval cultural direction, a fundamental problem for the unionist promotion of the Ulster-Scots narrative is its implied anti-unionism and non-Britishness, or, at least, a shrinkage of unionists' Britishness to cultural links with Scotland. Another problem is the antipathy of Ulster-Scots supporters towards their Scots Gaelic or Irish language-speaking 'other' who appear to be willing allies in the fight to protect lesser-used languages in EU. The absence of Scottish interest in Ulster-Scots identity and the lack of evidence that Ulster-Scots is spoken as a communal language in Ulster, or Scotland, is the biggest problem of all.

The institutions of the Agreement and the new Scottish Parliament signalled the beginning of shifting thresholds in the structure of the British Isles that created the possibility of increased Scottish participation in the affairs of Northern Ireland. Such involvement could support the unionist investment in an inclusive system of governance, as well as facilitating a coming to terms with the changing nature of governance in the British Isles and the EU. Such participation could also support the campaign for a recognition of Ulster-Scots as a legitimate cultural identity. However, the perceived ethnic ties that bind Scotland and Ulster should not be readily assumed. David Trimble supported Ulster-Scots as a cultural representation of unionism when commenting on the balance required with the Irish language to enable the new Northern Ireland government to be 'culturally pluralist'.[53] He had previously expressed uncertainty on whether unionists would ally with Scotland or England in the event of the break-up of Britain, suggesting a confusion of allegiance and identity.[54] Such ethnic ties that do exist with Scotland are not confined to the Protestant and unionist ethno-national allegiance. Broader Ireland–Scotland ties also persist through the Gaelic language, culture and sport. The establishment of the Irish Consulate in Edinburgh and the Research Institute for Irish–Scottish Studies at the University of Aberdeen prior to devolution represented initial contemporary steps at building Scottish–Irish links. Irish nationalists are likely to use Scottish–Irish links and the Agreement's British–Irish Council to pursue North–South (island of Ireland) infrastructural development. The Scotland–Ireland connection will represent a new direction for the nationalist–unionist political conflict, as well as a factor influencing a realignment of the unionist identity. Some unionists interpreted the active engagement of Irish Taoiseach Bertie Ahern with the newly devolved administrations in Scotland and Wales as evidence of this new direction.[55] This may account for a certain cooling in unionist enthusiasm for devolved 'east–west' interconnection and the British–Irish Council.

Conclusion

Unionism faces a crisis of identity in the contemporary climate of Northern Ireland, island of Ireland, British–Irish, European and global change. Maybe it was ever thus, since the reliance of unionists on a conditional British identity could not confer the cultural legitimacy, security and continuity required by an ethno-national identity. The progressive paradigm shift in the nature of governance in Northern Ireland, the island of Ireland, the British Isles and the EU presented Ulster unionist identity with unprecedented challenges and opportunities.

Previously, the lack of constitutional alternatives to Irish unity for unionists had ensured that 'Ulster ethnicity and Britishness [were] symbiotic states of being for a great majority of the Unionist community.'[56] Globalisation, EU multilevel governance, cosmopolitan localism, UK devolution and the dynamics of the Agreement presented a barrage of dynamic factors that are changing the nature of the state in the British Isles and the alignment of identities therein. Faced with this barrage, pro-Agreement unionists attempted to shift the unionist ideology from exclusion to inclusion in terms of their Irish nationalist 'other'. This attempted ideological shift was bound up with the beginning of upheaval in the alignment of unionist identity in terms of Protestantism, Britishness, Irishness and Ulster-Scots cultural dimensions. It is logical to conclude that continued development in the structure of governance in Northern Ireland, on the island of Ireland, in the British Isles (or British–Irish Isles) and in the EU; the radical reduction of violent communal conflict in Northern Ireland which borders on peace; the decline and relegation of British identity in the emerging multinational Britain; continued secularisation in the Republic of Ireland; and shifts in Irish nationalist ideology and political action will perpetuate further upheaval in terms of the Protestant, British, Irish and Ulster-Scots cultural alignment of the unionist identity.

9

Religion, Modernisation and Locality in Nineteenth-Century Mid-Antrim

Kevin James

The diversity and complexity of Ulster's Presbyterian population challenge historians to find appropriate frameworks within which we may understand their place in nineteenth-century Ireland. Recently popularised notions of a distinctive and historic 'Ulster-Scot' community attribute continuous cultural markers to an imagined community, identifying a core of Scottish ethnic base and assigning Presbyterian religion as a pre-eminent and continuous communal marker. This approach ignores the historic, intrinsic cultural heterogeneity in both Scottish and Presbyterian populations in Ulster – heterogeneity which undermines the assignment of coextensive religious and ethnic markers to a continuous 'Ulster-Scots' population or community. The patterns of Scottish settlement in Ulster were complex and varied, embracing a long chronology of sojourning and permanent migration during which different sections of the immigrant population created, and were received into, varying institutional, economic, social and cultural contexts. Smith has asserted the importance of seeking markers of communal continuity in the elaboration of collective identities, as a corrective to seeing them as products of modernisation alone.[1] But identifying cultural attributes – religion, for example – as persistent communal markers foundational to a broad and continuous 'Ulster-Scot' experience is problematic, insofar as it assigns a singular set of markers to a population whose experience may be construed as being so diverse as to militate against the identification of a continuous cultural group. Many settlers in the Glens of Antrim were Catholics of Scottish extraction whose settlement occurred prior to the seventeenth century. Other Scottish settlers arrived at various points in the seventeenth century, with different motivations, in different regions of the province, and as part of a variety of settlement patterns. The Presbyterianism privileged as a cultural foundation of the 'Ulster-Scots' population was not part of a cultural repertoire 'transplanted' by seventeenth-century Scottish Protestant settlers, and it had not assumed a formal structure outside the Episcopalian tradition in Ulster until the 1640s, when it attracted large numbers of adherents in the development of an indigenous Irish Presbyterianism whose social base was, at best, approximately coextensive with some areas of earlier seventeenth-century Scottish settlement. There were also a variety of competing and conflicting strains within Presbyterianism as it evolved in Ulster: just as Presbyterians in Ulster were divided politically during the events of 1798, so Remonstrant Presbyterians were critical of, and alienated from, the political and cultural projects of other Ulster Presbyterian populations in the nineteenth century: this process was expressed in fragmentation and institutionalised denominational divisions within the province's Presbyterian population.

Alternatively, the experience of some sections of the Ulster Presbyterian population in the nineteenth century may be construed as a collective encounter with processes of modernisation, which reoriented the political, social and cultural positions of parts of Ulster's Presbyterian population and was part of a broader process of more general Protestant community formation. Miller has identified this cultural transformation as a process in which many Presbyterians embraced a new political theology which facilitated greater cultural and political coherence among Ulster Protestants generally, eschewing a relatively insular Presbyterian worldview in favour of evangelicalism as they adapted to new economic exigencies and social and cultural circumstances in Ulster, Ireland and the United Kingdom.[2] This analysis draws our attention to the experience of Presbyterians in a region of Ulster in which they were historically preponderant – the Ballymena district – and outlines some of the social and institutional contexts in which urban Presbyterians lived, worked and were schooled. In particular, it engages the contexts in which the 1859 revivals occurred in the district's urban centre. These revivals have been central to Ulster Presbyterianism's self-identity as a point of 'renewal'.[3] It suggests the fundamental importance of exploring how conditions of modernity and processes of modernisation shaped community building among sections of Ulster's population.

Although the denominational complexion of urban mid-Antrim was diverse, the district's Presbyterians were affected in specific ways by a range of mid-nineteenth-century social, economic, institutional and cultural reorganisations in the district which involved fundamental changes to systems of production, encounters with the market, patterns of association and communal self-definition.

Ballymena was the urban centre of the district in which the revivals of 1859 began. It was a prosperous inland market town situated in the heart of mid-Antrim. The town's brown linen market was one of the largest in Ulster, and in the mid-nineteenth century, the mid-Antrim district was notable for its local structure of textile production (in which handloom weaving persisted into the twentieth century), a preponderance of Presbyterian residents (most notably in rural regions surrounding

Ballymena) and as the site of a series of extraordinary events in 1859, during which revivals centred at first on the rural district spread to Ballymena and beyond, capturing popular attention throughout Ulster, Ireland and large parts of the English-speaking world.

The revivals played a central role in community self-definition at a time when local economic and social institutions were reorganised. If we may refer to this process of interrelated social, economic and cultural transformation as modernisation, it must be acknowledged that modernisation has proven to be a challenging concept for social scientists to define.[4] The autonomy of social and cultural transformation from economic change – industrialisation, specifically – has informed much of the debate since Karl Marx and Max Weber formulated theories of economic, social, cultural and political change posited on different principles of causation, and which positioned the relationship between economy and culture in fundamentally different ways. The definition of modernisation employed in this analysis embraces a number of interrelated processes characteristic of one avenue of sociocultural development which accompanied industrialisation: the emergence of new communal identities and social hierarchies, the integration of communication networks, the formulation of legal relationships, the development of bureaucracies, occupational specialisation and higher levels of urbanisation.

The 1859 revivals began among Presbyterians in rural mid-Antrim and were characterised by a proliferation of outdoor meetings under lay leadership, the wide circulation of reports of individual cases of personal 'salvation' experienced in dramatic emotional ways, and by a putative 'regeneration' within local communities which paralleled these claims of sudden personal renewal. The revivals were formative in the cultural memory of modern Presbyterianism particularly, as their genesis was in regions of high Presbyterian concentration, and their memory was nurtured in the rural milieu as indigenous forms of communal renewal within the structures and doctrine of Presbyterianism. The focus in rural mid-Antrim was on the denominational community and its institutions and on forms of internal regeneration. In Ballymena, however, the revivals affected not only Presbyterians but also attracted robust support from local Episcopalian and Methodist clergy and populations in the town: the revivals contributed to developing a set of Protestant identities and projects which partly subsumed denominational identities, but there were important structural developments in the town which supported this Protestant cultural coherence.

The revivals were transmitted to Ballymena in 1859 through a network of personal contacts and institutional links between the town and its surrounding rural areas where the activity had begun. Urbanisation did not dissolve or dilute channels of interaction between the town and rural areas, but occasioned an intense interplay between communities, institutions and ideas throughout rural and urban parts of the district, in which developments in the rural regions exercised influence over the character of development in urban areas. Nairn has criticised modernist interpretations of nationalism for focusing on the forward momentum of urbanisation and industrialisation at the expense of the potentially powerful and emotive force of rurality in ideology and mobilisation.[5] He argues that by serving as a repository for the images and symbols of a collective identity – as a 'peasantry transmuted into a nation' – the rural world can provide an accessible ideological resource for wider community building in which land, blood and purity are durably intertwined.[6] The revivals may have reinforced the religious identity of Presbyterians in a rural district where their faith was dominant and provided a basis for Presbyterian communal development through the strengthening of its internal resources, but in Ballymena the revivals developed resonance and cultural salience to sections of the population who lived, worked, traded and socialised within a more socially heterogeneous and institutionally dense environment. There, the revivals contributed to the development of denominational institutions while also expanding wider Protestant institutions and alliances.

Rural mid-Antrim was characterised by a profile of mid-sized land holdings, a highly developed Presbyterian congregational network, and by the overwhelming preponderance of Presbyterians in large sections of the countryside. In March 1859, this relatively denominationally homogeneous countryside was the locus for a communal 'renewal' centred on, and expressed through, Presbyterian institutions such as the prayer meeting and the church: this was the basis for the revivals which began in the rural parish of Connor, populated principally by Presbyterian small farmers and weavers. Anticipated for some time, and occurring in the wake of American revivals and simultaneously with religious enthusiasms reported in other parts of the United Kingdom, the revivals spread quickly throughout the district. This process strengthened many of the core institutions of rural Presbyterianism, including prayer meetings and congregations, whose participants increased during the events of 1859. In the district's urban centre, it also served as an important generator of relationships between Presbyterians and Episcopalians and Methodists in particular, extending the range of contacts between urban Protestant denominations.

The first stirrings of revival were reported in Ballymena's rural environs. Within weeks, on town streets, on open fields adjoining the town, at market-day meetings and in Presbyterian congregations, prayer meetings and lay preaching intensified within the boundaries of the district's urban centre. The urban revivals were of a different character from those which occurred

Table 9.1. Religious profile of the census rural district of the parish of Connor, 1861

Parish	Population (No.)	Episcopalian (%)	Roman Catholic (%)	Presbyterian (%)	Other (%)
Connor	7,423	4.66	5.17	87.81	2.36

Source: PP 1863 [3204-IV], vol. LXI.

in rural areas: here the message of denominational and cultural renewal encountered a much more varied social environment and a denser institutional network, and found expression in new social alliances and new social oppositions. The two censuses which bracketed the 1859 revivals reflect changes in the population profile of the town which suggest that demographic and institutional developments may have created conditions in which the rural religious movement served ·as an instrument in specific aspects of local urban community building, reinforcing and endowing cultural salience to sets of social boundaries in the town which were expressed in its institutions.

Between 1851 and 1861, Ballymena's overall population increased by under 10 per cent. This population growth was gender- and denomination-specific and spatially concentrated within the town. Harryville, a ten-acre rural village which was appended to Ballymena in the early nineteenth century but which lay across the Braid Water in a separate parish within a separate barony, absorbed most of the town's population increase over the decade and more than doubled in size between 1851 and 1861.

If the bulk of urban population growth was concentrated in Harryville, an analysis of characteristics of the village's population helps to elucidate the profile of the expanding suburb. By 1861, Harryville's religious profile differed

Table 9.2. Population growth, Ballymena and Harryville, 1831–1861

Year	Ballymena	Harryville
1831	4,067	252
1841	5,152	397
1851	5,597	536
1861	5,600	1,169

Source: printed census returns for 1831, 1841, 1851, 1861: PP 1833 (254), vol. XXXIX, PP 1843 [504], vol. XXIV, PP 1856 [2134], vol. XXXI, PP 1861 [2865], vol. L.

significantly from that of Ballymena; indeed, Presbyterians formed a clear majority in the village, at over 54 per cent, suggesting that many of the migrants hailed from the village's rural environs. The countryside surrounding Harryville, populated by weavers, was denominationally more diverse than more thoroughly Presbyterian rural areas in the district and was a site of frequent sectarian conflict. The village of Harryville was described in the *Ordnance Survey Memoirs* in 1835 as primarily agricultural, with a limited institutional base.[7] Its surrounding townlands comprised weavers and farmers, with a high proportion of Roman Catholics. The annual Crebilly fair, held nearby, was notorious for sectarian conflict. The primary retail districts for the village lay in the commercial heart of Ballymena, on the other side of the Braid Water.

Table 9.3. *Denominational profile of Ballymena and Harryville, 1861*

Denomination	Harryville (%)	Ballymena (%)
Presbyterian	54.23	45.52
Roman Catholic	20.02	25.38
Episcopalian	17.02	21.98
Methodist	4.79	3.38
Baptists	0.77	1.34
Other	3.17	2.30

Source: PP 1863, vol. II, vol. LX.

Ballymena experienced urban population growth, a growing gender imbalance (particularly among newcomers in Harryville), together with the development of a spatially distinct community within the town which had the characteristics of a Protestant working-class enclave in proximity to a rural area with traditions of sectarian tension. These distinctive features of urban development in Ballymena suggest that the revivals were to play a different role in community definition than in more homogeneously Presbyterian regions of Ulster.

The revivals also found resonance in an area whose local educational institutions were increasingly organised around divisions between Roman Catholic and Protestants. Developments in the national education system had implications for social distances within and between populations in the town. By mid-century a form of denominational separation between Catholics and Protestants had developed within local schools. This polarisation was not a feature of Ballymena's educational bodies in the 1830s. In 1835, for instance, only in the local Diocesan School did one denominational group, Episcopalians, overwhelmingly predominate.

Table 9.4. Denominational profile of Ballymena schools, 1835

Denomination	No.	Presbyterian (%)	Episcopalian (%)	Roman Catholic (%)
Ballymena Town Free School	149	53.02	22.82	24.16
Guy's Free School	140	57.14	18.57	24.29
Female National School	100	51.00	34.00	15.00
Classical and Mercantile School	60	51.67	16.67	31.67
Diocesan School	50	16.00	80.00	4.00

Source: Angélique Day, Patrick McWilliams and Nórín Dobson (eds.), Ordnance Survey Memoirs of Ireland: Parishes of County Antrim VII 1831-5, 1937-8: Ballymena and West Antrim (Belfast 1993), pp. 112–14.

By the 1860s, however, almost all of the town's schools, including the National Schools which formed part of Ireland's pioneering centralised state-sponsored education system, were significantly denominationalised, as local school attendance figures in Table 9.5 confirm. Only in one small private institution were Roman Catholics present in approximate proportion to their share of the local population.

Enrolment in the town's Model School, in which many middle-class children were educated, testified to a similar process of sectarian division, as Table 9.6 illustrates.

Separation between Catholics and Protestants in the Model School unhinged a primary interface for middle-class urban residents. With reduced institutional contact between these groups, divergences between populations of urban Roman Catholics and Protestants became increasingly important in structuring perceptions of, and relationships between, the populations. Indicators suggest that limited structural differences between local Episcopalian, Methodist and Presbyterian populations had the potential to develop a degree of pan-denominational coherence if they were constructed in opposition to the local Roman Catholic population, whose structural characteristics – literacy rates, for example – diverged significantly from Protestant denominations. Among local females, interdenominational divergences between members of the largest Protestant denominations on one hand and Roman Catholics on the other were most pronounced. These features are significant because of an increasing gender imbalance in the community, particularly in the fastest-growing part of the town. There, an ideology expressing Protestant politico-cultural coherence and premised on the commonality of Presbyterian, Episcopalian and Methodist interests could build on structural features in the population which reflected a degree of *relative* homogeneity among Protestants.

Table 9.5. Ballymena: attendance at selected schools, by religion, on 25 June 1868

School	Status	No.	Episcopalian %	Roman Catholic %	Presbyterian %	Other %
Castle St	National	24	33.33	0.00	58.33	8.33
Castle St	Private		On	Holiday		
Guy's Wellington St	Free	270	23.70	1.48	73.33	1.48
Ballymoney St	Parochial	187	45.99	1.07	52.94	0.00
High St	Private	46	0.00	0.00	97.83	2.17
High St	Private	30	13.33	20.00	66.67	0.00
Georges St	Private	20	50.00	0.00	50.00	0.00
Harryville	National	93	19.35	0.00	80.65	0.00
Harryville	National	113	0.00	98.23	1.77	0.00

Source: Royal Commission of Inquiry into Primary Education, Ireland, part V, PP 1870 [C.6-V], vol. XXVIII.

Table 9.6. Attendance by denomination at the Ballymena Model School in the last week of December 1856, 1861 and 1867

Denomination	1854(%)	1861 (%)	1867 (%)
Presbyterian	60.53	73.77	77.60
Episcopalian	15.79	18.03	14.21
Roman Catholic	14.74	6.01	4.37
Other	8.95	2.19	3.83
Total No.	190.00	183.00	183.00

Source: Annual Reports by Head and District Inspectors of the Ballymena Model School in the Twenty-Third, Twenty-Eighth and Thirty-Fourth Reports of the Commissioners of National Education in Ireland, PP 1857-58 (457), vol. XX, PP 1862 (357), vol. XX, PP 1867-68 (426), vol. XXVI.

Table 9.7. *Literacy rates, Ballymena females over five, by denomination, 1861*

Denomination	No.	Read and write (%)	Read only(%)	Neither(%)
Presbyterian	1,511	53.28	36.33	10.39
Episcopalian	642	49.38	33.33	17.29
Methodist	108	48.15	42.59	9.26
Roman Catholic	802	31.42	38.28	30.30
Other	133	62.41	28.57	9.02

Source: PP 1863 [3204-III], vol. LX.

The demographic and institutional structure of the town during the period of the revivals promoted aspects of community building among Ballymena and Harryville's Presbyterians, and Protestants generally, which directed their attention away from interdenominational differences (which were still significant in their socioeconomic bases and theological positions) and towards community formation along a Protestant–Roman Catholic divide. An instability in local associational culture also provided 'space' in which rural evangelicalism was elaborated and expressed with denominational and, to a lesser extent, pan-denominational, institutions. In 1860, the local newspaper, the *Observer*, reported that the town's Harmonic Society, though not formally dissolved, had 'no practical existence'.[8] 'The instruments should have been given,' the editor opined, 'to young men belonging to and likely to remain permanently resident in the town.' Instead, the Harmonic Society had comprised 'merchants' clerks, shop-keepers' assistants, young tradesmen, and apprentices – all very respectable persons, no doubt, but, for the most part, only temporarily connected with Ballymena'. Similarly, the town's Fire Brigade, comprising fourteen first class and twenty-eight second class volunteers when it was established in 1854, was reported to have lost all but six of its original second class members by 1866.[9] Even the Young Men's Christian Association published a letter in the *Observer* in September 1859 in which the secretary, Robert Esler, asked: 'Surely Ballymena can spare 150 young men for one hour in the week to attend a meeting peculiarly their own and whose is the blame that the numbers have been as yet so inconsiderable?'[10] Under clerical and lay membership, such religious institutions would become revitalised and increasingly central to the local Protestant community's associational culture in the decade following the revival. This culture would provide infrastructure and a degree of institutional coherence to Protestant projects and discourses in subsequent decades.

Prior to the relatively belated emergence of an urban textile labour force in the mid-1860s, which accompanied the partial centralisation of production in the local textile industry, the revival movement which was formulated and expressed in rural mid-Antrim was received in Ballymena and Harryville and invested with cultural significance within the institutional and demographic contexts outlined in this analysis. Modernisation involved changes to social and cultural boundaries of local communities, which were affected by the distinctive pattern of urban growth in mid-Antrim and by the trajectory of development of its local institutions. These developments interplayed with cultural experiences such as the revivals to crystallise sets of identities consonant with new relationships between sections of the local population and endowed communal boundaries with powerful meanings. By the early 1860s, the town's Roman Catholics and Protestants were separated within the framework of local education. Additionally, denominational groups were characterised by clearer divisions between Roman Catholics and members of the town's main Protestant denominations than between the largest Protestant populations. Structures of voluntary association were weak, owing to rates of mobility linked to heavy internal migration. The revivals provided a strong impetus to stabilising structures and patterns of association through the establishment of a local voluntary network centred on churches and pan-Protestant projects such as Temperance. In spite of these developments, however, the initial stages of religious institutional consolidation occasioned very public theological controversies in the town between Roman Catholic and leading Protestant clergy over matters of Christian doctrine, but little violent sectarian conflict – owing perhaps to the relatively fixed institutional and cultural boundaries between Roman Catholic and Protestant populations described in this analysis, and to the high numerical imbalance between them. Ballymena was not traditionally a venue for such contests over claims to local space, although the *Observer* reported occasional sectarian conflict centred in the small back lanes and courts of the town, including Paper Mill Entry, described in 1857 as 'the Pound district' of Ballymena.[11] Religious revivals arrived in mid-Antrim not in contested urban space but from the countryside, through channels linking the town to processes of communal consolidation transpiring in a relatively denominationally homogeneous district of rural Antrim, where the infrastructure of Presbyterianism was strong and overwhelmingly inclusive of the local population. In the more heterogeneous urban environment, revivals combined with institutional and demographic developments to build a community whose coherence increasingly revolved around cultural and institutional separation from local Catholics and discourses of shared Protestant aspirations and projects: in this sense, mid-Antrim's rural and urban populations experienced different revivals, with different conse-quences. Although the revivals were understood by contemporaries as involving a 'renewal' of Presbyterianism generally, the impact in the urban milieu was important in the development of wider identities consonant with contemporaneous institutional developments. The creation and recreation of communal bonds through these revivals developed social and cultural bonds and reshaped relationships between populations in the town. These developments suggest qualifications to Nairn's assertion that the rural world exercises influence on the development of urban institutions and ideologies in processes of modernisation: it argues instead for the primacy of exploring differentiating features in rural and urban environments, and how they affected community building in these milieux. The rubric of an 'Ulster-Scot' or Ulster Presbyterian experience can simplify and generalise the experience of populations who were involved in complex acts of community formation in strikingly different social contexts through religious revival – one in the rural milieu, in which internal institutional renewal achieved primacy, and the other in more diverse urban space, which focused Presbyterians on forging and strengthening their alliances with Protestants. In more homogeneously Presbyterian rural districts, the revivals may have been situated exclusively within the structures of the Presbyterian population and therefore have been construed primarily as a part of a process of internal regeneration. The interaction between populations, institutions and ideologies in the formation and maintenance of communal identities in the urban centre of mid-Antrim suggests the importance of contrasting town and townland in nineteenth-century Ulster, and exploring the dynamics of interchanges between them, in order to examine paths of community formation in which cultures and structures combined to give meaning to new social boundaries, which in turn had implications for discourses and politics in urban and rural Protestant Ulster.

Ireland and Scotland: The Quest for Devolved Political Institutions, 1867–1914[1]

Alan O'Day

These nationalities will be inclined to help one another. Ireland has received signal assistance from Scotland and from Wales on the great and capital subject of her nationality. Should there be, and will there not be? – questions carrying forward, in which Scotland or Wales have a special interest or feeling, it is probable that Ireland, so long at least as she continues to have a voice through her members in British affairs, will reciprocate the boon.[2]

The opinions of the Welsh and Scottish upon this matter [federalism] are not of much moment to me. I have been sent here to endeavour to obtain Home Rule for Ireland, and it is no part of my duty to ask the English people to break up their existing system and establish different legislative assemblies in Wales or in Scotland.[3]

I maintain that the affairs of Scotland should not be decided by anything except Scottish opinion.[4]

Introduction

In 1889, Colonel John P. Nolan, a prominent Irish MP, favoured the Scottish demand for home rule 'because I think it will strengthen the Irish demand'.[5] Conversely, John Dillon in 1898 argued 'their only chance of getting an increased measure of Local Government for Scotland and Wales is to carry home rule for Ireland, and if it works successfully in that country the other will probably follow as far as the people of Scotland and Wales are desirous'.[6] In 1999 Northern Ireland, Scotland and Wales each was granted a devolved legislature, though their respective forms and powers differed, creating a hybrid constitutional mechanism. The outcome would have horrified A.V. Dicey, who, with devastating logic, savaged Gladstone's Irish home rule proposals.

Achievement of legislative powers in Scotland and Wales owed little to cooperation between the Celtic peoples or to the example set by Ireland since 1920–21. Gladstone and O'Connor cited at the head of the chapter were over-optimistic; William Redmond, more perceptively, articulated an underlying reason for that failure. The severe limits of Irish coordination with Scots and Welsh devolutionists occasions such slight notice in the literature that there is not in the usual sense a subtle difference of interpretation between various writers. Hechter pointed out: 'if England may be considered the core then at least four separate peripheries must be distinguished in the British Isles, namely, Wales, Scotland, Ireland and Ulster. Hardly any attention has been paid to the interaction of these multiple peripheries both with each other, and with respect to the core.'[7] Despite recent attention to core–periphery relationships, there is still little research on the relationships between the countries of the Celtic fringe. Robbins blamed the failure of a 'Celtic League' on acute religious and political differences. Kendle adopts a similar verdict in his study of United Kingdom devolutionists.[8]

It was not self-evident that religious and linguistic distinctions made Celtic cooperation any more difficult than alliances focused on the 'centre'. Kendle notes the fear of Irish nationalists that general schemes of federalism would delay, maybe obviate, home rule for Ireland. Evidence on contacts is sparse. Parnell took little interest in Scottish or Welsh cases, dismissing the Scots as having lost their nationality.[9] Infrequent trips to Scotland never took him to the Highlands. The few trips to Wales were to elicit support for Ireland's cause. The indifference contrasted with his well-informed participation in many British and imperial questions.

During his North American mission in early 1880, John Murdoch, owner and editor of *Highlander*, and a radical, land reformer and home ruler, joined Parnell's touring party. An enthusiast for a union of 'sea divided Gaels', Murdoch failed in his attempt to forge a connection.[10] Parnell severed Murdoch's participation abruptly in St Louis and had no known subsequent contact with him.[11]

Much the same applied to Wales. In October 1885, David Lloyd George thought that energies could be concentrated 'in one great agitation for National Self-Government'.[12] Widening the area of agitation appealed to Michael Davitt, and he spoke in Wales to that end in February 1886.[13] Tom Ellis 'drew the moral that race-consciousness should heighten the awareness of nationality and that Welsh and Irish nationalism should be merged with the Social Democrats in a great campaign of social regeneration'.[14] Little concrete contact ever emerged. In 1886 and 1887 John Dillon lent his name to the abortive attempt to form a Celtic League to promote 'common political objects' of the Highlands, Ireland and Wales.[15] Davitt visited the Highlands in 1887 and the following year linked the self-government cause for the Irish and Scots: 'If Scotland really desires home rule – if its national sentiment is evoked in favour of a national assembly in Edinburgh – the very manifestation of such a feeling among the Scottish people will make home rule for Ireland an assurance doubly sure.'[16] Like similar sentiments from William O'Brien in 1891, enthusiastic about 'these bonds of blood and clanship which once bound us to our Scottish soldier-colonists who conquered with Angus and knelt to Columkille',[17] these portended no deep or significant institutional arrangements.

At the turn of the century Douglas Hyde and Patrick Pearse both showed interest in fostering connections, but their individualistic enthusiasm occasioned controversy in their own ranks. When Hyde proposed to attend the Pan-Celt Conference planned for 1900 in Dublin, the committee of Coiste Gnothe responded that they 'would be sorry that any of their members should give time or money to an enterprise that could not help the Irish language'.[18] In 1906 the dream of a Gaelic confederation remained alive. *Guth na Bliadhna* foresaw that 'the drawing together of the Gaels of Scotland and Ireland is a natural consequence of the language movement in both countries'.[19] These were exceptions that prove the rule, and formal connections between Scots and Welsh proved no sturdier. In 1890 a meeting between representatives of national sentiment in the two countries met to consider cooperation, and in August 1910 there was a further effort to build a working relationship between the respective movements, but nothing consequential emerged.[20]

The absence of cooperation has implications for the difficulties faced by the Celtic regions in creating alliances for their mutual benefit, and for the success of the British state (except in southern Ireland) in thwarting demands for autonomy on its fringes. This absence of a coherent Celtic movement was not inevitable. Three vital factors might have worked in the opposite direction. First, Ireland and Scotland (also Wales) had parallel experiences and aspirations within the British imperium. Scotland and Ireland were incorporated into the British State relatively late, within less than a century of one another. Both derived benefits from the connection while still insisting upon the primacy of local traditions, customs, culture, legal arrangements and governing institutions. As Hechter maintained, 'by the nineteenth century, the existence of Celtic culture had become a weapon in that it could be used as a basis for anti-English political mobilisation in these traditionally disadvantaged regions', a point that can be applied with equivalent force to Wales as well.[21]

Second, if the demand for a degree of autonomy proved sharper in Ireland, it gained momentum in Scotland and Wales after Gladstone introduced the home rule bill in 1886. There was a logic to an alliance in and out of Parliament. After 1885, Ireland possessed 103 seats, Scotland had another 74 and Wales 34, and though not all of these in any country were ever going to become nationalist preserves, the potential aggregation could give the Celts a substantial bargaining chip with the representatives of the 'predominant partner'. Introducing the Government of Ireland bill, Gladstone seemed to invite Scots to replicate the Irish demand: 'The principle that I am laying down I am not laying down exceptionally for Ireland.'[22] Uncommonly explicitly for him, Gladstone later in 1886 contended:

> What is no less likely, and even more important, is the sense of nationality, both in Scotland and in Wales, set astir by this controversy may take a wider range than heretofore. Wales and even Scotland, may ask herself, whether the present system of entrusting all the affairs to the handling of a body, English in such overwhelming proportion as the present Parliament is and must probably always be, is an adjustment which does the fullest justice to what is separate and specific in their several populations.[23]

Third, the Scottish (and Welsh) movement made sufficient headway for an alliance to be attractive. In response to Gladstone's initiative, Dr G.B. Clark formed the Scottish Home Rule Association in May 1886, which lasted until 1914.[24] Though in the longer term replete with defects, it made an immediate impression. In November 1886 James Bryce enjoined Gladstone: 'the idea has not yet taken so much hold in Scotland but what it may be successfully discouraged. But it seems to be growing under the influence of a rather thoughtless agitation, conducted by people more active than weighty, and one cannot but fear that it may greatly injure the prospects of Irish self-government.'[25]

At its annual conference in September 1887 the Scottish Liberal Association adopted a home rule resolution and repeated the exercise the next year.[26] The outcome may have resulted from an 'unrepresentative' attendance,[27] but the movement nonetheless made strides and significant converts.

Gladstone did not endorse the movement, but during the Scottish Home Rule debate of April 1889 offered sustenance:

> I hold that Scotland and Ireland are precisely equal in the face of England with respect to their moral and political right to urge on the Imperial Parliament such claims as they may consider arise out of the interests and demands of those respective countries. They are precisely equal in this right, so that if I am to suppose a case in which Scotland unanimously, or by a clearly preponding voice, were to make a demand in the same manner as Ireland, I could not deny the title of Scotland to urge such a claim.[28]

Although he noted that the practical problems were very different, he, like Dillon, saw advantages for Scotland in the essential links between the two situations.[29] 'The whole subject will be worked through and through on the

Irish points. Scotland will reap the advantage of that; so that if there be some delay ... Scotland will be richly rewarded by the increased facilities she will have in advancing her claim.'[30]

Gladstone's prophesy missed the mark for both countries, but the Scottish cause advanced in the House of Commons. In 1894 a majority of Liberal MPs supported it, and in 1913 the Second Reading of the Scottish Home Rule bill passed by 204 to 159.[31]

The present investigation has two objects: to discover the extent of Irish nationalist exceptionalism in the context of national movements, and to assess the degree of interest that Irish party MPs held over time in wider parliamentary political affairs. Scottish parliamentary agitation for devolved government affords an opportunity to test both propositions. The argument advanced here is that the three countries, especially Ireland and Scotland, found sustained cooperation unattractive because they were each at different points in the potential evolutionary cycle of national movements. Hroch identifies three stages of a successful non-dominant ethnic movement: Phase A, intellectuals lacking a political intention seek to study and revive their country's history and traditions; Phase B, a political as well as a cultural programme is pursued; and Phase C, mobilisation of the masses. By the mid-1880s Ireland was firmly in Phase C, Wales at the beginning of Phase B, but Scotland only at the initial stage.[32] Hroch's diagnosis allows four theoretical insights to be integrated into the matrix: the stress upon the unique character of a nation or people; the core–periphery approach; and uneven development along with the distinction between nationalism and patriotism. The methodology of focus on parliamentary debates allows a snapshot of a key segment of national attitudes. Despite the limited franchise pre-1918, this method points to conclusions about the Irish which evidence from newspapers and private contacts would nuance but not disturb.

Irish Nationalists and Scottish Home Rule

It requires some source-mining to locate consistent and meaningful Irish interest and nationalist references to Scotland. In terms of references to home rule, colonial and foreign examples vastly outnumber those of Scotland and Wales combined. The evolving Irish position was supportive if reticent. Pre-1886, Irish spokesmen supported Scottish devolution in theory but held it had little practical significance. Between 1886 and the mid-1890s, there seemed possibilities of wider linkages, but from then until 1914 the Irish worried that Scottish aspirations would be tied to federalism, thereby delaying home rule for Ireland. These conclusions derive from analysis of three pamphlets by Isaac Butt, John George MacCarthy and Thadeus O'Malley; Irish home rule debates of 1874 and 1876; the

Government of Ireland bills 1886, 1893 and 1912; and parliamentary consideration of Scottish devolution or home rule in 1889, 1892, 1895, 1898 and 1913. The final sequence is as much one of omission as of actual expressions of opinion.

The federalisation of the United Kingdom debate began in 1831, with a pamphlet by Fr O'Malley, 'the father of federalism'. In November of the same year, William Sharman Crawford, better known for advocacy of tenant-right, wrote to Daniel O'Connell that he could support 'a national principle of local legislation' though not 'two parliaments with equal powers in all matters'.[33] The debate was revived in the 1840s as an essentially Protestant enthusiasm to counter the success of O'Connell's repeal campaign, a mainly Catholic campaign. In November 1844 Crawford, in the midst of federalist fever, drew up a plan heavily influence by the Canadian model. Under his scheme, Irish representation would be retained at Westminster.

> The principle of self government by representation should be carried out through every institution of the state; and local taxation, whether in a parish or a town, should be imposed and managed, and the bye-laws affecting the locality enacted by a body representing the locality which taxation or these laws affect, and the whole kept under control and regulation, by the central power of Imperial representation.[34]

O'Connell, in an effort to forge a cross-confessional alliance, momentarily appeared ready to substitute federalism for Repeal. His wavering drew criticism from within the Repeal Association. Thomas Davis rejected the federalist project because 'the aspiration of Ireland is for unbounded nationality ... The destiny of Ireland ... is for no qualified freedom'.[35] By late November 1844 O'Connell was anxious to distance himself from the federalist adventure. '"Federalists", I am told, are still talking and meeting – much good may it do them, I wish them all manner of happiness; but I don't expect any good from it ... I wish them well. Let them work as well as they can but they are none of my children, I have nothing to do with them.'[36]

This early foray into constructing a federal constitution, largely forgotten, merits closer attention. Charles Gavan Duffy's retrospective, *Young Ireland*, affords a useful glimpse of the episode by one critical of O'Connell's brief deviation. He called federalism a construct of Irish Protestants and English Radicals. Although allowing for Sharman Crawford's sincerity, he portrayed it as motivated by Irish Whigs' need to identify with, and promote, a 'national' cause in order to salvage their prospects at the forthcoming general election. Duffy noted that the temptation for some Repealers to shift allegiance to federalism arose because Repeal had failed to win over middle-class Protestants.

Federalism as it was then commonly understood meant little more than the creation of a Legislative Council with fiscal powers somewhat in excess of the fiscal powers of a grand jury, but not authorised to deal with the greatest concerns of a nation – domestic and international trade, the land code, education, national defences, and the subsidies to religious denomination.[37]

This was less than Catholic nationalists demanded. This critique assists our understanding of the subsequent reticence about federal schemes or 'home rule all round', particularly when these threatened to delay or undermine implementation of Irish home rule.

In the two decades after 1846, both Repeal and, more completely, federalism were in hibernation. Following the Fenian revolt in 1867, the self-government question resurfaced more forcefully. At the beginning of 1868 the Dean of Limerick organised a Declaration of the Catholic clergy for Repeal of the Union signed by 1600 clerics.[38] Among those feeling the impulse of the revival of national spirit was Isaac Butt. He took the lead in the Amnesty and land movements and was the foremost figure at the private meeting held at the Bilton Hotel, Dublin on 19 May 1870 which adopted a federal platform, marking the origins of the Home Government Association.

Butt quickly publicised the new movement in *Irish Federalism:Its Meaning, Its Objects and Its Hopes*. Anticipating later arguments, and alert to wider implications, he outlined plans which granted Ireland a Parliament for purely domestic affairs.[39]

I intend to propose a system under which England, Scotland, and Ireland, united as they are under one sovereign, should have a common executive and a common national council for all purposes necessary to constitute them, to other nations, as one state, while each of them should have its own domestic administration and its own domestic Parliament for its internal affairs. I say each of them, because, although my immediate concern is only with Ireland, I do not suppose that if Irishmen obtain the separate management of Irish affairs it is at all likely that Englishmen or Scotchmen would consent to the management of their domestic concerns by a Parliament in which Irish members had still a voice.[40]

This he qualified: 'Whether England and Scotland would still desire to have the internal affairs of Great Britain managed by one common Parliament is a matter entirely for themselves to desire.'[41] Scotland played no further part in his deliberation; Wales was ignored. The following year, John George MacCarthy's *A Plea for the Home Government of Ireland* appeared. There was a nod towards Scotland – 'though the Scottish case for autonomy is not as strong as that of Ireland, it is of considerable strength'.[42] He, too, omitted Wales.

In 1873 O'Malley issued *Home Rule on the Basis of Federalism*, citing his own longstanding credentials as a federalist. His early contributions advocating federalism had been published in 1831 and again in 1845 as one of the Repeal Prize Essays. His new pamphlet was more wide-ranging than Butt's and MacCarthy's, attributing federalist inspiration to the American system. He was more direct about the Scottish parallel. Editorially, *The Times* had raised the Scottish case, which O'Malley acknowledged.

I am thankful to The Times for insisting on home rule for Scotland and for England, being a *necessary corrolative* of home rule for Ireland. I am, if not the only home ruler who has maintained this 'necessary corrolative', certainly the sturdiest and most consistent in maintaining it. Every word the reader will see just now of what I say upon home rule for Scotland, he will find in my second Federalist, published just forty-two years ago.[43]

'In a very large proportion,' he argued, 'most of the grievances affecting Ireland, from the absence of self-government, may be traced to Scotland',[44] and 'when the benefit of home rule becomes apparent, and the question comes up for final settlement, Scotland will, of course, fall into line.'[45] Wales was ignored, but O'Malley visualised Scotland holding a fundamental place in any federal restructuring of the United Kingdom. Similarly, at the National Conference held in Dublin in November 1873 to form the Home Rule League, there was recognition of the Scottish dimension but, as usual, it did not loom large in the delegates' minds and no-one advocated developing links with the Scottish brethren.[46] Intriguing though these early expressions of fraternal sympathy with the Scots are, they were never translated into concrete contacts. T. O'Neill Russell, who called for cooperation of Gaelic speakers and an end to 'infernal ... prejudices that have kept the Highlanders and the Irish apart for hundreds of years' was a fairly regular contributor to Murdoch's *Highlander*, but this represented an individualist aspiration.[47]

The first major discussions of Irish home rule in the House of Commons were on 30 June and 2 July 1874. Butt asserted that Irish intervention in English and Scottish business 'had been a great damage to themselves, to the character of Parliament, and to English legislation'.[48] He reiterated his observation in *Irish Federalism*, stating 'if the Scotch Members wished to be separated from the English he should be ready to support them, but if they were satisfied with the English Legislature, he would not wish to disturb the existing arrangements'.[49] His close colleague, Mitchell Henry, did not speak directly about Scotland, though he proposed:

As against the world they must be an united Empire having one Sovereign, one Army, one Navy, one foreign policy; whilst, in their internal affairs, and admitting of those national diversities of thought and action which must exist in the case of peoples whose race and religion were as different as the resources and capabilities of the countries were different.[50]

Revealing even an absence of agreement on the broad principle, McCarthy Downing insisted 'there is no parallel between the cases of Scotland and Ireland'.[51] On 30 June 1876, a second major parliamentary discussion of Ireland's demand again exposed divergent opinions on Scotland. P.J. Smyth, an unrepentant Repealer, attacked the notion of 'federalism', stating that 'although Ireland only is named in the Resolution, Scotland is specifically included in the Federal arrangement'.[52] G.H. Kirk observed that 'a federation of the three Kingdoms was absolutely necessary for the foundation of a great Empire which would have itself respected throughout the world'.[53] While most Irish home rulers in both debates in the 1870s saw Scotland potentially as a part of any broad scheme of federalism, the northern kingdom did not occupy a significant position for any writer or speaker.

Home rule for Ireland entered the vocabulary of practical politics with the Government of Ireland bill in 1886. Introducing the bill on 8 April, Gladstone stated 'the principle that I am laying down I am not laying down exceptionally for Ireland'. Irish party MPs were concerned to counter the challenges of people like Chamberlain, and federalism had a minor part in this. T.M. Healy on 9 April answered Chamberlain's critique as follows: 'If the Members of the Government of this Empire bring forward a scheme of federation as a serious proposal, and not as a *tu queque* ex-Ministerial counter-plan, then the people of Ireland will be willing to join the subjects of the Empire in the consideration of the scheme.'[54]

Others, not including Parnell, revealed sympathy for the idea. On 13 May John Redmond 'looked forward to the day when it would be applied to England, Scotland, and Wales, as well as Ireland. Then the character of the so-called Imperial Parliament would be changed. It would be then only an Imperial Parliament, and all the Kingdoms, having their own National Parliaments, might be represented in it.'[55] The national party was keen to praise a concept then fashionable in liberal circles but sensed a trap in which discussion of constitutional reorganisation on a wide basis would be detrimental to realisation of home rule in Ireland. This was a recurrent theme of nationalist rhetoric after 1886. On 21 May, Justin McCarthy summarised.

This House of Commons has so much weighty work to do that it must be very long indeed, I fear, before it could frame and work out to practical success a broad, vast scheme of universal federation. But ... we in Ireland cannot afford to wait for that time. Our cause and our grievance will not bear the delay, and the question has reached a point when its settlement is imperatively called for; and we say to the House that the best thing to do is to form an Irish Parliament to begin with; and if at any time there should arise a demand for this scheme of federation, and if practical statesmen work it out, you have the Irish Parliament ready to be made a portion of the scheme … And if you have an Irish Parliament you have at least that one step towards an Imperial federation. But in the meantime, we want to do something.[56]

Despite sporadic interest, T.P. O'Connor accurately declared the 'plan and method of federation … is dead' in the absence of public opinion in England, Scotland and Wales in its favour.[57]

Scotland, subsumed into the controversy over federation or federalism, received little attention. Irish party MPs initially were caught flat-footed by Chamberlain's insertion of federation, a curious circumstance in view of its identification with federalist ideas since the beginning of the 1870s. They rapidly realised that this was a diversion along a path less dangerous to the centralised British state. Yet there could be no doubt that Gladstone's measure stimulated discussion about Scottish (and Welsh) devolution inside a framework concocted for Ireland.

In 1889 Irish party MPs voted in favour of the resolution for home rule for Scotland, but none spoke in the debate. In 1892 Colonel Nolan, a post-split Parnellite member, was the only nationalist to participate. The question arose again during the Government of Ireland bill in 1893, but the relatively small number of references to devolution pertained to federalism, usually the federalisation of the Empire. On 17 February, the Canadian politician Edward Blake, who had been co-opted into the anti-Parnellite party, argued that the ultimate solution

> was to be found in the shape of local institutions for other parts of the Kingdom, with an Imperial Parliament for all. He [Blake] was an advocate of that policy, though he knew the time for it had not yet arrived … The beneficial results of home rule in Ireland would go far to advance and bring into the region of practical politics the adoption of this plan.[58]

On 14 April he declared that imperial federation was a more distant prospect than United Kingdom federalism.

> The principle of home rule for the various divisions of the United Kingdom might long proceed the practical application of it, and when it was recognised that local opinion should rule in Scotland in Scottish concerns, that local opinion should rule in Wales in Welsh affairs, and in England in English affairs many of the difficulties which now gave rise to alarm would be solved in practice.[59]

Davitt proclaimed that 'Scotland will insist upon it, so will Wales'.[60]

When United Kingdom federalism was debated in March 1895, John Redmond took exception to the resolution because it 'placed the case of Ireland for home rule on precisely the same level as the cases of England, Scotland, and Wales. But the case of Ireland was an entirely exceptional one.'[61] Dillon dissented; he 'looked at the resolution from the point of view largely, though not entirely, of the interests of Ireland, and he thought they were bound by every consideration of expediency, and of their desire to push forward the cause of home rule to show their allies that so long as they were true to them the Irish Members would be true to them'.[62] Three years later Dillon shifted ground during discussion of the local self-government resolution, insisting on the 'priority of the Irish'.[63]

When the issue next made a serious appearance in the Government of Ireland bill, 1912, the nationalist leadership was still sympathetic to the concept of federalism but very reluctant to let it come forward before Irish home rule had been secured. Federalist credentials were suspect; many of its advocates were Conservatives who sponsored it as an alternative to Irish home rule. H.H. Asquith introduced the third home rule bill as 'the first step, and only the first step in a larger and more comprehensive policy'.[64] John Redmond upheld the management of local affairs by local bodies, though he embraced the idea without notable enthusiasm.[65] The one nationalist who did pick up the baton was William O'Brien. But federalism was mainly a preoccupation of British, not Irish, MPs.[66] T.P. O'Connor was the sole Irish MP to intervene in the debate on Scottish home rule in 1913, which passed its Second Reading with Irish support, saying: 'I speak in favour of this Bill because I want home rule all round.'[67]

Irish parliamentary commentary on Scottish devolution was not extensive but was generally sympathetic to its principle. Irish reservations tended to fall under three headings: doubts about the popularity of the cause in Scotland, concern that the Scots case might delay implementation in Ireland, and worries over the source and implications of federalisation. Few nationalists opposed the ideology behind Scottish devolution and gave support in sporadic parliamentary divisions.

Conclusion

This evidence does not radically reshape the perception that the Irish gave no more than irregular attention to Scottish (and Welsh) devolution. They could not reject it, for to do so had unfortunate implications for Ireland's case, but they never allowed themselves to form or be drawn into intimate associations with their Celtic counterparts. The same observation pertains to contemporary terrorism–paramilitary groups on both sides of the divide in Northern Ireland. Viewed through an alternative prism, however, the outcome takes on a predictability that does not depend on religious–linguistic differences in the way predicated by Robbins.

Nationalism stems from an assumption that each person belongs to a nation and that each nation is unique. As Walker Connor observed, 'the essence of the nation is a psychological bond that joins people and differentiates it, in the subconscious conviction of its members, from all non-members in a most vital way'.[68] Irish spokesmen, who spent innumerable hours explaining to the House of Commons the 'historic' claim of 'nationality' and the exceptional nature of Ireland's case, then found a problem extending the principle to other 'nations' within the United Kingdom as a meaningful doctrine capable of engendering cooperation between them. This practical difficulty was exacerbated because the Scottish and Welsh situations actually were distinguishable. Scotland and Wales had industrial regions and a working class that was integral to the 'nation'. In Ireland, the most industrialised area located in the north-east tended to disassociate itself from the 'nation,' and its working class was predominantly anti-national. The 'nation' in Ireland gained a content highlighting the distinctive experience of its people. A fundamental distinction was that the Irish national movement was at a different stage of development within Hroch's model from Scotland and Wales. Gladstone's advocacy of home rule stimulated the Scottish demand, but his flexibility also was important for containing that demand within the existing political structures. The core–periphery approach requires modification on account of this and also because the degree and type of disadvantage experienced by Ireland, Scotland and Wales was uneven. Uneven development is a useful tool for explaining periphery resentment of the dominant core, but it also helps us understand why various peripheries find mutual cooperation to gain redress difficult. As Hroch pointed out, national movements typically pose three groups of demand: first, the development or improvement of national culture; second, the creation of a completed social structure; and third, the achievement of equal civil rights and some degree of political self-administration, but the priority and timing between movements differs.[69] Ireland conformed more closely to an ethnicity–nationalism where loyalty was directed to the national group rather than the state and its institutions, as applied in Scotland.[70] Handleman's categories for ethnic identity reinforce the case. These he terms an *ethnic category* (a loose level of incorporation, where there is a perceived cultural difference between the group and outsiders); an *ethnic network* (where there is regular interaction between the group members, allowing the network to distribute resources among its members); an *ethnic association* (where members develop political organisations to express common goals); and an *ethnic community* (which possesses a permanent, physical territory over and above its political organisations).[71]

Within this frame of reference, the Irish comprised an ethnic community while the Scots primarily formed an ethnic category or sometimes an ethnic association. Finally, it is worth recalling the observation of E. Rumpf and A.C. Hepburn that the very flexibility of nationalist parties suggests that in the long run they will not be very reliable vehicles for the passage of wide-ranging social reform.[72] In the present context, this can be reformulated to mean that national movements find links unattractive when these do not advance their own interests.

Bullet Moulders and Blackthorn Men: A Comparative Study of Irish Nationalist Secret Society Culture in Mid-Nineteenth-Century Scotland and Ulster

Máirtín Ó Catháin

This essay spans a wide historical ravine covering the years 1848 to 1878. It seeks to examine two distinct strands of conspiratorial Irish nationalism in two separate locations: urban Ulster and urban Scotland. There is a short comparative allusion to European continental conspiratorial groups, but the main underlying theme is a concern with 'culture' and the role it plays in the formation and sustenance of secret societies. The approach adopted looks at serious sectarian disturbances and the arrests of Fenians in both Ulster and Scotland to retrieve information on the social background and modus operandi of Fenians and Ribbonmen.

The focus on Ulster and Scotland is prompted by the influx of Catholic migrants to the large urban centres which were undergoing broadly comparable industrialisation in both regions in the period in question. It is also a reflection of the fact that the majority of such migrants were from rural Ulster and lived in similarly atrocious social conditions in the slum quarters of towns such as Glasgow, Belfast, Derry, Airdrie, Lurgan and Greenock. In the mid- to late 1860s, Belfast had a Catholic population of almost 45,000 (or 30 per cent of the overall population), while Glasgow had the larger number (130,000), with the slightly smaller proportion of around about 28 per cent.[1] Hepburn has already pointed up the similarities between Belfast Catholics and their co-religionists in urban centres throughout the Irish diaspora. Two contemporary sources convey a striking duality of images between the two cities. The Belfast of 1853 in the Reverend W.M. O'Hanlon's *Walks among the Poor of Belfast*, and the Glasgow of 1858 captured under the title *Midnight Scenes and Social Photographs* by a writer calling himself 'Shadow', were focused on the poorest parts. Of the 'Briggait' district of Glasgow, which provided shelter to both Ribbon and Fenian secret societies, Shadow commented: 'Rags, poverty, disease and death are the appropriate emblems of the district.'[2] O'Hanlon decried the conditions in a comparable part of Belfast, Smithfield, as being 'for all that is foul and filthy, surpasses almost anything of the kind which has come under my eye'.[3] Such an environment, further coloured by high levels of drunkenness, crime and violence, is vitally important to bear in mind when we scan the social class base of secret society members, because systemic alienation could not be avoided by the skilled workers or artisans who continued to live in such communities any more than it could be by the rest of the working class. The picture is reflected elsewhere. In the Scottish port of Greenock, which had an Irish population that rose from 12 to 16 per cent between 1841 and 1881 and was mainly though not entirely Catholic, 61 per cent of Irishmen were in labouring or other unskilled occupations and living in overcrowded substandard housing in the centre of the old town. This compares with Derry with its large dock labour force and masses of rural migrants crammed into the Bogside, which continued to lack basic amenities such as adequate drainage, water supplies and privy houses at the beginning of the twentieth century.[4] Further comparisons could be drawn with the Scottish towns of Airdrie and Coatbridge alongside those of Lurgan and Portadown, even if only in terms of their practically ethnically homogenous residential and sectarian disturbance patterns.[5]

It is important to define the term 'culture' which informs this essay. A standard sociological definition has been chosen: 'the human creation and use of symbols and artefacts', which can constitute a way of life comprising 'codes of manners, dress, language, rituals, norms of behaviour and systems of belief'. Such cultures are brought into being primarily as a result of social factors and in response to pre-existing cultures. Overall, cultures so defined are characterised by their historical nature, their relativity and their diversity.[6]

Ribbonism and Fenianism are terms which need some explanation. Both, of course, have been used in a generic manner as a shorthand for various expressions of Irish nationalism from sources as diverse as the Royal Irish Constabulary, the Roman Catholic Church and numerous academic historians. Despite differences in emphasis, the works of Lee, Beames, Garvin and Murray commonly agree that the Ribbon societies had agrarian roots and were highly localised, yet loosely federated. They were loyal to a non-particular form of populist Irish nationalism. In rural areas they oper-ated a system of social intimidation and ostracism encompassing everything from threatening letters and cattle maiming to arson, assault and assassination.[7] It is the passage into an urban setting which is crucial here. Wright, Belchem and Kenny have already discussed the cultural transformation that Ribbonism underwent in towns such as Belfast,

Liverpool and in the coal belt of industrial Pennsylvania, where it assumed a proto-trades union role and served as a cohesive community defence mechanism.[8] With regard to Fenianism, it is much easier to define, insomuch as this refers to the Irish Republican Brotherhood (IRB), founded in 1858.

Ribbonism, as it is commonly understood, had its roots in the Defender tradition of the late eighteenth century, and through the example of individual societies such as the St Patrick's Fraternal Society or the Northern Union was widely spread throughout rural Ulster and was particularly strong in counties Down, Armagh and Monaghan. Great stress has been laid by many or most historians on Ribbonism's support role for an Irish Catholic tenantry which believed itself to be under siege from landlords, and its use as a bargaining tool with local elites for ameliorative measures relating to rents, evictions and resale of properties. Indeed, this rural Hobsbawm-inspired focus has long held sway. Thus far, most academics have chosen to concentrate on Ribbonism's relationship with the rural Catholic communities from which it emerged and with the authorities, to the downplay of its definitive aspect: its violent anti-Orangeism.[9] We know from the reports of seasoned police officers and their informers that Ribbonism in Ulster – and especially in an urban setting – was more than merely a Catholic defence association; it was in reality a fighting organisation directed at Orange parades and individuals suspected of Orange sympathies. This was an element that clearly came to light in the Belfast Ribbonmen trials of 1859, but it was no less evident in the consistently well-planned attacks which took place against parading Orangemen on their 'Twelfth' celebrations and which leap out at the reader from the pages of Ulster's provincial newspapers most years for the greater part of the nineteenth century.[10]

As soon as Orangemen felt confident enough about organising really large-scale Twelfth parades again around 1845 in the face of the largely ailing Party Processions legislation of 1832, Ribbon societies sought to attack them. This does not seem to have been done in either an orchestrated or collective manner but was localised and understood to be a duty of Ribbonmen. This proceeded on an ad hoc basis, often in the face of influential opposition, as in 1845 when Catholics in Armagh launched an obviously pre-planned feint and assault manoeuvre in the narrow streets of a residential area against local parading Orangemen. This came shortly after a speaking tour by a representative of the Loyal National Repeal Association who pleaded for toleration and non-interference.[11] The clever use of local geography became a recurring feature of urban Ribbon attacks and was often used as a direct offensive against Orangemen rather than a communal response to Orange incursions of Catholic areas. The Ribbon protagonists were regularly reported to be seen waving their blackthorn sticks and occasionally even carrying colours before making their attacks. These roles were reversed, though, on St Patrick's Day when, as in Downpatrick, Ballynahinch and Lurgan in 1848, parades by Ribbonmen – or 'Threshers/Thrashers' as they were also colloquially known in Down and Armagh – were attacked, albeit in a perceptibly less well-organised manner, by local Orangemen or their sympathisers.[12] In the wake though, of the massive Ribbon–Orange clash at Dollies Brae in 1849 which resulted in estimates of at least thirty Ribbonmen killed, the Party Processions Act virtually brought the parading tradition to a standstill for over twenty years. Riots did of course continue sporadically, and Ribbonmen were noted to have taken an organising role in them whether in Belfast in 1853, 1857 and 1864, at Derrymacash, near Lurgan in 1860 or in Derry in 1864 and 1869.[13]

This riotous era was the backcloth to the meeting of fifteen Belfast Ribbonmen, assembled in an upstairs room of Mrs Unity McKay's pub on the corner of Chichester and Great Edward Street (roughly the present location of Rumpole's pub), on the evening of the 12 December 1858. This group was arrested in session by a large party of constabulary acting on the tip-off of an informer calling himself Henri D'Alton and affecting a mixture of Spanish and French origins; in actual fact, as police later discovered, he was a stucco worker named Henry Toye or Tighe, son of a Belfast bricklayer from the slightly less exotic but no less interesting location of Eliza Street in the heart of the Markets district. Fourteen of these men eventually stood trial, indicted for being members of an illegal secret society and, after two separate hung and subsequently dissolved juries, were finally dismissed with the court's declaration that the law would recognise them as Ribbonmen were they ever again to find themselves in the dock.[14] The importance of the trial lies less in the strange charge and stranger verdict but rather in the wealth of information it provided about Ribbonism in Belfast at this time. While it would be foolish to suggest the sources from which this information emanated – informers such as Tighe and police officers – were accurate and uncontaminated by bias, it is possible to extrapolate from the trial details similar to those known more widely about the nature of Ribbon socities.[15] The evidence indicates that although the men arrested were almost entirely from one part of Belfast, the Markets, their society (probably the Knights of St Patrick) had ten similar branches, or 'numbers' as they were known, throughout the city. Their aim was clearly to oppose Orangeism, and this was stated by two of its members who turned Queen's evidence, though it also emerged that their weekly subscriptions were pooled to provide bail money for members caught fighting with Orangemen. It seems all of their meetings took place in public houses, often with the knowledge of the landlord or landlady in charge, and that they regularly learned new passwords and signs, known as the 'goods' well into the 1890s, which changed every quarter of the year. The men themselves were from relatively financially stable occupations, a number of them being clerks employed with city firms, a couple of publicans and a tailor alongside some artisans.[16] This class profile matched that of many early Fenians in other urban parts of the country, and the Under Secretary at the time, Sir Thomas Larcom, was convinced of a connection of some sort between the Phoenix Society in the south and the Ribbonmen in the north.[17] Ó Broin has already investigated the likelihood of this hypothesis and found little or no evidence for it, besides which, issues of nationality made no appearance whatever in the Belfast trials.[18]

The Belfast trials were unique in many respects because although Ribbon societies were discovered with some frequency in rural districts of Monaghan, Cavan and Fermanagh, the larger towns appear to have provided a greater measure of concealment for Ribbonmen – possibly aided by the fact that they became less focused on internal enemies and more concentrated on those external to them.[19] In this way the passage into new communities brought about a cultural transformation of Ribbonism which made it develop into an at times aggressive and at times defensive territorial organisation directed outwards against Orangeism and those forces generally outside the confines of districts such as the Pound, Smithfield or the Markets. It is probable that had the Ribbonmen tasked themselves more with policing their own community rather than its conflictual interface with other communities they would have found themselves more often before the courts of Belfast. How effective they actually were as a community defence association is another question altogether, although the evidence of the 1857 riots in Belfast indicates they were not able to do enough to protect their self-designated charges.[20]

Although in Scotland individual Irish Catholics, almost always from labouring backgrounds, were brought to trial on numerous occasions for being seen to lead mass attacks on Orange parades from the time of the very first formal processions of the early 1820s, there were no Ribbon trials. But police intelligence reports built on seized documents and surveillance of suspects dating from 1839 to 1841 reveal a significant Ribbon organisation based in Glasgow and in existence for some considerable length of time. It had numerous branches, in towns around Edinburgh and Glasgow. There were an average of only about twenty-four men in each 'number', according to one informant.[21] As Belchem has asserted in relation to the organisation in Liverpool, the Ribbon societies in Scotland appear to have provided political sanctuary and job opportunities for their brethren coming over from Ireland either 'on the run' or simply seeking to make a new start. The societies, like those in Belfast, were more firmly focused on opposing the progress of Orangeism in Scotland than they appear to have been in Liverpool. The men involved were mainly from lower (unskilled) working-class occupations rather than artisan backgrounds, although one of the Glasgow leaders in 1840 was a provisions dealer and his assistant a publican.[22] In 1862 police obtained Ribbon documents which implicated a Glasgow butcher and indicated the continued existence of the movement in Scotland, prompting the authorities to look into the extension of Irish security legislation to Irish communities resident in England and Scotland.[23] Ribbon involvement, if not orchestration, in anti-Orange premeditated attacks was definitely apparent in sectarian riots such as in the Ayrshire village of Dalry in 1847; Airdrie in Lanarkshire in 1851, when an Orange funeral was attacked; Maybole, Ayrshire in 1854; Kilbirnie, Ayrshire and Coatbridge in Lanarkshire in 1857; and Linwood in Renfrewshire in 1859.[24] As in Ulster, these attacks bore the hallmarks of some level of organisation and grew out of localised conditions of religious polarisation, complicated and exacerbated by socioeconomic competition. Where they were involved, the Ribbonmen, armed as ever with the increasingly stereotypical blackthorn club, attempted to use local geography to their advantage and paint themselves as community defenders; as in 1857, for example, when they led a crowd of people in defence of a Catholic chapel in a suburb of Glasgow which they believed Orange elements would attempt to destroy.[25]

Ribbon secret societies in Scotland and Ulster did not evaporate in the 1860s with the rise of the Fenian movement, and while Ribbon elements appear to have subsumed themselves into the IRB, the 1870s saw the re-emergence of Ribbonmen in a slightly different, more formal character.[26] In Ulster the IRB had first begun to develop under the efforts of a man from County Carlow named John Nolan. Belfast had a fairly solid organisation by 1862 and by 1864 had at least six circles, as they were known, containing about 1,000 men, while Ulster as a whole, including Belfast, had a total of just over 6,000. Derry appears to have had a much smaller organisation led by a Bishop Street publican named John Donlan. To compare, Scotland at this time (1864–65) had something in the region of 8,000 IRB men in circles of various sizes from Aberdeen in the north to Greenock in the west.[27] The Fenians in Ulster and Scotland, like the Ribbonmen, were closely linked throughout their existence, and almost every commander of the IRB in Scotland as well as most of the membership had their roots in Ulster. Regardless of whether the Fenian bullet moulders were based in Nitshill in Glasgow or the Pound Loney in Belfast, the same pattern of drill, arms gathering and ammunition manufacture was to be found amongst the Fenians in both areas, and a sizeable portion of the Scottish IRB was to be deployed to Belfast and Derry when the long-anticipated rising finally got under way.[28] There were, though, divergences in the social class base of Fenianism in both localities. An analysis of fifty-eight Ulster Fenians arrested in the years 1866 and 1867 reveals a breakdown of twenty-three skilled workers or artisans, twelve unskilled workers, ten soldiers, eleven in lower-middle-class occupations such as draper's assistants, a pawnbroker, shopkeepers and publicans, and two further unclassified individuals, a policeman and a gardener. This places the movement in Ulster more in line with Fenianism elsewhere in Ireland, though few towns could boast as one of their commanders a Crimean veteran with a wooden leg who ran a local barber's shop.[29] In Scotland, there was a greater proportion of labourers, dock iron workers and iron workers, with a smaller number of artisans such as shoemakers and blacksmiths (and no one-legged army pensioners-cum-barbers).[30]

Fenianism in Scotland and Ulster was very much attuned to a military ideal in the 1860s, and while perhaps not the 'Punch and Judy Jacobins' referred to by the Young Irelander, Thomas D'Arcy McGee, the Fenians did appear to enjoy the play of being makeshift secret soldiers working what one Glasgow IRB man in 1869 called 'the silent system'.[31] Military defeat was the only thing which could effectively dilute and eventually transform the militarist IRB of the 1860s into the 'civil' IRB that came after and dispensed with the formalities and ostentations of rank and uniform (even as late as the 1916 rising, a salutary indicator of this was that IRB leaders Thomas J. Clarke and Sean MacDermott were among a very few in the General Post Office dressed in civilian attire).[32]

As the 1870s commenced, the home rule movement made its appearance and secured the public support of most Catholics in Scotland and Ulster, and with the Party Processions Act and Party Emblems Act being withdrawn, the Ribbon societies also made their cultural adaptations. Taking part as would-be stewards, and thus accommodating themselves within the large home rule parades of the 1870s, Ribbonism's adherents came out into the open. Arrayed in the green sashes that the Ribbonmen had occasionally worn in Repeal demonstrations during the 1840s and more often behind closed doors, and armed with their apparently decorative but actually functional blackthorn sticks, the new Ribbonmen-cum-Hibernians of the 1870s began in an unarticulated though nonetheless demonstrative way their long association with constitutional nationalism.[33] This whole area still requires extensive research, but there are indicators, not least of which are the riots involving Ribbonmen after home rule demonstrations in Belfast and Scarva, Co. Down in 1872, in Magherafelt in 1873, in Partick, Glasgow in 1874 and 1875, and in Lurgan, Springburn, Glasgow and Hamilton in Lanarkshire in 1876 and 1877, all of which suggest substantial Ribbon involvement.[34]

In Europe, secret societies arose more out of necessity than choice after the suppression of the 1848 insurrectionary ventures and were more obviously political, or socialist, conspiracies than the Ribbon and Fenian movements in Ireland, which were motivated more by religion and nationality than socioeconomic issues. The Fenians did, though, draw inspiration from and evince a sympathy with the Blanquist secret societies as well as sharing an urban artisanal membership base, a formal military structure and a similar methodology which stressed the importance of the urban insurrection over the rural uprising.[35] By contrast, the Ribbon societies in rural Ireland bear some resemblance in terms of their class base and their activities to the various expressions of European social brigandage outlined by Hobsbawm. At the same time, the performance of Ribbonmen in an urban context is more readily comparable with nineteenth-century street gangs than any social or political organism of the time. Such gangs could be highly organised social yet secretive combinations, preoccupied with territorialism and most often drawn from the ranks of the unskilled working class – all elements compatible with Ribbonism.[36]

The question of a secret society culture as an explanation for conspiratorial groups has not been directly put in this essay. Instead, I have tried to illustrate that the culture in which both Ribbonmen and Fenians were embedded changed as a result of population movement and the passage of time. The idea of secrecy itself, and the use of codified language, signals and surreptitious gatherings were but some of the cultural indicators. The Ribbonmen had their so-called parish masters and numbers in both Scotland and Ulster alongside the centres, circles and military rank of the IRB men. Both bodies also met in public houses, no doubt as they were convivial places to meet, but more because of the fact that there were so few other places they could gather and not attract undue and unwelcome attention.[37] Further, the Ribbonmen and the Fenians produced cultural echoes which remained for many years afterwards: the blackthorn-wielding and stone-throwing 'Mollies' emerging out of a side street into the head of an Orange parade, or back-room bullet moulders and midnight drilling IRB soldiers. Both groups also had balladeers a-plenty to sing of their triumphs and tribulations.

These cultures were threatened by transplantation and changing circumstances, but they adapted in several important respects. Ribbonism readily found support in communities perceiving themselves to be under attack and isolated in strange and alien environments. Adapting to this, the Ribbonmen turned their attentions outwards from that community (which previously had regarded Ribbon societies with a mixture of suspicion and hostility) towards enemies real and imagined. Ribbonism also provided networks of sanctuary from the law, besides employment and social protection. With new political horizons, it grasped the chance to embolden itself via home rule parades which enabled it to demonstrate a marshalled, colourful and altogether imposing street presence, partly as a protection measure for the marchers and partly as a direct challenge to Orangeism.

For their part, the Fenians too were compelled to transform their conspiracy into a demilitarised, civil, entryist-type organisation with a smaller élite structure prepared for the long haul before another chance at insurrection. Even as the mythology surrounding the daring of the famed 'Bold Fenian Men' died down it was slowly replaced by one which whispered of 'the Organisation', with its arms smuggling, assassins, dynamiters and quiet preparation.

12

The Irish and the Scots in the English Orange Order in the Later Nineteenth Century[1]

Donald M. MacRaild

Introduction

While the Irish Catholic abroad built an impressive array of religious and political organisations underpinned by their contribution to the Catholic Church, the same was not true for the Irish Protestant. Although the Orange Lodge was often a symbol of sectarian negativity and cannot be compared with the substance of the Catholic parish network, preliminary evidence from Scots and Irish in northern England suggests a more positive associational role.

The Orange Order, and its interconnection within the Protestant migrant stream within Ireland, offers a useful laboratory for testing the extent to which militant Ulster Protestantism could be assimilated into similar British, English or Scottish identities.[2] Neal, on the Liverpool dimension, and McFarland and Walker, on Scotland, have demonstrated the linkages between Protestant Ireland and Britain by focusing on the Orange Order and its role within communities of heavy Irish settlement. More recently, Ruth Dudley Edwards has significantly extended understanding of the wider Orange movement.[3]

Sources remain a problem. Aside from Edwards' work, these studies mostly draw on 'higher-level sources' – that is, materials culled from outside the Order: newspaper reportage, the 1835 Select Committee, memoirs and the movement's own annual aggregate statistics. Edwards draws extensively upon contemporary accounts and the reminiscences of Orange members. In general, though, historians have not been able to gain access to the manuscript records of the Order, and many writers have sorry stories to tell of records destroyed, thus adding to the aura of secrecy that cloaks the movement.[4] As a consequence, despite our clear picture of the movement's public face, especially its 'walking' culture,[5] much less has been said about the mechanisms of individual lodges and the profile of their members.

Existing studies demonstrate that the Order maintained a relatively unchanging anti-Catholic world view. While this became enmeshed in political issues (education, home rule, partition of Ireland, imperial policy, etc.), the religious mindset was its most consistent feature. The Order maintained a Masonic-style ceremonial dimension – signs, readings, and peculiar attire – but was not necessarily connected to the Freemasons. The Orange Order was mostly working class in composition, which made it an alternative, rather than either a complement to or an associate of, Freemasonry. Well-to-do persons may have joined both organisations, but most ordinary members tended to be Orangemen alone.

Material for this chapter is drawn from several lodges in the north-east of England, mainly Hebburn, Jarrow, Wallsend, North Shields and Consett. Jarrow was considered Catholic and Hebburn Protestant. North Shields and Wallsend lie north of the Tyne. North Shields was an old fishing centre and port, an early rival to Newcastle for control of the river; Wallsend developed as a shipbuilding centre, as did Jarrow and Hebburn, although all of them had other industries such as coal mining, iron manufacture, chemicals and engineering. Consett was at the heart of an iron-making and coal-mining area twenty miles or so to the west of the Tyneside towns. It was an isolated, violent settlement, where relatively highly paid industrial work could be obtained by migrant labour, including numerous Irish. All of the towns in question attracted Irish and Scottish labour and became centres of Orange activity. While Hebburn remained the focal point for Tyneside Orangeism, with the greatest number of lodges and the eventual Orange Hall for the region, Consett also maintained a vibrant Orange community, remarkable not least because of the small size of the town.[6] The printed census does not make it possible to quantify the Irish- or Scots-born populations of these towns, as only larger units were analysed at this level. However, ethnicity is essential to an appreciation of the Orange Order in its British context, which must be located within a narrative of Irish migration in Britain.

Contexts

During the nineteenth century, Orangeism developed a global presence. It was transmitted to almost every place overseas where Irish Protestants settled. In Canada, where it enjoyed perhaps its highest profile and certainly its widest membership, Orangeism moved powerfully into the mainstream of the country's political and cultural life, especially after Ogle Gowan settled in Ontario in the late 1820s.[7] In America, the Orange Order has been considered much less important. This is partly because of the importance of the Catholic element of the Irish–American population, but it is also to do with the fact that ultra-loyalist and monarchical sentiment was ill-suited to the political culture of the new republic.[8] As Gordon demonstrated in his study of the New York Orange riots of 1870 and 1871, Orangeism could be just as much an emblem of a new identity as of an old or traditional sense of belonging.[9]

In the early days of the movement – notably in 1835 when the Select Committee report into Orange activity revealed a sprinkling of lodges in the far north of England[10] – it is likely that the Order had a mixed membership. It certainly enjoyed greater upper-class support in those days than it did subsequently, and in Liverpool members included Englishmen drawn from the ranks of the lower middle class. Employers in the Lancashire mill towns saw Orangeism as a useful reactionary bulwark against trades unionism and other, perhaps more dangerous, levelling tendencies. Most members outside Liverpool were probably Irish.[11] In the far north, after the Great Famine (1845–51), the ethnic emphasis shifted even more decisively in favour of these Irish Protestants. With this development, the movement north of Lancashire and Yorkshire began to look increasingly like its Scottish counterpart, spurred on by northern Irish migrants since the late eighteenth century. Such an assertion is underscored by the similar economic trajectories of heavy industrial centres such as Tyneside, western Cumbria and Clydeside in the 1860s. The mass production of steel during this decade coincided with both a further flow of migration from Ireland and the rebirth of Orangeism in the early 1870s.[12] The Scottish lodges remained almost exclusively Irish into the early twentieth century.[13] Scots themselves showed much less interest in the movement than might have been expected. The movement remained attractive mainly to the sons and daughters of Irish migrants, rather than being able to draw upon Scots support. As the twentieth century progressed, the Order in Scotland only became Scottish as the Irish themselves became Scots. As the grandsons and great-grandsons of migrants lost their Irishness and became assimilated into Scottish society, so too their movement lost its migrant-ethnic flavour.

Evidence from Canada suggests that Scots could make significant contributions to an Order dominated by the Irish.[14] In Ontario, places such as Stormont, Russell, Glengarry and Apple Hill developed Orange cultures that rested principally upon Scottish foundations.[15] In late twentieth-century England, a sizeable number of Scots can be found in the lodges of places like Corby, Northamptonshire, and other centres of a once vigorous Scots in-migration. Here they have joined the dominant 'English' working-class members and migrant northern Irish Protestants, often men with white-collar jobs in England.[16] Overall, the ethnic picture remains mixed. While the English clearly joined the English Order, Ulstermen and people of Scottish birth have historically been central players in the Orange story in Britain.

While sources outside the English Orange Order regularly point to the important influence of Scottish and Irish Protestant migrants in the maintenance of the movement, the Scots in northern England and the Irish Protestant in Britain have received little attention from historians.[17] Yet they were an important part of the ethnic–urban culture across the north. In the Famine and post-Famine years, the Irish were the more prominent of the two groups: in 1871, for example, the Irish-born in County Durham numbered 37,515 against the Scots-born figure of 21,559. Within thirty years, however, this relationship had changed considerably, with the Scots-born outnumbering the Irish-born by 27,489 to 22,496.[18] The major towns of the north contained some of the most significant Scottish and Irish populations in England. In 1881, Barrow-in-Furness had a population of just under 50,000, 10 per cent of whom were Irish; by 1911, the town had a higher proportion of those born in Scotland than any other borough in England, with Newcastle in second place.[19] Being the bigger place, however, Newcastle's overall Scottish population was much greater. Between 1891 and 1911, the city's Irish-born population dropped from 4,898 to 4,003, whereas its Scots-born populace grew from 11,085 to 11,990.[20]

Scottish migrants were part of a heavy and steady flow of skilled men who provided vital skills in the shipbuilding centres of Tyneside, Wearside, Barrow and elsewhere in the region. Tyneside shipbuilding owed much to the energies of Scotsmen such as William Clelland, who rose through the managerial ranks in the shipbuilding industry, eventually opening his own yard at Willington Quay, North Shields.[21] Both Scottish and Irish workers found work with Cleland and planted a trademark Orange lodge. In general terms, much less is known about the Scots than about the Irish Catholics who arrived in the same period. The Scottish migrants were well placed in the urban hierarchy of most northern towns by the mid-Victorian period. They were often the doctors and engineers, and regularly supplied the skilled labour. They were much less likely than the Irish to be unskilled. Although, like the Irish, they formed their own associational networks, organisations such as St Andrew's societies, Burns clubs and pipe bands cannot be compared to the impressive social, spiritual and political structures which the Irish Catholics built around their church and nation.[22]

Irish politics were of great concern to Orangemen in England, regardless of their ethnic origins. The home rule crises provided a focal point for their expressions of a conservative imperialist viewpoint, as well as a rallying call to new members. Members of lodges as far away from Ireland as the northeast were realistic enough to know that their counterparts in Ulster were in a far stronger position to fight against home rule. Northern Ireland was the centre of a political Orangeism that could only be dreamed about in Tyneside or even Glasgow. Local Orange lodges might swing a municipal election in Everton, Liverpool or Hebburn, but this was nothing compared to the clout that could be administered in Belfast. Orangemen in England knew this. That is why, when some members denounced the Grand Lodge decision to move from London to Belfast a large Unionist rally at which Sir Edward Carson was to speak, another member, Brother Williamson, defended the decision. As the minutes recorded, 'Brother Williamson gave a very good reason for doing so. His reason being in a nutshell, where the great trouble is at Present, is the proper place for us to demonstrate and show the sympathy and the help we were prepared to give.'[23]

Scottish and Irish Orange Members: A Preliminary Social Profile

The following section is based on the discussions of a small sample of Orangemen (94) captured in the monthly reports of two district meetings – No. 43, Jarrow and Hebburn and No. 46, Consett – between 1878 and 1883. The data were cross-referenced with the 1881 census. The Orangemen in question were not mere footsoldiers; they were holders of one of the five principal offices in their local lodges (which gave them the right to attend District meetings), those of Worshipful Master, Deputy Master, Chaplain, Treasurer and Secretary. Like the wider membership, these men were working class.

The average Orange officer was Irish, working class, thirty-three years of age, married and male. The sample contains only one woman, and while the region did have female lodges, no records survive from this period. Orange members were also more likely to be householders than lodgers, although many (18.1 per cent), were sons of members. Of the fourteen lodgers identified, none lived with known Orangemen.[24] The correlation between Orange membership and patterns of residence was not guaranteed. A systematic analysis of the residential patterns of Orangemen in this period, on the lines of Pooley and Letford's work on the ethnic geography of Liverpool in 1851 or Hepburn's study of spatial segregation of Belfast Catholics and Protestants, is yet to be undertaken.[25] Initial research suggests a strong degree of clustering, but nothing approaching ghettoisation. In the north-east sample, Irish-born were the most numerous – fifty-nine members (62.8 per cent) of the total. Scots were next with eighteen (19.1 per cent). The English had fifteen members (15.9 per cent), thirteen of those hailing from the north-east. This latter group were possibly the sons or grandsons of Irish- or Scots-born migrants.[26] While no lodge was entirely Irish or Scottish in composition, there was significant clustering in the Hebburn lodges.

The Orangemen of the region reflected the economy around them. There was a middle-class attachment to Orangeism in some areas, especially in the early part of the century. Walker demonstrates the close link between

Orange shipyard owners on Clydeside in the interwar years.[27] Both Swan and Hunter – co-owners of the famous Wallsend shipping concern – were members of North Tyneside lodges.[28] Such influential affiliations were absent south of the river, in Hebburn and Jarrow and further out in Consett. Records include the odd justice of the peace and the occasional small trader, but most of the Orangemen of Tyneside were proletarian. Approximately one half were unskilled workers, but more than 45 per cent were drawn from the ranks of the skilled. The occupational profile, according to the Registrar-General's classifications of 1891, shows only three members classed as non-manual: one commercial clerk, one grocer and one innkeeper. The proportion of skilled men was high, but then Protestant migrants were more likely than Catholics to be skilled, the Scottish population contained a significant skilled element, and the region to which these migrants had been drawn was noted for its high-wage, highly skilled industries.

Some recruiting grounds were more fertile than others. There was a strong bond between the men, their work and Orangeism. What is not known is which came first: Orangeism or a job. There is no direct evidence of Orangemen obtaining work because they were lodge men, or because workers encouraged new colleagues to join their society. It was probably a little of both. The potential mechanics linking lodge and workplace were evident in the fact that in the copperworks and chemical works in Hebburn, four foremen were also Orange officers. These men were long-serving members who appear in the records over many years. One of them, James Gibson, was Hebburn's most noted Orangeman, serving for nearly thirty years before his death in 1903. The role of these men as recruiting sergeants must have been important, yet there is nothing here to subvert D.G. Paz's claim that Orangeism was the 'Proletarian face of Protestantism'.[29]

The Irishness of Orangeism

Orangeism on Tyneside was not exclusively Irish, nor were individual lodges identical in their ethnic composition. Two Hebburn lodges, LOL 226 'Monkton True Blues' and LOL 264 'Johnstone's Heroes', provide a useful contrast. The two were placed at opposite ends of the town, one near the railway station, the other some way further out, near a colliery. The two lodges enjoyed reasonably good relations. They were long-lived and successful: both still exist today. Of the members of LOL 226 identified in the 1881 census, just four out of twenty-three were Irish, while a further eight were Scots. Together the two groups constitute a majority, but the Irish contingent was not the most important. The remainder come from a scattering of places, especially Durham and Northumberland, and include names such as Thompson, Muir and Bell, suggesting that these are the children of Irish or Scottish migrants. LOL 264 was completely different: here the Irish were dominant, with twenty-nine out of a total of forty-four coming from Ireland, and a further nine from Scotland. With the exception of six other members, this was very much the town's Irish lodge.

The master of this lodge was the Irish copperworks foreman, James Gibson. When he died in 1903,[30] the brethren of the district, i.e. all lodges in Jarrow and Hebburn, agreed to inaugurate the Gibson Memorial Fund. Their intention was to build an Orange Hall in his memory, and although it took them seventeen years, they eventually raised enough money (£500 against a total cost of £1,250) to buy the building on the corner of Station Road and Victoria Road, where it remains today. Although they fell short of the total needed, a plan was put forward to meet the costs of the debt. It was 'decided to make the Club entrance fee 10/s and [to issue] £1 share[s], but any one member could hold as many shares as he wished'. It was also suggested that 'it was best to register under the Industrial and Provident Friendly Society'. A former District Master, William McFarland, who was a cantankerous character, resigned over the issue, but Charles Johnstone, the serving District Master, persuaded him to return. Others who shared McFarland's concerns about indebtedness were probably turned round by the warning that 'the Roman Catholics or Sinn Fienners [sic] were trying to get it [the building]', and so the plan came to pass.[31]

Ireland provided the strongest of all ethnic bonds for these Orangemen. Lodges of origin and destination for arrivals and leavers were predominantly in Ireland and Scotland, although Barrow-in-Furness and Birkenhead were mentioned, suggesting that the Orangemen were part of a major cycle of labour migration between the north, Scotland and eastern Ulster.[32] Brother Robert Fleming of LOL 264 'Johnstone's Heroes', Hebburn, illustrates this connection. On 23 May 1908 the lodge agreed to send Fleming's certificate to Ireland 'free-gratis' once he had arrived and found a suitable lodge.[33] One month later, however, on 25 June 1908, the lodge agreed to send Fleming's certificate free to LOL 418 in Glasgow. He probably found work in Glasgow while on his way home to Ireland.[34]

This physical distance from Ireland diminished but did not dissolve the faith the English lodges set in their Irish counterparts. The lodges looked across the Irish Sea for a lead in certain matters. Constitutional problems were referred to districts and provinces, but when it came to buying new collarettes, music sheets, cloaks, swords, and other types of Orange regalia, they were bought not from Liverpool or Glasgow but from the Shankill Road in Belfast. Jarrow and Hebburn members were, by the early 1900s, taking holidays with their families back home. The minute books reported this if members were tying holidays with Orange business. When Edward Coyle, the Worshipful Master of LOL 395 'Enniskillen True Blues',

Wallsend 'informed the brethren that he was going to Ireland on his holidays and would be absent on our regular meeting night', he was 'instructed to call in Belfast and bring some samples of collarettes with him'. Coyle duly did this and presented the collarettes to the July meeting.[35] Stories of trips to Ireland featured in the entertainment that was part of most lodge meetings. Brother James Williamson of LOL 432 'Jarrow Purple Heroes' agreed to give an account of a holiday in Ireland. He told how 'the Orangemen of Armagh held a great demonstration in Armagh City on July 12th'. He also mentioned too the kindness he was shown by the members of LOL 35 Hilmore lodge who 'welcomed [him] and allowed [him] to march in procession on the twelfth day and also social in the evening'.

The Orangemen of England, like their Irish counterparts, remained true to a basic core of values. Religion to Orangemen meant upholding a simple bible Christianity that was devoid of 'ritualism' and 'priestcraft'. In Victorian Britain this was a deeply political issue. Orangeism involved excoriating Catholicism and maintaining what was viewed as a necessary level of vigilance to avoid being out-manoeuvred by the other side. A lot of energy was expended to ensure that lodges were not open to those who had Catholic friends, were married to Catholics or who attended Catholic ceremonies. Such rulings were harsh, as this quote from the minutes of LOL 226 indicated: 'Bro. Thomas Johnstone's case for marrying a Roman Catholic woman was put before the committee and they found he should be put before the district and expelled the order.'[36] At the first District meeting of 1911, LOL 432 'Jarrow Purple Heroes' asked the members 'to confirm their decision in expelling a Brother for marrying a Roman Catholic in a Roman Catholic Chapel and [with a service conducted] by a Roman Catholic Priest.'[37] Would-be members were simply denied the right of entry if they had Catholic connections, as happened in March 1884 when Robert Martin's membership was opposed 'on the grounds that his father was a Roman Catholic'.[38] A minute of 1914 recorded: 'There was a discussion upon the acceptance of Mr James Stothard into the Orange Order on the report that he was keeping company with a Roman Catholic young women. Bro. Fleming proposed that the proposer and seconder of Mr James Stothard see him and that they read the qualifications of an Orangeman over to him.'[39]

Politics was enmeshed in this. Lodges refused support to a Catholic candidate even if they were Unionist. In early 1912, the District committee sent the following resolutions to Edwin L. Orde Esq., President of Jarrow's Unionist Association:

First that we the Orangemen of Hebburn and Jarrow District will on no account whatever support Mr Grattan Doyle or any other Roman Catholic that may be brought forward as a candidate for the Jarrow Division. Second

Resolution that we ... do pledge ourselves to do our utmost to return as our candidate Mr Rose Innes or any other Protestant gentleman which the Unionist Association may select as their candidate.[40]

Mr Rose Innes was told 'that we [Orangemen] ... do pledge ourselves to support you to the utmost of our abilities and will leave nothing undone to return you as our MP if you stand as a candidate for this division'.[41] Such were the paradoxes of grassroots Orangeism.

The growing intensity of the Irish question in the 1880s and the perceived crisis of unionism enhanced the Irish nature of political discussions. Above all they stood for the preservation of a Protestant-led union. Unionism was not simply a matter for northern Irish Protestants but was important to many working-class people and bound together a formidable alliance of patriotic Tories and Liberal Party Empire. The language of Orange Conservative-Unionism revealed an especial Irish flavour. Members might make comment on some distant imperial battle, but the clearest statements of political belief concerned the Union. In 1888 Hebburn's LOL 264 'Johnstone's Heroes' pledged £1 to a movement called the Anti-Repeal Union, formed in Belfast in January 1886, in opposition to the moderate and middle-class Dublin-based Irish Loyal and Patriotic Union.[42] Orangemen dominated the northern anti-repeal organisation, and the brethren of the north-east clearly felt an affinity with it. This was the first of many such pledges made by the region's Orangemen, and its timing was acute.

Every lodge in the area was interested in Sir Edward Carson's efforts to preserve the Act of Union. Some lodges made monthly donations to the cause – not much, just a shilling or two, but if other lodges were doing the same, then the Orange fraternity outside the Ulster heartland may well have contributed a significant amount to Carson's war chest. Carson, undoubtedly the Orangeman's hero, merited numerous fulsome mentions in the minutes of the lodges, particular at the time of his visit to the north-east on 13 September 1913, when he addressed an anti-home rule meeting in Durham's Wharton Park. The District Master had urged all members to support the 'Champion of the Orange cause namely Sir Edward Carson'. Members also involved themselves in a well-attended torch-lit procession in Wallsend. They clamoured to sign Carson's 'Loyal English Covenant' which did the rounds of the Orange Districts, as it did in Ulster, and associated petitions were held open in the region for much longer than anticipated because of the levels of interest shown.[43] While 250,000 signed the covenant in Ulster, only 25,000 did in England, a measure of the English Orangeman's political power.[44]

The Orangemen showed strong support for Unionists in their constituencies, canvassing support for particular councillors and MPs and opposing home rulers and Catholics (even Catholics who were Unionist). In the Hebburn lodge in 1905, Brother J. Dutton, a longstanding member of the lodge, 'spoke regarding the canditure [sic] of Councillor Walker Holmes urging them to give him their vote, Bro. Carson supporting him with a few well chosen words'.[45] In an action that confirmed the solidarity of the Orange ideal, the next meeting, held on 31 March 1906, heard Brother Carson again speak 'regarding the candidature of Counc Holmes'. This time, 'it was agreed to give him [Holmes] the support of members'.[46] Members probably followed their officers' bidding. The Order's political strength lay in the guarantee that if members said something, they meant it. Their moral philosophy was a wider Protestant one, i.e. that membership of their sect or creed was itself proof of trustworthiness, as Max Weber noted in his essay on the Protestant spirit. Thus it is highly likely that we can deduce that what was said in the minute books about contributions to political movements or promised votes for particular councillors was a fair reflection of what came to pass.

For the Orangemen of northern England, their political culture and profile was shaped by relationships with the regional Unionist tradition and their Irish nationalist counterparts. In Cumbria, the Unionist bloc was powerful, with an average Unionist vote of 50 per cent being recorded across all the region's constituencies between 1885 and 1910.[47] There were vituperative exchanges with nationalists in the letters pages of local newspapers.[48] The Cumbria press paid considerable attention to the annual Orange parades, two to three columns of dense text describing the speeches, the marches and the violence which occurred almost annually in at least one of the region's industrial towns. Orange demonstrations in Cumbria could be as large 5,000 or 6,000 strong, with crowds of onlookers cheering or jeering the Orangemen as they marched around the streets. Irish Catholics came out in force to express their displeasure at the loud and uncompromising renditions of 'Kick the Pope', 'Croppies Lie Down' and other standard tunes.[49]

On Tyneside, with its liberal culture, the Orange Order was less influential. In the north-east, the average Unionist vote was 44.7 per cent,[50] and the dominant Liberal press paid much less attention to the Orangemen's views. When the towns of the north-east threw up successful challenges to the Liberal hegemony, the Orange Order and the wider Unionist bloc were not among the victors. The Orangemen in the Jarrow constituency (which included their Hebburn heartland) had no Pete Curran, the Glasgow-Irish Independent Labour Party member, Gasworkers' leader and pro-home ruler, who won the seat from the Liberals in 1907 and held it till 1910.[51] Nor did they have a Joseph Cowen, the famous Newcastle MP, notable supporter of Home Rule and opponent of coercion.[52] They did get support from local Unionist landowner, Lord Londonderry.[53] The Order had no need for separate representation in Parliament but worked within the framework of the Unionist Party.

Orange and Irish nationalist relationships in Cumbria or the north-east were never as serious as in Belfast. Even in the Irish Protestant enclaves in parts of Hebburn or Barrow, the jousting, while at times noisy and aggressive, never threatened severe disorder. There were riots between Orange and Green, beginning in Gateshead in 1856,[54] but none of these compared with the endemic and dangerous rioting culture than emerged in Liverpool.[55] An Irish Catholic postman and Irish National League activist named Henry Tumelty was killed when he took a bullet in the head at Cleator Moor in July 1884, during what was the most serious sectarian riot in the far north of England.[56] Rioting was common, particularly in Cumbria, but fatalities were extremely rare. Orange and Green meetings were turbulent, not least when gatecrashers from the enemy camp went along to cause trouble. At Jarrow, one of Tyneside's most Catholic towns, an anti-home rule meeting addressed by Dublin lawyer Mark Cooper was interrupted many times, with Orangemen and Catholics engaging in heated exchanges around the hall.[57] In the north-east, however, the oxygen of publicity was entirely the preserve of local nationalists. The approving reception offered to visiting Irish worthies such as T.P. O'Connor and John Redmond was a sign of the gap between the Orange and Green fraternities.[58]

Conclusions

What has been sketched here is a reflection on some aspects of a wider research project. The preceding discussion does not begin to demonstrate the full extent of the Orange phenomenon in the north-east, still less in the north more generally. More might have been said about the mechanics of Orangeism, its rituals and brotherhood, and its anxieties and enmities. The associational culture of Irish, Scottish and English Protestants was perhaps more important than we know, and Orangeism played a role in providing a permanent expression for a clear, if prejudiced, world view. Underpinned by its ethos of sociability, and bolstered, if somewhat haphazardly, by a collective self-help dimension, its appeal is fairly self-evident. It is tempting, nevertheless, to say that it is easy to understand why Irish Protestants and their Scottish counterparts played such a significant part in maintaining what its Liberal-press critics referred to in unflattering terms as 'the Bunkum of Ulsteria'.[59] The movement was, after all, ingrained in their culture; and in the period 1885–1920s, it had a particular political relevance.

13

'Into the Whirling Vortex of Modernity': Cultural Developments in the Scottish Gaidhealtachd, 1939–1965

John A. Burnett

The simplicity of the Isles life particularly close to the mainland is disappearing and modern conditions with their resultant haste are gradually taking its place. The single wire of a crude aerial is to-day a not uncommon sight beside the cottage on the wind-swept moorlands. The lone cottager to-day looks into the whirling vortex of modernity.[1]

As late as 1939, the Highlands and Islands were regarded by many outsiders, policy makers and inhabitants as a place apart with a distinctive set of values born of a unique culture.[2] For the discerning traveller such as Anderson, the population's alternative outlook was already under threat from 'modernisation'.[3] This paper examines the impact of changes introduced between 1939 and 1965 in the context of Irish experience and the nature of Highlands and Islands society pre-1939. The concept of culture has a double base: Geertz's notion that 'man is an animal suspended in webs of significance that he himself has spun, I take culture to be those webs, and the analysis of it to be therefore not an experimental science in search of law but an interpretative one in search of meaning', together with Raymond Williams' more refined definition of culture as that 'which expresses certain meanings and values not only in art and learning but also in institutions and ordinary behaviour'.[4] Therefore the emphasis is not just on the language, music, poetry and folklore of Scotland's Gaels, but on their 'way of life'. Throughout the period 1939 to 1965, commentators from a wide array of backgrounds referred to this phenomenon, often letting the reader form some implicit understanding of the term. Though conditioned by the legacy of the past, at its most basic it relates to the everyday lives and activities of the population of the Highlands and Islands. This essay will outline the tensions inherent in the modernisation of the Highlands and Islands as 'felt' by the Gaelic-speaking population struggling to maintain a distinctiveness of 'place'.

Features of pre-1939 Highland Society

'Modernisation' was nothing new in the 1930s. The defeat at Culloden only served to accelerate change.[5] Clearance, emigration and resistance left an enduring imprint in the collective psyche of the Gael that shaped attitudes through the twentieth century.[6] 'Exiles' encamped in Lowland cities joined sympathetic groups to champion the cause of the Highlander and contributed to the 'invention' of the Highlander. Changed popular perception attributed iconic status to the Gael within European Romanticism.[7] People and place were combined through royal patronage, service to the empire and their imagined status as an antidote to modernity. The extent to which the Gael was a willing and active participant in the discrete yet interlinked phases of 'Balmorality', 'empire' and 'Celtic twilightism' has received limited academic attention.[8]

The impact of this complex web of forces upon the *Gaidhealtachd* in late nineteenth- and twentieth-century Scotland and Britain has not received the scrutiny symptomatic of a robust debate around attitudes to the past in Ireland. In Ireland, not only has the cultural decline of the *Gaeltacht* been charted, but the 'myths of the West', the valorisation of the Gael, the unrealizable quest for 'authenticity' and 'tradition', and the 'binarist ideology' that underpins representations of rural Ireland have all been the subject of intense scrutiny and sometimes heated discussion.[9] Ideas emanating from both cultural and post-colonial theory have been introduced to challenge the dominant narratives.[10]

With Scotland's Gaels, our understanding of the way in which representations of the region have been 'manufactured' and then distilled within twentieth-century Scotland is not as advanced as in Ireland. Yet it is clear that in the interwar period the legacy of the past was all too evident in the Highlands and Islands as various individuals and groups debated the best course of action to stimulate economic development in the region while maintaining the 'cultural purity' of the indigenous population. A depressed economy and a demoralised people led to some stark exchanges as prominent figures both in the Highlands and the urban diaspora to the south sought to introduce an industrial programme into a region long dependent on the primary-sector activities of crofting and fishing.[11] Against a backdrop of worsening economic and social conditions, with worrying levels of unemployment and out-migration, the development of hydro-electric schemes was regarded in some quarters as a panacea for the troubled region.[12] Yet the contours of the debate surrounding this proposal were symptomatic of the general attitude towards the region and its people, born of powerful motifs mentioned earlier.

In a speech delivered to the Gaelic Society of Inverness on 19 March 1937, Sir Alexander MacEwen rounded on those who expressed antipathy to industrialisation in the Highlands, asking in exasperation: 'Good heavens! What is the natural development of the Highlands? Is it the dole and the continual outcry for grants and subsidies?'[13] Though he shared the Highland 'exiles' enthusiasm for improvements in transport and social services, MacEwen was more concerned with the consequences.[14] For him, subsidising Highland development had resulted in the Highland people regarding government help as 'the Mecca of their existence'.[15] He continued: 'That most of these grants are at present inevitable cannot be denied, but the system is thoroughly bad. It is sapping the independence and initiative of the people. It is utterly alien to the traditions and character of the past, and must be profoundly distasteful to the best minds in the Highlands to-day.' Despite the recognition from this astute Highland leader that the culture of the region was coming under pressure, the government eventually responded to the pleas for action based on a more comprehensive and rounded approach to Highland development. The Hilleary report of 1938 pleaded for policy decisions to be based on a more informed and precise understanding of the current situation in the Highlands and Islands, and less on emotive perceptions of the region and its people.[16] Because of the war, the recommendations were not acted upon, but the general thrust of the arguments was taken up by activists in the region and informed much of government thinking in the following decades. The tensions surrounding these conflicting views on the future of the Highlands and Islands form the basis of the remainder of this essay.

The Highlands and Islands and the Second World War

The Second World War had a dramatic impact on the Highlands and Islands of Scotland.[17] This related to the strategic importance of the region, the administrative changes taking place at a Scottish level and the renewed commitment to address the Highland problem of unemployment and depopulation. As in previous wars, the inhabitants of the north of Scotland enlisted for active service in disproportionate numbers, particularly in the merchant navy.[18]

The wild expanses of the Highlands and Islands offered a perfect environment for military training. The area known as the 'Rough Bounds', comprising Moidart, Knoydart and Glenelg, was heavily used by the newly formed commando units, while other 'behind the lines' units were brought up to the Rothiemurchus estate and the Great Glen area. Allied air crews made extensive use of the region, particularly to improve navigational skills and for low-level flying to avoid radar detection. The navy bases at Kyle of

Lochalsh, Invergordon and Scapa Flow were extended to cope with the increased activity centred on protecting the convoys of the North Atlantic. An aerodrome was built at Macrihanish on the Kintyre peninsula, and the ones at Benbecula and Stornoway were upgraded. The establishment of prisoner-of-war camps throughout the region and the relocation of evacuees increased contact with the outside world.[19] All this resulted in improved communications with the south.

Wartime demands for key resources heralded changes for the people of the Highlands and Islands. The aluminium plants at Kinlochleven and Fort William were brought under the control of the Ministry of Supply as overseas provisions dried up in the early years of the war. Most importantly, hydro-electricity schemes were extended. The 'vested interests' that had stalled earlier projects were now being overruled by the energetic wartime Secretary of State for Scotland, Tom Johnston. His appointment in 1941 marked a significant departure from earlier years, as he used the powers of the new Scottish state apparatus based in St Andrew's House to dramatic effect.[20] Finally, and in line with the overall drive for greater domestic food production, livestock production was augmented as the region's crofters benefited from sheep and cattle subsidies.

The symbolic importance of the region, and the impression that its people represented one of Scotland's 'finest assets', ensured that any development proposals would be heavily scrutinised and vigorously debated. Emboldened by an upturn in their political standing, the Scottish Labour party offered a prescient analysis of the difficulties in the north of Scotland:

> The 'lone shieling on the misty island' is always certain to bring a lump to the throat of the exile, but the probability is that had the shieling not been so lonely; had it possessed electric light, radio and a garage; had it been within reasonable reach of a cinema or good dance band and, above all, had the inhabitants had security and a decent standard of life, the exile would never have exiled himself. Unless we make life in the Highlands worth living for the Highlanders there is no solution to the Highlands problem.[21]

The party, mirroring the attitude of Tom Johnston, was optimistic providing problems were 'tackled with vigour, foresight and [noting] the accepted fact that Highlanders are ordinary Scottish people entitled as much as the rest of us to a full, free and happy life'.[22] Perhaps naively, the party was optimistic that Gaelic culture could survive these changes. 'Communal centres must open up a *modern* social life whilst at the same time encouraging and invigorating the [Highland] Games, Mods and other traditional forms of native culture.'[23] Scottish Labour's vision for the future of the Highlands reflected the influence of the war. As one Labour activist from Islay stated: 'We must plan or perish. The choice is develop or evacuate.'[24]

His calls for the establishment of a Highland Development Authority, despite widespread support in the region, went unheeded.

During the war, the main alternative to Labour's vision of a future Highland society came from the Scottish National Party (SNP).[25] In a series of emotionally charged pamphlets, the SNP were always ready to evoke the tragedy of Highland history to galvanise support among the Scottish electorate.[26] Donnachadh Mac' illedhuibh, a native Highlander, attacked the government's treatment of the Highlands:

> What lies behind the relationship of the Government to the Highlanders? Has there been a conscious purpose on its part – the destruction of the Highlanders as an obstacle to the unification of the 'British' peoples in a Greater England? Or is it merely a case of criminal neglect unparalleled under any civilised government?[27]

Always quick to condemn the wartime government's use of 'outsiders' to dictate Highland policy, there is a sense in which the SNP's attacks helped to push through concessionary legislation. Despite these powerful polemics, the SNP remained weak electorally. During the war the party underwent internal wrangling; ironically, the purges were designed to root out the cultural nationalist element.

Reconstructing the Highlands and Islands

Post-war government policy moved from reconstruction to a regional development based on natural resources and traditional industries. In many respects, the Labour administration's 1950 *A Programme of Highland Development* was taken as the blueprint for how to tackle the difficulties in the region. The report argued that since the 1940s new factors had emerged to allow a more radical approach to the Highland economy. The prohibitive and dilapidating effects of the previous era (i.e. the depressed nature of the agricultural and fishing industries) were no longer an impediment to economic growth because of the increased importance of home food production, the necessity for a large-scale programme of afforestation, the development of hydro-electric power in the Highlands and the greatly increased importance of the tourist trade. This provided the basis for a more constructive approach to the Highland problem, treating it effectively as one of economic development. The need was for plans to secure the full benefits presented by these fresh factors.[28]

The introduction of the welfare state was of immense importance in marginalised areas like the Highlands and Islands of Scotland. Though diluting the recommendations of the Beveridge Report, the 1944 White Paper 'Social Insurance' heralded a new approach to welfare provision, and successive governments between 1945 and 1965 remained committed to its underlying philosophy.[29] The main plank of the programme of Highland development was to bring the social amenities of the Highland region up to the standards enjoyed elsewhere in Britain, but underlying this desire was the aim of developing economic initiatives to stem the problem of depopulation.[30] The government pledged financial assistance for local authorities to provide basic services such as housing, water supply and drainage, health services, education, and transport. Two years earlier, in 1948, a new system of Equalisation Grants was introduced to ensure that poorer local councils were able to improve their provision of services to the standard of local authorities with wealthier resources.[31]

The 1947 National Health Service (Scotland) Act incorporated the special assistance given to the region from the Highlands and Islands (Medical Services) Scheme of 1913. The earlier act was designed 'to overcome the geographical obstacles to the provision of medical services for the people of the Highlands'.[32] This allowed for domiciliary medical care, with financial and other assistance provided for doctors and nurses to cover their rural practices. Hospital facilities at Inverness and Stornoway were extended, and an air ambulance service was set up. The 1947 act consolidated and improved on these measures, with a new maternity department in Inverness and an extension of specialist services. New general hospitals for Skye and Shetland and an institution for the mentally impaired were built. The Education (Scotland) Act of 1946 had much to commend it, according to the Labour government, as it gave local authorities statutory powers to over-come the difficulties faced by isolated communities.[33] The extra finance for the transport, bursaries and hostels required came from Equalisation Grants and the Education (Scotland) Fund. Improvements in other educational sectors, notably technical education and facilities for evening classes and extracurricular activities, were delayed until the 1950s.

State assistance allowed local authorities to embark on a significant housing programme, including the importation of over 1,000 of the ubiquitous Swedish timber houses. The net result of this more focused and sustained strategy was the completion of over 6,000 houses between 1945 and 1950 compared with around 9,300 in the twenty-year period from 1919 to 1939.[34] Under the Agriculture (Scotland) Act of 1948, crofters were able to modernise their distinctive black houses as well as farm buildings. The Labour government of 1950 emphasised the provision of adequate water supplies and drainage as being 'perhaps the most important single improvement which can be made in the amenities of the Highlands'.[35] Bearing in mind the 'immense arrears to be overtaken', the government pledged further help for Highland authorities. They already received the maximum rate of grant available (85 per cent) through the Rural Water Supplies and Sewerage Act of 1944, and extra funding for those in the Highland Development Area, under the Distribution of Industry Act (1945), followed.

The government recognised that many of the problems associated with the Highlands and Islands stemmed from geographical isolation.[36] The Labour government of 1945–50 recognised that without a fundamental overhaul of the transport network 'the maintenance of proper standards of life' would be impossible. This was all the more important bearing in mind the concerted efforts to reinvigorate the traditional industries of agriculture and fishing as well as hopes afforded to the manufacturing and tourist sectors; both wholly dependent on a modern and efficient communications system. The Trunk Roads Act of 1946 paved the way for five more arterial roads to be built, including the 'Road to the Isles' (Fort William to Mallaig) and an important connection from Glengarry to the port of Kyle.[37] All of these roads were already included in the Crofter Counties Scheme, but because of the slow progress the Labour government decided to take on the sole responsibility for their maintenance and reconstruction.[38] The *Programme of Highland Development* report recognised the difficulties which Highland councils faced in trying to upgrade the numerous unclassified roads scattered throughout the region, let alone the many communities with no viable road connection at all. The government therefore pledged additional funds to be made available through the Department of Agriculture for the construction of roads and bridges. An extensive construction programme of piers and boat slips was also undertaken and, under prompting from the Advisory Panel to the Highlands and Islands, financial assistance was given to lessen the crippling freight and transport costs on the ferry services.[39]

All of these proposals and initiatives contained in *A Programme for Highland Development* were carried out, to a greater or lesser degree, by successive governments up to 1965. Though politicians sometimes disagreed over the detail, there was a consensus of opinion on the need for a range of initiatives to bring about parity with the rest of Britain in terms of economic and social programmes. The establishment of the Highlands and Islands Development Board in 1965 exemplified this approach and confirmed that the region was generally perceived by planners, civil servants and politicians as a development zone.[40] Although the Highlands and Islands were treated as an administrative construct, the extent to which this planning zone was coterminous with a distinctive culture was becoming increasingly problematic for those who presented the region in ethnic terms.[41]

Impact on the Culture of the Highlands

In those parts of the Highlands and Islands where wartime activities occurred, there were dramatic effects for the local population. Services were stretched to the limit as they catered for the large presence of servicemen and women stationed in the region. The demands of the home front, particularly with regard to agricultural production, brought marginal land into cultivation, and unproductive estates were requisitioned.[42] Aside from the physical changes to the landscape, working practices were also affected, with tractors used in certain parts of the region, even on smallholdings.[43] The spread of radio accelerated, one Glasgow Gael claiming that 'when war came everyone was hungry for news, so by the time the war stopped nearly every family who had someone far away from home had a radio'.[44] These developments helped usher in a less cautious attitude to change.

Other aspects of government policy emanating from the wartime experience were widely felt. The introduction of the welfare state was particularly welcome, evident in this 1950 description of Glenelg on the western seaboard of the Highlands: 'The old order is gone, we do not wish it back. Gone too from our glens, we hope, is the grim spectre of want, which has for long haunted them.'[45] Highland parishes appreciated the specific improvements for the elderly and the sick with the introduction of old people's homes and easier access to hospitals. One observer noted that the improvements in the welfare of the elderly made the decision to leave the family household that bit easier.[46]

Although political battles were fought over the pace of change, successive governments from 1939 to 1965 remained committed to bettering the transport links and hastening the spread of electricity and fresh water supplies. The closer contact with the 'outside' world was appreciated. 'The Highlands are generally becoming more uniform in outlook with the more populated districts. In Laggan most people now get a daily paper and have a wireless set so that the parish no longer feels so remote from the rest of the country and from the world.'[47]

By 1966, even places like Harris in the Outer Hebrides were able to enjoy the benefits of improved communication with the rest of the country, a development which had 'completely transformed the outlook of the people'. Despite a sense of sadness that 'the old days and many of the old ways have gone', the general opinion seemed to be that 'the gains outweigh the losses'.[48] Generally, the measures introduced by the state were regarded as a positive development. Yet not all Highlanders were as enthusiastic about the transformation taking place.

Better transport routes, allied to a growing awareness of alternative lifestyles, hastened the drift of population. Most fundamentally, some social commentators perceived that the root cause of continued depopulation was a dissatisfaction with a 'way of life' based on agriculture.[49] In the parish of Watten in Caithness, one observer claimed: 'Despite the subsidies paid to assist marginal holdings to continue to cultivate crops and pay better wages, the young people fly from the land. The girls especially, though born and reared on the land, rarely take agricultural work as a vacation, and to see a woman working in the fields is an unusual spectacle.'[50]

Undoubtedly, working and living conditions in the region had improved. The availability of fresh milk from mobile vans hastened the switch from cattle to sheep, an animal that was easier to keep. The re-seeding schemes introduced in the 1950s altered the land-use patterns on upland grazing, the use of artificial fertilisers removed the need to gather seaweed from the shore, while the tenancy rights introduced with the 1955 Crofters' Act allowed for a more individualised approach to crofting.[51] Relative to the rest of society, the dominant attitude among young people was that the traditional lifestyle, albeit more comfortable than before, was unappealing.[52] Throughout the period 1939–65, young men continued to leave the region to learn a trade or to join the army or merchant navy, while young women entered the nursing profession, became domestic servants or found work in the expanding retail trade.[53] Reflecting on the 1960s, one islander said: 'Young people grow up expecting to get away. You minded your parents, you weren't wild – you just waited until you got away. Even if home jobs were available, we'd still leave.'[54] The increased contact with the 'outside' world, with its emphasis on materialism and modernism, was seen as deleterious in a number of other respects.

Even religion, which was a significant, if not dominant, element in many parts of the Highlands and Islands, was affected by the economic and social changes taking place after the war. Although it was the most resistant facet of local culture, some felt that the changes in the post-war period had 'resulted in a more independent attitude to life' and 'an end to the fatalistic and gloomy religious attitude'.[55] Others, with a different definition of independence, argued that the increase in welfarism was harmful because 'the spirit of independence is killed and only more and more is demanded. There is a different spirit abroad everywhere, a spirit of restlessness and lack of discipline through want of supervision from the home.'[56] These comments from 1952 were directed at the whole parish, not just 'the younger ones'. The pervasiveness of the transformed attitudes was blamed directly on the combined effect of two world wars and the loss of men from the townships.[57] Others attacked the growing influence of the city, often with the implicit understanding that industrialism itself was the greater threat.

> Those who have tried to graft certain aspects of city life on to the Highland way of life have not been very successful, for in most cases the poorer, rather than the better features, have been emulated and the result has been not to elevate but to lower the tone of the community. Gambling, especially

on the football pools, is prevalent. Sunday as an 'odd-job-day' is still very much the exception. Sunday newspapers are delivered to certain homes. A considerable proportion of the younger ladies indulge in smoking.[58]

This sense of an attack on a 'traditional' way of life was felt throughout the Highlands and Islands, but in those places where the Gaelic language was strong, other factors emerged.

The extent of the cultural decline in one of its strongholds, South Uist, can be gauged by the reaction of a local bard on his return from war service. At just thirty-nine years of age and in the prime of his artistic talents, Donald Allan MacDonald was beginning to feel alienated from the people for whom he had already composed so many songs in the pre-war period. The bard felt culturally distanced from his own people, especially the younger generation – trapped in a cultural vacuum. Unable to write Gaelic, he was unwilling to adapt to the demands and opportunities of a new social order which downplayed the oral tradition and its celebration.[59] One of the reasons for this dilution in Gaelic culture was the decline of the ceilidh house, or *tigh-ceilidh*.[60] By the 1960s and the advent of electricity in places like Barra, 'despite its advantages', this new form of power was seen as having 'a strong adverse effect on the old social life' in that 'many people now prefer to stay at home and watch television instead of going to *ceilidhs* or attending the drama productions in the local halls and schools'.[61] Others, though recognising the decline, offered some grounds for optimism. 'Gaeldom as a culture is flowering no more and the plant is sick, though scions from the old stock grafted into a fresh environment bloom anew.'[62]

This sense of a cultural dichotomy of a traditional Gaelic culture belonging to the older generation and an emerging hybrid for the youth of Gaeldom was picked up by a Gaelic commentator, D.F. MacKenzie. Writing in the 1948 edition of *Alba*, he attacked the 'pseudo-culture' emerging in the *Gaidhealtachd*:

> What is known as modern Highland culture may be explained as one of two things – as the natural old age and senility of real Gaelic culture, or as a reincarnation in a new form. It certainly has none of the marks of youthful or adult civilisation. It has none of the sincerity, spontaneity, dynamic self-consciousness or proud awareness of itself which is a necessary accompaniment of healthy culture. Nor does it spring from the people. It is no longer 'local', but is brought to bear on them from above. Language is the true currency of culture. The next census will reveal that the Gaelic language is rapidly dying out in Scotland, and the young people in the last bastions of Gaelic, along the West Coast and in the Islands, have thrown it off as an out-moded garment, and are rapidly adopting the more fashionable garb of young Hollywood.[63]

MacKenzie's prediction that the 'senile' culture of the oral tradition would be replaced by a 'synthetic' form imposed from above was certainly evident by the mid-1950s as the communications industry took root. In popularising Gaelic songs the new artists were making the product a marketable commodity, while the local oral dimension of traditional songs disintegrated.

With the changing conditions (and fashions) in the *Gaidhealtachd*, the forums for cultural exchanges, besides the *tigh-ceilidh*, were diminishing. *Reiteachs*, or engagement parties, were carried out in parts of the Islands in order for families to become acquainted with one another and discuss matters relating to the croft.[64] With improvements in transport and changing attitudes among the younger population, the *reiteach* declined. Prior to the war, wedding celebrations were often conducted in the family home, but with the growth in the number of hotels, a more formal approach to this key social event became the norm. More and more weddings and other family celebrations were taking place in Inverness and Glasgow.[65] This reflected the improvements in communications and the increasing vitality of the urban Gaelic communities, as well as the close family ties which endured throughout the period. The frequency of visits between relatives may have remained constant or even increased, but the rationale for returning had altered. No longer a vital element in maintaining a working croft, relatives returned for social reasons.[66] The significance of these visits, and the more permanent return of temporary migrants, should not be underestimated.[67]

Despite the dilution within Gaelic culture, there were folkbearers, important carriers of tradition, who resented 'the rush and bustle of what we call progress' or lived in townships where the standards of living had not advanced greatly.[68] This led some Gaels to adopt a rather complacent attitude towards the preservation of their culture. Others clung to the achievements of the past, unwilling to embrace the way in which the culture had moved on. This was understandable, because past struggles were fresh in the memory and in many respects conditioned attitudes to the present.[69] The tide of history was against those who remained tied to the past. The reality of the situation was that many of the younger Gaels were abandoning their language and culture, often with the tacit approval of their elders.

Paradoxically, a 'renaissance' in Gaelic arts coincided with the sharp decline of the language in its natural setting. Complacency and a lack of coordination among Gaelic activists prevented any decisive action being taken. It was only through the enthusiasm of Calum MacLean, working initially under the auspices of the Irish Folklore Commission and then the School of Scottish Studies, that the rich folklore of the Gaels was being preserved.[70] Members of the School, and others, recorded precious material, often with a sense of regret that the task had not been started earlier, such was the alacrity with which the folklore was dying out.

These urban Gaels were important in adapting the culture to the modern era.[71] This did not necessarily mean an inferior cultural product. There was a coterie of Gaelic literary figures whose prodigious talents did herald something of a renaissance in the artistic world of post-war Gaeldom.[72] Although the Second World War had 'severely affected' Gaelic publishing, by the early 1950s a new, purely Gaelic, magazine had been launched. *Gairm*, edited by Derick Thomson was, like its bilingual counterpart *An Gaidheal* (run by the Reverend T.M. Murchison), based in Glasgow.[73] These activists, writers, poets and singers were very much active in the urban Gaelic communities, while maintaining strong ties to their homelands. Their experience of war and their wider appreciation of European culture informed much of their work. These Gaelic writers showed a deeper understanding of the wider political context which affected the Highlands and Islands and addressed issues relating to identity, language and nationalism. Certainly some urban Gaels played an important role in keeping alive the pan-Celtic movement despite the negative attitude in Europe towards cultural minorities and nationalist movements in general.[74] By the late 1960s, Gaelic activists were once more on the offensive, and the earlier connections made with other cultural minorities proved useful.

Conclusion

'Every profound change in the flow of civilisation, particularly every change in its economic bases, tends to bring about an unsettling and readjustment of cultural values.'[75] Sapir's conclusion that it was usually easier for a 'genuine culture to subsist on a lower level of civilisation' would have found its supporters in the 1920s Highlands and Islands of Scotland.[76] Sir Alexander MacEwen, vocal campaigner for Highland development, would have concurred with these sentiments, torn as he was between the desire for an improvement in his people's economic prospects and social wellbeing and the cultural regression that seemed to be necessary.

The discourse of development is 'loaded', and constructions of the 'rural' and the 'traditional' are complex issues which certainly merit further analysis in the case of the Scottish Highlands and Islands.[77] Though Irish scholars have demonstrated that the concepts of culture and modernity are deeply problematic, nevertheless the issue of how to maintain and support a culture, a 'way of life', within a 'whirling vortex of modernity' occupied the minds of a large number of Gaels and those interested in the Highlands and Islands throughout the middle decades of the twentieth century. The alacrity with which the Highlands developed in the years between 1939 and 1965 was the direct result of the exigencies of war, the reconstruction programme and subsequent government-inspired initiatives. This critical juncture in

Highland society resulted in a fundamental overhaul of the material conditions and standards of living in the region.

The effects on the culture of the Highlands and Islands were profound. For a significant number, a 'way of life' based on the land and the sea was no longer the norm. Even where crofting and fishing remained, working practices had altered considerably. During the period 1931 to 1961 there was a dramatic downturn in the fortunes of the Gaelic language, with a fall in the number of speakers from 136,135 to 80,978.[78] Gaelic monoglots were 'on the verge of extinction' by the 1960s and the language continued to recede to the north-western seaboard, while significant numbers of speakers resided in some cities of the central belt.[79] Many Gaelic activists were not surprised by the decline in the language noted in the census returns, with some predicting that it was in danger of dying out completely.[80] During this period of 1939–65, the divergence between Gaeldom and the Highlands becomes increasingly apparent. Though there were, and indeed are, many 'highlands' within the Highlands, the perception of the region as an ethnic zone was dominant within the literature. By the 1960s, however, this 'reading' was being challenged and the Highlands treated more as an administrative and planning zone. A corollary of that move towards deconstructing the Highlands as the *Gaidhealtachd* of Scotland was that Gaeldom's centre of gravity arguably moved to Glasgow. The changes to the cultural matrix of Gaeldom had a long gestation period, but the events of the 1940s and 1950s undoubtedly accelerated the trends already in place.

That said, by 1965, optimistic noises were again being heard in the Highlands and Islands. Many believed that a new chapter in the region was beginning as the opportunities afforded by further scientific advance – the 'white heat of technology' – could again be applied to a Highland 'way of life'. The 'threat' to its survival, almost always externalised, was now being used more purposefully. Cultural pessimism, though still present within Gaeldom, was being replaced by a hardened resolve to build on links to other European cultural minorities and extract greater concessions from the state. The emergence of a skilful Gaelic lobby by the latter part of the decade, and the more politicised nature of the debate, evident in the language being deployed, reflects Raymond Williams' argument that though each new era of technological change is held up to be a 'threat', at its 'base' there is a 'political and social position'.[81]

The failure, or unwillingness, to appreciate the fundamental transformation in the cultural foundations of Gaeldom during the middle decades of the twentieth century is understandable, as is the recurrent claim that the seeds of revival are being sown. Despite an upturn in the economic and social vitality of the region in subsequent decades, problems remain. The tensions apparent in the earlier period have taken on a different guise as resentment comes to replace the resignation of the recent past. Only by addressing these problems and their deep-seated nature will the Gaelic language and culture survive. As Gaeldom enters the 'post-modern' age, it is worth reflecting on the words of a noted Gaelic scholar and folklore collector, the late John Lorne Campbell.[82] Because we are so conditioned by the present, it is difficult to convey the sense of loss felt by those who witnessed the cultural transformation ushered in by the economic and social changes of the 1939 to 1965 period.

Twenty-odd years ago [c.1940] Barra was an island where, one felt, time had been standing still for generations. It is always extraordinarily difficult to convey the feeling and atmosphere of a community where oral tradition and the religious sense are still very much alive to people who have only known the atmosphere of the modern ephemeral, rapidly changing world of industrial civilisation. On the other hand there is a community of independent personalities where memories of men and events are often amazingly long (in the Gaelic-speaking Outer Hebrides they go back to Viking times a thousand years ago), and where there is an ever-present sense of the reality and existence of the other world where people live in a mental jumble of newspaper headlines and BBC news bulletins, forgetting yesterday's as they read or hear today's, worrying themselves constantly about far-away events which they cannot possibly control, where memories are so short that men often do not know the names of their grandparents, and where the only real world seems to be the everyday material one.[83]

14

Land, People and Identity: Popular Protest in the Scottish Highlands after 1918

Iain Robertson

The cultural significance of land to ordinary Highlanders was deeply embedded in the events of popular protest in the Scottish Highlands after 1918. Current explanations are too reliant on the view of the 'crofting community' as an undifferentiated mass, which obscures the varying and conflicting processes evident within protest. The analysis offered here questions the notion of a single regional class consciousness and the efficacy of the class model as a means to the comprehension and explanation of Highland protest.

Highland Protest: Causes and Events

Since the second half of the eighteenth century, the intention of Highland protest was consistently to resist the imposition, from the top of the social structure, of capitalistic change and to maintain and reassert traditional land holding and working practices. Change was also geographic, originating in the south and east, coming late to the north-west and the islands.[1]

The ideology and practice of the clan was a product of feudalism, kinship and locality and functioned to regulate access to the resources of subsistence, namely cultivable land. Land gave the clan meaning. The power, paternalism and patronage of the clan chiefs who allocated land were accompanied by a belief that clan members had permanent, hereditary rights of occupation.[2] During the seventeenth century, these obligations of reciprocity were loosened by the move from food to cash rents and by the increasing influence of Lowland models of landlord behaviour on the chiefs. Together with demographic pressures, this impelled the transformation of landholding, land working and tenurial practices.[3] By 1800, the aim of maximising estate income rather than retaining large populations on clan land resulted in the shift to sheep farming and the displacement of the bulk of the population from the interior to marginal land on the coast.

This first phase of clearance brought a new form of agricultural organisation: crofting. In Gaelic the term 'croft' means a small piece of arable land, and the 'crofter' was one who held a croft of land.[4] Crofts began small and got smaller under the impact of population growth and partible inheritance. Combined with the poor quality of the land, this ensured that crofting was at best subsistence agriculture, with any cash income being provided by part-time industrial by-employment.[5] The speed of this fundamental change enabled the tenantry to retain their traditional beliefs regarding landholding. It was these beliefs that would generate acts of popular protest.

The development of crofting created other social groups distinguished in terms of access to land. Crofters were the landholders. They would often share or sublet part of the croft to cottars, usually near-relatives. Squatters, again often relatives, would, by agreement with the rest of the township, settle on part of the common grazing. Though permeable and crossed by kinship ties, these divisions brought differences in aspiration crucial to the explanation of Highland protest.[6] Crofters wanted to enlarge existing crofts to make them viable, while cottars and squatters wanted crofts of their own.

As extensively documented by commentators such as Richards, Hunter, MacPhail and Withers[7], and despite the brutality and thoroughhnesss of the clearances of the 1830s and 1840s, protest did occur and was essentially reactive and aimed at the prevention of clearance. The protest of the 1880s was proactive, typically conducted by the descendants of those cleared, and aimed to recover land expropriated under the drive to make room for sheep and deer. The characteristic action was the land raid: the forced seizure of specific but often quite small parcels of land, cultivation of which by their forebears, the raiders believed, gave them rights of occupation and utilisation. The land raid, an attempt to reclaim supposed lost rights, was sustained into the 1890s but revived after the First World War.

Land and Highland Protest after 1918

The two principal government departments involved with the agitation for land were the Scottish Office and The Board of Agriculture for Scotland. From November 1918, these received an increasing volume of correspondence from the crofting tenantry expressing their frustrations and motives to protest. In January 1921, Donald Mackay wrote that he had been 'patiently waiting for long promised land which is now as far off as it was when the [Pentland] Bill was passed in 1911'. He blamed the political will of the Scottish Secretary. The letter threatened to seize land at Garrynahine Farm on Lewis.[8]

The need for land remained the dominant motive in post-1918 Highland protest. This desire, as at Newtonferry, North Uist, could be economic. In November 1920, Angus Macdonald and others wrote: 'Such employment as we can obtain is far from sufficient ... and we have nothing to look for employment and livelihood but the land.' They concluded with a threat to seize land. A month later the Scottish Office received a threat to raid Gress Farm, Lewis. The potential raiders claimed there were 'extensive farms capable of producing good crops ... given up to the rearing of sheep', while 'the landless are Suffering [sic] severely from want of milk, potatoes and vegetables and are housed under appalling conditions. Being merely squatters on other men's crofts they have no rights ... to cultivate any ground or erect proper dwellings.' In both cases, raid followed threat.[9]

Protest was triggered by economic downturn, notably the collapse of fishing, but the key motivation remained ideological. Land raiding was legitimated by the belief amongst the land-working population that they were reclaiming land that was rightfully theirs. In February 1919, a petition from North Tolsta, Lewis concluded: 'we shall also fight to get the land if steps are not taken to see us settled on the land of our ancestors which we consider is ours by right.' In 1920 a group from Valtos on Skye wrote: 'this meeting appeals to the Board of Agriculture to take steps to restore to the people the adjoining land of Scorrybreck from which our forefathers were cruelly evicted.' In 1934, the Board of Agriculture received a threat from the Park district of Lewis to seize land that still 'shows signs of our Forefathers [sic] labour'. The implications of this belief, what Smout calls 'land preference',[10] was admitted by the Board of Agriculture in 1926: 'Further sub-division is not in the true interests of the communities concerned [but] the applicants ... see patches of land scattered throughout the forests of a character that they would be quite content to have, and agitation for them will continue.'[11]

This belief, which Withers identified as a unifying 'regional or class consciousness', found its most convincing and coherent expression in the oral tradition.[12]

Popular Memory and Highland Protest

For the post-First World War land agitation, the oral tradition is strongest on the island of Raasay.[13] Agitation predated the war, but the principal act of protest came in May 1921. After earlier threats to raid, seven men from the adjoining island of Rona seized land at the south end of Raasay formerly attached to the townships of Fearns and Eyre. Immediately interdicted (served with a legal notice preventing further trespass), the raiders continued with their occupation, began cultivation and house building, and were arrested for breach of interdict in the late summer of 1921. After imprisonment, the raiders simply reoccupied the claimed ground. Purchase of the land under the terms of the 1919 Land Settlement (Scotland) Act by a reluctant Board of Agriculture followed (as it did in virtually every raid which followed this pattern) and raiders allocated holdings. Their success continued to inspire those less successful to threaten raids until at least 1929.[14]

According to popular memory the raiders' ancestors had been

removed from these areas of Fearns and Eyre. And they were desirous of getting back to what their ancestors had had. So there was some of the MacKays, the famous MacKay pipers were in Eyre and Fearns. And then there were MacLeods there, some of their ancestors were in Fearns and Eyre also.

Question: Is there any idea that they felt that the land belonged to them? That's right. They thought that they weren't taking anything out of the hands of the [Laird?] or anything else but what was their property, what they took out of their hands by removing them, their ancestors. They weren't a people that were careless, who didn't care whether they were doing good or not, whether they were breaking the law or not, that's not the kind of people they were at all. They were very desirous in keeping the law … although they had, for the benefit of their families, they had to break it in this sense just to take it at that time before it was allotted to them, but there was no time, there was no sign of it being allotted to them if they hadn't taken that step because some of them had been in the services during the fourteen–eighteen war.[15]

All informants are in accord. The raiders were descendants of those cleared from Fearns and Eyre, and this was crucial both to the decision to seize land and the location of the seized land.

Some of them from Rona decided to raid the south end and that included Eyre and Fearns as near as possible, I suppose convenient to where they had been originally evicted from.

Question: This was important to them was it? Oh yes, very important. And in fact my, I actually heard my father say that he says 'if you are going to raid why don't you raid a decent bit of ground more convenient' and 'no we don't want that bit of ground we want … where they came from'.[16]

A strong aspect of popular memory, which fails to appear in the written record, was the close communal links between raiders and the remainder of the crofting population. On the return of the Raasay men from jail, a local piper met them

at the pier when they came off the boat from Inverness and they went to the Raasay House where the Department representatives were, they were stationed there at that time and started to pipe round there and the crofters, the raiders following. Then they came to Fearns and that was the first thing I remember regarding them, seeing the piper behind our house on the road.[17]

These communal links were not confined to the locale from which those seizing land came.

> Once it became apparent that the Rona men had been arrested their friends in Braes [Skye] heard of it and they were very much in favour of the raiders and quite a few of these gallant men of Braes, some of them who were ex-servicemen, came across ... So they went to the pier. The raiders, they all went quietly to the pier and when they arrived there about four o'clock, that was the time the boat would be on the way to Portree, there was a crowd of Braes people and they were prepared, the Braes people were prepared to make a stand y'see to stop the police y'see, they said that what they would do if the police showed any resistance that they would put them off the pier but a och the raiders didn't like to make any noise or any stir, they said to them that they were prepared to go quietly. So they did.[18]

These unequivocal and widely shared popular memories are 'the core of the tradition' and thus have implications 'beyond the experience of this one event'.[19] And yet the claim to land as principal motive does not appear in the historical record. From the archive the motive appears to be the poor conditions on Rona.[20] Memory is not an infallible depository of facts but 'an active process of creation of meanings' which, together with the gaps and silences created, can be seen as 'an expression and representation of culture'.[21] Land raiding and the belief in rights to land were expressions and representations of culture, and while the oral tradition has no prior claims over the archival it does permit a more culturally based explanation. The discrepancy over principal motive can be understood if the act of protest is regarded as a text underlain by competing discourses. When writing to the authorities, the raiders expressed themselves in terms of the dominant political–economic discourse of the day and not oral tradition.

It is through the utilisation of the oral tradition, alongside archival evidence, that we may more fully trace the complex nexus of place, people, kinship and history, out of which emerged the belief within the crofting tenantry of rights to land. These attitudes to land and place were not uncontested. Acts of protest revealed lines of schism within crofting society between crofters and cottars, and which were generative of protest. There is evidence of conflict within protest, between groups within the land-working population and over access to land, as well as consensus.

Conflict within Protest

Divergence between crofters and cottars was based on their ambitions and beliefs regarding land and land rights. At Balranald, North Uist, crofters, basing their claims on the belief that the land in question was theirs by right, moved to exclude cottars from the raiding party in order to ensure that land was exclusively broken up for enlargements. In Lemreway, Lewis, crofters also acted to advance their own interests. The consequence was a threat to raid the farm of Orinsay by ten 'squatters' from the township who were being forced out by 'the Committee and Crofters [sic] of Lemreway'.[22] In some cases, the cottar or squatter being excluded from the croft was the crofter's brother, a weakening of kinship bonds which was often related to overcrowding. Neil MacRitchie, who claimed to be under threat of expulsion by his brother, shared a croft at Gravir with three other families plus three unmarried sisters.[23]

The division between crofter and cottar over access to land emerged as each recognised distinct and opposing interests. In March 1922 the Board of Agriculture was planning to divide up Nunton farm for enlargements to crofts. The response of the local cottars was that 'unless the Board ... faithfully promises us that they shall hold back their present scheme ... from the one and only farm in Benbecula available for settling landless ex-soldiers, and that without delay to settle us and any other ex-soldier or soldiers, as you shall think fit on the said Nunton farm we shall avail ourselves of the land'.

On Tiree, cottar applicants for disputed land wrote: 'When there was fighting to be done we had first chance to be shot; not your precious crofters. Likewise when there is land set out ... we shall have first share of it, or there will be trouble. In fact we shall have it all, with no crofter companions.'[24]

Tensions such as these could be long-lived. On the island of Barra, despite successive government attempts to facilitate access to land, protest had been virtually continuous since the 1880s. The determined nature of the 1917 raid was blamed by the Board of Agriculture's local official on population growth and the effects of war. At this time raiding was begun by cottar–fishermen from the east side of the island who wanted small plots for crofts and to continue fishing. Given the finite amount of land available this generated conflict. Crofter families from the west side of the Island, about 100 in number, many of whom were tenants of the Board of Agriculture, wanted the same land to extend their own crofts. They responded to the initial seizures by threatening reciprocal action. Tension between the two groups grew as the raided area expanded and house building began, and the Board of Agriculture felt compelled to purchase the farm. While negotiations were taking place, a near-anarchic situation developed, at times coming close to violence, as both groups began cultivating crops and allowing their cattle to roam across the farm. The official view was that purchase and subdivision of the farm would 'exhaust all lands available or suitable in Barra and bring to an end the Barra land problem'. This view proved incorrect. Such was the enduring feeling for land, the purchase failed to quell both land agitation and the accompanying tension between those who had land and those who did not.[25]

Sustained tension was also apparent on Bernera. Here the threats to raid first came from cottars from Tobson, who claimed: 'We are warned by this Township Crofters to clear off our stock.'[26] Subsequently the crofters wrote setting out their position. In the township there were as many squatter families (twenty) as there were crofter families.

That means heavy Congestion on poor Crofters. These squatters has [sic] got more stock than many of the crofters ... we can't put up with them any longer upon us. I am requested by the crofters to ask you to remove the squatters ... before the end of September ... or else we shall pay no rent or tax ... The state of our Township will be sent to the Prime Minister. Poor crofters' widows and orphans ruined to poverty by Ex-servicemen heaped upon them.[27]

In this instance, the priority given by the Board of Agriculture to settling ex-servicemen only added to the tension, which continued despite the creation of Crior township and the relocation of some cottars there. Crior had been set up without summer grazing. In 1930 the Bernera crofters withdrew permission previously given for access to such grazing, and Crior threatened a rent strike if they did not get rights to a moor or other holdings.[28]

This tension between crofters and cottars was most evident in areas of overcrowding but, given that crofters and cottars were often close relatives, the tension was also created by the feeling that past occupation and inheritance gave both an equally valid claim to the land. At Scorrybreck, claimants of land 'from which our forefathers were driven' objected 'to servicemen or others from outside' getting 'any part of this land from which our forefathers were cruelly evicted'. When the Board proposed to create crofts rather than enlargements, the Scorrybreck crofters wanted the Board 'to reconsider their scheme so that justice be done in restoring the lands of our ancestors to us' and threatened a raid if the Board did not.[29] The same arguments were used in disputes over Quendale links in Shetland.[30]

The complex conflicts generated by competing claimants, the belief in rights to land and the finite nature of the available land all operated on the west coast of Harris in 1925. Northton, Scaristaveg and Scaristavore ran conjointly from south to north. Northton was a crofting township established by the Congested Districts Board early in the twentieth century. Scaristaveg was a cleared crofting township and Scaristavore an existing township. With the compliance of the proprietor, Northton cattle had been able to range freely across the three townships, but the prospect of new holdings on Scaristaveg threatened this. Consequently, Northton crofters applied for enlargements. When these were not forthcoming they threatened a raid on Scaristaveg. These actions revealed tensions within Northton. In November 1925 cottars from the township threatened to raid the same land. They repeated this threat in March 1926, arguing that new holdings should have preference over enlargements. On the morning of the 25th they telegrammed the Board of Agriculture that they had carried out their threat. That afternoon a second telegram from the Northton crofters informed the Board that they had 'made these three raiders stop'. In early April the cottars wrote again, stating that they were still in possession and arguing that because they were without crofts they had 'a right to take possession of the land and ... the Northton crofters, who already have crofts, have no right to interfere'.[31]

It was not just the Northton township that was interested in Scaristaveg. Cottars from Scaristavore had seized land on the farm shortly before the Northton tension became apparent. This was prompted by the belief that the Scaristavore proprietor was working with the local crofters to ensure that the farm was broken up for enlargements. Once in possession, the cottars were given help to maintain and extend their occupation by the Northton crofters.[32] Events on the north-west coast of Harris add a further strand to the complex nexus of alliance and fracture evident in acts of protest and surrounding access to land. Neither written nor remembered records indicate why the Northton crofters acted as they did, but this was not a conflict over scarce resources – there was sufficient land to satisfy the demands of two different groups. The suspicion remains, therefore, that the Northton crofters were supporting the Scaristavore cottars as a means of suppressing the ambitions of their own cottars. The Northton crofters wanted a specific block of land and acted to maintain that claim. They did not take up an oppositional stance to cottars generically, just to those cottars who threatened their claim. But whatever the reason, conflict between crofters and cottars emerges very clearly here.

As first suggested by Withers,[33] conflicts within crofting society revealed by land protests suggest that to see such events as manifestations of class conflict solely between homogenous crofting communities and landowners can no longer be applied. Rather, evident fractures between crofters and cottars may well accord with Reed's view of nineteenth-century English rural protest. He believes[34] that there is a fluidity to class structure based on transient alliances and oppositions. If we follow Reed, what we may be witnessing within Highland protest are the normal and complex processes of negotiation, confrontation and fracture within a class. There is a problem with this analysis, however. It cannot take into account the fact that the actions taken by crofters and cottars look at times like the actions of separate and opposed classes. Nor does it explain how fracture and alliance can be visible at the same time and often in the same event. To admit all of this blurs and attenuates the boundaries between classes to such an extent that they become meaningless; a problem which renders it imperative to examine forces and alliances which run counter to the processes of class.

Non-Class Conflict

As with protest as a whole, the 1914–18 war had a significant impact on conflict around identities other than those of class. One conflict came from the temporary and enhanced powers taken by the government under the Defence of the Realm Act (1917). Deer forests were opened up to crofting agriculture, a move which brought government into conflict with local landowners, thereby adding to the multiple conflicts of interest.[35]

More directly, within crofting society war service was a major catalyst for disturbance. With demobilisation, the demand for land, given the economic conditions of the time, far exceeded the capabilities of agencies of government to meet it, causing great frustration and generating many acts of protest. This frustration was compounded by the belief that recruiting officers had failed to fulfil their promise that at the end of the war land would be made available for the landless in return for war service. In December 1920 the Board of Agriculture's local officer for North Uist reported his conversation with those who had seized land at Lochmaddy. They had 'joined up ... on account of the direct promise made ... by Captain Beaton, of land'. This promise was not fulfilled. The seizure of land thus followed. Similarly, in South Uist the Drimore raiders claimed that their raid was prompted by the lack of action on a 'definite and precise promise of land made to them ... when they joined up for service'. They believed that 'if they were in default of law and order' then 'so were others in not fulfilling the promise of land made'.[36] They believed, then, that local recruiting agents had a moral obligation to meet their promises. This sense of a moral obligation was shared by some local authorities and altered their attitude to the crofting tenantry and to the justice of claims to land. In July 1920 the Rev. Roderick MacGowan wrote from the Free Church manse, Kiltarlity, that the local ex-servicemen 'have a claim on me, because as Chairman of a Tribunal I sent a good many of them away to War, and following the government I promised them land on their return'. He later wrote supporting the threat to raid made by the ex-servicemen.[37]

Alongside the impact it had on protest more generally, the war also exacerbated tensions within crofting society and opened up the possibility of a new layer of identity. The 1919 Land Settlement Act gave preference to ex-servicemen when allocating land (virtually) regardless of their situation, with groups claiming land identifying themselves solely as ex-servicemen. This created the potential for conflict between those who went to war and those who did not. On Lewis in 1923 the tension between the two groups forced the Board of Agriculture to abandon the ex-service preference. At Galson the officer undertaking the creation of smallholdings advised that giving preference to ex-servicemen would exclude a large number of 'married men who are either squatters or living with relatives', the 'root cause' of land disturbance on the island. Consequently he offered holdings to all those from the area without land (forty-eight families), regardless of ex-service qualification. This did not prevent disturbance. Applicants divided into two groups on the basis of war service, and when the officer attempted to carry through his plan 'threats and accusations were indulged in by the two sections ... and general pandemonium ruled for several minutes'. The allocation was abandoned. Fearful of even greater disturbance, the Board of Agriculture nevertheless agreed to waive the war service preference and the allocation went through.[38]

Elsewhere the situation was still more complicated. At Drimore in South Uist, as I have already noted, raiders were objecting to their exclusion from a proposed scheme for enlargements. They were motivated by the failure to fulfil recruiting promises of land. They also expressed the war service divide, arguing that the scheme gave 'land to Old Age Pensioners ... while ex-servicemen who have fought and bled for 4 years are left in the cold'. There was the same tension around the division of Balephetrish farm on Tiree, where the civilian cottars threatened a raid against ex-service preference.[39] On Barra the situation was reversed. Civilians seized land and the Board legitimated their position, thereby creating resentment amongst ex-servicemen.[40]

These new tensions question the class-conflict model, and yet a note of caution is justified. South Uist, Tiree and Barra were all locations of crofter–cottar tensions. What may in fact be occurring here is the working out of these tensions in whatever form possible.

Popular Protest after 1918: A Diverse Experience

For Highland social protest after 1918 the significant registers of identity are class, kin and land. In all of these there were cross-cutting processes at work which indicate layers of conflict between crofters and cottars. Access to land was a particularly divisive issue within the crofting tenantry given the continued cultural significance of land to ordinary Highlanders as a central pillar of crofting society and mentality. Beliefs and claims surrounding access to land were inevitably conflictual given the finite nature of available land; competing demands reveal deeper rifts within crofting society. Nevertheless, this conflict between crofters and cottars must be set in the context of continued cooperation between the two groups in protest events.

Kin and place, which together form a significant part of the local structure of feeling, were crucial factors, as they were in Ireland.[41] While kinship was the means by which the belief in rights to land was sustained over time and space, kin and township links also proved divisive. It is precisely this complex web of cooperation and conflict, often taking the same form, that requires a more nuanced, reflexive and discursive explanation than that offered hitherto. The land-working population was not a homogenous class, and conflict in the post-1918 Highlands was not solely between crofting community and agencies of local and national government. It was both wider and more fine-grained than that. What we might need to recognise is an emergent tripartite, if not quadripartite, conflict of interests. The recognition is made more urgent by the integration of the oral tradition.

Written sources record only particular 'moments' of an incident.[42] Oral evidence often records different 'moments' from the same incident. One cannot replace the other, but taken together they can provide a more complete record of motivation. But a different understanding brings different problems.[43] The evidence presented here comes through the additional filter of language and from a particular negotiation between researcher, informants and the wider social structure. Utilisation of the oral tradition of particular places and events is part of a conscious effort to advance a thicker description of acts of popular protest. But, as Duncan has argued, this is inevitably a re-presentation, a disruption of the extra-textual field of representation. In this disruption some elements are highlighted and others deleted. 'As such, the world within the text is a partial truth, a transformation of the extra-textual world, rather than something wholly different from it.'[44]

Oral and written evidence not only offer partial truths but also the chance to uncover the discourses that comprise a protest event. This essay retains land as a central motif of Highland class relationships and protest, but notes the visibility of that motif at several different levels and registers. The gaining and maintaining of land was central to crofting identity. At least from the 1880s, one very important aspect of this gaining and maintaining was the land raid. The land raid was an act of protest against the earlier expropriation of worked land, and an expression of class and cultural conflict. As an expression of cultural conflict it was also an expression of an ideologically derived belief in a right to land. But as an expression of class conflict between the landowning and land-working classes it was also an expression of class conflict within the land-working classes. Protest over access to land could be, and was, all of this at once and the same time. Protest attests to a complex process that demands a complex explanation. The project in Highland historiography has been to put 'the crofter at the centre of his [sic] own history'.[45] It may be that what we should be restoring is not one history but many. And from that position of strength it would then be possible to move beyond the Highlands to encompass other areas where land was such a critical determinant.

PART FOUR

CONSUMER DISCIPLINES

15

The Business of Health: The Hydropathic Movement in Scotland and Ireland Compared, 1840–1914

Alastair Durie

Tourism was an industry in which both Scotland and Ireland became increasingly interested between 1840 and 1914. In Ireland this was prompted not just by the example of the growing popularity of Scotland as a tourist destination, but also by the absence, post-Famine, of reasonable alternatives for development in many areas. *The Times* in February 1864[1] spoke of the whole country as 'having beauties that many a travelled Englishman has not the least conception of. The time will come when the annual stream of tourists will lead the way, and when wealthy Englishmen … will seize the fairest spots and fix here their summer quarters. We see in the beauty of Ireland a surer heritage than in hidden mine or fertile soil.' Whereas Scotland became a major tourist area for visitors from England, America and the Continent, and attracted a growing flow of moneyed tourists, Ireland's progress was fitful, partly – or so conventional wisdom has it – because it lacked both a sufficient domestic base of people with time and income to spare or a significant urban working class. Domestic tourism was largely a preserve of the Anglo-Irish and rural elite. That may well have held back domestic tourism, but that leaves the question of the foreign contingent, much prized for their propensity to stay longer and spend more, who could and should have been drawn if Ireland had matched Scotland.

Ireland did have a range of natural attractions to the educated tourist to rival any in Scotland. The Giant's Causeway was on the European itinerary. There were ruins, castles and scenery in abundance, spas of considerable reputation, notably at Lisdoonvarna, and fishing a-plenty to tempt the sporting traveller. Unfortunately, it lacked grouse in sufficient quantity to act as a magnet to draw away some of the golden stream of English sportsmen who flowed north every August to the Scottish Highlands, to the great benefit of the railway companies, the landed estates and local suppliers. Like Scotland, a number of coastal seaside resorts – as at Portrush, Newcastle, Bray and Kilkee[2] – developed to cater for both the day excursionist and the summer settler, although, as with the resorts in Scotland, they could not compare with the mass resorts of England or even the Isle of Man. In one particular Ireland could offer more than mainland Britain, with its own rival to Lourdes at Knock. It may just have been coincidence that one of the key beneficiaries – a local coach hirer – of the flow of pilgrims to Knock was the father of one of the first to be cured.[3] Scotland's belated answer in the early 1920s was the sanctuary at Carfin.[4]

Access to Ireland and within Ireland, as was true for Scotland, was much improved by the coming of steamer services, coastal, Irish Sea and transatlantic. Many transatlantic passengers disembarked at Cork for two or three days of hectic sightseeing before crossing to the mainland. The railways promoted tourism through publicity and special fares. The much-criticised fares and service improved in the later nineteenth century.[5] The standard of accommodation and service in Ireland, at one time unquestionably dire, was much debated. By the later nineteenth century some authorities insisted that Ireland's hotels could rival any in Europe: 'the haphazard and slovenly way in which Irish hotels were managed has become almost a thing of the past';[6] Baddeley's *Thorough Guide* was much more guarded. 'The writer upon Irish hotels, who desires to be just to the landlord, and at the same time faithful to the traveller, is awkwardly placed.' While allowing that great advances had been made, Ward felt that unpunctuality and untidiness were besetting sins – 'so that breakfast was served two minutes before departure' and worst of all a 'carelessness about those sanitary arrangements which nowadays are seen as essential'.[7]

Tourism was, and remains, composed of many streams. There were those in quest of scenery and culture, others after sport and recreation, and more in search of health. For some, travel itself was a sufficient tonic, with a change of locality and air, a stay in a relaxing place with a good climate, and a beach or walks. Sea air and bathing was much favoured, primarily during the spring and summer. There were also inland health resorts, especially the spas, where people went to 'take the waters', not for an overnight miracle but a planned cure based on a calculated therapeutic regime under supervision of diet, exercise and water. By definition, the spa experience and culture, which lasted for weeks or even months, was for the better-off, those able to afford the costs of travel, accommodation and treatment. It was a highly profitable business for the communities concerned, especially as growing numbers of friends and relatives accompanied the patients, for whom a programme of excursions and entertainments had to be provided. Continental spas attracted the greatest number of British and Irish health seekers in the eighteenth and nineteenth centuries, although some English resorts enjoyed a high reputation. If Scottish visitors were to be found in number every season at Scarborough, Harrogate and other northern spas, there was usually a large Irish contingent at Bath. 'You need not tell me how full the town is of Irish at present,' commented one lady to her friend in January 1799.[8]

Neither Scotland nor Ireland was able to mount a sustained challenge in this key field of tourism. There were Scottish spa towns, notably Moffat (which had a long pedigree), Bridge of Allan and Strathpeffer, which despite its northerly location achieved quite a degree of success in late Victorian times; Ireland had quite a number,[9] of which Mallow, Lucan (near Dublin) and Lisdoonvarna ('the queen of spas in Ireland') were the best-known. 'Such extraordinary cures have been lately been effected that the Irish medical profession keeps on sending patient after patient to Lisdoonvarna' reported one observer in the early 1870s.[10] But for all the hopes invested in the development of these spa resorts for both domestic and foreign health seekers, they failed to rival the appeal of the Continent. *The Dublin Journal of Medical Science*[11] noted in 1842 that while Dr Granville had explored every spa in England, major and minor, for his comprehensive guide, he had not visited Ireland. This the reviewer regretted. 'National predilections do not so far mislead our judgement as to make us think that our spas are of such importance as to be likely to attract foreigners to our shores, but surely we possess many mineral waters which though now neglected are capable of conferring health on invalids who cannot afford to go north.' The same complaint was to be repeated time and time again, but to little effect.

The focus of this essay is a key element within health tourism, namely the hydropathic movement,[12] which got off to a good start in both Scotland and Ireland in the early 1840s. Whereas by the mid-1880s in Scotland the hydro–hotel had become a very distinct part of the physical, cultural and medical landscape, in Ireland there was little. St Ann's near Cork was the only establishment of any as against eighteen or nineteen in Scotland. Those at Peebles, Crieff and Moffat were large undertakings, capable of accommodating two or three hundred guests. One English visitor on a bicycle tour through Scotland in 1882 remarked that whereas in England any imposing detached building was pretty certain to be either a lunatic asylum or a workhouse, in the north it was likely to be a hydropathic establishment. Relative to England where Malvern and Matlock were key centres of hydropathy, Scotland was as over-represented in this type of health business as Ireland was under-represented. Why was there this difference in experience? Was it a failure of demand or supply, a function of inadequate promotion, or a more effective opposition by the medical establishment in Ireland?

Hydropathy got a equal start in both countries in the 1840s followed by slow development. The gap in provision widened in the later 1860s. There was no parallel in Ireland to the frenzy of investment in Scotland between1878 and1882, when ten came into operation, and another two at Oban and Morningside were abandoned when virtually complete. There were a few additions subsequently, and enlargements of existing businesses, but the picture thereafter until 1914 was one of steady state. The absence of corresponding progress in Ireland was remarkable. Dr Haughton had an establishment at Bray in the 1860s, and Dr W. Alfred Johnson, son of the pioneering hydropathic doctor at Malvern who had treated amongst others Florence Nightingale, ran a hydro at Delgany which was extensively advertised in the British press. There was talk in 1888 of a venture at Rostrevor, and a Hydropathic & Spa Hotel was opened at Lucan in September 1891,[13] but essentially the story of hydropathy in Ireland was the story of one centre, St Ann's near Cork. The practice which became quite common after about 1910 in Scotland, of hotels with pretensions calling themselves hydros even though they lacked any medical department or curative regime or equipment, had no equivalent in Ireland. In Scotland a hydro meant something; in Ireland it did not.

Hydropathy was but one of a number of alternative therapies – usually denounced by the medical profession as quackery – which were on offer during the first half of the nineteenth century, including herbalism, homeopathy, mesmerism and phrenology. What they had in common was that they rejected the tools of conventional medicine: leeching, bleeding and drugging. Harsh and demanding, orthodox medicine had a poor and unpleasant track record: indeed one authority suggested that many Victorians suffered from ill-health induced, not cured, by medical treatments. Not for hydropathy the use of drugs such as morphine or mercury. Instead, what was substituted was a series of repeated water treatments – usually cold – to flush, sweat or draw out foreign matter in the system to a programme, taking at a minimum several weeks and often longer, worked out by the resident doctor and closely supervised. What mattered was not the properties of the water (as was central at the spas) but its action. A system of baths, showers and sessions wrapped in a wet sheet was at the heart of hydropathy, complemented by a plain cuisine in which alcohol made no appearance, and a regime of exercise and conversation. The famed Scottish preacher Dr Donald Macleod spent some weeks in September 1865 at a Scottish hydro and reported:

> Here I am in a state of perpetual thaw: ceaseless moisture, always under a
> wet blanket, and constantly in danger of kicking the water bucket – water,
> water everywhere. I have been stewed like a goose, beat on like a drum,
> battered like a pancake, rubbed like corned beef, dried like a Finnan
> haddock, and wrapped up like a mummy in wet sheets and blankets. My
> belief is that I am in a lunatic asylum – but am too mad to be sure about it.[14]

Initially, enthusiasts claimed too much for hydropathy – a tendency with all alternative therapies. But hydropathy toned down its role as a panacea and focused on the treatment of specific skin and other complaints, as well as nervous conditions, thus becoming more respectable. By the later nineteenth century, mainstream medicine was incorporating elements of hydrotherapy into the orthodox curriculum. One contemporary surgeon (Dr Mayo) concluded in 1845 that the regime of relaxing baths, fresh air, controlled diet, rest and exercise could do no harm and that many invalids could be restored to health by the accessories of hydropathy alone, or by following the cold water cure with the omission of the cold water! In the context of a world in which many overate, overdrank and overdrugged themselves, the cold water cure was safe and effective in restoring health in certain ailments.[15]

It certainly attracted a clientele of some standing: Tennyson, Darwin – who rigged up a douche shower in his back garden – and Carlyle. Dickens sent his wife to Malvern to try a change of air and cold water.[16] Not all benefited, and some, having tried it, were hostile. Jane Welsh Carlyle, 'like a fool', allowed herself out of a scientific curiosity to try a 'packing' (being wrapped in a wet sheet, a key element for hydropathic patients) at Ben Rhydding. Her experience convinced her that Dr Macleod, the famed hydropathist in charge, was only a 'good-natured humbug'.[17] Macaulay was vehemently against it. He wrote from Malvern in August 1851 that he was not undergoing any of the quack cures for which Malvern is famous. 'I sit in no wet sheet. I subject the nape of my neck to no water spout. I dine at seven and do not absolutely reject the cider cup.' Most who tried pronounced themselves the better for the regime, and a fair proportion, like the Scottish philanthropist and temperance enthusiast John Hope, returned year after year.[18] Most years from 1848 until his death in 1893, Hope was to be found two or three times at one hydro or another. Moreover, he arranged for church workers and temperance agents in need of a rest to spend time there at his expense, an example followed by others. The woollen manufacturer, David Paton of Tilliecoultry, created a special fund to subsidise the stays of United Presbyterian ministers and missionaries at Crieff; Mary Slessor may have been a beneficiary. The Scottish hydros were for the respectable and were patronised, as one journalist said, 'by the unco good of all denominations'. When Robert Brown, later Provost of Paisley, stayed at Rothesay for some weeks early in 1862, he observed that the number of patients in residence was generally between twelve and twenty, and that several clergymen were amongst them. 'They were all very intelligent, indeed extra so, and we were most agreeable amongst ourselves.'[19] Agreeable, respectable and douce – these were the hallmarks of the Scottish hydros' clientele.

The hydropathic movement originated on the Continent. At Graffenberg in Silesia a medically unqualified 'peasant', Vincent Priessnitz, established a water cure institution in 1826, which in the following decade and a half attracted patients from all around Europe, who came either as patients or observers. Doctors like William Paterson were among the British visitors who, on their return, set up hydropathic premises of their own. Dr Patterson's small hydro at Rothesay was the first in Scotland. It opened in 1843.

An important role was played by amateur enthusiasts ('motivated solely by philanthropic feelings').[20] Captain Claridge was involved in the formation of a Hydropathic Society at London in March 1842 and undertook an extensive promotional lecture tour in Ireland and Scotland during the summer of 1843. On 23 June he was in Limerick, where his lectures – up to two hours in length – were well supported by members of the local Society of Friends; two weeks later he was in Cork before moving on to Wexford and Dublin. He was enthusiastically received, and hydropathic societies were founded to carry on the work in all of these places. The Hydropathic Society at Enniscorthy was active for several years. Claridge's final port of call in Ireland was Belfast, where there was a good turnout – 'a numerous and respectable audience', including many of the local medical profession – but less enthusiasm and no actual outcome.[21] Early in September he crossed to Scotland and held meetings in Glasgow, where the Lord Provost chaired a meeting; Glasgow, where a Hydropathic Society was founded, proved more fruitful ground than Edinburgh, where he rounded off his speaking tour in the early autumn.

The nature of the support and the reaction of the medical profession were key features of this tour. In the early phase of the movement, and for many of the pre-1914 years, temperance and hydropathy shared the same sponge. The platform parties at Claridge's meetings in Glasgow and the committee members of the hydropathic societies were alike full of those devoted to the temperance cause, both clerical and lay. Hydros in Scotland were almost, without exception,[22] resolutely temperance, with the prohibition on alcohol persisting until the turn of the century or indeed beyond: Crieff Hydro was probably the last hotel in Britain to remain 'dry'. Only in 1983, after long debate, was a table licence obtained.[23] Investors in the hydropathic movement included John Davie of Dunfermline, a retired merchant and founder member in 1830 of the first total abstinence society in Scotland. Like many hydropathists, Davie was a man of many causes: Chartism, Peace, Vegetarianism and Women's Suffrage, and he was against tobacco as much as alcohol. He provided much of the capital for the hydro at Melrose ('the Waverley').[24]

The connection was less apparent in Ireland, but it was there. Claridge's visit coincided with Father Mathew's temperance campaigning, then making a considerable impact. Mathew, 'the Apostle of Temperance', knew and approved of hydropathy. He was a patient at St Ann's during his last months, and he sent one of his temperance medals to Priessnitz in September 1845, praising him as one who had 'much promoted the cause of Total Abstinence'.[25] *The Limerick Reporter*[26] carried enthusiastic stanzas addressed to Captain Claridge after his visit there:

> Hail! Claridge, aqueous friend of man.
> Thou Patron and promoter
> Of promptest cure, and simplest plan
> Of cure – the cold-water cure.
> A grateful world turns its gaze –
> In admiration at you.
> And shares its mutual need of praise
> Twixt you and Father Mathew.

As elsewhere, the medical profession in Ireland was split. Some were hostile, root and branch, quick to plant and publicise cases in which the water cure had failed. Others urged caution. A few were sufficiently interested to take matters further. Two Cork physicians, Drs Barter and Wherland, set off for England to inspect hydropathic establishments prior to opening their own premises. Wherland, on his return, advertised that he had been to Bath, Cheltenham, Malvern, London, Stanstead Bury, Liverpool and Dublin and that: 'Having been kindly permitted to witness and to test the various kinds of applying water in the cure of disease on ladies and gentlemen of the first rank and respectability, he has no doubt as to its efficacy and safety when judiciously and properly applied under medical advice.'[27] His Cork Hydropathic opened within days of his return on 14 August 1843, offering a mixture of day-patient and residential care for the cure of chronic diseases, in particular nervous debility, gout and rheumatism. Barter was available for consultation three days a week in Cork while St Ann's was being equipped. Two other establishments in the vicinity were opened within the year at Youghal – primarily a baths establishment – and at Monkston, where Dr Curtin was the resident physician for many years.[28] Cork seemed well set to become a centre of hydropathic treatment. Dublin was also touched by the movement in 1843, and a Dr Feldman from Vienna set up an establishment at Blackrock, predictably called 'New Grafenberg'. Feldman's initial reception, thanks to his reputation as a seasoned practitioner, was favourable despite his high charges; his terms were about one-third higher than elsewhere. Blackrock was enlarged, but its popularity did not last.[29] It failed, and Feldman moved on, only to fail again in London. Another hydro was in operation at Delgany in the early 1860s, but little is known of it.[30] Early progress in Ireland was well ahead of that in Scotland, where to Dr Paterson's pioneering residential establishment on Rothesay was added only one new operation, that of Dr Rowland East at Kirn Pier near Dunoon, set up in 1846 after his return from Austria. There were, however, a number of hydropathic practitioners who could be consulted by those who wanted to try it for themselves at home. A distinctive feature of early hydropathy is Scotland was its link to an older therapeutic tradition, that of sea water and sea air. East, for instance, emphasised that: 'Hitherto the Hydropathic Establishments, both of Great Britain and the Continent have been almost exclusively confined to localities very far inland. Mr East has selected Dunoon in order that a new element can be introduced as a collateral agent – the sea air – and he feels convinced of the attendant advantage.'[31]

If the two countries differed little in the initial reception and business institutionalisation of hydropathy, a widening gap began to develop from the mid-1860s. Neither added many establishments in the 1850s. In Scotland, Aberdeen became an important outpost of the movement; Dunoon closed when Rowland East deserted medicine for the Anglican ministry, and Robert Wylie's Arvullin lasted less than a year. Archibald Hunter, an upholster with no medical training, opened Gilmorehill in the West End of Glasgow in 1856. None of these rivalled the scale of English ventures at Ben Rhydding, Matlock or Malvern. In Ireland there was little progress. Barter, the most prominent figure, identified with the promotion of Turkish baths[32] as a central therapeutic feature to any hydro and a facility to be made more generally available. He had his own baths built at St Ann's and was active in the formation of baths companies at Cork, Dublin, Limerick and London. Amongst his patients was Edward Haughton, a Quaker, who was sent as a sickly youth to St Ann's and, after qualifying in medicine at Edinburgh, became an enthusiastic advocate of his mentor's baths system.

Little is known about the Irish hydro clientele, but it is known that the tariffs were much the same as at hydros in Britain and, therefore, at a level that restricted access to the reasonably well-off. Barter spoke in 1856 of physicians and gentry being amongst those who had stayed at St Ann's and that 'noble personages resort to the establishment for months'.[33] How many and from where is impossible to determine. Unlike the leading English and Scottish resorts, lists of visitors are not available for Ireland. Nor is there census enumeration data for Ireland of the calibre of that for Scotland after 1851. Analysis of these sources for Forres in the mid-1860s and for Shandon in the early 1880s revealed a catchment area which was more than local or regional. About a quarter of Shandon's visitors came from England or from further afield. Curtin's hydro at Monkston had some English guests, but there were no data to support any systematic assessment. St Ann's, having been a small house with a series of cottage annexes, was more than doubled in capacity by the addition in the mid-1850s of twenty-two bedrooms so that it could accommodate eighty to ninety people. Barter claimed that in the first three years of its operation, when the residential capacity was much smaller, he had treated over 600 people,[34] but some may have been outpatients.

Even in the early days, not all of those staying at the hydros were patients. There were relatives, servants, companions and even children at Barter's, and therefore a need to provide conversation, recreation and amusement. The first hydros were places of cure, but the second generation of Scottish hydros from the mid-1860s onwards were increasingly catering not just for patients but for visitors looking for good company, reasonable cuisine and entertainment, people who had become 'fagged with labour and worry, and stand in good need of holiday rest'.[35] Inebriates, and those with contagious or socially unpleasant afflictions, were turned away. By the later nineteenth century the resident doctor was no longer the central figure. Instead the key person was the house entertainer (usually female), and the baths were less important than the golf course, bowling green or billiards table. This change in emphasis and function was evident to observers.

> A tolerably extensive and varied experience of Scottish hydropathics has led me to the conclusion that they are frequented only to a limited extent by invalids of the class for which they were primarily intended. At all of them one does meet with cadaverous and sallow faced individuals who attend strictly to regim ... But the number of those who are impelled by quite different motives, the liking for comparatively cheap and on the whole comfortable living in the midst of picturesque scenery, and by the attractions of a free and easy and quasi-refined society is certainly very much larger.[36]

One of the most significant functions of a hydro, *The Times* added, was its role as a marriage market, much to be recommended to those who had returned from the colonies in search of a helpmeet. Or, as another contemporary source put it, 'marriages may be made in heaven but they are arranged in Hydropathic Institutions.'[37]

The widening of function served to promote the increasing numbers of hydropathic limited companies being floated in the 1870s. In Scotland it became a mania, with over £500,000 subscribed within a relatively short time. The prospectus of the Callander Hydropathic Company, which appeared in the Scottish press in April 1878, stressed that the purpose was to erect a hydropathic establishment which would combine the advantages of a sanatorium with additional accommodation for the large numbers of tourists to the Trossachs who 'regularly frequent this favourite resort'.[38] The original company went into liquidation within a few years, as did many new ventures south and north of the Border, the result of a combination of over-expansion in the market, underestimation of the costs of construction for these large purpose-built hotels, a failure to allow for the lack of off-season trade, and difficult economic conditions in the wake of the collapse of the City of Glasgow Bank in 1878. But the sector was essentially sound, and the great majority found new owners, albeit at bargain basement prices. Only two new hydros were to be built in Scotland after 1882. Several were rebuilt after major fires, which suggests that they remained viable financial prospects. Dividend levels were very healthy from 1890 onwards. Crieff never paid less than an annual dividend of 9 per cent, and Forres did even better.

There was no parallel in Ireland to this remarkable expansion in Scotland. St Ann's, a 'fairy colony'[39] as one visitor called it, did soldier on after the death of Barter in 1871. Ownership continued with the family, but the medical side was devolved to the management of a series of residential physicians until a medically qualified grandson, Dr Richard Barter, came on the scene in 1914. Its residential and other facilities were expanded several times, thanks in part to its conversion to a limited company. By 1886, it could accommodate some 200 visitors, the medium-size range for such hotels. It had a croquet lawn, fishing nearby and, for the robust, hunting to hounds in the winter. It had close links with two new golf courses laid out in the vicinity just after 1900. The design of the Muskerry course was the work of the physician in residence at St Ann's, Dr Ainslee Hudson.[40] Visitors staying at the hydro were given generous discounts on weekly tickets. Local businesses and services benefited. The Muskerry Tramway carried a consid-erable amount of first-class traffic to and from the Hydro. St Ann's matched the business performance of its Scottish counterparts. The 1901 census returns[41] showed some seventy-five guests in residence drawn from the middle and professional classes of Ireland: landowner, engineer, architect, master manufacturer and journalist were among the guests' occupations. Over half were Catholic, but appreciable numbers were Church of Ireland and Presbyterian. St Ann's was able to tap into a growing market at the turn of the century, which raises the question of why other institutions could not follow suit. There was some demand: the hydros of Scotland, England and even the Isle of Man[42] benefited from Irish patronage. Why could Irish establishments not retain at home some of these visitors as well as draw in guests from Britain and the wider world? Was it a weakness in domestic demand? Scottish hydros relied on a steady, loyal middle-class and profes-sional clientele: respectable and religious, happy – if young and active – to spend hours in the baths or outside on the tennis courts or golf course, to join in charades, entertainments or even hymn singing, or – if older – just to enjoy 'the endless small talk' of ministers, ailments and sudden deaths, which delighted some and appalled others. Dickson McCunn, John Buchan's retired Glasgow grocer, 'rancorously hated hydropathics having once spent a black week under the roof of one in his wife's company',[43] but he was more than happy for his wife and others of her ilk to enjoy a holiday there, providing that he was not required to go. Nothing unseemly would occur. Unaccompanied wives, maiden aunts and miscellaneous relations could all be assured of a place at any time of the year. Christmas and Easter, when special programmes were mounted, tended to attract a younger and more boisterous set.

Another problem in Ireland may have been a shortage of investment capital. Scots were prepared to invest – not always wisely – in the many hydropathic ventures in Scotland of the 1860s and 1870s. Some were drawn from the ranks of the very rich – the Clarks and the Coats of Paisley – while others were lawyers, ministers, doctors, accountants and the like, but there were also people of lesser standing. The list of subscribers in 1881 to the Oban Hills venture, which came to nothing, included a railway guard, a groom and a police constable. Scottish capital was prepared to forage outwith Scotland. Andrew Philp, a temperance hotelier with whom Thomas Cook did considerable business, headed a Scottish syndicate which bought Conishead Priory near Barrow in the late 1870s for conversion into a hydro; Philp's son, William Cornfold, was the first resident doctor. Philp Senior added Glenburn and Dunblane hydros, as well as a temperance hotel at Harrogate, to his portfolio. Neither he nor any others looked to any development in Ireland. If anything, the tide was the other way. The largest single investor by some margin in the Deeside Hydropathic Company in 1913 was a Belfast shipbuilder, Charles Allen.

In the hydropathic sector Ireland lagged far behind Scotland, and it remains an unresolved question why nothing of the kind was attempted at either Lisdoonvarna or Killarney, both of which had potential. The First World War saw quite a number of establishments taken over as military hospitals, including Craiglockhart and Peebles, and the hydro movement began to lose ground. A number shut down or were converted to other uses. St Ann's continued, 'deserving of mention' as T.D. Luke noted in his magisterial survey of *The Spas and Health Resorts of the British Isles*, published in 1919. His judgement was that Irish health resorts had been little developed and that 'in the present disturbed state of politics it is to be feared it will remain so for some time to come'. This was an area of health tourism – health through leisure and pleasure rather than by cure – from which Scotland had benefited, and Ireland would have been advantaged if it had.[44]

16

Philosophy and the Individual in Commercial Society: Towards an Interpretation of David Hume's Treatise of Human Nature, Books I and II[1]

Christopher J. Finlay

Although usually interpreted in terms of the intellectual, literary and philosophical concerns of its author, *A Treatise of Human Nature* by David Hume is a text which needs to be understood in part as a response to changing economic and social conditions in Scotland and England in the 1730s, especially those associated with consumerism.[2] This essay suggests that the arguments in Books I and II of the *Treatise* constitute a philosophical response to the practical experience of a society in the process of commercialisation and that Hume's theory incorporates intellectual and psychological features related to the purchase and consumption of goods.

The interpretation is presented in four parts. The first outlines the methodological framework for the study of human nature that Hume set out, particularly in the introduction to the *Treatise*. The second part analyses Hume's theory of the passions, particularly the 'indirect' passions, articulated in Book II of the *Treatise* and attempts a reconstruction of the individual mentality implied by Hume's theory. In the third part, the social contexts through which Hume is known to have moved during the years preceding his composition of the *Treatise* are examined, with particular attention to evidence for the existence of mentalities of the kind characterised by Hume in his theory of the passions. The fourth part shows how the theory of the understanding presented in Book I of the *Treatise* completes the construction of the human individual analysed in the second part.

Hume's Empirical Methods: The Observation of Common Life

As the subtitle of the *Treatise* – 'Being an attempt to introduce the experimental Method of reasoning into moral subjects' – suggests, Hume's methodology for the investigation of human nature was modelled on the experimental natural philosophy that emerged in the seventeenth century. The empirical bias of Hume's method derived from Baconian and Newtonian emphasis on the need for observation.[3] As a method for the study of human nature in philosophy, however, this presented problems. In natural philosophy as practised by the investigators of non-human nature, the production of controlled and artificially contrived experiences through experiment provided empirical information. In the investigation of human nature this was problematic. Hume contrasted the methodological requirements of the two domains of philosophy, writing that with non-human nature, 'when I am at a loss to know the effects of one body upon another in any situation, I need only put them in that situation, and observe what results from it.' With human nature, if he '[endeavoured] to clear up after the same manner any doubt ... by placing myself in the same case with that which I consider ... tis evident this reflection and premeditation would so disturb the operation of my natural principles, as must render it impossible to form any just conclusion from the phaenomenon'. As a philosopher of human nature, Hume was not in a position to manipulate his subjects or to control their environments in the way that a member of the Royal Society could with his.[4] Solving the problem of how to find an 'experimental' method suitable to moral philosophy (the basis of which, for Hume, was the study of human nature) therefore pushed the focus of Hume's philosophy towards a more intimate engagement with common life. He stated that 'we must therefore glean up our experiments in this science from a cautious observation of human life, and take them as they appear in the common course of the world, by men's behaviour in company, in affairs, and in their pleasures'.[5] Hume's project to imitate the methods of natural science as far as possible therefore compelled him to observe and explain the occupations and practices of men as he found them in the society surrounding him.[6]

Hume's Theory of the Passions

On the basis of the kind of observations described in the introduction to the *Treatise*, Hume presented an analysis of human individuals which laid out both their intellectual and emotional–psychological characteristics (in Books I and II respectively). Hume notoriously regarded the human propensities and capacities so described as largely immutable features of human nature and hence outside any given historical conditions.[7] Closer examination of the mentality described in his analysis of the passions shows that the individuals observed by Hume gave his theory a much more historically specific shape, albeit one presented as a universal pattern.

Of the two volumes of the *Treatise* published in 1739, the first was entitled *Of the Understanding* and the second *Of the Passions*. It is in the latter book particularly that evidence is to be found for the kinds of phenomena that Hume observed and sought to understand as the 'experimental' philosopher of human nature. By examining and characterising the psychological construction of Hume's individual presented in Book II, it is possible to establish the kinds of phenomena with which his philosophical theory was meant to engage.

Individuals, according to Hume's theory, were exceedingly anxious about their social status. At the centre of their self-awareness stood the feeling of pride or, in adversity, the feeling of humility.[8] Pride compensated for the inability of the human understanding to construct a consistent and permanent idea of the self;[9] the sense of the self relied instead on the individual's awareness of how others regarded him, and on the pleasurable or displeasurable feelings which this provoked. The regard – or in Hume's terminology, the love or hatred, esteem or contempt – in which an individual was held by others depended on the extent to which he could display ownership of certain kinds of objects. The objects which caused both pride in one's self and esteem in the spectator were typified by property and riches,[10] but also extended through a wide range of personal attributes and social and familial connections associated with the possessor in an analogous way to the relation of property. The key feature of objects which caused pride and esteem – in short, the sense of social status – is that they possessed the power to cause pleasure. Clothes, houses, books, 'a fine scritoire',[11] did so directly by providing utilities for the person who possessed them; riches provided pleasure less directly, by representing or measuring the power to acquire objects which themselves embodied the power to cause pleasure. Further requirements for the desirability of such objects were that they could be owned or used conspicuously, as well as exclusively, and that such objects were possessed by as few other individuals as possible.

Hume characterised his 'system' for explaining the indirect passions using the formulation 'that all agreeable objects, related to ourselves, by an association of ideas and of impressions, produce pride, and disagreeable ones, humility'.[12] In section II.1.vi Hume lists the further requirements for the desirability of objects as *limitations* of this *system*. What the list amounts to is a series of observations on the manner in which individuals develop the pride which they feel through their close, proprietorial, and conspicuous relationship with certain objects or qualities.

The first limitation is the requirement of a close relation between the object and the self who is the object of pride. As Hume observes, 'tis only the master of the feast, who, beside the same joy [as his guests], has the additional passion of self-applause and vanity'.[13] The guests will experience joy but not the same pride as the host, despite the close proximity to themselves of the objects that cause this pride. The first limitation which Hume therefore places on his initial system – 'that every thing related to us, which produces pleasure or pain, produces likewise pride or humility' – is that 'there is not only a relation requir'd, but a close one, and a closer than is requir'd to joy'.[14] The close relation by which the host is associated with the feast is proprietorship.

The second limitation is that the object must be peculiar to ourselves as possessors, 'or at least common to us with a few persons'. Hume observes that people 'likewise judge of objects more from comparison than from their real and intrinsic merit; and where we cannot by some contrast enhance their value, we are apt to overlook even what is essentially good in them'.[15] Objects owned or otherwise closely associated with the self enhance the possessor's pride to the extent that they distinguish him from those who possess no such thing. In this sense, the motivation which pride gives is emulative. Pride is strongest when the person feeling this passion finds himself a member of an exclusive proprietorial group.

The third limitation stipulates that the possessive relationship with the cause of pride be a conspicuous one. Hume states that it is necessary that 'the pleasant or painful object be very discernible and obvious, and that not only to ourselves, but to others also'.[16] Membership of a small group of owners must be clearly visible to those outside the group if it is adequately to distinguish its members from those who do not possess its attributes or objects. The fourth and the fifth limitations relate closely to an issue discussed in Hume's treatment of the will and the understanding.[17] Hume observes that in society, individuals engage their intellects in evaluating the motives and powers of the other people whom they encounter. Due to the inconstancy of human volition, he argues, it is necessary to use general rules in order to categorise individuals into classes of person. The attributes of a person are generalised on the basis of their constant repetition into a notion of character, and the general attributes or habits of a number of people may be understood under a broader grouping defined by its status or its typical activities. The fourth limitation requires, therefore, that there be some degree of constancy in the relation between the cause of pride and its possessor. Hume observes that 'what is casual and inconstant gives but little joy, and less pride'.[18] The final limitation presents the wider importance of developing general rules through which the status of possessors is evaluated: 'general rules,' Hume writes, 'have a great influence upon pride and humility, as well as on all the other passions. Hence we form a notion of different ranks of men, suitable to the power or riches they are possest of.'[19]

Thus, Hume's anatomical portrait of human nature presents man as naturally emulative. This is strongly evident where he writes that

> [it] is evident we must receive a greater or less satisfaction or uneasiness from reflecting on our own condition and circumstances, in proportion as they appear more or less fortunate or unhappy, in proportion to the degrees of riches, and power, and merit, and reputation, which we think ourselves possess of. Now as we seldom judge of objects from their intrinsic value, but form our notions of them from a comparison with other objects; it follows, that according as we observe a greater or less share of happiness or misery in others, we must make an estimate of our own, and feel a consequent pain or pleasure. The misery of another gives us a more lively idea of our happiness, and his happiness of our misery. The former, therefore, produces delight; and the latter uneasiness.[20]

Social status and mobility are managed using competitive display, and the purpose of engaging in such competition is to establish visible superiority over rivals in terms of social status.

Hume's analysis, however, suggested that such instincts for social rivalry occurred within a limited arena. According to Hume, individuals compete with those who are sufficiently similar to themselves to merit comparison, as well as distant enough to be beyond the reach of familial affections. Beggars do not emulate kings, and kings feel no need to put on a show to prove themselves above beggars. The sense of rivalry is usually played out between individuals who respect the same kinds of goods, typically things such as tasteful clothing and furnishing and personal attributes relating to education, taste and refinement. Rivals tend to have the same sorts of quantities of socially significant property.

> [It] is worthy of observation concerning that envy, which arises from the superiority of others, that 'tis not the great disproportion betwixt ourself and another, which produces it; but on the contrary, our proximity. A common soldier bears no such envy to his general as to his sergeant or corporal; nor does an eminent writer meet with so great jealousy in common hackney scriblers, as in authors, that more nearly approach him. It may, indeed, be thought, that the greater the disproportion is, the great must be the uneasiness from the comparison. But we may consider on the other hand, that the great disproportion cuts off the relation, and either keeps us from comparing ourselves with what is remote from us, or diminishes the effects of the comparison.[21]

This implies that the observations on which this theory was intended to explain involved the behaviour of members of the same class emulating one another, or members of different classes – for example, landed and commercial – who were sufficiently close in terms of their cultural attributes to feel mutual rivalry.

The Source of Hume's Observations

This characterisation of the psychology and intellectual capacities of Hume's individual can now be placed in the contexts in which Hume observed his contemporaries during the 1730s.

First of all, it is useful to highlight Hume's own social background. Hume's father, who died when David was two, was a lawyer practising in Edinburgh, and a landowner.[22] As the second son, David Hume was left without an estate and his patrimony was too limited to afford a genteel style of life without finding what he called some further 'settlement'.[23] He had to make his way among the middle, professional and merchant classes. The pressure to do so became especially acute in 1734. Suffering from a period of ill health partly as a result of this, Hume went to Bristol that year to work with a firm of sugar merchants. He left the firm later in the year on account of a disagreement with his employer.

Hume's connections were reasonably high on the social ladder, with Henry Home, later Lord Kames, helping him to establish links in London in 1738.[24] His financial situation left him without the independence needed for the status associated with landed property, and the loss of his job in Bristol after only a few months marked a failure to establish himself as a member of the merchant middle class. Hume travelled to France after leaving the firm of merchants in Bristol. In 1735 he gave up on genteel society, fleeing from the expenses of Rheims to the cheaper social environment at La Fleche to fulfil his immediate literary–philosophical ambitions while saving himself excessive expense. Hume, therefore, came from a gentry background, found himself having to pursue a middle-class mercantile career at which he failed, and still wished to retain genteel status. He had therefore an anomalous relationship with both the gentry *and* the middle class, being neither a complete outsider nor an insider in relation to both. In addition, he was a Scot who felt himself to be an outsider within the English (and then the French) culture in which he found himself.[25] As a consequence of these various shifts in geographical, social and cultural context, Hume was in a position to observe and contrast a wide range of environments.

The features of consumerism visible in the social contexts encountered by Hume in the 1730s resembled the context implied by his anatomy of human nature. The consumption of non-subsistence goods increased in Britain across a wide range of social ranks throughout the eighteenth century. Growing numbers of people had sufficient cash in excess of subsistence needs, permitting the use of terms like 'rising expectations' and the more specific 'social emulation' to characterise English society quite widely in the eighteenth century.[26] Consumer society of one kind or another may be presupposed in a wide range of contexts within Britain. Despite periods of rising food prices and the existence of large groups of poor, there was a sufficient increase in prosperity among the middle-income groups and a rise in the numbers who could afford non-subsistence goods in the population as a whole to maintain demand for manufactured goods throughout the century. John Rule also agrees with other scholars that the 'bottom line income above which recipients can be presumed to have enjoyed at least the modicum of comfort above subsistence and simple "decency" ... need not be drawn very high'.[27]

There was a widely visible increase in the pursuit of fashionable trends, at least in the consumption of higher classes of goods, those which we may loosely term 'luxuries' as opposed to 'necessities' or 'decencies'. In his study of the history of fashion, Christopher Breward found that

> the impact of fashionable trends in all areas of production and consumption, from architecture through interior decoration, household furnishings, tableware, food, gardening, print and literature, music, theatre, [and] textiles, underwent something of a metamorphosis. Through innovations in manufacturing techniques, supply structures and retail strategies, a degree of luxury, comfort and fashionability was made available to a market no longer restricted to either the elite or the metropolitan.

He describes 'a group of consumers, who although not new, formed the most distinctive segment of a society increasingly identified, not through the sartorial trappings of hierarchies based on status at birth, but on commercial acumen and material possessions which represented worldly success'.[28]

Although post-Union economic development remained slow in Scotland until the 1750s, the propertied classes did manifest changes in their consumer behaviour, smaller in scale and milder in drama than those in London, Bristol and other prosperous English towns. In his *History of the Scottish People*, Smout refers to a 'revolution in manners' among the Scottish Lowland landowners.[29] There was already evidence of this slow spread of consumer culture in Scotland in the 1720s and 1730s, in the form of changes in the design of houses, furniture, and culinary habits of the gentry throughout the eighteenth century, and Smout argues that one can see 'the early stages of the revolution in the way of life of the eighteenth century lairds which was to be far-reaching in itself and to have far-reaching consequences for other people'.[30] The reasons for this change in manners among Lowland Scots landowners are not entirely to be found in increased rents available for expenditure. A further cultural element was involved in the formation of new manners for the Scots. Smout states: 'Obviously, it could not have been sustained (at least in its purely material aspects) unless the gentry as a whole had enjoyed larger real incomes in the late eighteenth century than they did at the beginning.' But rents did not rise significantly until decades after 1720, so it is also necessary to bear in mind 'the desire to copy England'. The root of this desire was two-fold.

> Highly educated Scots felt themselves backward, boorish and uncouth in the company of the wealthier squirearchy of England with whom they came increasingly in contact. Few landed Scots doubted that England began with a more polite and more desirable civilisation than their own, or that it was a duty of patriotism to match and even to outshine the southerners' model whether it was in teacups, in good tone or … in farming.

There emerged a need in the wake of the Union for propertied Scots to imitate and emulate English culture. On the other hand, there were also more immediate models for social and cultural emulation. Smout refers to

> the challenge and the influence of the newcomers to the landed classes: colonial adventurers, war profiteers and merchants who not only had a wide experience of the polite world abroad but also capital (accumulated from other sources than rents) which they could splash in ostentatious display. It was painful for an older laird to see this without making at least an effort to match it.[31]

Hume's portrayal of human individuals as consumers, deeply concerned with social status, seems to reflect this kind of awareness in Scotland that commercial success of the kind seen in England was something to imitate.

Hume had immersed himself, albeit briefly, in the more commercially advanced context of Bristol, and it seems likely that some of his observations were made at this time. Writing in the 1720s, Daniel Defoe said of Bristol that it was 'the greatest, the richest, and the best Port of Trade in Great Britain, London only excepted'.[32] Marcy describes Bristol as 'first and foremost a city of trade and commerce', whose predominance in this activity 'drew many visitors to the city'.[33] It was to this environment that Hume arrived in 1734 with the intention of making his fortune and pursuing a new kind of career.

Peter Borsay's work on the impact of changing and widening commercial practices on the landscapes and cultures of English towns, including Bristol, during the eighteenth century establishes what he called 'an English urban renaissance'.[34] Concentrating on the creation of new urban spaces within which the culture and social display associated particularly with the development of the commercial middle class could take place, he found that the early part of the eighteenth century was somewhat more dynamic than it was given credit for by economic and social histories still perplexed by the origins of the British industrial revolution. Leisure and luxury affected the development of provincial towns during the late seventeenth and the eighteenth centuries.

A key feature that emerged during the first half of the eighteenth century was the appearance of 'leisure facilities' serving the needs and desires of upper and middling social groups. A primary example is the town assembly, which became a common feature of the provincial town from the end of the seventeenth century onwards.[35] The main function of such leisure facilities was 'personal display'. The creation of walks on which people could promenade in their best apparel related such facilities to both consumption and the symbolic value of conspicuous possession in the town. The increasing prominence of sporting activities provided further opportunities, and the arts became a focal point for tasteful consumption and a further arena within which one could be seen to enjoy, and be able to afford, certain kinds of goods. By 1760 provincial theatres were established as regular features of provincial towns as well as the capital, and Bristol itself had its own first permanent establishment from 1729 onwards.[36]

For Borsay, the use of surplus wealth in this way marked 'a different style of living', which he characterises as part of the 'world of social competition'. The key feature of this new world was 'the pursuit of status' marked by the increase in those in possession of surplus wealth. 'Such a growth unquestionably took place during [this period]. The town was to play a crucial role in servicing the increasing demand for status, and absorbing the pressures being laid upon the social structure.'[37]

The town provided 'the instruments of battle' required for a new incidence of individualistic social competition over status. In the new arena, Borsay observes that

> physical and mental possessions can be used as a way of transforming wealth into social status. In this sense the new sophisticated urban economy can be seen as a munitions factory in the pursuit of status. When the milliners, drapers, mercers, jewellers, and so forth, dispensed their luxury products, it is hard to imagine their customers were unaware of the uses to which they could put their purchases. [38]

The town provided the resources and necessary *loci* through which the cultural and practical information required for new social roles was circulated. This was achieved in theatres, concerts, coffee houses and other public spaces, where knowledge and insight were exchanged in Addisonian fashion in order to equip the individual with the means to cultivate 'an educated and genteel mind'. The guidelines for such transactions and practices were dictated by fashion, establishing criteria concerning 'the status value of any particular object ... they also allowed, because of fashion's essentially fluid nature, these guidelines to be changed at a frequency commensurate with the level of demand for status at any given time or place'.[39] John Smail's analysis of middle-class culture, focusing on the case of Halifax, clarifies further the picture of the kind of social scene in which Hume found himself in 1734. Changes occurred in the kind of goods to which expenditure was directed among merchants, with a significant proportion of money being 'siphoned off to support a more luxurious lifestyle'. Consumers typically had their eyes set on the capital in order to identify the fashionable models which were to be imitated, or emulated, although they could be highly selective in their choices.[40]

The meanings which typically accrued to the consumption of goods purchased in imitation of centres outside the locality were strongly associated with the enhancement of visible status. The possession and consumption of certain kinds of goods could enhance the self-awareness of the social group and help to distinguish them from their social inferiors. As Smail observes, 'the use of certain services and the possession of certain goods helped to define the members of an increasingly distinct group' and 'implicit in the very genesis of the eighteenth century consumer culture was the attempt by middling people to demonstrate their social worth by purchasing goods associated with a higher status.'[41] The middle ranks should not be regarded as simply trying to emulate their social betters, although even if they did not buy consumer goods in order to become aristocrats, Smail says they did purchase 'in part with the intent of establishing their social credentials'.[42] Geoffrey Holmes' analysis of the professions[43] shows that these contributed a high degree of spending power, as well as a high social profile, to the strength of the middle class as a whole. The conspicuous consumption of goods was used to identify members of a group whose social status was grounded in economic factors, and it helped not only to mark their rising self-esteem as a group, but also to mark the exclusion of non-members who were associated with lower social orders.

This middle-class group was typical of the kind of society into which Hume entered when he headed for England in 1734 to try out the new scene of life that he associated with merchant business. His failure to gain the status and independence associated with elder sons from his own social background forced Hume, in the 1730s, to try the kinds of economic and professional activities in which male members of the middle class were engaged.

The commercial and professional middle classes were not the only or even the principal participants in eighteenth-century consumerism, however. A crucial mainstay in the rise of consumerism in English society was provided by the landed gentry, even where it rested on political and economic strengths that are more closely associated with a traditional society; Hume's background and connections associated him strongly with this social stratum. The deployment of wealth and prestige in distinguishing them-selves from others made members of the landed elites of Britain important in establishing the culture in which fashionable imitation and social emula-tion generated economically and socially significant motives for individuals.

The self-conscious consumption practices of Scots gentry were matched by the growing participation of the English gentry in forms of consumerist display sometimes regarded as more typically middle class. There was an element of status insecurity in this. In his *History of England*, Hume had remarked upon the 'inflation of honours' originating in the early seven-teenth century[44] The size of the nobility doubled, and the creation of the hereditary but non-noble title of baronet in 1611, as well as the growing landholdings of the gentry, led to a narrowing of the cultural distance between landed gentry and the peerage proper.[45] Even while the greater landed class exercised a 'domination' over the rest of society, its hegemony was marked by tensions arising from a lack of self-confidence, which waxed and waned through the second half of the seventeenth century and the first half of the eighteenth. Land-based wealth, status and power gave rise to a self-awareness on the part of this class, characterised by 'a collective aware-ness of inherited and unworked-for superiority'. This was reinforced during the period between 1650 and 1750, but Rosenheim observes that its cementing was based more on 'a sense among the landed of anxiety and even fear' than on 'confidence in a future based on ... persistence through time'.[46] Some of the reasons for this uncertainty arose during the difficult period of the mid-seventeenth century. The deep separation appearing between popular and elite political cultures was a particular source of concern, espe-cially as the possibility of divisions among the elite could raise prospects of political vulnerability. Increasing awareness of the 'fragility' of the social and political privileges of the aristocracy and the broader landed class manifested itself in the gestures of self-display which marked elite culture. Gestures such as 'hanging portraits, landscaping grounds, decorating houses, adorning themselves with *à-la-mode* clothes' marked a need to reinforce a sense of cohesion, and while these gestures were not always visible to lower social orders, they are nonetheless 'explicable as the deployments of cultural claims to superiority intended to fortify their social position against challenge'.[47]

Thus, the psychological propensities attributed by Hume to individuals generally were prevalent at different levels of eighteenth-century British society, and in both Scotland and England. Hume's geographical and social movements at this time placed him in positions where he could observe these propensities in action, providing him with the empirical foundations for a synthetic construction of psychology that may be either middle class and mercantile or aristocratic and landed, or indeed both. It was a mentality that was increasingly prevalent in flourishing commercial consumer societies. This is not to suggest that Hume's theory simply and directly reflected a concrete reality, but that he attempted to make sense of his social environment through the construction of a philosophical understanding of human nature.

The Passions and the Understanding

While the second book of the *Treatise* bears the imprint of social experience by providing explicit treatments of concrete objects, feelings and practices, the relationship between philosophical theory and practical context also has a bearing on the constructive parts of the book on the understanding. Each of the first two books presented a different layer of the individual, a different part of the same 'compleat chain of reasoning', as Hume called it in the advertisement for the first two books.[48] The association of ideas in the understanding occurs as a result of, and is facilitated by, the prompting of the passions, according to Hume's theory of mental processes; and the second book of the *Treatise* (particularly Part 3) suggests that it is the passions that enlist the powers of the understanding in order to assist in achieving the ends determined by desires and aversions.[49]

What Hume presented in the first book of the *Treatise* was an explanation of the intellectual means available to individuals to apprehend the environment in which they found themselves, and to discover effective means of intervening amongst them.[50] The understanding presents the intellectual means to achieve the ends determined by the passions, notably the acquisition of objects that cause pleasure and the generation of social esteem which can be earned by conspicuously possessing them. In order to comprehend a complex, chaotic and rapidly changing social environment in which individualistic competition played an important role and was related to the intellectual and practical complexities of commerce, both from the point of view of consumers and of merchants and other participants, the individual required an efficient intellectual apparatus. The seemingly random wilfulness of the actions of others, no longer bound by the prescriptive rules of tradition in many areas of life, required renewed attention. Not only the subtleties of polite social interaction between potential social rivals, but also the key instrument of social power in this sphere, money, required specialised intellectual equipment and renewed theoretical attention.[51] With social interaction and the establishment of social status closely tied to the possession and consumption of goods, money obtained a new and complex significance for individuals and required effective management in the commercial transactions of getting and spending. In his analysis of pride and its causes in Book II of the *Treatise*,

Hume remarks that 'if the property in any thing, that gives pleasure either by its utility, beauty or novelty, produces also pride by a double relation of impressions and ideas; we need not be surpriz'd, that the power of acquiring this property, shou'd have the same effect'.[52] The theory of causal beliefs from Book I Part 3 provides the basis for his explanation of the effectiveness of money, and its esteem value, by explaining how an individual comes to believe in the operation of causes – or, as Hume sometimes calls them, 'powers'. He explains that 'riches are to be consider'd as the power of acquiring the property of what pleases; and 'tis only in this view they have any influence on the passions'.[53] His reference to non-bullionist conceptions of money was consistent with the idea that the meaningfulness of the monetary medium lay in its capacity to represent a belief.

> Paper will, on many occasions, be consider'd as riches, and that because it may convey the power of acquiring money: And money is not riches, as it is a metal endow'd with certain qualities of solidity, weight and fusibility; but only as it has a relation to the pleasures and conveniences of life. Taking then this for granted, which is in itself so evident, we may draw from it one of the strongest arguments I have yet employ'd to prove the influence of the double relations on pride and humility.[54]

Smail stressed the importance of changing financial accounting practices and the increasing use of credit in the formation of communal self-awareness among businessmen in the eighteenth century.[55] The complexities of such new techniques made demands on the intellect of the individual. Hume experienced this during his brief spell at the Bristol firm of merchants in 1734, and this awareness may be seen to be reflected in his repeated use of accounting metaphors to illustrate the capacities of the understanding.[56] The ability to appreciate the potency of monetary wealth as a means not only of conducting effective business and trade, but of conducting a personal and social life in which social esteem had to be earned through self-conscious display, required intellectual apprehension. The fluidity of the medium and the increasing extent of its capacity to measure value and move goods and persons, which now manifested itself increasingly in the everyday life of at least the middle and upper ranks of society, is a change whose demands on the participating individual must not be underestimated.

Conclusion

The adaptation of the experimental method to the study of human nature by David Hume established a peculiarly direct relationship between the life and experience of the philosopher and the content of his philosophical theories. The *Treatise* has, therefore, an especial need of historical contextualisation and interpretation. By stating explicitly that observation of his contemporaries in their ordinary conduct of life in company, in their affairs and in their pleasures formed the foundation of his theories, Hume inadvertently points towards a window through which we can discover historically specific contents within his ideas. These contents are most strongly evident in Book II, *Of the Passions*.

In Book II, Hume presents an analytic framework within which the principal motivational propensities of the individual are to be comprehended. Desire and aversions, hopes and fears are presented in Book II, Part 3 as the direct motives for human actions. The passions of pride and humility, love and hatred orientate the direct passions, motivating human actions, especially the selection of desirable objects, and thus mediate between perceptions of the self, perceptions of others and perceptions of objects.

Under the influence of the indirect passions, Hume's individual is concerned with the manner in which he or she may be compared with other individuals in terms of two things: success in acquiring objects which bestow pleasure, which, as Hume explains, are understood to embody the 'power' to bestow pleasure; and an individual's power to acquire further objects that will provide pleasure – in other words, wealth. Through the estimation of the self in terms of pride and of others in terms of esteem, the individual measures the relations of power and success and thus establishes the relative status in society of himself and the individuals surrounding him.

This mentality may be characterised as consumerist. It describes the kind of person found most commonly in advanced commercial societies; a person who uses the purchase and conspicuous consumption of goods to display social status and who measures the status of others by their success in doing the same thing. This mentality was prevalent in both urban and, to a lesser extent, rural contexts in Britain from at least the early eighteenth century onwards. Hume's movements during the 1730s, when he was taking his observations for the *Treatise*, took him to different points on the social and geographical map: from a family of the landed gentry of Scotland, frequenting both the rural Lowlands and Edinburgh, to the merchant society of Bristol, through London and even, at a late stage, to France, where his earlier impressions may have been reinforced at Rheims. From these social vantage points, Hume was in a position to observe the changing landscapes of British social and economic life, and to interpret the kind of individual mentalities that emerged.

PART FIVE

HISTORY
IN THE PRESENT

17

History on the Walls:
A Photo-Essay on Historical Narrative
and the Political Wall Murals of
Belfast in the Late 1990s

R.J. Morris

The North of Ireland has an intensely visual culture.[1] This has been frequently recognised, but less comment has been made on the creative historical content of this culture.

Until the early 1980s, the wall murals for which Belfast has gained considerable fame were dominated by the Orange symbols of King William crossing the Boyne, and the Red Hand of Ulster. Paradoxically, these have almost gone from the urban culture of Belfast, where the use of such spaces is dominated by paramilitary cultures with their state usurpatory ambitions. Such 'traditional' symbols are best seen in Protestant villages such as Ballycarry in County Antrim.

If 1690 was the first date in Ulster history, then 1912 and 1916 came next.

This memorial to the Ulster Division in the Battle of the Somme placed on the gable end of the Northern Ireland Housing Executive housing scheme at Monkstown in North Belfast does not face a sectarian divide.

Instead it marks the class division of public and owner–occupier housing, conveying its history lesson to residents and passing motorists alike.

The message is repeated in various forms across Protestant Belfast. Mount Vernon, in the fractured territorial politics of North Belfast, celebrated a winner of the Victoria Cross.

The paintings create a visual historical continuity. The establishment of the original Ulster Volunteer Force in 1912 was the formal beginning of the organised armed defence of Ulster. The year 1916 marked the slaughter on the battlefield of the Somme.

These dates were visually linked in the murals to the creation of a new generation of Protestant paramilitary organisations in the 1970s.

In East Belfast, with its more secure Protestant ownership of space, the message is continued.

The history of 1912–69 is constantly associated with images of First World War battlefields.

Very little knowledge of Irish history is needed to recognise the importance of 1916. In Protestant Belfast, the date represents not the Dublin Post Office, the Easter Rising and the executions that followed, but the blood sacrifice of the Protestant People which formed the basis of the claim to remain within the United Kingdom. This history of the defenders and sacrifice is linked visually with aggressive and assertive images. Blood sacrifice at many different levels plays a very deep and basic part in the art of legitimating killing.

Mount Vernon is the most direct.

The relative security of East Belfast can afford a more theoretical position.

Here the wall politicians provide lessons in the theories of national identity and are not afraid to deepen their sense of history beyond 1689 and, by doing so, appropriate some myths and symbols that might be associated with other identities.

On the Republican walls, the sense of history is still vital but much more fragmented. It is harder to find a 'story'. This may, in part, be an aspect of a world view that has more to do with the compulsions of an unchanging historical destiny than with the defence of a historical tradition.

Easter 1916 is more evident than the Battle of the Boyne in urban Belfast.

The Famine of the late 1840s was a crucial event. In some cases, as here

in Ballymurphy, the mural artists employ the contemporary language of atrocity inflation. For Europeans of the 1940s' and 1950s' generation, 'genocide' and 'holocaust' have very specific meanings. The artists also quote numbers that should have historians reaching for the demography literature. In other places, they prefer simple portraits of death and starvation, aware that the massive failure of any regime to keep a population alive was a very basic challenge to its legitimacy.

Overwhelmingly, Republican visual history is about the last three or four decades. History began in 1969.

On wall after wall the mood is one of memorialisation. Sometimes memorials take very simple forms, as here in Logan Street in the Lower Falls.

The compelling message is one of legitimacy derived from death and sacrifice. These reminders are deeply embedded in the urban scenery of the Republican areas of Belfast. They are rarely used as boundary markers but face inwards, asserting identity and history to those who live in those areas,[2] as in this reminder of the women prisoners in the H Blocks near to Clowney Street in the Falls Road.

The dead hunger strikers of the early 1980s peer out from wall after wall. In places, as here in the New Lodge area of North Belfast, they are presented as savage and menacing. There is no need here to be reminded that these deaths were used to legitimate killing as well as to legitimate claims to usurp and reform the state.

In the Lower Falls of the 1990s, the images of the hunger strikers portray more comfortable people. They are cheerful, friendly young boys, dated only by their 1970s haircuts.

The same style provided reminders of the young children killed by the rubber bullets of the security forces. Again this was an attack on the legitimacy of government.

The visual messages of the Republican areas are quite different from those of the Loyalist parts of Belfast. The former are more dynamic and display a wider variety of cultural assertions. There is a deliberate internationalism. In many cases, this reflects a simple identity with 'national liberation struggles' in other parts of the world.

In other places, the themes of aboriginal inhabitants and land struggles are adopted with clear references to the settler–native narrative of Republican history.

The Republican murals provide a more confident marking out of space. Ballymurphy conveys a presentist air of cheerful aggression. Here, history clearly ends tomorrow.

History may not actually be written by the winners, as another memorial from the Lower Falls implies, but on the walls of Belfast it is being written by the most creative and dynamic exponents of the past.[3]

Notes

INTRODUCTION

1. L.M. Cullen and T.C. Smout (eds.), *Comparative aspects of Scottish and Irish economic and social history, 1600–1900* (Edinburgh 1977); T.M. Devine and David Dickson (eds.), *Ireland and Scotland. Parallels and contrasts in economic and social development* (Edinburgh 1983); Rosalind Mitchison and Peter Roebuck (eds.), *Economy and society in Scotland and Ireland, 1500–1939* (Edinburgh 1988); S.J. Connolly, R.A. Houston and R.J. Morris (eds.), *Conflict, identity and economic development* (Preston 1995).

2. Rosemary Richey, 'The eighteenth-century estate agent and his correspondence. County Down: a case study' (Chapter 3 of this volume).

3. T.M. Devine, *The transformation of rural Scotland: social change and the agrarian economy 1660–1815* (Edinburgh 1994).

4. Cullen and Smout, *op. cit.*, pp. 4–8.

5. Patrick Gallagher ('Paddy the Cope'), *My story* (Dungloe 1947).

6. See the Andy Whiteman website (www.caledonia.org.uk/land) for a survey of radical and reformist views; also Robin Callendar, *How Scotland is owned* (Edinburgh 1998).

7. Frank McDonald, *The construction of Dublin* (Kinsale 2000).

8. David McCrone, *Understanding Scotland. The sociology of a stateless nation* (London 1992); Owen Dudley Edwards (ed.), *A claim of right for Scotland* (Edinburgh 1989).

9. Sarah Nelson, *Ulster's uncertain defenders. Loyalists and the Northern Ireland conflict* (Belfast 1984); Michael Farrell, *Northern Ireland: the Orange State* (London 1980).

10. *The future of multi-ethnic Britain. The Parekh Report* (The Runnymede Trust, London 2000); Karen Barkey and Mark von Hagen (eds.), *After Empire. Multi ethnic societies and nation building. The Soviet Union and the Russian, Ottoman and Habsburg Empires* (Boulder and Oxford 1997).

11. Benedict Anderson, *Imagined communities*, revised edition (London 1991).

12. Edward W. Said, *Orientalism. Western conceptions of the Orient* (London 1978); Catherine Hall, *White, male and middle class. Explorations in feminism and history* (Cambridge 1992); Frank Wright, *Northern Ireland: A comparative analysis* (Dublin 1987).

13. Roy F. Foster, 'Varieties of Irishness' in Maurna Crozier (ed.), *Cultural traditions in Northern Ireland* (Institute of Irish Studies, Queen's University Belfast 1989).

14. The most recent statement in this tradition is probably the polemic by Francis Fukuyama, *The end of history and the last man* (London 1992).

15. Marshall Berman, *All that is solid melts into air. The experience of modernity* (New York 1982).

16. Peadar O'Donnell, *The big windows* (first published 1955; reprinted Dublin 1986); Peadar O'Donnell, *The knife* (first published 1930; reprinted Dublin 1980).

17. Graeme Morton, *Unionist nationalism. Governing urban Scotland, 1830–1860* (East Linton 1999).

1. RURAL CHANGE IN ULSTER AND SCOTLAND, 1660–1815

1. My thanks are due to the Director of the Public Record Office of Northern Ireland (hereafter PRONI) for permission to quote from the collections in his custody.

2. S.J. Connolly, R.A. Houston, and R.J. Morris (eds.), *Conflict, identity and economic development: Ireland and Scotland, 1600–1939* (Preston 1995), pp. 7–8.

3. T.S. Devine, *The transformation of rural Scotland: social change and the agrarian economy 1660–1815* (Edinburgh 1994).

4. P. Roebuck, 'The economic situation and functions of substantial landowners, 1660–1815: Ulster and Lowland Scotland compared'; and G.E. Kirkham, 'To pay the rent and lay up riches: economic opportunity in eighteenth century north-west Ulster' in R. Mitchison and P. Roebuck (eds.), *Economy and society in Scotland and Ireland 1500–1939* (Edinburgh 1988), pp. 81–92, 95–104.

5. T. Scott (ed.), *The peasantries of Europe from the fourteenth to the eighteenth centuries* (London 1998), p. 18.

6. G. Hill, *An historical account of the Plantation in Ulster at the commencement of the seventeenth century, 1608–1620* (Belfast 1877); N.P. Canny, 'Hugh O'Neill, Earl of Tyrone, and the changing face of Gaelic Ulster', *Studia Hibernica*, 10 (1970), pp. 7–35.

7. J.C.W. Wylie, *Irish land law* (London 1975), pp. 17–21, especially 19–20.

8. M. Perceval-Maxwell, *The Scottish migration to Ulster in the reign of James I* (London 1973), especially Chapter VII; V. Treadwell, 'The Survey of Armagh and Tyrone, 1622', *Ulster Journal of Archaeology*, 3rd series, XXIII (1960) and XXVII (1964).

9. R. Gillespie, *Colonial Ulster: the settlement of East Ulster 1600–1641* (Cork 1985), pp. 212–15.

10. J.H. Andrews, *Plantation acres: an historical study of the Irish land surveyor and his maps* (Belfast 1985), pp. 4–18, 56–59.

11. R. Gillespie, *Settlement and survival on an Ulster estate: the Brownlow leasebook 1667–1711* (Belfast 1988).

12. Gillespie, *Colonial Ulster*, pp.28–43; J. Ohlmeyer, *Civil War and Restoration in the three Stuart kingdoms: the career of Randal MacDonnell, Marquis of Antrim, 1609–1683* (Cambridge 1993), pp. 33–42; P. Roebuck, 'The making of an Ulster great estate: the Chichesters, Barons of Belfast and Viscounts of Carrickfergus, 1599–1648', *Proceedings of the Royal Irish Academy*, 79, C (1979), pp. 1–25.

13. J.H. Ohlmeyer, 'Civilizing of those rude partes: colonization within Britain and Ireland, 1580s–1640s' in N. Canny (ed.), *The Oxford history of the British Empire, Vol. 1: the origins of Empire* (Oxford 1998), p. 138.

14. Gillespie, *Colonial Ulster*, pp. 122–29, 199–206; R.C. Simington (ed.), *The Civil Survey 1654–6. Vol. III: Counties of Donegal, Londonderry and Tyrone* (Irish Manuscripts Commission 1937), *passim*, but see pp. 254, 257, 264–67; J. Agnew, *Belfast merchant families in the seventeenth century* (Dublin 1996), pp. 42–47.

15. R.M. Smith, 'The English peasantry, 1250–1650' in Scott, *The peasantries of Europe*, pp. 361–62.

16. Wylie, *Irish land law*, pp. 35, 66, 184–85.

17. 14 & 15 Car. II c.19.

18. Wylie, pp. 17–23.

19. Smith, 'English peasantry', pp. 339–71; Martin Dowling, *Tenant right and agrarian society in Ulster 1600–1870* (Dublin 1999), especially Chapter 2.

20. I. Whyte, *Agriculture and society in seventeenth century Scotland* (Edinburgh 1979), p. 271.

21. *Ibid.*, p. 44–7.

22. Devine, *Transformation of rural Scotland*, pp. 50, 62–64.

23. *Ibid.*, p.114.

24. Isaac Macartney to Charles Herron, 3 November 1705 (PRONI, Letterbook of Isaac Macartney, D/501, pp. 220–1).

25. Hamilton Maxwell, Drumbeg, to Agmondisham Vesey, Dublin, 15 August 1722 (PRONI, Kirk-Vesey papers, T/2524/17).

26. James Hamilton to Abercorn, 21 January 1780 (PRONI, Abercorn MSS, D/623/A/44/6).

27. Brabazon Noble to Lord Dacre, 24 April 1760 (PRONI, Barrett-Lennard MSS, T/2529/6/C34/200). See also W.A. Maguire, *The Downshire estates in Ireland: the management of Irish landed estates in the early eighteenth century* (Oxford 1972), pp. 111, 112–16; also A.P.W. Malcomson, *John Foster: the politics of the Anglo-Irish ascendancy* (Oxford 1978), pp. 311–12.

28. Devine, *Transformation of rural Scotland*, p. 63.

29. Earl of Abercorn to James Hamilton, 2 September 1773 (Abercorn MSS, D/623/A/21/51).

30. Earl of Abercorn to John Hamilton, Strabane, 12 April 1774 (Abercorn MSS, D/623/A/21/87).

31. Earl of Abercorn to James Hamilton, 31 December 1775 (Abercorn MSS, D/623/A/22/52).

32. James Hamilton to the Earl of Abercorn, 8 March 1772 (Abercorn MSS, D/623/A/40/17).

33. James Hamilton to the Earl of Abercorn, 30 May 1767 (Abercorn MSS, D/623/A/37/75).

34. Devine, *Transformation of rural Scotland*, p. 60.

35. *Ibid.*, p. 70.

36. *Ibid.*, p. 61.

37. *Ibid.*, p. 73.

38. James Hamilton to the Earl of Abercorn, 2 August 1771 (Abercorn MSS, D/623/A/39/135).

39. William Henry, 'Hints towards a natural and topographical history of the Counties of Sligo, Donegal, Fermanagh and Lough Erne' (National Archives of Ireland, Ms 2533).

40. J. Kelly (ed.), *The letters of Lord Chief Baron Edward Willes* (Aberystwyth 1990), pp. 30–31.

41. 'Scheme of Robert Stevenson' (PRONI, Massereene-Foster MSS, D/562/1270) .

42. W.H. Crawford, 'The evolution of the urban network' in W. Nolan, L. Ronayne and M. Dunlevy (eds.), *Donegal: history and society* (Dublin 1995), pp. 381–404; W.H. Crawford, The evolution of the urban network' in A.J. Hughes (ed.), *Armagh: history and society* (Dublin 2001).

43. Walter Harris, *The ancient and present state of the County of Down* (Dublin 1744), pp. 49, 71.

44. W.H. Crawford, 'The construction of the Ulster road network 1700–1850' from papers collected for a symposium on 'The History of Technology, Science, and Society' at the University of Ulster, 1989.

45. Examples of the colonisation of marginal lands in mid-Ulster are to be found in W.H. Crawford and R.H. Foy (eds.), *Townlands in Ulster: local history studies* (Belfast 1998), pp. 135–236.

46. James Hamilton to Abercorn, 19 March 1767 (Abercorn MSS D/623/A/37/63).

47. Abercorn to James Hamilton, 12 April 1767 (Abercorn MSS D/623/A/18/90).

48. James Hamilton to Abercorn, 9 July 1784 (Abercorn MSS D/623/A/45/32).

49. Devine, *Transformation of rural Scotland*, p. 133.

50. *Ibid.*, pp. 125–34.

51. *Ibid.*, p. 140.

52. *Ibid.*, p. 141.

53. T.W. Freeman, *Pre-famine Ireland: a study in historical geography* (Manchester 1957), p. 35.

54. *Ibid.*, p. 56.

55. *Ibid.*, p. 54.

56. P.M.A. Bourke, *'The visitation of God'? The potato and the Great Irish Famine* (Dublin 1993), pp. 16–21, especially the sketch maps on p. 21.

57. F. Wright, *Two lands on one soil: Ulster politics before home rule* (Dublin 1996), p. 510.

2. DEBT AND THE SCOTTISH LANDED ELITE IN THE 1650S

1. David J. Menarry, 'The Irish and Scottish landed elites from Regicide to Restoration' (unpublished PhD, University of Aberdeen 2001).

2. Robin Jeffs *et al.* (eds.), *The English Revolution III, Newsbooks 5, Mercurius Politicus*, 19 vols. (London 1971), III, p. 65.

3. Hamish Scott (ed.), *The European nobilities in the seventeenth and eighteenth centuries*, 2 vols. (London 1995); Keith Brown, *Noble society in Scotland: wealth, family and culture from the Reformation to the Revolution* (Edinburgh 2000); 'Aristocratic finances and the origins of the Scottish revolution', *English Historical Review*, CIV (1989); 'Noble indebtedness in Scotland between the Reformation and Revolution', *Historical Research*, LXII (1989); Jane H. Ohlmeyer and Éamonn Ó Ciardha (eds.), *The Irish Statute Staple Books, 1596–1687* (Dublin 1998).

4. The New British and Irish Histories have been the subject of a great deal of historiographical debate; see, for example, Brendan Bradshaw and John Morrill (eds.), *The British problem, c.1534–1707* (London 1996); Keith Brown, 'British history: a sceptical comment', in Ronald Asch (ed.), *Three nations – a common history? England, Scotland, Ireland and British history c.1600–1920* (Arbeitskreis Deutsche England-Forshung, XXIII, Bochum 1993); Jane H. Ohlmeyer, 'The wars of the three kingdoms', *History Today*, XLVIII (1998); John Adamson, 'The English context of the British Civil Wars', *History Today*, XLVIII (1998); Glenn Burgess, 'Scottish or British? Politics and political thought in Scotland c.1500–1707', *HJ*, XLI (1992); and the papers presented to the American Historical Review Forum: The New British History in Atlantic Perspective in 1999 by David Armitage, Jane Ohlmeyer, Ned C. Landsman and Eliga H. Gould, published in the *American Historical Review*, CIX (1999).

5. John R. Young, *The Scottish Parliament, 1639–1661: a political and constitutional analysis* (Edinburgh 1996), Chapter 9; Ian Michael Smart, 'The political ideas of the Scottish Covenanters, 1638–88', *History of Political Thought*, I (1980), pp. 167–79.

6. T. Thomson and C. Innes (eds.), *The Acts of the Parliament of Scotland*, 12 vols. (London 1814–72), (hereafter *APS*) VI.ii, pp. 157, 276, 435, 559; David Stevenson (ed.), *The government of Scotland under the Covenanters, 1637–1651* (Scottish History Society (hereafter SHS), Edinburgh 1982), pp. 85, 97, 98, 101; Sir James Balfour, *Historical works*, 4 vols. (Edinburgh 1825), III, pp. 408–9; Bulstrode Whitelocke, *Memorials of the English affairs*, 4 vols. (Oxford 1853), III, p. 18; *Calendar of state papers, domestic series, 1641–60*, 20 vols. (London 1860–97), (hereafter *CSPD*) (1649–50), pp. 96, 325, 361, 403; S R Gardiner (ed.), *Letters and papers illustrating the relations between Charles II and Scotland in 1650* (SHS, Edinburgh 1894), p. 74; Alexander F. Mitchell and James Christie (eds.), *The Records of the Commissions of the General Assemblie of the Church of Scotland, 1646–52*, 3 vols. (SHS, Edinburgh 1896–1909), II, pp. 447–60; *H. of C. Journals* (UK), VI, p. 431. Allan I. Macinnes, *Clanship, commerce and the House of Stuart 1603–1788* (East Linton 1996), pp. 90, 108; David Stevenson, *Revolution and counter-revolution in Scotland, 1644–51* (London 1977), pp. 135–40; Young, *Scottish Parliament*, pp. 218–27, 234–36.

7. Young, *Scottish Parliament*, p. 257.
8. Gardiner (ed.), *Charles II and Scotland*, p. 25.
9. Young, *Scottish Parliament*, p. 257.
10. Stevenson, *Revolution and counter-revolution*, Chapter 5; Young, *Scottish Parliament*, Chapter 11.
11. F.D. Dow, *Cromwellian Scotland 1651–1660* (Edinburgh 1979), pp. 14–23.
12. C.H. Firth (ed.), *Scotland and the Commonwealth* (SHS, Edinburgh 1895), pp. 340–1; Balfour, *Historical works*, vol. IV, pp. 345–46.
13. *APS*, VI.ii, pp. 809–10.
14. *Ibid.*, p. 809. At the Union of the Crowns (1603) the exchange rate between Scotland and England was fixed at 12:1; that is 1*l*. stg = 12*l*. Scots. All amounts are in sterling unless stated otherwise.
15. Dow, *Cromwellian Scotland*, p. 38; Lesley M. Smith, 'Scotland and Cromwell: A study in Early Modern government' (unpublished DPhil, University of Oxford 1980), p. 65.
16. *APS*, VI.ii, p. 773.
17. Firth, *Commonwealth*, p. 49.
18. Dow, *Cromwellian Scotland*, pp. 52–53.
19. Brown, *Noble society*, pp. 95–96.
20. Dow, *Cromwellian Scotland*, p. 32; C.S. Terry (ed.), 'The Cromwellian Union', (SHS, Edinburgh 1902), p. xxiv.
21. Smith, 'Scotland and Cromwell', pp. 120–21.
22. Dow, *Cromwellian Scotland*, p. 56; Smith, 'Scotland and Cromwell', Chapter 5.
23. *Parliament, the Civil War and the conquest and administration of Scotland: Sir William Clarke Manuscripts in Worcester College Oxford* (Worcester College, Oxford) (hereafter *Clarke Papers*), (Harvester Microfilm Publications 1979), Reel 2, 1/11, ff. 85v–9r.
24. See Charles Fraser Mackintosh (ed.), *Antiquarian notes: a series of papers regarding families and places in the Highlands* (Inverness 1865), p. 214; J.Y. Akerman (ed.), *Letters from Roundhead officers* (Bannatyne Club, Edinburgh 1856), pp. 59–60.
25. *Clarke Papers*, Reel 2, 1/10, f.96.
26. Terry (ed.), *The Cromwellian Union*, p. 17.
27. Smith, 'Scotland and Cromwell', p. 123.
28. M.V. Hay (ed.), *The Blairs papers, 1603–1660* (London 1929), p. 48.
29. T. Thomson (eds.) *et al.*, *Registrum Magni Sigilli Regum Scotorum* (hereafter *RMS*) (Edinburgh 1882–1914), (1652–60), pp. 99, 159, 220, 229–30, 266–68.
30. *CSPD* (1651–52), pp. 213, 349, 437; (1652–53), pp. 55, 204, 225.
31. See J. Graham Stewart, *A treatise on the Law of Diligence* (Edinburgh 1898); Smith, 'Scotland and Cromwell', Chapter 5.
32. National Library of Scotland (hereafter NLS), Ms.3159, f.21r; NLS, Wod. Oct. XXXVII, p. 35; J Macknight (ed.), *Memoirs of Sir Ewen Cameron of Locheil* (Abbotsford Club, Edinburgh 1842), p. 97; David Laing (ed.), *A diary of public transactions and other occurences, chiefly in Scotland from Jan 1650 to June 1667, by John Nicoll* (Bannatyne Club, Edinburgh 1875), p. 116.
33. Firth, *Commonwealth*, pp. 160–61, 239. *Clarke Papers*, Reel 10, 3/1, f.126r.
34. Firth, *Commonwealth*, pp. 160–61, 227, 243, 289. *Clarke Papers*, Reel 10, 3/1, f.126r.
35. *RMS* (1652–60), pp. 32–33, 38–39, 44–45, 88–89.
36. *Clarke Papers*, Reel 10, 3/2, f.19.
37. Smith, 'Scotland and Cromwell', p. 122; J.B. Paul (ed.), *The Scots peerage*, 9 vols. (Edinburgh 1904–14), V, p. 546.
38. Firth, *Commonwealth*, pp. 238, 240–41, 243–44, 257, 259, 265, 270–71, 273, 275; James Maidment (ed.), *The Spottiswoode miscellany*, 2 vols. (Spottiswoode Society, Edinburgh 1844–45), II, pp. 135–43.
39. Firth, *Commonwealth*, pp. 241, 265, 273; Firth, *Protectorate*, pp. 9, 68.
40. Firth, *Commonwealth*, p. 289.

41. *Ibid.*, pp. 266–67.
42. *Ibid.*, p. 289.
43. See T.C. Barnard, *The English Republic* (London 1982), pp. 37–43.
44. Firth, *Protectorate*, pp. 20–21.
45. C.H. Firth and R.S. Rait (eds.), *Acts and ordinances of the interregnum*, 3 vols. (London 1911), II, p. 883.
46. Firth, *Protectorate*, pp. 90, 98.
47. *APS*, VI.ii, p. 888; Firth, *Protectorate*, pp. 158–61, 165–68, 177–79.
48. Firth and Rait (eds.), *Acts and ordinances*, II, p. 898.
49. See Dow, *Cromwellian Scotland*, p. 183.
50. Laing (ed.), *Nicoll's diary*, p. 143.
51. Smith, 'Scotland and Cromwell', p. 125.
52. *Ibid.*
53. *Clarke Papers*, Reel 12, 3/9, 18 September 1654.
54. *Ibid.*, 3 October 1654, 7 October, 13 October, 7 November.
55. *Ibid.*, 12 December 1654, 16 December, 19 December, 12 January 1655.
56. *Ibid.*, 20 March 1655; BL, Add. Ms.38,848, f.27.
57. BL, Add. Ms.38, 848, f.27, and *CSPD* (1655), p. 181.
58. P.J.S. Little, 'The political career of Roger Boyle, Lord Broghill, 1636–1660' (unpublished PhD, University of London 2000).
59. *CSPD* (1655), pp. 284, 319.
60. *Ibid.*, p. 364.
61. Dow, *Cromwellian Scotland*, p. 183.
62. Loudon to Lothian, 12 February and 18 March 1656: National Archives of Scotland (hereafter NAS), GD 40/2/V/89–90.
63. *CSPD* (1655–56), pp. 203, 224, 274–75; Laing (ed.), *Nicoll's diary*, pp. 178–80; NLS, Ms.7001, pp. 6, 8.
64. *CSPD* (1655–56), pp. 274–75.
65. NAS, CS 4/24–5. Registration ended on 14 April 1657.
66. Some of the entries are difficult to read, and there are variations in what individuals included in their lists. The calculation of exact figures in all cases proved impossible. Therefore, all the totals quoted, which have been rounded to the nearest hundred, must only be regarded as a rough guide. NAS, CS 4/24, pp. 29 (Preston of Craigmillar), 34 (Renton of Lamberton), 88 (Loudon), 94 (Douglas), 104 (Buchan), 125 (Roxburgh), 138 (Hartfell), 160 (Findlater), 168 (Queensberry), 173 (Callendar), 170 (Tullibardine), 190 (Drummond), 205 (Perth), 282 (Galloway), 341 (Forrester), 372 (Kinghorne); 4/25, pp. 54 (Cranston), 65 (Kenmore), 87 (Barclay of Collernie), 94 (Woolmet), 96 (Dudhope), 98 (Auchmutie of Gosford), 102 (Meldrum of Tillibodie), 138 (Rothes), 175 (Murray of Stanhope), 202 (Winton).
67. NAS, CS 4/24, pp. 36 (Herries), 75 (Linton), 81 (Home), 88 (Loudon), 94 (Douglas), 104 (Buchan), 115 (Nithesdale), 125 (Roxburgh), 138 (Hartfell), 142 (Annandale), 152 (Elibank – first entry), 160 (Findlater), 168 (Queensberry), 172 (Callendar), 175 (Lovat), 179 (Tullibardine), 182 (Mar), 190 (Drummond), 199 (Morton), 205 (Perth), 211 (Cardross), 213 (Frendraught), 221 (Kirkcudbright), 224 (Airlie), 261 (Ramsay), 282 (Galloway), 335 (Dunfermline), 341 (Forrester), 347 (Lindores), 372 (Kinghorne); 4/25, pp. 30 (Dumfriess), 31 (Ogilvy), 42 (Balmerino), 54 (Cranston), 65 (Kenmore), 81 (Kingston), 83 (Elibank – second entry included in the calculation of the arithmetic mean), 96 (Dudhope), 101 (Sutherland), 137 (Boyde), 138 (Rothes), 157 (Caithness), 158 (Argyll), 175 (Wigton), 202 (Winton).
68. See, for example, NLS, Ms.2263 (iii), f.234v; *Mercurius Politicus*, XIII, (1655), p. 212.
69. Laing (ed.), *Nicoll's Diary*, p. 184. Louise B. Taylor (ed.), *Aberdeen Council letters*, 6 vols. (London 1942–61), III, pp. 270, 277, 287–88.
70. *APS*, VI.ii, p. 786.

3. THE EIGHTEENTH-CENTURY ESTATE AGENT AND HIS CORRESPONDENCE. COUNTY DOWN: A CASE STUDY

1. List of the nobility in Counties Antrim and Down worth more than £100 p.a. as divided into papist, dissenter and churchman [early eighteenth century] (R.I.A. Ms.24 K19).

2. D.R. Hainsworth, *Stewards, lords and people: the estate steward and his world in later Stuart England* (Cambridge 1992), pp. 43, 186, 237; general County Down estate correspondence; Natt. Nesbitt to the Earl of Abercorn, 19 April 1757 (Public Record Office of Northern Ireland (hereafter PRONI) Abercorn Ms. T2541) printed in W.H. Crawford and B. Trainor (eds.), *Aspects of Irish social history 1750–1800* (Belfast 1969), p. 18. For further works on the role of the land agents see Peter Eden, *Dictionary of land surveyors and local map makers of Great Britain and Ireland 1530–1850*, 2 vols. (London 1997); Richard J. Colyer, 'The land agent in nineteenth century Wales', *Welsh History Review*, VIII (1997), pp. 401–25; Gary Firth, 'The roles of a West Riding land steward, 1773–1803', *Yorkshire Archaeological Journal*, LI (1979), pp. 105–15; Edward Hughes, 'The eighteenth century estate agent' in H.A. Cronne, T.W. Moody and D.B. Quinn (eds.), *Essays in British and Irish history in honour of James Eadie Todd* (London 1949), pp. 185–99; Martin W. Dowling, *Tenant right and agrarian society in Ulster 1600–1870* (Dublin 1999); Pamela Horn, 'An eighteenth century land agent: the career of Nathaniel Kent (1737–1810)', *Agricultural History Review*, XXX (1982), pp. 1–16; G.E. Mingay, 'Estate management in eighteenth century Kent', *Agricultural History Review*, VI (1956), pp. 108–13; F.M.L. Thompson, *English landed society in the nineteenth century* (London 1963); David Spring, 'Agents to the Earls of Durham in the nineteenth century', *Durham University Journal*, XXIV (1962–63), pp. 104–13; Leland J. Bellot, 'Wild hares and red herrings: a case study of estate management in the eighteenth century English countryside', *Huntington Library Quarterly*, LVI (1993), pp. 15–39; David Dickson, 'An economic history of the Cork region in the eighteenth century (unpublished PhD thesis, Trinity College Dublin 1977); W.H. Crawford (ed.), *Letters from an Ulster land agent 1774–85: the letter books of John Moore* (Belfast 1976); E.M. Jancey, 'An eighteenth century steward and his work', *Transactions Shropshire Archaeological Society*, LVI (1957–60).

3. Hainsworth, *Stewards*, pp. 1–2, 8; correspondence of Robert Isaac and Henry Hatch, 19 September 1747 to 16 December 1747 (PRONI Downshire Ms. D607/A/50–5).

4. Dowling, *Tenant right and agrarian society*, p. 59.

5. Henry Hatch to Lord Blundell and William Trumbull, 7 February 1746 (PRONI Downshire Ms. D607/A/23); James Gwyn to Henry Hatch, 28 June 1746 (*ibid.*, D607/A/23).

6. Henry Hatch to Lord Blundell and William Trumbull, 1 July 1746 (*ibid.* D607/A/23).

7. Dickson, 'An economic history of the Cork region in the eighteenth century', p. 231; Henry Hatch to Lord Blundell and William Trumbull, 6 September 1746 (PRONI Downshire Ms. D607/A/23); John Moore to Arthur Annesley, 29 April 1775, printed in W.H. Crawford (ed.), *Letters*, p. 4; Henry Hatch to Lord Blundell and William Trumbull, 27 Aug. 1747 (PRONI Downshire

Ms. D607/A/23); same to same, 24 June 1747 (*ibid.* D607/A/23); James Savage to Henry Hatch, 6 December 1755 (*ibid.* D607/A/136).

8. Same to same, 3 December 1755 (*ibid.* D607/A/134); James Gwyn to same [c.1755] (*ibid.* D607/A/128).

9. John Willock to same, 17 October 1762 (*ibid.* D607/A/235).

10. Robert Isaac to same, 21 November 1747 (*ibid.* D607/A/53).

11. Same to same, 14 September 1748 (*ibid.* D607/A/91); Thomas Squire to Michael Ward, 13 July 1742 (PRONI Castleward Ms. D2092/1/5/142); John Moore to Arthur Annesley, 22 June 1782, printed in Crawford (ed.), *Letters*, p. 39.

12. Hainsworth, *Stewards*, p. 51.

13. Sean Connolly, 'Eighteenth century Ireland' in D. George Boyce and Alan O'Day (eds.), *The making of modern Irish history* (London 1996), p. 22.

14. Robert Isaac to Henry Hatch, 21 November 1747 (PRONI Downshire Ms. D607/A/52-3).

15. Hainsworth, *Stewards*, pp. 4, 24.

16. Robert Isaac to Henry Hatch, 3 December 1755 (PRONI Downshire Ms. D607/A/134).

17. John Bateman, *The great landowners of Great Britain and Ireland*, second edition (NY 1971), p. 11; Thomas Harrison Montgomery, *A genealogical history and pedigree of the family of Montgomery* (Philadelphia 1863), p. 132.

18. Hainsworth, *Stewards*, p. 7; E.M. Jancey, 'An eighteenth century steward and his work', p. 35.

19. A.C.W. Merrick (ed.), *Old Belfast families* (Belfast 1991), pp. 258-60.

20. Leslie Stephens (ed.), *Dictionary of national biography*, 63 vols. (London 1888), L15; Crawford (ed.), *Letters*, p. i.

21. A.G. Malcolm, *The history of the General Hospital Belfast* (Belfast 1851), pp. 35, 38, 43, 63; John Killen, *A history of the Linen Hall Library 1788–1988* (Belfast, 1990), *passim*; C.J. Woods (ed.), *Journals and memoirs of Thomas Russell 1791–5* (Dublin 1991), pp. 47, 49, 108, 153; Merrick (ed.), *Old Belfast Families*, pp. 258-60.

22. The Rev. James Clewlow to Michael Ward, 2 March 1740 (PRONI Castleward Ms. D2092/1/3/88); the Rev. Edward Bayly to Sir Nicholas Bayly, 2 August 1757 (PRONI Anglesey Ms. D619/22/I/3); the Rev. George Vaughan to [William Mussenden], 20 February 1772 (PRONI Mussenden Ms. D354/1035).

23. Visitation of Dromore, 1730 (R.C.B. Ms.31).

24. Lease, Michael Ward to John Jolly, 3 January 1709 (Ms. in private hands, County Down); lease, Lord Limerick to same, 31 August 1725 (*ibid.*).

25. Thomas Squire to Michael Ward, 13 July 1741 (PRONI Castleward Ms. D2092/1/5/1).

26. Crawford (ed.), *Letters*, p. vii.

27. Aynsworth Pilson, 'Memoirs of notable inhabitants of Downpatrick', 1838 (PRONI Pilson Ms. D356/8); Kathryn Southwell to Edward Southwell, 8 July 1749 (PRONI Southwell Ms. T1254/1).

28. John Slade to Lord Hillsborough, 7 April 1779 (PRONI Downshire Ms. D607/B/76).

29. Robert Maxwell's account with James Crawford, 23 August 1746 (PRONI Maxwell Ms. D1556/16/14/1).

30. Henry Hatch to Lord Blundell and William Trumbull, 24 June 1747 (PRONI Downshire Ms. D607/A/23); Crawford (ed.), *Letters*, p. vi.

31. Hainsworth, *Stewards*, p. 37; J.R. Wordie, *Estate management in eighteenth century England: the building of the Leveson-Gower fortune* (London 1982), pp. 42, 46.

32. James Savage to Henry Hatch, 6 October 1766 (PRONI Downshire Ms. D607/A/276).

33. Henry Hatch to Lord Blundell and William Trumbull, 27 August 1747, 23 July 1754 (*ibid.* D607/A/23).

34. John Moore to Arthur Annesley, 9 February 1784, printed in Crawford (ed.), *Letters*, p. 47; same to same, 1

November 1784 (*ibid.* p. 55).

35. John Moore to [Mrs Annesley], 5 August 1776 (*ibid.* pp. 16–17).

36. Same to Arthur Annesley, 3 May 1783 (*ibid.* p. 43).

37. Same to same, 9 February 1784 (*ibid.* p. 48); same to same, 22 June 1783 (*ibid.* p. 63).

38. Same to [Mrs Annesley], 5 August 1776 (*ibid.* pp. 16–17).

39. *D.N.B*, LVII, p. 254.

40. Hainsworth, *Stewards*, p. 103.

41. John Moore to Arthur Annesley, 5 July 1777, printed in Crawford (ed.), *Letters*, p. 19.

42. Reply by John Trotter to the address published by Cromwell Price, *Belfast Newsletter*, 27 February 1761.

43. John Moore to Arthur Annesley, 5 January 1784, printed in Crawford (ed.), *Letters*, p. 46; same to same, 9 February 1784 (*ibid.* p. 47).

44. Sandra A. Millsop, 'The Provosts of Bangor', *Journal of Bangor Historical Society*, III (1984–85), pp. 43–45; Robert Ward to Michael Ward, 3 February 1746 (PRONI Castleward Ms. D2092/1/6/125).

45. Tony Canavan, *Frontier town: an illustrated history of Newry* (Belfast 1989), pp. 101–2; John Hutcheson to Sir Nicholas Bayly, 22 July 1779 (PRONI Anglesey Ms. D619/21/C/183).

46. 46 Edward Trotter to [—], 23 February 1771 (PRONI Southwell Ms. T582/1/667); John Sainsbury to Lord Hillsborough, 31 December 1783 (PRONI Downshire Ms. D607/B/123A–B).

47. List of the high sheriffs of County Down [c.1790] (Ms. in private hands, County Down).

48. Thomas Lane to Lord Downshire, 1 October 1797 (PRONI Downshire Ms. D607/B/1268); John Slade to Lord Hillsborough, 19 March 1780 (*ibid.* D607/B/109); Crawford (ed.), *Letters*, p. vii.

49. A.P.W. Malcomson, 'The parliamentary traffic of this country' in Thomas Bartlett and D.W. Hayton (eds.), *Penal era and golden age: essays in Irish History 1690–1800* (Belfast 1979), p. 143.

50. John Slade to Lord Hillsborough, 15 March 1779 (PRONI Downshire Ms. D607/B/70); T.G.F. Paterson, 'The volunteer companies of Ulster 1778–1793', *Irish Sword*, VII (1965–66), pp. 204–30.

51. John Slade to Lord Hillsborough, 15 March 1779 (PRONI Downshire Ms. D607/B/70).

52. Eden, *Dictionary of land surveyors*, *passim*.

53. Henry Waring, 'A scheme for the improvement of the estate and town of Rathfriland', 2 March 1764 (PRONI Castleward Ms. T1181/1).

54. Henry Waring to Bernard Ward, 24 August 1764 (PRONI Castleward Ms. D2092/1/8/109).

55. Crawford (ed.), *Letters*, p. vi; Robert Isaac to Henry Hatch, 19 September 1747 (PRONI Downshire Ms. D607/A/50). For English examples see Horn, 'Eighteenth century land agent' and Mingay, 'Estate management in eighteenth century Kent'.

56. James Savage to [Henry Hatch], 16 April 1764 (PRONI Downshire Ms. D607/A/247).

57. John Moore to Arthur Annesley, 5 October 1782, printed in Crawford (ed.), *Letters*, p. 39; same to same, 15 February 1783 (*ibid.* p. 42); same to same, 28 February 1784 (*ibid.* p. 49); same to Mr Chester, 27 December 1775 (*ibid.* p. 10).

58. Grand jury presentments at Co. Down [n.d.] (PRONI Tennison-Groves Ms. T808/15015); John Trotter to [—], 23 February 1771 (PRONI Southwell Ms. T582 (1), fol.131).

59. George Vaughan to [William Mussenden], 20 February 1772 (PRONI Mussenden Ms. D354/1035).

60. *Belfast Newsletter*, 6 February 1772.

61. The Rev. James Porter, *Billy Bluff and the Squire*, edited by Brendan Clifford (Belfast 1991), pp. 5–21.

4. SCOTTISH INFLUENCES ON IRISH
FARMING TECHNIQUES

1. The difficulty of developing links between specific objects and techniques and general social structure is well illustrated by Marx's discussion of commodities as a 'crystallisation of social labour'. Marx identifies labour, and the value arising from it, as creating the fundamental connection between artifacts and the relations of production. However, the labyrinthine calculations involved in calculating the amount of labour 'fixed' in any particular implement, tool or machine makes the task of working through specific connections impractical. Karl Marx, 'Wages, price and profit' in Karl Marx and Frederick Engels, *Selected works* (Moscow 1970 (1980)), pp. 202–3.

2. Jonathan Bell, 'Social anthropology and the study of material culture in Irish Museums', *Annales del Museo Nacional de Antropologia*, vol.1 (Madrid 1994).

3. Alexander Fenton, *The shape of the past*, vol.1 (Edinburgh 1985), p. 8.

4. Jonathan Bell, 'Changing farming methods in County Derry, 1700–1900' in G. O'Brien and W. Nolan (eds.), *Derry and Londonderry* (Dublin 1999), p. 405.

5. Henry F. Berry, *A history of the Royal Dublin Society* (London 1915), p. 35.

6. *Ibid.*, p. 50.

7. Arthur Young, *A tour in Ireland*, vol. 2 (Dublin 1780), p. 95.

8. Michael Partridge, *Farm tools through the ages* (Reading 1973), p. 162.

9. Alan Gailey, 'The introduction and spread of the horse-powered threshing machine to Ulster's farms in the nineteenth century', *Ulster Folklife*, vol. 30 (Holywood 1984), p. 40.

10. John Dubordieu, *Statistical survey of the County of Down* (Dublin 1802), pp. 53–54.

11. Joseph Archer, *Statistical survey of the County of Dublin* (Dublin 1801), p. 44;

Gailey, 'Threshing machines', p. 40; D.A. Beaufort, 'Materials for the Dublin Society Agricultural Survey of County Louth' in C.C. Ellison (ed.), *Journal of the County Louth Archaeological and Historical Society*, vol. 18:1 (Dundalk 1973), p. 124.

12. Gailey, 'Threshing machines', p. 40.

13. *Ibid.*, p. 41.

14. *Irish Farmer's Gazette* (1849), p. 342.

15. John Sproule, *The Irish Industrial Exhibition of 1853: a catalogue of its contents* (Dublin 1854), p. 218.

16. G.E. Fussell, *The farmer's tools, 1500–1900* (London 1952), p. 162.

17. Martin Doyle, *A cyclopaedia of practical husbandry*, revised edition, W. Rham (London 1844), p. 553.

18. *Purdon's practical farmer* (Dublin 1863), p. 296.

19. Pierce Ltd., *The story of Pierce* (Wexford, c.1970), p. 1.

20. Gailey, 'Threshing machines', p. 47; T. O'Neill, 'Tools and things: machinery on Irish farms 1700–1981' in Alan Gailey and Dáithí Ó Hógáin (eds.), *Gold under the furze* (Dublin 1982), p. 110.

21. *Purdon*, p. 67.

22. Joseph Lambert, *Agricultural suggestions to the proprietors and peasantry of Ireland* (Dublin 1845), p. 28.

23. Thomas Hale, *A compleat body of husbandry* (Dublin 1757).

24. John Wynn Baker, *A short description and list ... of the implements of husbandry, made in the factory at Laughlinstown, near Cellbridge, in the County of Kildare* (Dublin 1767–69), pp. 10–11.

25. Young, *Tour*, vol. 2, p. 34.

26. *Ibid.*, p. 123.

27. Fussell, *Farmer's tools*, p. 49.

28. H. Townsend, *Statistical survey of the County of Cork* (Dublin 1810), p. 613.

29. Hely Dutton, *Observations on Mr Archer's statistical survey of the County of Dublin* (Dublin 1802), p. 33.

30. Dubordieu, *County Down*, p. 50.
31. R. Thompson, *A statistical survey of the County of Meath* (Dublin 1802), p. 114.
32. William Shaw Mason, *A statistical account, or parochial survey of Ireland*, vol. 3 (Dublin 1814), p. 633.
33. *Munster farmers magazine*, vol. 1 (Cork 1812), pp. 342 and 850.
34. *Ibid.*, vol. 2 (1813), pp. 85–87.
35. *Ibid.*, pp. 85–87.
36. John Sproule, *Irish Industrial Exhibition*, p. 202.
37. Mervyn Watson, 'North Antrim swing ploughs: their construction and use', *Ulster Folklife*, vol. 28 (Holywood 1982).
38. Watson, 'Swing ploughs', pp. 20–21.
39. Fussell, *Farmer's tools*, p. 129; Sproule, *Irish Industrial Exhibition*, p. 216.
40. W. Howatson, 'Grain harvesting and harvesters' in T.M. Devine (ed.), *Farm servants and labourers in Lowland Scotland* (Edinburgh 1984), p. 129.
41. J.C. Loudon, *An encyclopaedia of agriculture* (London 1813), p. 373.
42. Jonathan Bell and Mervyn Watson, *Irish farming* (Edinburgh 1986)
43. Gavin Sprott, *The tractor in Scotland* (Edinburgh 1978), pp. 3–8.
44. *Ibid.*, p. 12.
45. L.E. Cochran, *Scottish trade with Ireland in the eighteenth century* (Edinburgh 1985)
46. Cormac Ó Grada, 'Seasonal migration and the post-famine adjustment in the west of Ireland', *Studia Hibernica*, xiii (1973), p. 51; Roger Wilson Leitch, 'Seasonal Workers … 1770–1970', vol. 2 (unpublished PhD thesis, University of Dundee 1990), pp. 221–25.

5. ARCHIVES OF ABUSE AND DISCONTENT? PRESBYTERIANISM AND SEXUAL BEHAVIOUR DURING THE EIGHTEENTH AND NINETEENTH CENTURIES

1. O. Hufton, *A history of women in Western Europe: Vol. 1, 1500–1800* (London 1997), p. 260.
2. A. Blaikie, *Illegitimacy, sex and society: northeast Scotland, 1750–1900* (Oxford 1993), pp. 185–210; C. Brown, *Religion and society in Scotland since 1701* (Edinburgh 1997), Chapter 4; P.E.H. Hair, *Before the Bawdy Court* (New York 1972); M. Ingram, *Church courts, sex and marriage in England, 1570–1640* (Cambridge 1987); D. Levine and K. Wrightson, 'The social context of illegitimacy in early modern England', in P. Laslett, K. Oosterveen and R.M. Smith (eds.), *Bastardy and its comparative history* (London 1980), pp. 158–75; R. Mitchison and L. Leneman, *Sexuality and social control: Scotland, 1660–1780* (Oxford 1989); G.R. Quaife, *Wanton wenches and wayward wives* (London 1979); J.A. Sharpe, 'Defamation and sexual slander in early modern England', *Borthwick Papers* (York n.d.); M. Todd, *The culture of Protestantism in early modern Scotland* (New Haven 2002).
3. J.M. McPherson, *The Kirk's care of the poor with special reference to the northeast of Scotland* (Aberdeen 1941), pp. 120–23; G. Henderson, *The Scottish ruling elder* (London 1935), p. 109, notes that in Grange, Banffshire in 1803, 248 females were so examined by midwives.
4. M. O'Riordan, *Catholicity and progress in Ireland* (London 1906), p. 272.
5. J. Forbes, *Memorandums made in Ireland in the autumn of 1852* (London 1853), p. 246.
6. R. Lynd, *Home life in Ireland* (London 1909), p. 52. For literary references to Ulster morals, see Angela's pregnancy outside marriage in F. McCourt, *Angela's ashes: a memoir of childhood* (London 1996). Malachy, the father, is suspected by a cousin of Angela's of

having 'Presbyterians in your family, which would explain what you did to our cousin ... Our little cousin no sooner gets off the boat than you are at her. We have morals in Limerick, you know, morals. We're not like jackrabbits from Antrim, a place crawling with Presbyterians.' (pp. 6–7). Also see B. MacNamara, *The valley of the squinting windows* (Dublin 1996 edition). Mrs Brennan, hearing that Mary Cooney is home from Belfast and is suspected of being pregnant outside marriage, says 'Aye, and to think that it was in Belfast, of all places, that it happened. Now, d'ye know what I'm going to tell ye, Farrell? "Tis the bad, Orange, immoral hole of a place is the same Belfast!"' (p. 20).

7. A. Day, 'Habits of the People; Traditional Life in Ireland 1830–1840, as recorded in the Ordnance Survey Memoirs', *Ulster Folklife*, Vol. 30 (1984), pp. 22–36.

8. S.J. Connolly, *Priests and people in pre-famine Ireland, 1740–1845* (New York 1982), pp. 187–88.

9. D.H. Akenson, *Between two revolutions: Islandmagee, County Antrim, 1798–1920* (Ontario 1979), p. 122.

10. D.H. Akenson, *Small differences: Irish Catholics and Irish Protestants, 1815–1922* (Kingston and Montreal 1988), p. 37.

11. R.F.G. Holmes, *Our Irish Presbyterian heritage* (Belfast 1985), pp. 55, 58 and 60.

12. J.M. Barkley, *A short history of the Presbyterian Church in Ireland* (Belfast 1959), pp. 104–6.

13. For the sexual discipline of the Quakers in Ireland see R.L. Greaves, *God's other children: Protestant non-conformists and the emergence of denominational churches in Ireland, 1660–1700* (Stanford 1997), pp. 335–37.

14. Route Presbytery Minutes 1701–1706, 143 pages Typescript. Moira and Lisburn (Seceder) Presbytery Minutes 1774–1786, 170 pages Typescript.

Down Presbytery Minutes 1707–1715, 386 pages Typescript. Route Presbytery Minutes 1811–1834, 338 pages Typescript. Down (Associate) Presbytery Minutes 1785–1795, 84 pages Typescript. Tyrone Presbytery Minutes 1781–1809, 269 pages Manuscript. (Presbyterian Historical Society). The terms Seceder and Associate are synonymous.

15. Down Presbytery Minutes 31 May 1710, p. 179.

16. Moira and Lisburn (Seceder) Presbytery Minutes 4 August 1775, p. 18.

17. Down Presbytery Minutes 8 January 1706, pp. 7–8.

18. For examples of: criminal conversation see Moira and Lisburn (Seceder) Presbytery Minutes 18 November 1778, p. 5; uncleanness see Route Presbytery Minutes 18 June 1704, p. 94; incest see Route Presbytery Minutes 9 May 1704, p. 90; fornication with birth of an illegitimate child see Down (Associate) Presbytery minutes 23 August 1786, p. 11; indecent behaviour see Moira and Lisburn (Seceder) Presbytery Minutes 11 January 1775, p. 12; whoredom see Down (Associate) Presbytery Minutes 22 August 1787, p. 19.

19. General Synod of Ulster, *The constitution and discipline of the Presbyterian Church*, (Belfast 1825), pp. 68–69.

20. For example, see the long-running case of the Rev. John Greer who, being charged with adultery and indecent behaviour, was rebuked, deposed from office and laid under 'ye lesser excommunication'. Moira and Lisburn (Seceder) Presbytery Minutes, various pages.

21. Cahans Kirk Session Minutes M865–M885 (Presbyterian Historical Society) 5 August 1753, p. 31.

22. Cahans Kirk Session Minutes 14 June 1753, p. 29.

23. Connor Kirk Session Minutes (Presbyterian Historical Society) 14 March 1708 (no pagination).

24. C. Kinealy, 'Presbyterian Church Records', in J.G. Ryan (ed.), *Irish church records* (Glenageary 1992), p. 77. For other comments see *First report from His Majesty's Commissioners for inquiring into the condition of the poorer classes in Ireland*. Appendix A (B.P.P.1835, XXXII), p. 112, also J. Boyle, 'Ordnance Survey Memoir Parish of Island Magee, Co. Antrim April 1840', in *Ordnance Survey Memoirs of Ireland Parishes of County Antrim 111 1833, 1835, 1839–40 Vol 10* eds. A. Day and P. McWilliams (Belfast 1991), p. 37.

25. Connor Kirk Session Minutes (Presbyterian Historical Society) 4 April 1708.

26. Connor Kirk Session Minutes 10 December 1732.

27. Connor Kirk Session Minutes 17 March 1725.

28. Connor Kirk Session Minutes 21 April 1709. In a similar case the midwife demanded of Margaret Cragg 'when in hard labour who was the father of her child' (Connor Kirk Session Minutes 8 August 1704). For a similar case in Carnmoney see J. Stevenson, *Two centuries of life in Down,1600–1800* (Belfast 1990 edn.), p. 175. Also see S.H. Bell, *December bride* (Belfast 1990), p. 130.

29. Connor Kirk Session Minutes 28 May 1706.

30. A. Day and P. McWilliams (eds.), *Ordnance Survey memoirs of Ireland parishes of County Antrim 1, 1838–9 Vol 2* (Belfast), p. 59.

31. D.H. Akenson, *Small differences*, p. 35.

32. See R.F.G. Holmes, *Our Presbyterian heritage*, p. 58.

33. L. Stone, *The family, sex and marriage in England, 1500–1800* (Harmondsworth 1979), p. 400.

34. K.M. Boyd, *Scottish church attitudes to sex, marriage and the family, 1850–1914* (Edinburgh 1980), p. 4.

35. Barkley in 1963 wrote that 'Discipline – even for sexual offences – has died out except in the Presbytery of Route. In some sixty current Session Minute Books, examined by the present writer, from twenty Presbyteries, fifty contain no cases of discipline since 1912. Of the remaining ten, six only provide one or two instances, whereas four, all from the Route, contain cases of discipline for breaches of the seventh commandment, and allied faults, to the present time.' J.M. Barkley, *The eldership*, p. 99. It is intriguing to observe the vestigial elements of the Kirk Session sexual discipline system still in operation in the closing decade of the twentieth century. In 1995 an elder in Ballyhenry Presbyterian church accused a member of the congregation of having an adulterous relationship. Although the remarks were made in the supposed confidentiality of the Session and apologies were subsequently issued on the instructions of the Presbytery, a Presbyterian Church statement noted that 'it is within the laws of the Presbyterian Church for the Kirk Session of a congregation to investigate the behaviour of its members and if necessary take appropriate measures of censure'. This case was notable because of its exceptional nature. *The Belfast Telegraph*, 17 November 1995.

36. R.F.G. Holmes, *Our Irish Presbyterian heritage*, p. 73.

37. Ibid., p. 73.

38. J.M. Barkley, *The eldership*, pp. 56–57.

39. Holmes quotes A.F. Scott Pearson on the settlers 'frontier' experience developing characteristics of 'courage, watchfulness, suspicion … acquisitiveness, adventurousness, dourness, diligence'. R.F.G. Holmes, *Our Presbyterian heritage*, p. 9. Crawford, referring to Irish Presbyterians' Scottish background, noted 'a Puritancial strain which showed itself in church architecture, the conduct of worship, disciplined attendance, the keeping of the Sabbath, dress and behaviour'. R.G. Crawford, *Loyal to King Billy: a*

portrait of the Ulster Protestants (Dublin 1987), p. 43.

40. Connor Kirk Session Minutes 24 February 1717.
41. Connor Kirk Session Minutes 28 February 1727.
42. S.H. Bell, *December bride*, p. 164.
43. W. Mair, *A digest of laws and decisions ecclesiastical and civil relating to the constitution, practice, and affairs of the Church of Scotland* (Edinburgh and London 1887), p. 224.
44. Connor Kirk Session Minutes 16 January 1719.
45. L. Leneman and R. Mitchison, 'Scottish illegitimacy ratios in the early modern period', *Economic History Review*, XL (1987), p. 44.
46. Mitchison and Leneman, *Sexuality*, pp. 13–14.
47. Quaife, *Wanton wenches*, notes that in early modern Somerset illicit sexual acts recorded by the church courts were widespread at a time when recorded illegitimacy was rare. L. Leneman, 'The study of illegitimacy from Kirk Session records', *Local Population Studies*, 31 (1983), pp. 29–33, finds that although the Blair Atholl Old Parish Register recorded only 13 illegitimate baptisms from 1775 to 1779, the Kirk Session mentions some 32 fornication cases over the corresponding period.
48. I.M. Clark, *A history of church discipline in Scotland* (Aberdeen 1929) provides coverage of the structure and functions of Kirk Sessions.
49. Henderson, *Scottish ruling elder*, pp. 242–45.
50. Rothiemay (Church of Scotland) Kirk Session Minute Books, 23 August 1827 to 18 June 1848 (CH2/416/5) and 25 June 1848 to 5 May 1872 (CH2/416/6), SRO, Edinburgh and 3 August 1872 to 2 November 1945, Rothiemay Parish Church Vestry (hereafter R/KSMB), 9 September 1927.
51. R/KSMB 8 February 1829, 13 September 1829, 16 May 1830, 16 July 1837, 5 October 1828. Fines

were divided between the two parties. On the virtual irrelevance of irregular marriage – as opposed to irregular banns – see T.C. Smout, 'Scottish marriage, regular and irregular, 1500–1940' in R.B. Outhwaite (ed.), *Marriage and society: studies in the social history of marriage* (London 1981), pp. 204–36; A. Blaikie, 'Scottish illegitimacy: social adjustment or moral economy?', *Journal of Interdisciplinary History*, XXIX (1998), pp. 221–41 (p. 227).
52. R/KSMB 14 June 1835. The session discontinued fines simply because 'it does not appear lawful'. However, W. Cramond, *Illegitimacy in Banffshire: facts, figures and opinions* (Banff 1888) cites the Banff session resolving to end fines 'in consequence of the exaction of the said penalty having a tendency to lead to unscriptural and papistical views in the minds of those on whom the Session might have occasion to impose them' (p.10).
53. For a fuller analysis of Kirk discipline in Rothiemay and Marnoch during this period, see Blaikie, *Illegitimacy*, pp. 185–210.
54. See Blaikie, *Illegitimacy*, pp. 175–78.
55. *Ibid.*, pp. 73–75.
56. R/KSMB 2 November 828, 27 January 1833, 7 May 1837.
57. Interestingly, although the Rothiemay session refers to twenty-one certificates of poverty being granted between 1827 and 1860, between 1860 and 1904 only two appear to have been issued.
58. R/KSMB 20 January 1833, 13 September 1835, 31 December 1837, 4 May 1873, 1 September 1890.
59. M.Gray, 'Farm workers in north-east Scotland' in T.M. Devine (ed.), *Farm servants and labour in Lowland Scotland, 1770–1914* (Edinburgh 1984), pp. 10–28.
60. I. Carter *Farm life in north east Scotland* (Edinburgh 1980), pp. 157–59.
61. R/KSMB 6 August 1888, 14 November 1869, 5 May 1890.

62. R/KSMB 10 June 1860, 13 August 1894, 17 February 1900.

63. Marnoch (Free Church) KSMB 15 June 1843 to 16 January 1890, Marnoch Parish Church Vestry, 8 January 1872, 6 July 1874. See also 10 February 1858 and 6 March 1859; Marnoch (Church of Scotland) KSMB, 29 January 1842–1896, Marnoch Parish Church Vestry, 6 April 1884; R/KSMB 5 March 1848.

64. Blaikie, *Illegitimacy*, p. 187.

65. Mitchison and Leneman, *Sexuality*, comment: 'it appears a very constant pattern in the eighteenth century that the allegation of fornication was not made until a woman was visibly pregnant, usually in the sixth or seventh month' (p. 136).

66. See Boyd, *Scottish church attitudes*; Blaikie, *Illegitimacy*, pp. 32–65.

67. J. Obelkevich, *Religion and rural society: South Lindsey, 1825–1875* (Oxford 1976), pp. 313–31; Mitchison and Leneman, *Sexuality*, p. 240.

68. R/KSMB 4 June 1876

69. A.A. MacLaren, *Religion and social class: The Disruption years in Aberdeen* (London, 1974), pp. 221–55, provides potted biographies of city elders.

70. T.C. Smout, 'Aspects of sexual behaviour in nineteenth-century Scotland' in A.A. MacLaren (ed.), *Social class in Scotland: past and present* (Edinburgh 1976), pp. 55–85 (p. 80).

71. Mitchison and Leneman, *Sexuality*, pp. 238, 203.

72. R/KSMB 4 August 1895; Clark, *Church discipline*, p. 166.

73. Mitchison and Leneman, *Sexuality*, p. 230.

74. See, for example, Smout, 'Aspects', p. 81.

75. See the discussion in Blaikie, 'Scottish illegitimacy', pp. 229–32.

76. E. Shorter, 'Illegitimacy, sexual revolution and social change in modern Europe', *Journal of Interdisciplinary History*, 11 (1977), pp. 237–72.

77. P. Laslett, K. Oosterveen and R.M. Smith (eds.), *Bastardy and its comparative history* (London 1980), pp. 41–8; see also Mitchison and Leneman, *Sexuality*. Locality persistence is examined in detail in Blaikie, 'Scottish illegitimacy'.

78. R. Adair, *Courtship, illegitimacy and marriage in early modern England* (Manchester 1996), p. 21.

79. W. Alexander, *Notes and sketches illustrative of northern rural life in the eighteenth century* (Edinburgh 1877), p. 213.

80. Mitchison and Leneman, *Sexuality*, p. 182.

81. *Ibid.*, p. 243.

82. L. Leneman and R. Mitchison, *Sin in the city: sexuality and social control in urban Scotland, 1660–1780* (Edinburgh 1998), p. 160.

83. Mitchison and Leneman, *Sexuality*, pp. 61–64.

84. Marriage was irregular if celebrated by a 'papist priest', in the Established Church, by a 'debarred' clergyman of any church, or in disobedience to parents (Barkley, *The eldership*, p. 42). There are many such examples of irregular marriage in Kirk Session minutes. For instance, on one day alone, 13 October 1796, irregular marriage formed six out of eight items of Carnmoney Session business. On 31 March 1796, four out of five items of business related to irregular marriage. The Memoirs of Templepatrick also note that when military regiments were stationed nearby, some local Presbyterian females became victims of an improvised marriage whereby a man and woman became man and wife simply by jumping over a sword together. When the regiment left, the military personnel left their improvised wives behind them ('Congregational Memoirs – Templepatrick', *The disciple*, 11, 16 (April 1883), pp. 108–112).

85. Such scarcity is itself interesting since, during both the eighteenth and twentieth centuries, irregularity was far

more common in Scotland. The
Victorian phase of high marital
conformity could suggest either the
triumph of sessional control or – more
likely in the north-east – official
marriage being offset by rebellious non-

marriage supplanting earlier irregularity.

86. R. Benedict, *The chrysanthemum and
the sword: patterns of Japanese culture*
(London 1947).
87. C. Brown, *The death of Christian
Britain* (London 2000).

6. MORE IRISH THAN THE IRISH? NUPTIALITY AND FERTILITY PATTERNS ON THE ISLE OF SKYE, 1881–1891

1. The support of the Economic and
Social Research Council is gratefully
acknowledged, as are grants from the
Population Investigation Committee
and the British Academy. We are also
grateful to the General Register
Office for Scotland for permission to
transcribe the contents of the civil
registers of Skye.

2. T.W. Guinnane, *The vanishing Irish:
households, migration and the rural
economy in Ireland, 1850–1914*
(Princeton 1997), p. 6; C. Ó Gráda,
'New evidence on the fertility
transition in Ireland 1880–1911',
Population Studies 28, 4 (1991) pp.
535–47 (p. 535).

3. Guinnane, *The vanishing Irish*, p. 284.

4. Ireland's civil registers began in 1864,
those of England and Wales in 1837.
Registration in Scotland began in
1855.

5. M. Flinn, J. Gillespie, N. Hill, A.
Maxwell, R. Mitchison and T.C.
Smout, *Scottish population history from
the seventeenth century to the 1930s*
(Cambridge 1977); D. Morse, 'The
decline of fertility in Scotland'
(Unpublished PhD thesis, University
of Edinburgh 1988); M. Anderson and
D. Morse, 'High fertility, high
emigration, low nuptiality; adjustment
processes in Scotland's demographic
experience, 1861–1914, Part 1',
Population Studies, 47 (1993), pp. 5–25,
'——, Part 2', *Population Studies*, 47
(1993), pp. 319–43; M. Anderson,
'Fertility decline in Scotland, England
& Wales, and Ireland: comparisons
from the 1911 Census of Fertility',

Population Studies, 52 (1998) pp. 1–20;
M. Anderson 'Highly restricted
fertility: very small families in the
British fertility decline', *Population
Studies*, 52 (1998), pp. 177–99.

6. Anderson and Morse, 'High fertility';
Anderson, 'Fertility decline';
Anderson, 'Highly restricted fertility'.

7. Bracadale and Duirinish largely
comprise the McLeod estate, while
Portree, Sleat, Snizort and Strath
form the MacDonald estate. Kilmuir
was largely owned by a Major Fraser.

8. Scottish civil registers are open to
inspection on payment of a search fee
at New Register House, Edinburgh.
Special permission has to be sought
from the General Register Office for
Scotland to pursue the study of a
particular geographic area.

9. The linking procedure is outlined in
R. Davies and E. Garrett, 'Moving
between censuses: linking individuals,
households and families, a case study
from the Inner Hebrides',
unpublished paper presented to the
1996 annual conference of the British
Society for Population Studies, St
Andrews.

10. The marriage certificate also indicates
where the marriage took place, for
under Scottish law weddings did not
have to be conducted in a place of
worship.

11 .It is hoped in the later stages of the
project to link in other documents,
such as the reports and papers
generated by the Royal Commission
on the Condition of the Crofters and
Cottars in the Highlands and Islands

of Scotland (1883 onwards) to add additional detail to our understanding of life on the island at this time.

12. For discussion of migration patterns in Skye between 1881 and 1891, see R. Davies and E. Garrett 'Over the sea to Skye: migration to, from and around the parishes of the Isle of Skye, Scotland 1881–1891'. Unpublished paper presented to the British Society for Population Studies annual conference, Utrecht, September 2000.

13. A.T.A. Learmouth, 'The population of Skye', *Scottish Geographical Magazine* 66 (1950), pp. 77–103.

14. In 1891, 33 per cent of Skye's population was aged less than 15, while 14 per cent was aged 60 or over.

15. The figures for England and Wales and Scotland are taken from Anderson and Morse 'High fertility', Part 1, Table 2, p. 8.

16. The number of fishermen may well be under-counted, some being at sea on census night, although inshore fishermen who returned to land so as not to break the Sabbath may well have been captured by the Sunday night census.

17. Marriages taking place from 1 April 1881 to 31 May 1891, 596 marriages in all.

18. There is a small chance that due to transcription errors, alternative translations of Gaelic names into English, or extremely unusual family circumstances, a few individuals remained resident on Skye but went unidentified by the linkage process.

19. Amongst fishermen there is a greater risk that they may have been away at sea on census night 1891, although the presence of their families would have identified them as 'absent residents' during linkage. It is possible that some deaths at sea were not registered on the sailors' home island.

20. M. Anderson, 'Why was Scottish nuptiality so depressed for so long?' in I. Devos and L. Kennedy, *Marriage and the rural economy: Western Europe since 1400* (Brussels 1999).

21. D. Fitzpatrick, 'Marriage in post-famine Ireland' in A. Cosgrove (ed.), *Marriage in Ireland* (Dublin 1985), pp. 116–131, Table 2 quoted in Guinnane, *The vanishing Irish*, pp. 94–5. Guinnane warns of the caution necessary when interpreting SMAMs, especially when 'extensive' out-migration is suspected. The SMAMs for Ireland as a whole for the 1860s birth cohort were 31.0 for men and 27.5 for women.

22. Guinnane, *The vanishing Irish*, p. 100

23. The high number of widowers amongst the crofter grooms is not related to the high proportion of crofter grooms who had lost their fathers: 82 per cent of bachelor crofter grooms had lost their fathers.

24. The average age of crofter brides rose to 29.6 when marriages involving widows are included. No fisherman married a widow.

25. Exceptions to the 'companionate' model of marriages may well have been the middle classes and coalminers. Both of these groups appear to have had considerable age gaps between spouses. See S. Szreter and E. Garrett, 'Reproduction, compositional demography, and economic growth: family planning in England long before the fertility decline', *Population and Development Review*, 26,1 (2000), p. 67

26. See Anderson 'Why was Scottish nuptiality so depressed', for a discussion of why rural Scots evinced 'more caution in approaching marriage' than their counterparts in England and Wales.

27. One advantage of using the 45–54 age group is that it markedly reduces any effect of age heaping on the age 50. This is very important on Skye, where heaping on ages ending in 0, particularly in the later decades of life, is marked.

28. In addition, a further 16 per cent of the females aged 45–54 were

widowed, but only 4 per cent of the men.

29. Guinnane, *The vanishing Irish*, Tables 4.2 and 4.3.

30. *Ibid.*, p. 95, pp. 200–8 indicates that celibacy in Ireland had increased markedly by 1911. It was not until then that female rates reached those of Skye in the 1880s. Unfortunately, our data do not at present allow us to track the celibacy rates for Skye over time.

31. Guinnane, *The vanishing Irish*, Map 7.1, p. 200. Guinnane devotes a whole chapter to discussion of 'the decline of marriage', i.e. the rise in celibacy in Ireland.

32. J.W. Eaton and A.J. Mayer, 'The social biology of very high fertility among the Hutterites: the demography of a unique population', *Human Biology* 25,3 (1953), pp. 206–63.

33. The Princeton indices have been used to map the historical course of fertility decline in Europe. See A.J. Coale and R. Treadway, 'A summary of the changing distribution of overall fertility, marital fertility and the proportion married in the provinces of Europe' in A.J. Coale and S.C. Watkins, *The decline of fertility in Europe* (Princeton 1986), pp. 31–181. R.I. Woods, *Population analysis in geography* (London 1979), pp. 118–21, gives a very clear account of their calculation.

34. M. Teitelbaum, *The British fertility decline: demographic transition in the crucible of the Industrial Revolution* (Princeton 1984).

35. C. Ó Gráda, *Ireland before and after the Famine, explorations in economic history, 1800–1925*, second edition (Manchester 1993), Table A5 – as quoted in Guinnane, *The vanishing Irish*, 1997, Table 8.2, p. 249

36. Ó Gráda, 'New evidence' and C. Ó Gráda, 'Correction to Ó Gráda 1991', *Population Studies* 29, 4 (1992), p. iv; see also Guinnane, *The vanishing Irish*, Appendix 8A, pp. 270–71

37. We have no evidence of children registered as though they had been born to their grandmother, but we have seen one or two instances in the census of grandchildren being returned as children, although these may have been transcription errors on the part of the enumerator rather than a deliberate attempt to mislead.

38. The number of single women living on Skye dropped between 1881 and 1891, so to calculate the illegitimacy rate (the number of illegitimate births per 1,000 single women), the number of unmarried women in each five-year age group in 1881 and 1891 was averaged, the resultant figures being totalled before being divided into the number of illegitimate births registered. Technically, widows are at risk of illegitimate birth too, but they were not included in this calculation.

39. Flinn *et al.*, *Scottish population history*, Table 5.4.3, p. 353.

40. Agricultural districts: see E. Garrett, A. Reid, K. Schürer and S. Szreter, *Changing family size in England & Wales: place, class, and demography, 1891–1911* (Cambridge 2001); E.A Wrigley, R. Davies, J. Oeppen and R.S. Schofield, *English population history from family reconstitution* (Cambridge 1997), Table 7.1.

41. Flinn *et al.*, *Scottish population history*, Table 5.3.6, p. 345.

42. M. Anderson, 'Fertility decline', p. 11. From the ASMFRs shown in Table 3 it may be calculated that the TMFR for the Hutterites was 10.9 children per woman, for the Irish Quakers: 9.6, for England & Wales 1800–24: 7.7 and for the Agricultural areas of England and Wales in 1891: 6.3.

43. See discussions in Wrigley *et al.*, *English population history* concerning female fecundity.

44. R. Floud, K. Wachter and A. Gregory, *Height, health and history: nutritional status in the United Kingdom, 1750–1980*. (Cambridge 1990), pp. 200–6, for example, show rural Scots and Irish men to be

considerably taller than their English counterparts.

45. The 170 women married in their twenties on Skye in the period 1881–85 were observed to be still resident on the island in the 1891 census. Eighty-eight of the women had married aged 20–24, and eighty-two had married aged 25–29.

46. One other option is that they may have been more likely to report a stillbirth or miscarriage as a live birth. See E. Garrett & R. Davies, 'Birth spacing and infant mortality on the Isle of Skye, Scotland in the 1880s: a comparison with the town of Ipswich, England', *Local Population Studies*, 71 (Autumn 2003), pp. 53–74.

7. CREATING NEW FORMS: CIVIL SOCIETY IN NORTHERN IRELAND

1. R. Rose, *Governing without consensus* (London 1971), p. 75.

2. Eco in fact describes this as 'a great peace breaking down, a great international power that has unified the world in language, customs, ideologies, religions, art and technology, and then at a certain point, thanks to its own ungovernable complexity, collapses'. 'Living in the new Middle Ages' in *Faith in fakes* (London 1986), p. 74.

3. *Ibid.*, pp. 76–77.

4. *Ibid.*, p. 79.

5. *Ibid.*, p. 79–80.

6. John O'Farrell on BBC2's Dispatch Box, 3 July 2001, on being asked why Jill Dando's killer and Pete Sampras' exit from Wimbledon knocked Northern Ireland off the front pages of the tabloids.

7. J. Ruane and J. Todd, 'Why can't you get along with each other?: Culture, conflict and Northern Ireland' in E. Hughes (ed.), *Culture, politics and Northern Ireland* (1993), p. 36.

8. K.A. Miller, 'Revising revisionism' in D. Keogh and M. H. Haltzel, *Northern Ireland and the politics of reconciliation* (Cambridge 1993), p. 60. Miller argues that 'unless we address the fundamental economic and social problems and inequalities inherent in "modernisation", we will not only fail to find long-term solutions to the Northern Ireland crisis, but we also may witness similar explosions of nationalist, racist and fascist ideologies and movements among frustrated and marginalised groups throughout post-Cold War Europe.'

9. U. Eco, 'Chaosmos: the Return of the Middle Ages' in R. Kearney, *States of mind: dialogues with contemporary thinkers on the European mind* (Manchester 1995), p. 77.

10. R. Kirkland, *Literature and culture in Northern Ireland: moments of danger* (London 1996), pp. 8–11.

11. The Northern Irish state cannot be said to have been hegemonic if we understand hegemony as 'not limited to matters of direct political control but [that which] seeks to describe a more general predominance which includes, as one of its key features, a particular way of seeing the world and human nature and relationships'. It is 'different from ideology in that it is seen to depend for its hold not only on its expression of the interests of the ruling class but also its acceptance as "normal reality" or "commonsense" by those in practice subordinate to it'. R. Williams, *Keywords: a vocabulary of culture and society* (London 1988), p. 145.

12. *Irish News*, 11 April 1998.

13. A. Ferguson, *An essay on the history of civil society*, edited by F. Oz-Salzberger (Cambridge 1995), p. 182.

14. G. Morton, 'Civil society, municipal government and the state: enshrinement, empowerment and

legitimacy', *Urban History*, 25:3 (1998); K. Kumar, 'Civil society: an inquiry into the usefulness of an historical term', *British Journal of Sociology*, 44:3, September 1993, pp. 390–91, C. Hann and E. Dunne, *Civil society: challenging Western models* (London 1996).

15. C.G.A. Bryant, 'Social self-organisation, civility and sociology: a comment on Kumar's 'Civil society', *British Journal of Sociology*, 44:3, September 1993, p. 397–400.

16. Various policy initiatives aimed to strengthen civil society. The Good Friday Agreement set up a Civic Forum which is a recognition of the importance of civil society in its strictest sense: Strand One Section 34 of the Agreement states: 'A consultative Civic Forum will be established. It will comprise representatives of the business, trade union and voluntary sectors, and such other sectors as agreed by the First Minister and Deputy First Minister. It will act as a consultative mechanism on social, economic and cultural issues.'

17. R. Putnam, 'Bowling alone: America's declining social capital', *Journal of Democracy*, 6:1, January 1995, p. 67.

18. M.W. Foley and B. Edwards, 'The paradox of civil society', *Journal of Democracy*, 7:3, (1996), p. 38.

19. *Ibid.*, p. 43.

20. *Ibid.*, p. 46.

21. D. Miller, 'The new battleground?', *Planet: the Welsh internationalist*, No. 102, Dec. 1993/Jan. 1994, pp. 74–79.

22. K. Kumar, 'Civil society', pp. 382–3.

23. Prof. J. Darby's contribution to A. Pollack *et al.*, *A citizens' inquiry: The Opsahl Report on Northern Ireland*, (Dublin 1993), p. 4.

24. M. Walzer, *Obligations: essays on disobedience, war and citizenship* (Massachusetts 1970), p. 46.

25 J. Locke, *Two treatises of government*, edited by P. Lazlett (Cambridge 1988), par. 95.

26. It has been argued that this has simply created two vetoes as well as two majorities. P. Emerson, 'Party politics', *Fortnight*, April 2000.

27. The Agreement, Strand One, Point 6.

28. M. Elliott, *The Catholics of Ulster: a history* (London 2000), p. 470.

29. NICRA, *'We Shall Overcome' ... The history of the struggle for civil rights in Northern Ireland, 1968–1978* (Belfast 1978).

30. The Lord Mayor of Belfast, Sir Joseph Cairns, remarked that Northern Ireland had been reduced to the level of a 'fuzzy wuzzy nation' and referred to himself as a 'Britishman', a 'dying breed'. Tom Paulin, *Ireland and the English crisis* (Newcastle 1984), p. 137.

31. J. McGarry and B. O'Leary, *Explaining Northern Ireland* (Oxford 1996), pp. 111–12.

32. By the spring of 1974, the UWC had become a 21-person committee drawn from workers at Harland and Wolff, Short Brothers, the power stations, engineering works and the new industrial estates. Politicians Paisley, West and Craig had been co-opted onto the committee under the chair of Glenn Barr, a Vanguard Assembly member and UDA officer from Derry. J. Bardon, *A history of Ulster* (Belfast 1994), p. 707.

33. The British Army was more equivocal and lacked purpose in breaking the strike. R. Fisk, *Point of no return* (London 1975), pp. 87–88.

34. M. Walzer, 'The civil society argument' in C. Mouffe (ed.), *Dimensions of radical democracy: pluralism, citizenship, community* (London 1992), pp. 89–107; Foley and Edwards, 'Civil society', p. 48.

35. H. Griffiths, 'Community relations and voluntary involvement' in J. Darby *et al.*, *Violence and social services in Northern Ireland*, (London 1978), pp. 165–200; J.W. McAuley, 'Cuchullain and an RPG-7: the ideology and politics of the Ulster Defence Association' in E. Hughes (ed.), *Culture and politics*, p. 45.

36. *Guardian*, 19 November 1991, cited in Bardon, *Ulster*, p. 827.
37. Equally, the peace process was a recognition that there was no military victory to be had in Northern Ireland.
38. B. Rolston, 'Gagging for it', *Fortnight*, June 1995.
39. D. Butler, *The trouble of reporting Northern Ireland* (Aldershot 1995), p. 65.
40. *Ibid.*, p. 73.
41. R. Wilson, *The media and intrastate*

conflict in Northern Ireland, Democratic Dialogue Papers.
42. When Ian Paisley asserted in a BBC interview that everyone knew the BBC was Vatican Television, the interviewer Noel Thompson's assurance that the BBC was neutral on all things drew on a rhetoric that is almost as old-fashioned as Paisley's. *Hearts and Minds*, BBC, 21 June 2001.
43. Eco, *Fakes*, p. 75.
44. *Ibid.*, p. 84.

8. ARISE THEREFORE ULSTER-SCOT: ULSTER UNIONIST IDENTITY AND THE RECONFIGURATION OF THE ISLES

1. V. Bognanor, *Devolution in the United Kingdom* (Oxford 1999), p. 287.
2. Great Britain–Northern Ireland Office, *The Belfast Agreement: an agreement reached at the Multi-Party Talks on Northern Ireland* (Stationery Office, London 1998). For a comprehensive analysis of the institutions and the equality, criminal justice and police reform issues of the Agreement, see E. Meehan, 'The Belfast Agreement: distinctiveness and cross-fertilisation in the UK's devolution programme', *Parliamentary affairs* (1999), 52:1, pp. 19–51; and B. O'Leary, 'The nature of the British–Irish Agreement', *New Left Review* (1999), 233, pp. 66–96.
3. C. McCall, *Identity in Northern Ireland: communities, politics and change* (Basingstoke 1999).
4. In *Ulster's uncertain defenders: Protestant political, paramilitary and community groups and the Northern Ireland conflict* (Belfast 1984), Sarah Nelson painted a convincing picture of the sense of insecurity and siege experienced by Ulster Protestants.
5. R. Axtmann, 'Globalization, Europe and the state: introductory reflections', in R. Axtmann (ed.), *Globalization in Europe: theoretical and empirical investigations* (London 1998),

pp. 1–22.
6. W. Wallace, 'The sharing of sovereignty: 'The European Paradox', *Political Studies* (1999), 47:3, pp. 511–12.
7. C. Pentland, *International theory and European integration* (London 1973), pp. 117–19.
8. A. Moravcsik, 'Preferences and power in the European Community: a Liberal intergovernmental approach', *Journal of Common Market Studies* (1993), 31:4, pp. 473–524.
9. W. Wallace, 'The sharing of sovereignty: the European paradox', *Political Studies* (1999), 47:3, pp. 503–6.
10. C. McCall and A. Williamson, 'Fledgling social partnership in the Irish Border Region: European Union community initiatives and the voluntary sector', *Policy and Politics* (2000), 28:3.
11. J. Shaw, 'Postnational constitutionalism in the European Union', *Journal of European Public Policy* (1999), 6:4, pp. 583–87.
12. J. Mitchell, 'What could a Scottish Parliament do?' in H. Elcock and M. Keating (eds.), *Remaking the Union: devolution and British politics in the 1990s* (London 1998), pp. 76–80.
13. L. Moreno, 'Local and Global: Mesogovernments and territorial

identities', *Nationalism and Ethnic Politics* (1999), 5:3 and 4, p. 62.

14. Member of the Legislative [Northern Ireland] Assembly.

15. Interview with author, 19 September 1995

16. Political party representation in the 108-seat Northern Ireland Assembly is made up of both pro-Agreement and anti-Agreement parties. The pro-Agreement parties include the UUP, 28 seats; the SDLP, 24 seats; Sinn Féin, 18 seats; Alliance, 6 seats; the Women's Coalition, 2 seats; and the Progressive Unionist Party (PUP), 2 seats. Anti-Agreement parties include the DUP, 20 seats; the Northern Ireland Unionist Party (NIUP), 4 seats; the United Unionist Assembly Party (UUAP), 3 seats; and the UK Unionist Party (UKUP), 1 seat.

17. S. Bruce, *God save Ulster!: The religion and politics of Paisleyism* (Oxford 1989); Democratic Unionist Party (DUP), *The surrender of Maastricht: what it means for Ulster* (Belfast 1992).

18. 'Playing the Orange card' is a euphemism usually reserved for British politicians who pander to sectarian Orange or unionist interest for the purposes of electoral gain or short-term political expediency. It is sometimes accompanied by the threat of mass mobilisation and violence. The leading UK Conservative Lord Randolph Churchill was most closely associated with playing the Orange card for the purpose of maintaining British authority within and without the UK. In response to the movement for Irish home rule which coalesced into the formation of the Irish Parliamentary Party in 1874, he declared that 'Ulster will fight and Ulster will be right'.

After the 1992 UK General Election, John Major was accused by Irish nationalists of playing the Orange card. His Conservative party's slim parliamentary majority required him to seek the support of the UUP. He achieved this through reaching a non-specified 'understanding' with its then leader James Molyneaux and using the language of a 'born again unionist' (P. Mitchell, 'The party system and party competition' in P. Mitchell and R. Wilford (eds.), *Politics in Northern Ireland* (Boulder 1999), p. 110.

19. P. O'Malley, *The uncivil wars: Ireland today* (Belfast 1983), p. 151.

20. Since 1995, Irish nationalist residents of the Garvaghy Road have had some success in their campaign to prevent Protestant Orangemen parading from Drumcree into Portadown via the Garvaghy Road. Many Orangemen understand this denial of their 'traditional right to march' as one of siege on Drumcree hill and as a metaphor for siege in Northern Ireland generally.

21. P. Maume, 'Young Ireland, Arthur Griffith and Republican ideology: the question of continuity', *Éire–Ireland* (1999), 34:2, p. 155.

22. *News Letter*, 23 October 1989.

23. R. Rose, 'Is the United Kingdom a state? Northern Ireland as a test case' in P. Madgwick and R. Rose (eds.), *The territorial dimension in United Kingdom politics* (London 1982), p. 101.

24. Cited in J.M. McAuley, 'Mobilising Ulster Unionism: new directions or old?', *Capital and class* (2000), 71, pp. 37–64.

25. L. Colley, *Britons: forging the nation 1707–1837* (London 1992), p. 8.

26. G. Walker, 'The Northern Ireland problem and Scottish–Irish relations' in T.M. Devine and J.F. MacMillan (eds.), *Celebrating Columba: Irish–Scottish connections 597–1997* (Edinburgh 1999), p. 161.

27. T. Wright and A. Gamble, 'The end of Britain?', *The Political Quarterly* (2000) 71:1, p. 2.

28. R. Hansen, 'British citizenship after the Empire: a defence', *The Political Quarterly* (2000), 71:1, p. 46.

29. J. Loughlin, *Ulster Unionism and British national identity since 1885* (London 1995), p. 220.

30. Interview with author, 29 June 2000.
31. J. McMillan, 'Britishness after devolution' in G. Hassan and C. Warhurst (eds.), *A different future: a modernizer's guide to Scotland* (Glasgow 1995), p. 287.
32. G. Dawe, *The rest is history* (Newry 1998), p. 112.
33. B. Graham, 'Ulster: a representation of place yet to be imagined' in P. Shirlow and M. McGovern (eds.), *Who are 'the people'? Unionism, Protestantism and Loyalism in Northern Ireland* (London 1997), pp. 40, 53.
34. Z. Bauman, *Globalization: the human consequences* (Cambridge 1998).
35. J. Loughlin, *Ulster Unionism and British national identity since 1885* (London 1995), p. 227.
36. N. Porter, *Rethinking Unionism: an alternative vision for Northern Ireland* (Belfast 1996).
37. *Irish News*, 18 May 2000.
38. *Irish Times*, 23 September 1999.
39. I. Adamson, *The identity of Ulster: the land, the language, and the people* (Bangor 1982); I. Adamson, *The Ulster people: ancient, medieval and modern* (Bangor 1991), and interview with author, 16 June 2000.
40. P. Robinson, *Ulster-Scots: A grammar of the traditional written and spoken language* (Bangor 1997), p. 1.
41. Ulster-Scots has the features of a cant, that is, a second dialect relearned to distinguish ethnicity. See

M. Görlach, 'Ulster-Scots: a language?' in J. M. Kirk and D. P. Ó Baoill (eds.), *Language and politics: Northern Ireland, the Republic of Ireland and Scotland* (Belfast 2000).
42. Ulster-Scots Language Society, *An introduction to the language* (Belfast 1995), p. 1.
43. F. O'Connor, 'A Trimble of anticipation', *Magill* (January 1999), pp. 14–16; C. Ryder, 'Ulster-Scots will trip off the tongue', *Irish Times* (13 May 1999).
44. C. C. O'Reilly, *The Irish language in Northern Ireland: the politics of culture and identity* (Basingstoke 1999), p. 178.
45. *Ibid.*, pp. 22–23.
46. *Irish News*, 22 March 1996.
47. I. Herbison, *The rest is silence: some remarks on the disappearance of Ulster-Scots poetry* (Ballymena 1996), p. 10.
48. Interview with author, 19 June 2000.
49. Interview with author, 29 June 2000.
50. *The Belfast Agreement*, p. 19.
51. *Irish Times*, 1 May 1997.
52. M. Görlach, 'Ulster-Scots: a language?'.
53. In the *Sunday Times*, 1 December 1998.
54. *Irish News*, 8 May 1991.
55. *Irish Times*, 1 March 2001.
56. J. Loughlin, *Ulster Unionism and British national identity since 1885* (London 1995), p. 230.

9. RELIGION, MODERNISATION AND LOCALITY IN NINETEENTH-CENTURY MID-ANTRIM

1. Anthony D. Smith, *Nations and nationalism in a global era* (Cambridge 1995). See also Clifford Geertz, 'Primordial ties' reprinted in John Hutchinson and Anthony D. Smith (eds.), *Ethnicity* (Oxford 1996), pp. 40–45.
2. David W. Miller, 'Presbyterianism and "Modernisation" in Ulster', *Past and Present* 80 (1978), pp. 66–90.
3. Ernest Gellner, *Nations and*

nationalisms (Oxford 1982) and 'Modular man is a nationalist' in *Conditions of liberty: civil society and its rivals* (London 1994), pp. 103–8; also Benedict Anderson, *Imagined communities: reflections on the origins and spread of nationalism* (London 1983). See also Miroslav Hroch, 'Real and constructed: the nature of the nation' in John A. Hall (ed.), *The state* of the nation. *Ernest Gellner and the theory of nationalism* (Cambridge 1998), pp. 91–106. For a critique of modernist theories of nationalism, see John Hutchinson, 'Ethnicity and modern nations', *Ethnic and Racial Studies* (July 2000), 23:4, pp. 651–69.

4. For an early and influential assessment of the relationship between industrialisation and modernisation, see E.A. Wrigley's 1972 essay 'The process of modernisation and the industrial revolution in England', reprinted in Robert I. Rotberg (ed.), *Social mobility and modernisation* (Cambridge 2000), pp. 89–123.

5. Tom Nairn, 'The curse of rurality: limits of modernisation theory' in Hall, pp. 107–34. In his investigation of the conditions in which forms of nationalist formation occur, David D. Laitin argues that these circumstances are partially dependent on rural social structures. See his article 'National revivals and violence', *European Journal of Sociology* 36 (1995), pp. 3–43. Sabrina Petra Ramet underlines the different character of urban and rural Serbian nationalist mobilisation in 'Nationalism and the "idiocy" of the countryside: the Case of Serbia', *Ethnic and Racial Studies* 19 (1996) 1, pp. 70–87.

6. Nairn, p. 108.

7. Angélique Day, Patrick McWilliams and Nóirín Dobson (eds.), *Ordnance Survey Memoirs of Ireland, vol. 23, Parishes of County Antrim VII: 1831–5, 1837–8: Ballymena and West Antrim* (Belfast 1993), pp. 52–66.

8. *Observer*, 2 June 1860.

9. *Observer*, 24 March 1866.

10. *Observer*, 24 September 1859.

11. *Observer*, 3 October 1857 and 10 October 1857.

10. IRELAND AND SCOTLAND: THE QUEST FOR DEVOLVED POLITICAL INSTITUTIONS, 1867–1914

1. I wish to thank Carla King for reading and commenting upon this draft, A.C Hepburn for a number of useful observations and the editors for pruning the verbose text. I am grateful also to my aunt, Col. Helen E. O'Day for her support.

2. W.E. Gladstone, *The Irish question: I. The history of an idea, II, Lessons of the election* (London 1886), p. 20

3. W.H.K. Redmond, reported in *Hansard* (Commons) 4th ser., 54, 1743, 15 March 1898.

4. T.P. O'Connor, reported in *Ibid.*, 5th ser., 53, 516, 30 May 1913.

5. *Ibid.*, 4th ser., 3, 1706, 29 April 1892.

6. *Ibid.*, 4th ser., 54, 1720, 15 March 1898.

7. Michael Hechter, *Internal colonialism: The Celtic Fringe in British national development, 1536–1966* (London 1975), p. 347.

8. Keith Robbins, 'Core and periphery in modern British history', *Proceedings of the British Academy* 70 (1984), p. 292; John Kendle, *Ireland and the federal solution: the debate over the United Kingdom Constitution, 1870–1921* (Kingston and Montreal 1989), p. 65.

9. Kenneth O. Moran, *Wales in British politics 1868–1922* (Cardiff 1970), p. 70; James Hunter (ed.), *For the people's cause: from the writings of John Murdoch, Highland and Irish land reformer* (Edinburgh 1986), p. 54.

10. John D. Wood, 'Transatlantic land reform: America and the Crofters' Revolt 1878–1888', *Scottish Historical Review* 63 (April 1984), p. 88.

11. William O'Brien and Desmond Ryan (eds.), *Devoy's post bag 1871–1928* (Dublin 1948), I, pp. 332–33; T.W. Moody, *Davitt and Irish Revolution 1846–82* (Oxford 1982), pp. 358–59.

12. Quoted in Kendle, *Ireland and the federal solution*, p. 82.

13. Carla King, *Michael Davitt* (Dublin

1999), p. 46.

14. Morgan, *Wales in British politics*, p. 70.

15. Quoted in James Hunter, 'The Gaelic connection: the Highlands, Ireland and nationalism, 1873–1922', *Scottish Historical Review* 54 (1975), p. 192.

16. Quoted in *Ibid.*, p. 188.

17. Quoted in *Ibid.*, p. 191.

18. Quoted in Ruth Dudley Edwards, *Patrick Pearse: the triumph of failure* (London 1977), p. 31.

19. Quoted in H.J. Hanham, *Scottish nationalism* (London 1968), p. 124.

20. Kendle, *Ireland and the federal solution*, pp. 71, 113.

21. Hechter, *Internal colonialism*, p. 343.

22. *Hansard*, 3rd ser., 304, 1081, 8 April 1886.

23. Gladstone, *The Irish question*, p. 20.

24. Kendle, *Ireland and the federal solution*, p. 62; Hanham, *Scottish nationalism*, p. 92.

25. Quoted in Kendle, *Ireland and the federal solution*, p. 63.

26. Quoted in Hanham, *Scottish nationalism*, pp. 92–93.

27. I.G.C. Hutchinson, *A political history of Scotland 1832–1924: parties, elections and issues* (Edinburgh 1986), p. 172.

28. *Hansard*, 3rd ser., 335, 101–2, 9 April 1889.

29. *Ibid.*, 102.

30. *Ibid.*, 108.

31. James G. Kellas, *Modern Scotland*, revised edition (London 1980), p. 145.

32. See Miroslav Hroch, *Social preconditions of national revival* (Cambridge 1985); 'Nationalism and national movements: comparing the past and the present of Central and Eastern Europe', *Nations and Nationalism*, II, 1 (1996), pp. 35–44.

33. Quoted in B.A. Kennedy, 'Sharman Crawford's federal scheme for Ireland' in H.A. Cronne, T.W. Moody and D.B. Quinn (eds.), *Essays in British and Irish history in honour of James Eadie Todd* (London 1949), p. 237.

34. *Ibid.*, p. 246; details of the scheme, pp. 250–51.

35. Quoted in Sir Charles Gavan Duffy, *Young Ireland: a fragment of Irish history* (London, Paris and New York 1880), p. 591.

36. Quoted in *Ibid.*, p. 599.

37. *Ibid.*, p. 577.

38. E.D. Steele, 'Cardinal Cullen and Irish nationality', *Irish Historical Studies* 19 (March 1975), p. 258.

39. Isaac Butt, *Irish federalism: its meaning, its objects, and its hopes*, second edition (Dublin and London 1870), p. 15.

40. *Ibid.*, pp. 15–16.

41. *Ibid.*, p. 16.

42. John George MacCarthy, *A plea for the home government of Ireland* (London 1871), pp. 127–28.

43. Rev. Thadeus O'Malley, *Home rule on the basis of federalism* (London and Dublin 1873), p. 4.

44. *Ibid.*, p. 19.

45. *Ibid.*, p. 21.

46. *Proceedings of the Home Rule Conference held at the Rotunda, Dublin on the 18th, 19th, 20th and 21st November 1873* (Dublin 1874).

47. Hunter, 'The Gaelic connection', p. 184.

48. *Hansard*, 3rd ser., 220, 703, 30 June 1874.

49. *Ibid.*, 715.

50. *Ibid.*, 905, 2 July 1874.

51. *Ibid.*, 954.

52. *Ibid.*, 230, 754, 30 June 1876.

53. *Ibid.*, 783.

54. *Ibid.*, 304, 1211, 9 April 1886.

55. *Ibid.*, 305, 969, 13 May 1886.

56. *Ibid.*, 1672–73, 21 May 1886.

57. *Ibid.*, 306, 1577, 710, 851, 31 May, 1 and 3 June 1886.

58. *Ibid.*, 4th ser., 8, 1757, 17 February 1893.

59. *Ibid.*, 11, 423, 14 April 1893.

60. *Ibid.*, 60, 11 April 1893.

61. *Ibid.*, 302, 537, 29 March 1895.

62. *Ibid.*, 543.

63. *Ibid.*, 54, 1718, 15 March 1898.

64. *Ibid.*, 5th ser., 306, 1403, 11 April 1912.

65. *Ibid.*, 1449.

66. *Ibid.*, 1468.

67. *Ibid.*, 53, 514, 30 May 1913.

68. Walker Connor, 'Beyond reason: the nature of the ethnonational bond' in

John Hutchinson and Anthony D. Smith, *Ethnicity* (Oxford 1996), p. 70.

69. Miroslav Hroch, 'National self-determination from a historical perspective' in Sukumar Perival (ed.), *Nations and nationalism* (Budapest and

London 1995), pp. 66–67.

70. Connor, 'Beyond reason', p. 69.

71. Hutchinson and Smith, *Ethnicity*, p. 6.

72. E. Rumpf and A.C. Hepburn, *Nationalism and socialism in twentieth-century Ireland* (Liverpool 1977), p. 223.

11. BULLET MOULDERS AND BLACKTHORN MEN: A COMPARATIVE STUDY OF IRISH NATIONALIST SECRET SOCIETY CULTURE IN MID-NINETEENTH-CENTURY SCOTLAND AND ULSTER

1. A.C. Hepburn, *A past apart: studies in the history of Catholic Belfast 1850–1950* (Belfast 1996), p. 4; J.E. Handley, *The Irish in modern Scotland* (Cork 1947), p. 46; Bernard Aspinwall, 'Scots and Irish clergy ministering to immigrants, 1830–1878', *Innes Review*, XLVII:1 (Spring 1996), p. 51; C.M. Oakley, *The second city* (Glasgow 1946), p. 47. Despite the known presence of a number of Protestants in the Fenian movement in Ulster, I have used Catholicism as a demographic indicator because the overwhelming majority of secret society men were Catholics.

2. Hepburn, *Past apart*, pp. 144–45; 'Shadow', *Midnight scenes and social photographs* (Glasgow 1858), p. 43.

3. W.M. O'Hanlon, *Walks among the poor of Belfast* (Belfast 1853), p. 45.

4. R.D. Lobban, 'The Irish community in Greenock in the nineteenth century', *Irish Geography*, VI:3 (1971), pp. 270–71, 275, 277; Terence Duffy, 'Urban living conditions and public health in Derry, 1815–1885', *Derriana* (1983), pp. 70–3.

5. Alan B. Campbell, *The Lanarkshire miners* (Edinburgh 1979), pp. 180–89; Frank Wright, *Two lands on one soil: Ulster politics before Home Rule* (Dublin 1996), pp. 397–406.

6. David Jary and Julia Jary, *Dictionary of sociology* (Glasgow 1991), p. 139.

7. J. Lee, 'The Ribbonmen' in T. Desmond Williams (ed.), *Secret*

societies in Ireland* (Dublin 1973); M.R. Beames, 'The Ribbon societies: lower-class nationalism in pre-Famine Ireland' and Tom Garvin, 'Defenders, Ribbonmen and others: underground political networks in pre-Famine Ireland', both essays in C.H.E. Philpin (ed.), *Nationalism and popular protest in Ireland* (Cambridge 1987); A.C. Murray, 'Agrarian violence and nationalism: the myth of Ribbonism', *Irish Economic and Social History*, XIII (1986).

8. Wright, *Two lands*, pp. 187, 296–97; John Belchem, 'Freedom and friendship to Ireland: Ribbonism in early nineteenth century Liverpool', *International Review of Social History*, 39 (1994); Kevin Kenny, *Making sense of the Molly Maguires* (Oxford 1998).

9. Garvin, 'Defenders', pp. 221–28; W.E. Vaughan, *Landlords and tenants in mid-Victorian Ireland* (Oxford 1994), pp. 189–202; K. Theodore Hoppen, *Ireland since 1800: conflict and conformity* (London 1989), pp. 48–51; Murray, 'Agrarian violence', pp. 71–73.

10. Public Record Office, London (now known as the National Archives; hereafter PRO(L)), Colonial Office papers, anti-government organisations reports and Royal Irish Constabulary (RIC) reports (Northern Division), CO/904/15, 16 and 18; H.B.C. Pollard, *The secret societies of Ireland: their rise and progress* (Kilkenny 1998), pp. 24–29; Kevin Haddick-Flynn,

11. *Orangeism: the making of a tradition* (Dublin 1999), pp. 274–75; Wright, *Two lands*, pp. 400–1.

11. Peter E. Newman, *Companion to Irish history* (Oxford 1991), p. 147; *Northern Whig*, 15 July, 24 June and 3 July 1845.

12. *Belfast Newsletter*, 21 March 1848; Anonymous, *Orangeism in Ireland and throughout the Empire Vol. II* (London n.d.), pp. 349–50; The blackthorn sticks were the pre-eminent symbol of the faction fighters and were carried over into the Ribbon tradition (see Patrick O'Donnell, *The Irish faction fighters of the nineteenth century* (Tralee 1975), pp. 15–18, 28; Anthony Buckley and Kenneth Anderson, *Brotherhoods in Ireland* (Cultra 1988), p. 37).

13. Anonymous, *Orangeism*, pp. 351–64; and Richard Niven, *Orangeism as it was and is* (Belfast 1899), pp. 44–48. Niven gives a useful summary of the Dollies Brae inquiry complete with maps and illustrations (pp. 55–157); Haddick-Flynn, *Making of a tradition*, pp. 276–80; *Belfast Newsletter*, 13 July 1853, 16 September 1857; Andrew Boyd, *Holy war in Belfast* (Tralee 1969), pp. 10–44; James Connor Doak, 'Rioting and civil strife in the City of Londonderry during the nineteenth and early twentieth centuries' (Unpublished MA thesis, Queen's University Belfast 1978), pp. 111, 125–35.

14. *Belfast Newsletter*, 13 December 1858, 4, 6, 8 and 16 April, and 3 August 1859; Marcus Patton, *Central Belfast: An historical gazetteer* (Belfast 1993), pp. 162, 144.

15. Vaughan, *Landlords*, p. 200; and PRO(L), Colonial Office papers, government document 'The Ribbon movement (now Ancient Order of Hibernians) in Ireland' (undated), CO/904/16/75/1.

16. *Belfast Newsletter*, 13 December 1858 and 1 April 1859; National Archives of Ireland (hereafter NAI), Crime Branch Special, S Files, report from 1891 on meeting of Belfast Ribbonmen, 4479/S.

17. National Library of Ireland (NLI), Larcom papers, MS. 7517.

18. Leon Ó Broin, 'The Phoenix conspiracy', *Irish Sword*, 14 (1980–81), p. 160.

19. *Northern Whig*, 15 July 1845 for trial report of typical rural Ribbon society and its activities near Clones in Co. Monaghan.

20. Samuel Clark and James Donnelly Jnr., 'The unreaped harvest' in Samuel Clark and James Donnelly Jnr. (eds.), *Irish peasants: violence and political unrest 1780–1914* (Manchester 1983), p. 424; Hoppen, *Ireland since 1800*, pp. 17, 58; Wright, *Two lands*, p. 244; Boyd, *Holy war*, pp. 34–36.

21. *Glasgow Herald*, 17 July 1829 and 14 September 1835 for trials of 'Ribbonmen'; PRO(L), Colonial Office papers, reports and letters re Ribbonism in Scotland, 1839–41, CO/904/8.

22. Belchem, 'Freedom and friendship', pp. 36, 45–46; and PRO(L), Colonial Office papers, letters dated 11 and 14 December 1840 from P. McGloin to Dublin Castle re Glasgow Ribbonmen; James E. Handley, *The Irish in Scotland* (Glasgow 1964), pp. 40–41. The 1840 killing of an English ganger by two Irish railway labourers in rural Lanarkshire led to much speculation about the operation of a Ribbon system among Irish immigrants, something underlined years later by the clerical ban on Ribbon societies after an intensive investigation which found evidence of the organisation's activism in the industrial heartlands of Lanarkshire (see Hugh P. Hagan, 'Ancient Order of Hibernians in Scotland, 1880–1914' (Unclassified, unpublished thesis, Ruskin College Oxford, 1987), pp. 13–14).

23. PRO(L), Home Office papers, letters dated 30 August, 2 September, 1 December 1862 and 2, 12 and 23 January, 6 February and 18 March

1863, HO/45/7522 re various aspects of Ribbonism in Scotland.

24. William S. Marshall, *The Billy Boys* (Edinburgh 1996), pp. 32–37; Alan B. Campbell, *The Lanarkshire miners* (Edinburgh 1979), pp. 316–19; W.S. Brownlie, *The proud trooper* (London 1964), pp. 71–72.

25. Campbell, *Lanarkshire miners*, pp. 180–87, 317. This church defence tactic was one often felt to be the preserve of Ribbonmen such as in the Dumbarton riots of 1855, the Partick riots of 1875 and the Belfast riots of 1864 (see *Glasgow Herald*, 10 August 1875; Handley, *Irish in Scotland*, p. 254; and Boyd, *Holy war*, pp. 56, 70–71).

26. Jeremiah O'Donovan Rossa, *Rossa's recollections 1838–1898* (Shannon 1972), pp. 302–3. In 1859, John O'Mahony, founder of the Fenian Brotherhood, met the secretary of the Belfast Ribbonmen, then on trial, who promised all help to the 'Phoenixes' and the loyalty of their members in Ulster, Scotland and England; Brendán Mac Giolla Choille, 'Fenians, Rice and Ribbonmen in Co. Monaghan, 1864–67', *Clogher Record*, Vol. VI, No. 2 (1967). It was noted soon after his arrest in February 1866 on a charge of Fenianism that Belfastman Owen McKeever had been charged and acquitted of murder and taking a leading role in the 1864 riots (see *Belfast Newsletter*, 27 February 1866, and Boyd, *Holy war*, p. 73).

27. John Devoy, *Recollections of an Irish rebel* (New York 1929), pp. 28, 103; R.V. Comerford, *The Fenians in context* (Dublin 1985), pp. 118–19; Ira B. Cross (ed.), *Frank Roney: An autobiography* (New York 1976), pp. 51–57; William D'Arcy, *The Fenian movement in the United States 1858–1886* (New York 1971), p. 45; *Belfast Newsletter*, 8 March 1867; NAI, Fenian Files, R Series, report dated 16 January 1868 on Derry Fenians, 516/R; Seán Ó Lúing, *Fremantle Mission* (Tralee 1965), p. 12.

28. Private information re John Torley, Scottish IRB leader from 1873 to 1897, donated by Patrick G. Torley, Clydebank, Glasgow, 1994; NLI, Patrick McCormick MS. 15,337, pp. 1–2; *Belfast Newsletter*, 8 March 1866 and 9 March 1867; *Derry Journal*, 6 January 1866. The practice of moulding bullets was a common activity among European insurrectionary groups in the nineteenth century, although it was often undertaken during or in the latter stages of an uprising as ammunition became more scarce. The Fenians, however, appear to have made it something of a cottage industry in urban areas, and raids by the police which captured bullet moulds were salaciously pored over in the newspapers.

29. *Belfast Newsletter*, 21, 22, 23, 26, 27 and 28 February, 1, 3, 5 and 9 March, 24, 28 and 29 November, 7, 10 and 20 December 1866, and 4 January, 8, 9 and 14 March 1867; NAI, Fenian Files, Index of Names Book, 1866–71 (VIIIB/W.P.3/5), pp. 325–26; Mitchell Library, Glasgow City Archives, Chief Constable of Glasgow's letter books, letter dated 28 February 1866 from Chief Constable James Smart to Divisional Superintendent Alexander McCall, Calton, Glasgow, E4/2/14.

30. Elaine W. McFarland, 'A reality and yet impalpable: the Fenian panic in mid-Victorian Scotland', *Scottish Historical Review*, LXXVII:2: No. 204 (October 1998), p. 209; NAI, Fenian Files, R Series, report dated 29 November 1869 by Head Constable Thomas Kerins (RIC, Glasgow) on Glasgow Fenian amnesty meeting, 5084/R, Fenian Files, Index of Names Book, 1866–71 (VIIIB/W.P.3/5), pp. 66, 95, 274, 280, 290, 320, 618, 644 and 889; *Derry Journal*, 13 January 1866; *Glasgow Herald*, 1 April 1867.

31. Leon Ó Broin, *Charles Gavan Duffy* (Dublin, 1967), p. 116; NLI, Luby papers, MS. 331–33, p. 15; Peter

Alter, 'Traditions of violence in the Irish national movement' in Wolfgang J. Mommsen and Gerhard Hirschfeld (eds.), *Social protest, violence and terror in nineteenth and twentieth century Europe* (London 1982), pp. 142–43; *Glasgow Herald*, 29 November 1869.

32. F.S.L. Lyons, 'Fenianism, 1867–1916' in T.W. Moody (ed.), *The Fenian movement* (Cork 1968), pp. 39–41; Charles Townshend, *Political violence in Ireland* (Oxford 1983), p. 239; Kevin B. Nowlan, 'Tom Clarke, MacDermott, and the IRB' in F.X. Martin (ed.), *Leaders and men of the Easter Rising: Dublin 1916* (London 1967); John Newsinger, *Fenianism in mid-Victorian Britain* (London 1994), pp. 75, 79.

33. Buckley, Anderson, *Brotherhoods*, pp. 41–42; Hagan, 'Ancient Order of Hibernians', p. 30; Beames, 'Ribbon societies', pp. 261–62; Hepburn, *Past apart*, p. 158.

34. Boyd, *Holy war*, pp. 89–119; *Belfast Newsletter*, 16 and 17 August 1872, 20 March 1873, 16 August 1876 and 16 August 1877; Sam Hanna Bell, *Erin's orange lily* (London 1956), pp. 115–16; and Anonymous, *Lilliburlero Vol. II* (Lurgan, 1988), pp. 42–45; *Glasgow Herald*, 18 August 1874, 9, 10, 11, 16 and 21 August 1875; *Glasgow Observer*, 19 August 1905.

35. Townshend, *Political violence*, p. 28; Desmond Ryan, *The phoenix flame* (London 1937), pp. 48–49; Pollard, *Secret societies*, pp. 38–41; Arthur Lehning, *From Buonarotti to Bakunin* (Leiden 1970), pp. 36–57, 150–83; David Millar, *Anarchism* (London 1984).

36. Garvin, 'Defenders', pp. 220–21, p. 239; Murray, 'Agrarian violence', p. 72; Herbert Asbury, *The gangs of New York* (New York 1928); R.G. MacCallum, *Tongs Ya Bas* (Glasgow 1994); Kellow Chesney, *The Victorian underworld* (London 1970).

37. Buckley, Anderson, *Brotherhoods*, pp. 58, 45–46; Douglas H. Johnson, 'Criminal secrecy: the case of the Zande secret societies', *Past and Present*, 130 (February 1991). It was believed by some in authority that publicans maintained their involvement with Ribbonism to generate business (see PRO(L), Colonial Office papers, report dated 21 November 1841 by John O'Brien, Stipendiary Magistrate, Sligo, CO/904/8).

12. THE IRISH AND THE SCOTS IN THE ENGLISH ORANGE ORDER IN THE LATER NINETEENTH CENTURY

1. This chapter forms an outline of ideas developed in D.M. MacRaild, *Faith, fraternity and fighting: The Orange Order and Irish Migrants in the North of England, c.1850–1920* (Liverpool, 2005). My thanks to the Lodge of Education and Research which allowed a non-member to access its north-east records, and to the Leverhulme Trust which awarded me a Research Fellowship from September 1999 to January 2000 (ref. no. RF&G/3/9900135) to work on the wider project upon which this chapter is based. The research included in this paper is part of a collaborative ongoing project, 'peoples and migration', which is organised under the auspices of the AHRB Centre for North-East England History. Finally, my thanks to the editors of this volume who made a number of useful suggestions which improved the text.

2. Expressly English and Scottish because, as Paul O'Leary shows, the Orange Order was virtually non-existent in Wales: *Immigration and integration: the Irish in Wales, 1798–1922* (Cardiff 2000). There were some lodges in north-west Wales (for example, Wrexham) and

in border towns such as Shrewsbury. However, the movement did not penetrate chapel Wales in the way that it reached Presbyterian Scotland or both Anglican and Dissenting England. Low levels of Irish Protestant immigration to Wales constituted the vital factor here.

3. Frank Neal, *Sectarian violence: the Liverpool experience, 1819–1914* (Liverpool 1988); Elaine McFarland, *Protestants first: Orangeism in nineteenth-century Scotland* (Edinburgh 1990); Graham Walker, 'The Orange Order in Scotland between the wars', *International Review of Social History*, XXXVII:2 (1992); Ruth Dudley Edwards, *Faithful tribe: an intimate portrait of the loyal institutions* (London 1999).

4. Donal McCracken states that South African Orangemen destroyed their records in 1961 when their country became a republic. See his 'Odd man out: the South African experience' in Andy Bielenberg (ed.), *The Irish diaspora* (London 2000), p. 268, n.27.

5. Tom Fraser (ed.), *Following the drum: the Irish parading tradition* (Basingstoke 2000), contains numerous considerations of the Order's walking tradition, both in Ireland and Britain, past and present.

6. Consett was a hive of industrial activity, and in 1875 its iron industry employed 5,000 to 6,000 men and produced the largest number of iron ship plates in the country. N. McCord, *North East England: the region's development, 1760–1960* (London 1979), pp. 119–20.

7. For the Canadian tradition, see C.J. Houston and W.J. Smyth, *The sash Canada wore: a historical geography of the Orange Order in Canada* (Toronto 1980). The way Ogle Gowan developed and used the political potential of Orangeism is fascinating. See D.H. Akenson, *The Irish in Ontario: a study in rural history*, second edition (Montreal, Kingston, London and Ithaca 1999), pp. 169–92, 193–96.

8. C.J. Houston and W.J. Smyth, 'Transferred loyalties: Orangeism in the United States and Ontario', *American Review of Canadian Studies*, 14, 2 (1984).

9. M.A. Gordon, *The Orange riots: Irish political violence in New York City, 1870 and 1871* (Ithaca and London 1993), Chapter 1.

10. In 1835, there were just twelve lodges in the far north of England: Kendal, Whitehaven (2), Carlisle (2), South Shields, North Shields, Wallsend, Sunderland, Newcastle upon Tyne (2) and Morpeth. See *Select Committee report on the origin, nature and extent of Orange institutions in Great Britain and the colonies*, BPP (1835), Appendix 19, pp. 141–44.

11. Hereward Senior, *Orangeism in Ireland and Britain, 1795–1836* (London 1966), p. 152

12. This is demonstrated in the Cumbria case. D.M. MacRaild, *Culture, conflict and migration: the Irish in Victorian Cumbria* (Liverpool 1998), Chapter 6.

13. E. McFarland, *Protestants first! Orangeism in nineteenth-century Scotland* (Edinburgh 1990).

14. Houston and Smyth, *Sash Canada wore*, Table 4, p. 94.

15. *Ibid.*, p. 95.

16. Admittedly, this point is based upon nothing more than a sense of the movement's public face. There is no statistical evidence to support or deny the claim.

17. For the Scottish dimension, see Graham Walker, 'The Protestant Irish in Scotland' in T.M. Devine (ed.), *Irish immigrants in Scottish society in the nineteenth and twentieth centuries* (Edinburgh 1991).

18. *Census of England and Wales (1871), Birthplaces of the people*, Table 18, p. 541; *Census of England and Wales (1801), Birthplaces of males and females in the Ancient County of Durham*, Table 36, p. 78.

19. J.D. Marshall, *Furness and the Industrial Revolution* (Beckermet, 1981), Epilogue.

20. *Census of England and Wales (1891), Birthplaces of males and females enumerated in counties and in each Urban Sanitary District of which the population exceeds 20,000 Persons*, Table 8, p. 480; *Census (1901), Birthplaces of males and females in the Ancient County of Durham*, Table 36, p. 78; *Northumberland*, Table 36, p. 74, *Cumberland*, Table 36, p. 53; *Census of England and Wales (1911) Birthplaces of males and females enumerated in the Administrative County and in each County Borough, Northumberland*, Table 30, p. 84, *Cumberland*, Table 30, p. 77.

21. *Shields Daily News*, 27 October 1884.

22. St Andrew's societies, Burns suppers and pipe bands remain a vibrant aspect of northern England cultural life, whereas Irish culture tends to mean little more than social clubs.

23. LOL 395, 'Enniskillen True Blues', Minute Books, 25 April 1914.

24. A sample of 94 Orange members found in the 1881 census indicates the following demographic breakdown: men (93); women (1). Married (67 (71.3%)); heads of household (62 (66.0%); lodger (14 (4.9%)); son (17 (18.1%)). MSS Minutes (accounts and rolls of district) No. 43 and 46, 1878–1883; *Census of England and Wales*, 1881.

25. L. Letford and Colin Pooley, 'Geographies of migration: Irish women in mid-nineteenth century Ireland' in P. O'Sullivan (ed.), *The Irish world wide: history, heritage, identity*, 6 vols (Leicester 1992–96), IV: *Irish women and Irish migration*, is a model for further research, as are Hepburn's pioneering works on Belfast, now usefully collected in one edition: *A past apart: studies in the history of Catholic Belfast, 1850–1950* (Belfast 1996), especially Chapters 4–7.

26. MSS Minutes (accounts and rolls of district) No. 43 and 46, 1878–1883; *Census of England and Wales*, 1881.

27. Walker tells of a presentation made to the Ulster-born shipyard employer, Edward Douglas, who, on retirement in 1921, received a presentation from fifty of his Orange foremen. 'Orange Order in Scotland between the wars', pp. 184–85.

28. North Tyneside records are fragmentary. Charles Swan was a member and Worshipful Master of LOL 395 'Enniskillen True Blues'. Unfortunately, lodge records do not survive from the period when he was active. However, both he and Hunter are mentioned in the North Shields District (No. 43) minute books in the late 1870s (e.g., annual accounts for 1877).

29. D.G. Paz, *Popular anti-Catholicism in mid-Victorian Britain* (Stanford 1992), p. 4. What is more contestable is his claim that the movement was marginal 'geographically, politically, and socially'. Clearly, it was socially limited; all working-class political organisations were limited, to some degree, in the 1880s. Orangeism certainly cannot be compared with the trade union movement or the Primrose League in either its class power or class status. But the movement was an important conduit for a mixture of religious and ethnic values, and in some barely perceptible way it strengthened members, not least by endorsing their unity of purpose.

30. LOL 264 'Johnstone's Heroes', Minute Book, 12 December 1903.

31. District 46, Minute Book, 13 March 1920.

32. The shipbuilding dimension of this migratory flow is mentioned in S. Pollard and P. Robertson, *British shipbuilding, 1870–1914* (Cambridge and London 1979), p. 163.

33. The tag 'free-gratis' was granted only in exceptional circumstances for Orangemen with exemplary records. Most had to pay a small fee of one or two shillings for their certificate, as well as clearing back dues.

34. LOL 264 'Johnstone's Heroes', Minute Book, 23 May 1908; 25 June 1908.

35. LOL 395 'Enniskillen True Blues', Minute Books, 20 June 1910; 23 July 1910.

36. LOL 339 'Monkton True Blues', Minute Books, 1 October 1904. Unfortunately, there are no records for the District at this time to verify the expulsion, although later rulings suggest the lodge's decision was usually upheld.

37. District No. 46, Minutes, undated [February?] 1911.

38. LOL 264 'Johnstone's Heroes', Minute Books, 22 March 1884.

39. LOL 264 Minute Books, 21 February 1914.

40. District 46 Minute Books, 11 May 1912.

41. District 46 Minute Books, 11 May 1912.

42. LOL 264 'Johnstone's Heroes', Minute Books, 25 February 1888.

43. No. 46 District, Minute Books, 23 August 1913.

44. P. Buckland, *Ulster Unionism and the origins of Northern Ireland, 1886–1922* (London 1973), pp. 56–57.

45. LOL 264 'Johnstone's Heroes', Hebburn, Minute Books II, 3 February 1906.

46. LOL 264, Minute Books II, 31 March 1906.

47. J.D. Marshall and J. Walton, *The Lake counties from 1830 to the mid-twentieth century* (Manchester 1983), Table 5.1, p. 111.

48. For the emphasis upon the racialised language of pro-Union Orange viewpoints, see MacRaild, '"Principle, party and protest": the language of Victorian Orangeism in the north of England' in Shearer West (ed.), *The Victorians and race* (Leicester 1996), pp. 136–39.

49. For the size and violence of Cumbria's Orange tradition, see MacRaild, *Culture, conflict and migration*, Chapter 7; for the parading tradition, see MacRaild, '"The bunkum of Ulsteria": The Orange parading tradition in Cumbria' in

Fraser, *Following the drum*, pp. 44–59.

50. H. Pelling, *Social geography of British elections, 1885–1910* (London 1967), Table 36, p. 332.

51. A.W. Purdue, 'Jarrow politics, 1885–1914: the challenge to Liberal hegemony', *Northern History*, XVIII (1982), pp. 182–98.

52. Joan Hugman, 'Joseph Cowen of Newcastle and radical liberalism' (Unpublished PhD, University of Northumbria, 1993); also Nigel Todd, *The militant democracy: Joseph Cowen and Victorian radicalism* (Whitley Bay 1991).

53. Londonderry was a close friend of Sir Edward Carson and chaired one of Carson's most important northern meetings. See *Evening Chronicle*, 18 September 1913.

54. Press coverage was extensive and quite favourable to the Orangemen (who were seen as victims). For example, *Newcastle Chronicle*, 14 July 1856.

55. John Belchem, *Merseypride: essays in Liverpool exceptionalism* (Liverpool 2000), and Belchem (ed.), *Popular politics, riot and labour: essays in Liverpool history, 1790–1940* (Liverpool 1992). Also, Neal, *Sectarian violence*, passim.

56. MacRaild, *Culture, conflict and Migration*, pp. 188–89.

57. *Wallsend Herald and Advertiser*, 1 March 1912

58. For one of T.P. O'Connor's many trips to the north-east, *Newcastle Evening Chronicle*, 4 and 5 November 1913; *Evening Chronicle*, 15 November 1913. Redmond was struck by a tomato as he sat on the train to Newcastle. However, it was thrown by a suffragette, not an Orangeman.

59. The words of an Irish nationalist organiser in Barrow-in-Furness (F.J. Devlin, letter, *Barrow Herald*, 10 June 1893). The Liberal press was just as likely to use this sort of language to denounce the Order's militant expression of belief.

13. 'INTO THE WHIRLING VORTEX OF MODERNITY': CULTURAL DEVELOPMENTS IN THE SCOTTISH GAIDHEALTACHD, 1939–1965

1. I.F. Anderson, *To introduce the Hebrides* (London, 1933), p. 216.
2. There has been a long and comprehensive discussion about the emergence of this dichotomy between the 'Highlands' and 'Lowlands' of Scotland. See the bibliography in C.W.J. Withers, *Gaelic Scotland: the transformation of a cultural region* (London 1988) for suitable texts; A. Collier, *The crofting problem* (Cambridge 1953), p. 4.
3. Anderson wrote a number of books describing his travels in the region, such *as The sunset shore: along Scotland's sea-girt west* (London 1934) and *Across Hebridean seas* (London 1937).
4. C. Geertz, *The interpretation of cultures* (New York 1973), p. 5; R. Williams, *The long revolution* (London 1961), p. 41; E. Sapir, *Culture, language and personality: selected essays*, edited by David G. Mandelbaum (Berkeley 1956), pp. 83–84.
5. R.A. Dodgshon, *From chief to landlords: social change in the Western Highlands and Islands, c. 1493–1820* (Edinburgh 1998); A.I. MacInnes, *Clanship, commerce and the House of Stuart, 1603–1788* (East Linton 1996).
6. For a more detailed discussion of these issues consult J.A. Burnett, 'Ethnic culture in transition? Gaelic Scotland 1939–1965' (Unpublished PhD, University of Sunderland 2000), Chapter 1; E. Richards, *A history of the Highland Clearances*, 2 vols. (London 1982 and 1985); T.M. Devine, *Clanship to crofters' war: the social transformation of the Scottish Highlands* (Manchester 1994); T.M. Devine, *The great Highland famine* (Edinburgh 1988); C.W.J. Withers, *Gaelic Scotland*; J. Hunter, *The making of the crofting community* (Edinburgh 1976); E.A. Cameron, *Land for the people? The British government and the Scottish Highlands, c. 1880–1925* (East Linton 1996), pp. 1–15.
7. C.W.J. Withers, *Urban Highlanders: Highland–Lowland migration and urban Gaelic culture, 1700–1900*, p. 47 and *passim*; I. MacDonald, *Glasgow's Gaelic churches: Highland religion in an urban setting, 1690–1995* (Edinburgh 1995).
8. R. Burnett, '*Tir nam beann, nan glean 's nan gaisgeach*: colonialism, complicity and the Gael', paper presented to *Rannsachadh na Gàidhlig*, Scottish Gaelic Studies 2000 Conference, University of Aberdeen, 2–4 August 2000; A. MacKillop, '*More fruitful than the soil*': *Army, Empire and the Scottish Highlands 1715–1815* (East Linton 2000).
9. T. Brown, *Ireland: a social and cultural history 1922–79* (Glasgow 1981); L. Gibbons, *Transformations in Irish culture* (Cork 1996); D. Kiberd, *Inventing Ireland: the literature of the modern nation* (London 1996); T. Varley and C. Curtin, 'Defending rural interests against nationalists in 20th century Ireland: a tale of three movements' in J. Davis (ed.), *Rural change in Ireland* (Belfast 1999), pp. 58–83.
10. C. Graham and R. Kirkland (eds.), *Ireland and cultural theory* (Basingstoke 1999), p. 1 and *passim*.
11. See E.A. Cameron, 'The Scottish Highlands: from Congested District to Objective One' in T.M. Devine and R.J. Finlay (eds.) *Scotland in the twentieth century* (Edinburgh 1996), pp. 153–69; E.A. Cameron, 'The Scottish Highlands as a Special Policy Area, 1886 to 1965' in *Rural History*, 8:2 (1997, pp. 195–215; J.L. Campbell, 'The subsequent history of Barra' in J.L. Campbell (ed.), *The book of Barra* (Stornoway 1998), p. 219. The attraction of the city versus the

drudgery of island life is evident in A.E. MacInnes, *Eriskay, where I was born* (Edinburgh 1997).

12. K.J. Lea 'Hydro-electric power developments and the landscape in the Highlands of Scotland' in *Scottish Geographical Magazine*, 84 (1968), pp. 239–47; P.L. Payne, *The hydro: a study of the major hydro-electric schemes undertaken by the North of Scotland Hydro Electricity Board* (Aberdeen 1988), pp. 29–30; C. Harvie, *No gods and precious few heroes: Scotland since 1914* (Edinburgh, 1993), pp. 46–47; Cameron, 'Objective One', p. 157.

13. Even factories were preferred, 'rather than starving both their souls and bodies on dole-supported crofts'. See *Transactions of the Gaelic Society of Inverness* (hereafter *TGSI*), 38 (1962), pp. 159–63. MacEwen was at one time the Lord Provost of Inverness and a political candidate for the Scottish National Party.

14. Colin MacDonald, *Echoes of the glen OR Mac-Talla nan Gleann* (Edinburgh 1936), p. 9.

15. Sir A.M. MacEwen, *The thistle and the rose: Scotland's problem to-day* (Edinburgh 1932), pp. 234–35.

16. Scottish Economic Committee (Committee on the Highlands and Islands), *The Highlands and Islands of Scotland: a review of the economic conditions with recommendations for improvement* (Edinburgh 1938).

17. For a penetrating insight into the effects of the war and its immediate aftermath, see F.F. Darling (ed.), *West Highland survey: an essay in human ecology* (Oxford 1955), *passim*.

18. J. A. Burnett, 'Wartime visions of the Highlands and post-war reality', paper delivered as part of the Arkleton Seminar Series, University of Aberdeen, January 2000.

19. *Ibid.*

20. M. Lynch, *Scotland: a new history* (London 1992), pp. 436–37; Harvie, *No gods*, pp. 102–4.

21. Scottish Labour Party, *Plan for post-war Scotland* (Glasgow 1941), p. 13.

22. *Ibid.*, pp. 11–13.

23. *Ibid.*, p. 13.

24. Alastair MacNeill Weir, *Highland plan* (Glasgow 1945), p. 3.

25. J. Burnett, 'Ethnic culture', pp. 85–127.

26. O. Brown, *Scotland – nation or desert* (Glasgow, n.d., but 1943?); O. Brown, *Hitlerism in the Highlands* (Glasgow n.d., but 1941?); D. Young, *Fascism for the Highlands* (Glasgow 1943).

27. D. Mac' illedhuibh, *Death to the Highland Scot? An exposure of British government policies in Scotland* (Glasgow 1944), p. 3.

28. *A programme of Highland development* (Edinburgh 1950, Cmnd 7976), para 4.

29. I. Levitt, *Poverty and welfare in Scotland, 1890–1948* (Edinburgh 1988); White Paper, 'Social Insurance' (Cmd 6550, 1944).

30. *Highland Development*, para 7, p. 10.

31. *Ibid.*, para 10, p. 7; para 11, p. 8.

32. *Ibid.*, paras 16–18, p. 9.

33. *Ibid.*, paras 19–21, pp. 9–10.

34. *Ibid.*, para 12, p. 8.

35. *Ibid.*, para 14, p. 8.

36. *Ibid.*, 'Transport', para 22, p. 10.

37. Kyle was the departure point for steamer services to ports in the Inner and Outer Hebrides.

38. *Highland development* (1950), paras 23–25, pp. 10–11; p. 24.

39. *Ibid.*, para 8, p. 7; para 11, p. 22.

40. I. Levitt, 'The creation of the Highlands and Islands Development Board, 1935–65', *Northern Scotland*, 19 (1999), pp. 85–105.

41. The planning zone of the seven 'Crofting Counties' that were created in the late nineteenth century was in fact an administrative boundary that covered many discrete 'Highlands'. See Cameron, 'Objective One' and Cameron 'Special Policy Area'. Unfortunately, there is a tendency to simplify these issues in the literature on the Highlands and Islands. Thus, although Caithness is beyond what is generally accepted as the Highland cultural line, people in that county

certainly 'felt' Highland. There is a danger in generalising on this subject, and Highland identity is a complex issue that merits further analysis.

42. A.D. Pilkington, 'The Parish of Reay', May 1952, p. 150 and Rev. A.K. Fairlie and D.K. Sutherland, 'The Parish of Thurso', June 1950, p. 178, both extracts in J.S. Smith (ed.), *The third statistical account of Scotland: the county of Caithness* (Edinburgh 1988); interview with Gaelic speaker resident in Edinburgh, May 2000, reflecting on wartime in North Uist.

43. Pilkington, 'Parish of Reay', p. 150.

44. A.E. MacInnes, *Eriskay*, p. 16.

45. Rev. N. MacDonald, 'The Parish of Glenelg, 1950' in H. Barron (ed.), *The third statistical account of Scotland: the county of Inverness* (Edinburgh 1985), pp. 360–63; similar views in Rev. N. MacDonald *et al.*, 'The Parish of Harris', March 1953, revised Aug 1966, in Barron, *The county of Inverness*, pp. 586–89.

46. Interview with Gaelic speaker resident in Edinburgh, May 2000.

47. Rev. T. J. Titterington, 'The Parish of Laggan' in Barron, *The county of Inverness*, p. 337.

48. MacDonald *et al.*, 'The Parish of Harris', p. 588.

49. Taylor Commission Evidence: 'N.A.S.', AF81/4; Crofters' Commission, *Annual Report for 1957* (Edinburgh 1958), p. 7.

50. W. Bain, 'The Parish of Watten' in Smith, *The county of Caithness*, p. 189. The extent to which the inhabitants of Caithness, a county beyond the historic Highland cultural line, identified with the homogenous image of the region is a moot point.

51. S. Parman, *Scottish crofters: An historical ethnography of a Celtic village* (Fort Worth 1990), p. 49. Parman's research was conducted between 1970 and 1971 in a crofting township in the Isle of Lewis. It is worthwhile noting that Parman's work was not uncritically received, and indeed anthropologists and enthnographers

have studied other parts of the region. For a brief discussion of this treatment of the Highland population, consult S. MacDonald, *Reimagining culture: histories, identities and the Gaelic renaissance* (Oxford 1997).

52. Interviews with Gaelic speakers resident in Benbecula, Edinburgh and Glasgow, May 2000.

53. Titterington, 'The Parish of Laggan', p. 338.

54. Quoted in Parman, *Scottish crofters*, p. 74.

55. MacDonald *et al.*, 'The Parish of Harris', p. 588.

56. Pilkington, 'The Parish of Reay', pp. 150, 153.

57. *Ibid.*, p. 153.

58. Rev. Angus D. MacDonald, 'The Parish of Moy and Dalarossie' in Barron, *The county of Inverness*, p. 166.

59. J.A. MacDonald (ed.), *Orain Dhòmhnaill Ailean Dhòmhnaill na Bainich: The songs of Donald MacDonald, 1906–92* (Benbecula 1999), pp. 51–52. In an article entitled 'The poetry of Donald Allan MacDonald', the Rev. Fr. J.A. MacDonald claimed: 'With the Second World War, a sea-change came over the community for which he had created his poetry and these social structures and occasions which had sustained his compositions now went into rapid decline. As the audience for his compositions went into ever decreasing decline, our bard ceased to practice his art.' See *TGSI*, 58 (1992–94), p. 40.

60. For Colin MacDonald, whose parental house used to be the *tigh-ceilidh* when he was a youngster in Ross-shire, 'A *ceilidh* was not a fore-ordered thing: it was a natural growth. Only round a kitchen peat-fire could it flourish. Nobody was bidden. Anybody came. There was absolute social equality. The sartorial peak never rose beyond a clean collar and brushed whiskers. The talk just came – easily – naturally. One topic led to another. Each was free to talk

or listen. Although, naturally, some excelled, never was the *ceilidh* a "show-off" place for the individual. There was utter camaraderie, utter "off-guard".' See MacDonald, *Echoes of the glen*, p. 31.

61. A.F. Smith and J. MacKinnon, 'The Parish of Barra', March 1955, revised Aug 1966, in Barron, *The county of Inverness*, p. 561.

62. F.F. Darling and A. Morley, 'The social situation' in Darling (ed.), *West Highland survey*, p. 281.

63. D.F. MacKenzie, 'Highland pseudo-culture' in *Alba*, 1 (1948), p. 63. Parman (*Scottish crofters*, p. 7), referring to a township in Lewis between 1970 to 1971, claimed: 'The Highlanders themselves vary in their use of these cultural constructs. Some of them have become self-conscious spokepersons for Highland ethnicity as poets, playwrights and politicians. Others are frequently embarrassed by the attention called to their cultural distinctiveness, covet the possessions portrayed in mail-order catalogs [sic] and disdain homemade products, downgrade their language and customs, and poke sly fun at the earnest *Sasunnachs* ... who wear the kilt and win the gold medals at the Gaelic song contests.'

64. *Reiteachs* were common in the rural parts of Lewis and Harris. The issue of cultural diversity is an important one and more work needs to be done on the differences of 'localism'.

65. MacInnes, *Eriskay*.

66. Interviews with Gaelic speakers resident in Edinburgh and Glasgow, May 2000.

67. *Ibid.*; Parman, *Scottish crofters*, p. 155.

68. Rev. C.N. MacKenzie *et al.*, 'The Parish of South Uist', Sept 1951, revised Jan 1957, in Barron, *The county of Inverness*, p. 626.

69. *Crofting conditions: Report of the Commission of Enquiry* ('Taylor Commission') (Edinburgh 1954, Cmnd 9091).

70. Though the history of how folklore collecting started and developed deserves analysis, there is an insight into the early history of the School of Scottish Studies, and the role of Calum MacLean specifically, in S. O'Suilleabhain, 'Memoir' in Calum I. MacLean, *The Highlands* (Inverness 1975), pp. vii–xvii. The school was set up by people connected to Edinburgh University interested in studying ethnology throughout Scotland. For the aims and objectives of the school, consult J. Orr, 'The School of Scottish Studies', *Scottish Studies*, 1, pp. 1–2.

71. The extent to which 'cultural fictions' were a creation of the Scottish urban Gaelic communities merits further research. For details of the Irish experience see Gibbons, *Transformations*, pp. 82–93.

72. Sorley Maclean's *Dain do Eimhir agus Dain Eile: Poems to Eimhir and other poems* (Glasgow 1943) is regarded as the inspiring catalyst for other poets such as Iain Crichton Smith, Derick Thomson and George Campbell Hay. See D.J. MacLeod, 'Gaelic: the dynamics of a Renaissance', in W. Gilles (ed.), *Gaelic and Scotland: Alba agus a' Gaidhlig* (Edinburgh 1989), pp. 222–29.

73. D.J. MacLeod, 'Gaelic Prose' in *TGSI*, XLIX (1974–76), p. 216.

74. P. Berresford Ellis, *The Celtic Dawn: A History of Pan Celticism* (London, 1993), pp. 88–89; *An Aimsir Cheilteach*, September 1947; interviews with Gaelic speakers resident in Lewis, 1995.

75. E. Sapir, *Culture, language and personality: selected essays*, edited by David G. Mandelbaum (Berkeley 1956), pp. 95, 96.

76. Certainly, Sapir's thesis has found support within the academic community. See R. Williams, *Towards 2000* (London 1983), pp. 128–89.

77. R. Burnett, 'The Cheviot, the stag and the last Munro: constructs of wilderness, the Highlands and subalternity', paper to *A' Chànain, Am*

Mac-Meanma agus Cruth na Tìre ann an Gàidhlig na h-Eireann is na h-Albann, Sabhal Mòr Ostaig, An t-Eilean Sgitheanach 3–5 Sultain 1999.

78. GRO, *Census 1961 Scotland*: Vol. 7, 'Gaelic' (Edinburgh 1966).

79. K.D. MacDonald, 'The Gaelic language, its study and development' in I. Grimble and D.S. Thomson (eds.), *The future of the Highlands* (London 1968), p. 179.

80. *An Gaidheal*, March 1949, p. 31, which discusses the article by F. Fraser Darling and R. S. Barclay, 'Recent changes in crofting populations' which appeared in Scottish Agriculture, 28:3 (Winter 1948–49); Rev. T. M. Murchison, 'The census and Gaelic', *An Gaidheal*, 46 (September 1951), pp. 83–84.

81. R. Williams, *Towards 2000*, p. 133.

82. Campbell himself represented a school of thought, born out of Catholic conservative reactionism, which railed against the threat of modernism. For a classic example of presenting the 'rural' as a bulwark against socialism, urbanisation and industrialism, consult G. Scott-Moncrieff, *The Scottish Islands* (London 1952). For a deeper understanding of the factors influencing the Catholic Highlands during this period see R. Burnett, '"The long nineteenth century": Scotland's Catholic Gaidhealtachd' in R. Boyle and P. Lynch (eds.), *Out of the ghetto? The Catholic community in modern Scotland* (Edinburgh 1998), pp. 163–92.

83. J.L. Campbell, 'Introduction', pp. 15–40, in his *Tales of Barra told by the Coddy* (Edinburgh 1960), pp. 24–25.

14. LAND, PEOPLE AND IDENTITY: POPULAR PROTEST IN THE SCOTTISH HIGHLANDS AFTER 1918

1. The best recent survey of the complex changes in Highland society in this period is C.W.J. Withers, *Gaelic Scotland* (London 1988), pp. 57–255. Also M. Gray, *The Highland economy, 1750–1850* (Edinburgh 1957) pp. 57–141; A. I. Macinnes, *Clanship, commerce and the House of Stuart, 1603–1788* (Edinburgh 1996); R.A. Dodgshon, *From chiefs to landlords* (Edinburgh 1998).

2. Macinnes, *Clanship*, pp. 8–24; Dodgshon, *Chiefs* pp. 7–8; R.A. Dodgshon, '"Prentense of blude" and "place of thair dwelling": the nature of Highland clans, 1500–1745' in R.A. Houston and I.D. Whyte (eds.), *Scottish society 1500–1800* (Cambridge 1989), pp. 170–97 (hereafter Dodgshon, 'Nature').

3. Dodgshon, 'Nature', pp. 170, 193; Dodgshon, *Chiefs*, pp. 233–45.

4. J. Hunter, *The making of the crofting community* (Edinburgh 1976), pp. 15–21; F. Thompson, *Crofting years* (Edinburgh 1997), pp. 13–14.

5. Withers, *Gaelic Scotland*, pp. 281–9; 311–19.

6. It is only Withers who begins to engage with these divisions when considering protest, and then he does not see these as seriously challenging his view of protest as expression of class consciousness, preferring instead to see Highland protest as a 'tripartite affiliation of land working classes'. C.W.J. Withers, 'Rural protest in the Highlands of Scotland and in Ireland, 1850–1930' in S.J. Connolly, R.A. Houston, and R.J. Morris (eds.), *Conflict, identity and economic development: Ireland and Scotland 1600–1900* (Preston 1995), pp. 182.

7. E. Richards, *A history of the Highland Clearances* vol. 1 (London 1982), vol. 2 (London 1985); Hunter, *Making*; Withers, *Gaelic Scotland*; I.M.M.

MacPhail, *The crofter's war* (Stornoway 1989).

8. Hunter, *Making*, pp. 192–95; D. MacKay to The Scottish Office (hereafter SO), 17 January 1921 (Scottish Records Office (hereafter SRO) AF67/65).

9. A. Macdonald and others, Newtonferry to SO, 22 November 1920 (SRO AF 67/150); D. Campbell and M. Graham to SO, 20 December 1920 (SRO AF 67/328).

10. T.C. Smout, *A century of the Scottish people* (London 1986) p. 67.

11. Petition from North Tolsta, Lewis to Board of Agriculture for Scotland (hereafter BoA), 8 February 1919 (SRO AF 83/363); letter resulting from public meeting at Valtos school, Skye, to BoA, 22 March 1920 (Department of Agriculture for Scotland (hereafter DAFS) files 5863/M, Scorrybreck); letter from Park, Lewis to BoA, 13 July 1934 (DAFS 5543, Park); Board of Agriculture to SO 12 April 1926 (SRO AF 67/66). Please note that on the request of the Department of Agriculture, and because these remain active files, all names have been withheld from DAFS material.

12. John Macdonald, Back, Lewis to SO, 11 December 1919 (SRO AF 67/147); Withers, *Gaelic Scotland*, p. 329.

13. Over the course of an extended visit to Raasay in 199, interviews were conducted with five individuals (names withheld), all of whom were either raiders, had a direct connection to the raiders, or were first-generation descendants of raiders. I am very grateful for the hospitality, consideration and openness shown to me by the islanders.

14. Sir Arthur Rose to SO, 2 August 1921, Charles Weatherill to Rose, 12 August 1921, Sir Robert Greig to SO, 28 September 1921 (SRO AF67/149); Letters to Board of Agriculture, 2 January 1922 (DAFS 14113, Raasay); Letter to Board of Agriculture, 16 June 1922 (DAFS 14113/3, Raasay);

Letter to Board of Agriculture, 28 January 1929 (DAFS 14113/M Raasay).

15. Interview, Callum M. Raasay, 30 September 1991.

16. Interview, John M. Raasay, 2 October 1991.

17. Interview, Callum M. Raasay, 31 September 1991.

18. *Ibid*.

19. S. Schrager, 'What is social in oral history?', *International Journal of Oral History*, 4:2 (1983) pp. 76–98.

20. DAFS 14113, Raasay.

21. A. Portelli, 'The peculiarity of oral history', *History Workshop*, no. 12 (1981), p. 106; I. Passerini, 'Work, ideology and consensus under Italian Fascism', *History Workshop*, 8 (1979), p. 86.

22. Letter from ten squatters of Lemreway to SO, 16 December 1919 (SRO AF 67/147)

23. Neil MacRitchie to Board of Agriculture, 26 February 1918 (SRO AF 83/354); other examples come from DAFS files 6110 Borve, Harris and 35267 Luskentyre, Harris, in letters dated 12 February 1928 and 6 June 1922. The details of those living on the croft in Gravir were provided to me by Angus MacLeod, Lewis. I am grateful to Angus for allowing me access to this information and for his many letters and the patience he showed in our discussions.

24. Archibald MacDonald and others to Scottish Office, 4 March 1922; (SRO AF67/154); John MacDonald and others to Board of Agriculture, 24 March 1922 (SRO AF83/267).

25. T. Wilson to Scottish Office, 7 November 1917 (SRO AF 67/143); Police report, 25 February 1920 (SRO AF67/148); Reports by sub-commissioner to Board of Agriculture, 19 Feb 1920, 25 June 1920, 3 July 1920 and 11 July 1920 (DAFS 1164/C).

26. Letter from N. Macdonald and others to Scottish Office, 24 January 1921 (SRO AF 67/65).

27. Malcolm Macdonald and others to Board of Agriculture, 24 January 1921 (SRO AF67/65); Township Grazings Committee to Board of Agriculture, 9 August 1921 (SRO AF83/751).

28. Eleven Tobson cottars to Scottish Office, 26 August 1926 (SRO AF 67/66); Croir township clerk to BoA, 28 July 1930 (SRO AF 83/751).

29. Letter from public meeting of Stenscholl to Lealt Eastside ex-servicemen and crofters, to BoA, 6 April 1922 (DAFS 5863/C, Scorrybreck) and nine ex-servicemen to BoA, 8 October 1921 (SRO AF 83/695).

30. Nine ex-servicemen to BoA, 8 October 1921 (SRO AF 83/695).

31. John MacCuish and two other cottars to BoA, 16 November 1925, Angus McQueen to BoA on behalf of Northton crofters, 31 December 1925, John MacCuish and others to BoA, 22 March 1926, telegram John MacCuish to BoA, 25 March 1926, telegram McQueen to BoA on behalf Northton crofters, 25 March 1926, John MacCuish and others to BoA, 8 April 1926, John MacCuish to BoA, 9 May 1928 (SRO AF 83/800).

32. D. Stewart to BoA, 15 March 1926 and 18 March 1926 (SRO AF 83/795).

33. See Footnote 5.

34. J. Sider, *Culture and Class in Anthropology and History* (London 1986), pp. 7–8, 170–71; M. Reed, 'Class and Conflict in Rural England: Some Reflections on a Debate' in M. Reed and R. Wells (eds.), *Class,*

Conflict and Protest in the English Countryside 1700–1880 (London 1990), p. 23

35. For a full discussion of the full range of conflicts evident in Highland protest, see I. Robertson, 'Governing the Highlands: the place of popular protest in the Highlands of Scotland after 1918', *Rural History,* 8:1 (1997), pp. 109–24.

36. L.Leneman, *Fit for heroes? Land settlement in Scotland after World War One* (Aberdeen 1989), p. 205; N. Maclean to Board of Agriculture, 14 December 1920 (SRO AF67/65), same to same, 11 December 1920 (SRO AF83/207).

37. Rev. R. MacGowan to SO, 3 July 1920 (SRO AF67/150).

38. Sub-commissioner C. MacDonald to Board of Agriculture, 20 November 1923 (SRO AF83/769).

39. Sub-commissioner E. Scott to Board of Agriculture, 19 April 1922 (SRO AF 83/252).

40. For examples of this, see DAFS 1164/M/1.

41. D. Fitzpatrick, 'Class, family and rural unrest in nineteenth century Ireland' in P.J. Drudy (ed.) *Ireland: land, politics and people* (London 1982).

42. E.P. Thompson, *Customs in common* (London 1993) pp. 309–10.

43. P. Thompson, *The voice of the past* (London 1988), pp. 196–233.

44. J.S. Duncan and D. Ley (eds.) *Place/culture/representation* (London 1993) pp. 8–10

45. Hunter, *Making,* p. 5.

15. THE BUSINESS OF HEALTH: THE HYDROPATHIC MOVEMENT IN SCOTLAND AND IRELAND COMPARED, 1840–1914

1. *The Times,* 29 February 1864.

2. See John Heuston, 'Kilkee. The origins and development of a West Coast Resort', and K.M. Davies, 'For health and pleasure in the British fashion: Bray, Co Wicklow, as a

tourist resort' in Barbara O'Connor and Michael Cronin (eds.), *Tourism in Ireland,* Part I (Cork 1993).

3. John White, 'The Cusack papers: new evidence on the Knock apparition', *History Ireland,* 4(4), 1996, pp. 39–43.

4. See Edwin Muir, *Scottish journey* [1935], (Edinburgh 1979), pp. 170–77.

5. J.W.P. Rowledge, *A regional history of railways. Vol. XVI: Ireland* (Trowbridge 1995).

6. Ward, Lock & Co., *Limerick* (c.1900).

7. Baddeley and Ward's *Thorough guide to Ireland* (London 1901), Introduction, p. xv.

8. Mrs C. Grumbleton, 29 January 1799, cited in Trevor Fawcett (compiler), *Voices of eighteenth century Bath* (Ruton 1995), p. 56.

9. For a full review of Irish spas, see D. Edgar Flinn, *Ireland: its health resorts and watering places* (London 1888).

10. C.W. Scott, *Round about the islands, or sunny spots near home* (London 1874), p. 27.

11. *The Dublin Medical Journal*, 20 (1842), p. 121.

12. A good popular account of hydropathy is that of E.S. Turner, *Taking the cure* (London 1967), Chapters 10–13. See also Alastair J. Durie (with J. Bradley and M. Dupree), *Water is best. The hydropathic movement in Scotland, 1840–1940* (forthcoming 2006).

13. The venture at Lucan was in the hands of a limited company, the Lucan Hydropathic and Spa Hotel Company Limited (Glasgow Royal College of Physicians, Pamphlet Collection). Flinn, *Health Resorts*, pp. 113–14 quotes from the prospectus for a projected hydropathic and sanatorium establishment at Rostrevor.

14. *Memoir of Donald MacLeod, D.D.*, by his brother, Norman MacLeod (London 1876), vol. 2, p. 206.

15. Dr John Harcup, *Preface to the Malvern water cure. Or victims for weeks in wet sheets* (Malvern 1992).

16. *The letters of Charles Dickens*, vol. 6, 1850–1852 (Oxford 1988), p. 9, fn 4.

17. J.W.C. to John A Carlyle, 23 July 1849, *The collected letters of Thomas and Jane Welsh Carlyle*, vol. 24, April 1849 to December 1849 (Duke and Edinburgh 1995), p. 143.

18. David Jamie, *John Hope, philanthropist and reformer* (Edinburgh 1900).

19. I owe this reference to Dr Fred Hay who is preparing a study of Provost Brown, drawn from his unpublished diaries.

20. *The Belfast Newsletter*, 18 August 1843, of Claridge.

21. *The Northern Whig*, 22 August 1843 noted that Claridge concluded his lectures by calling for the institution of a society on the lines of those established elsewhere, but there seems to have been no uptake.

22. Craiglockhart did relax its total abstinence rule to allow invalids and visitors who were proscribed the use of wine to bring their own to dinner, but they had to produce a duly authorised medical certificate. 'Craiglockhart hydropathic and pension, important intimation', *The Scottish Banking and Insurance Magazine*, September 1884, p. 224.

23. G. Christie, *Crieff Hydro 1868–2000*, second revision (Crieff 2000), p. 144.

24. *The Dunfermline Journal*, 4 May 1889, 'Sketch of a Worthy Citizen'. See also P.T. Winskill, *The Temperance Movement and its workers* (London and Edinburgh 1893), vol. 2, Chapter LI, 'The Maine Law agitation in Scotland'.

25. John Gibbs, Letters from Graefenberg in the years 1843, 1844, 1845 and 1846; with the report and extracts from the correspondence of the Enniscorthy Hydropathic Society (London 1847).

26. 29 June 1843. I am indebted to Ms Breffni Hannon of Limerick City Library for this reference.

27. *The Cork Examiner*, 5 August 1843.

28. Curtin died in 1876 and the establishment survived him only by a few years. Colman O'Mahony, *The maritime gateway to Cork* (Tower 1986), p. 72.

29. *The Athenaeum*, Saturday 25 May 1844, advertisement for Dr Feldman's hydropathic establishment.

30. *The Scotsman*, 7 July 1862 carried an

advertisement for the hydropathic establishment at Delgany, in the midst of the renowned scenery of Wicklow, fifteen miles from Dublin. 'The air is as bracing, the water as pure, and the scenery as beautiful as at Malvern.'

31. R. East, *The principles and practices of the water cure popularly expounded* (London, Edinburgh and Glasgow 1850).

32. His publications included *The Turkish bath. Uses and abuses* (Cork 1860).

33. Dr Barter, *Descriptive notice of the rise and progress of the Irish Gräffenberg* (Bradford 1858) pp. 20–21.

34. John Gibbs, Letters, p. 277.

35. *The Dunfermline Journal*, 22 September 1877.

36. *The Times*, 11 September 1878.

37. *The Scottish Banking and Insurance Magazine*, 1 July 1979, p. 181.

38. *The Glasgow Herald*, April 20 1878.

39. Scott, *op. cit.*, p. 44. 'Dr Barter's Bath is in the centre of a village ornée, built in a luxurious garden. It is called a hydropathic establishment, but this long-sounding title gives no idea of the pretty colony of St Ann's.

Wherever I turned I met a rose-covered cottage or a summer house . . . and I cannot imagine a more delightful spot for the nervous or hard-worked.'

40. See Stephen O' Leary, 'St Ann's Hydro, a medical and social analysis' (Undergraduate dissertation, University College, Cork 1995).

41. Taken on 4/5 April 1901, The Parish of Kilnamucky, 72/19, County Cork.

42. The Mona Cliff Hydro at Douglas, Isle of Man (no date, but c.1910) carried amongst its advertising an endorsement from a Dublin party, Mrs R.S.C.: 'Second visit in a month. Thoroughly satisfied'.

43. John Buchan, *Huntingtower* (Edinburgh and London 1922), p. 17.

44. Acknowledgement: the Wellcome Trust for the History of Medicine provided a travel and subsistence grant for research in Irish sources. The staff at the Boole Library of University College, Cork, the City and the County libraries there, and their colleagues at Limerick and Wexford were of the greatest assistance.

16. PHILOSOPHY AND THE INDIVIDUAL IN COMMERCIAL SOCIETY: TOWARDS AN INTERPRETATION OF DAVID HUME'S TREATISE OF HUMAN NATURE, BOOKS I AND II

1. This essay is based on a paper presented at the conference on 'Ireland and Scotland 1600–2000' held at Queen's University Belfast in June 2000. The paper was, in turn, based on part of the argument from my doctoral dissertation, 'Inventing the commercial consumer: an historical interpretation of David Hume's theory of the individual in Books I and II of *A Treatise of Human Nature*' (University of Dublin 2001).

2. Another approach to Hume's *Treatise* based on similar assumptions about the relationship between Hume's ideas and the social contexts in which they were

developed may be seen in Steven Wallech, 'Elements of Social Status in Hume's *Treatise*', *Journal of the History of Ideas*, 45:2 (1984), pp. 207–18.

3. James Noxon is sceptical, in his *Hume's philosophical development: a study of his methods* (Oxford 1973), of the validity of interpreting Hume's philosophical method as 'experimental' in a properly Newtonian sense since mathematics forms no serious part of Hume's solutions to problems in the *Treatise* (p.112) For a study that is more positive about the Newtonian ideas in the *Treatise*, see N. Capaldi, *op. cit.*

(1975), especially Chapter 3, entitled 'Hume's Newtonian paradigm'. For the importance of experimental observations, see p. 62. See also Michael Barfoot, 'Hume and the culture of science in the early eighteenth century' in M. A. Stewart (ed.), *Studies in the philosophy of the Scottish Enlightenment* (Oxford 1990).

4. There are instances in the *Treatise* where Hume alludes to the possibility of using experiments of a certain kind to prove theorems concerning human nature. See, for example, the edition of *A treatise of human nature* edited by L.A. Selby-Bigge and P.H. Nidditch (Oxford 1978), pp. 301–2, where he recommends that the reader attempt experiments with objects that produce feelings of pride. (Subsequent page references to the *Treatise* are from this edition, cited hereafter as *Treatise*; upper-case Roman numerals refer to the Book number, Arabic numerals refer to the Part and lower-case Roman numerals refer to Section number where relevant.)

5. *Treatise*, p. xix. James Noxon notes that Hume's idea of 'experiment' was more limited than the meaning given to it by the Royal Society, for example.

6. An important argument which emphasises the centrality of 'common life' to Hume's philosophy was made by Donald Livingston in *Hume's philosophy of common life* (Chicago 1984). See also Christopher J. Finlay, 'Enlightenment and the university: philosophy, communication, and education in the early writings of David Hume', *History of Universities* XVI (1) 2000, pp. 103–34.

7. The idea that human nature is always and everywhere the same has been held against Hume as a historian by R.G. Collingwood, for example. See R.G. Collingwood, *The idea of history*, revised edition by Jan van der Dussen (Oxford 1994), pp. 81–85.

8. The first of the three parts in Book II analyses pride and humility; the second part examines love and hatred,

which are regarded as arising from the same conditions as pride and humility but are directed towards others. The third part deals with the *direct* passions, i.e. desire and aversion and hope and fear, and the operation of the will.

9. This problem is articulated in *Treatise*, I.4.vi.

10. Hume writes at the beginning of section II.1.x ('Of property and riches') 'but the relation, which is esteem'd the closest, and which of all others produces most commonly the passion of pride, is that of *property*'. *Ibid.*, p. 309.

11. *Ibid.*, p. 281.

12. *Ibid.*, p. 290.

13. *Ibid.*, p. 290.

14. *Ibid.*, p. 291.

15. *Ibid.*, p. 291.

16. *Ibid.*, p. 292.

17. *Ibid.*, II.3.i.

18. *Ibid.*, p. 293.

19. *Ibid.*, p. 293.

20. *Ibid.*, p. 375.

21. *Ibid.*, p. 378.

22. See Ernest C. Mossner, *The life of David Hume*, second edition (Oxford 1980), pp. 7–8. Mossner confirms Hume's claim that 'his father's family was "a Branch of the Earl of Home's or Hume's"'. For the source of Hume's remark on this, quoted by Mossner, see David Hume, *Essays, moral, political and literary*, edited by Eugene F. Miller (Indianapolis 1985), p. xxxii.

23. In a letter to Henry Home written in December, he remarked that he 'cannot overcome a certain shamefacedness I have to appear among you at my years [he was born in 1711], without having yet a settlement, or so much as attempted any', and asked: 'how happens it, that we philosophers cannot as heartily despise the world, as it despises us?' *The letters of David Hume*, edited by L.Y.T. Greig (Oxford 1932), p. 24.

24. It was Henry Home who provided Hume with a letter of introduction

with which to approach Joseph Butler in 1738.

25. Hume attempted to adapt to English cultural mores by imitation as well as by suppressing his Scottishness as far as possible. See Alasdair MacIntyre, *Whose justice? Which rationality?* (Notre Dame, Indiana 1988), especially Chapter XV, 'Hume's anglicising subversion'. For analysis of the self-consciousness of eighteenth-century Scots with regard to their use of the English language (including, as an appendix, Hume's own list of Scotticisms that he published with the 1752 edition of his *Political discourses*), see James G. Basker, 'Scotticisms and the problem of cultural identity in eighteenth century Britain' in John Dwyer and Richard B. Sher, *Sociability and society in eighteenth century Scotland* (Edinburgh 1993).

26. John Rule, *The vital century: England's developing economy, 1714–1815* (London and New York 1992), p. 256.

27. *Ibid.*, p. 256.

28. Christopher Breward, *The culture of fashion: a new history of fashionable dress* (Manchester 1995), p. 110.

29. See T.C. Smout, *A history of the Scottish people, 1560–1830* (London 1970), pp. 285–91.

30. *Ibid.*, p. 286.

31. *Ibid.*, p. 291.

32. Quoted in Peter T. Marcy, 'Eighteenth century views of Bristol and Bristolians' in P. McGrath (ed.), *Bristol in the eighteenth century* (Newton Abbey 1972), p. 14.

33. *Ibid.*, p. 14.

34. Borsay (ed.), *The eighteenth century town: a reader in English urban history, 1688–1820* (London and New York 1990).

35. *Ibid.*, p. 161.

36. Borsay, *op. cit.*, p. 163. For the details on Bristol's own theatre see Kathleen Baker, 'The Theatre Royal, Bristol: the first seventy years' in P. McGrath (ed.), *op. cit.*

37. Borsay, *op. cit.*, p. 175.

38. *Ibid.*, p. 176.

39. *Ibid.*, p. 176.

40. *Ibid.*, p. 93.

41. John Smail, *The origins of middle-class culture: Halifax, Yorkshire, 1660–1780* (Cornell University Press 1994, pp. 100–1.

42. Smail, *op. cit.*, p. 101; and Colin Campbell, 'Understanding traditional and modern patterns of consumption in eighteenth century England: a character-action approach' in John Brewer and Roy Porter (eds.), *Consumption and the world of goods* (London and New York 1994).

43. Geoffrey Holmes, *The professions and social change in England, 1680–1730* (Oxford 1981), pp. 313–23.

44. David Hume, *The history of England*, vol. 6 (London 1773), Chapter XLV.

45. Rosenheim, *op. cit.*, p. 1.

46. *Ibid.*, p. 2.

47. *Ibid.*, p. 2.

48. Book III, *Of morals*, was not published until November 1740.

49. In Book II, Part 3, Hume asserts that 'Reason is, and ought only to be the slave of the passions, and can never pretend to any other office than to serve and obey them.' *Ibid.*, p. 415.

50. In Book I, Part 3, Hume explains the means of establishing beliefs about causal relationships as the key operation of reason in dealing with experience. The kinds of causal relationships that concerned him, however, were particularly those involving the actions of human individuals, as is evident, for instance, from I.1.iv, paragraph 5.

51. Hume dealt with the nature and use of money at a societal level in his *Political discourses* published in 1752. See, in particular, 'Of money' in David Hume, *Essays, moral, political and literary*, edited by Eugene F. Miller (Indianapolis 1985).

52. *Treatise*, p. 311.

53. *Ibid.*, p. 311.

54. *Ibid.*, p. 311.

55. John Smail, *op. cit.*), pp. 82–101.

56. As he does, for instance, in *Treatise*, II.3.iii.

17. HISTORY ON THE WALLS: A PHOTO-ESSAY ON HISTORICAL NARRATIVE AND THE POLITICAL WALL MURALS OF BELFAST IN THE LATE 1990s

1. Bill Rolston, *Murals and conflict in Northern Ireland* (London and Cranbury, NJ 1991); Neil Jarman, *Material conflicts. Parades and visual displays in Northern Ireland* (Oxford 1997); Anthony D. Buckley (ed.), *Symbols in Northern Ireland* (Belfast 1998); Neil Jarman, *Displaying faith. Orange, Green and Trades Union banners in Northern Ireland* (Belfast 1999).

2. Neil Jarman, 'Painting landscapes: the place of murals in the symbolic construction of urban space', in Anthony D. Buckley (ed.), *op. cit.*, 81–98.

3. The photographs reproduced here were taken by the author in 1999 and 2001.

Index